NEW DIRECTIONS IN GERMAN STUDIES
Vol. 39

Representing Social Precarity in German Literature and Film

Edited by
Sophie Duvernoy, Karsten Olson,
and Ulrich Plass

BLOOMSBURY ACADEMIC
NEW YORK · LONDON · OXFORD · NEW DELHI · SYDNEY

BLOOMSBURY ACADEMIC
Bloomsbury Publishing Inc
1385 Broadway, New York, NY 10018, USA
50 Bedford Square, London, WC1B 3DP, UK
29 Earlsfort Terrace, Dublin 2, Ireland

BLOOMSBURY, BLOOMSBURY ACADEMIC and the Diana logo
are trademarks of Bloomsbury Publishing Plc

First published in the United States of America 2024

Cover design: Andrea F. Busci
Cover image: screenshot from "'Kuhle Wampe," directed by Slatan Dudow.
© Praesens-Film AG, 1932. All rights reserved.

Library of Congress Cataloging-in-Publication Data
Names: Duvernoy, Sophie, editor. | Olson, Karsten, editor. | Plass, Ulrich, editor.
Title: Representing social precarity in German literature and film / edited by Sophie
Duvernoy, Karsten Olson, and Ulrich Plass.
Description: New York : Bloomsbury Academic, 2023. |
Series: New directions in German studies ; vol. 39 | Includes bibliographical references
and index. | Summary: "An exploration of representations of social precarity in German
literature and culture from the 19th to 21st centuries"–Provided by publisher.
Identifiers: LCCN 2023014037 (print) | LCCN 2023014038 (ebook) |
ISBN 9781501391477 (hardback) | ISBN 9781501391514 (paperback) |
ISBN 9781501391491 (pdf) | ISBN 9781501391484 (epub) |
ISBN 9781501391507 (ebook other)
Subjects: LCSH: Human security in literature. | German literature–History
and criticism. | Human security in motion pictures. |
Motion pictures–Germany–History. | LCGFT: Essays.
Classification: LCC PT134.H857 R47 2023 (print) | LCC PT134.H857 (ebook) |
DDC 830.9/93356–dc23/eng/20230504
LC record available at https://lccn.loc.gov/2023014037
LC ebook record available at https://lccn.loc.gov/2023014038

ISBN: HB: 978-1-5013-9147-7
           ePDF: 978-1-5013-9149-1
           eBook: 978-1-5013-9148-4

Series: New Directions in German Studies

Typeset by Integra Software Services Pvt. Ltd.

To find out more about our authors and books visit www.bloomsbury.com
and sign up for our newsletters.

Contents

Figures

Tables

Notes on Contributors

Sophie Duvernoy is a translator and writer. She received her PhD in German Literature from Yale University in 2023. Her translation of Gabriele Tergit's *Käsebier Takes Berlin* was published by New York Review Books in 2019 and shortlisted for the 2021 Schlegel-Tieck translation prize. She is the recipient of a 2023 Translation Grant from the National Endowment of the Arts, and is currently working on a translation of Gabriele Tergit's *Effingers*. Her writing and translations have appeared in the *Paris Review Online, Los Angeles Review of Books, No Man's Land,* and *The Offing.*

Patrick Eiden-Offe is a Heisenberg Scholar at the Zentrum für Literaturforschung in Berlin, and is working on the project *Georg Lukács: An Intellectual Biography.* He has previously held visiting professor positions at the University of Illinois at Chicago, the University of Hamburg, the Ruhr-University of Bochum, and the Humboldt-University in Berlin. Dr. Eiden-Offe is the author of *Hegels "Logik" lesen: Ein Selbstversuch, Die Poesie der Klasse: Romantischer Antikapitalismus und die Erfindung des Proletariats, Das Reich der Demokratie: Hermann Brochs "Der Tod des Vergil,"* and is currently working on the book *Über Über.*

Thomas Heise is a German documentary filmmaker. His last film *Heimat is a Space in Time* won the Caligari Prize at the 2019 Berlinale Film Festival. He was born in 1955 in East Germany and trained as a printer before he studied at the Academy of Film & Television in Potsdam-Babelsberg. All his East German films and projects, among them *Why Make a Film about These People,* were censored or blocked. Since the 1990s, his films have been internationally recognized and have won distinctive prizes and awards.

Mary Hennessy is Assistant Professor of German at the University of Wisconsin-Madison. She earned her PhD in German Studies from the

University of Michigan. Her research interests include German film and media, gender and feminist theory, and critical theory. Her current book project examines women's multiple (often hidden) roles in the production of media in order to retheorize relationships of gender, labor, and technological change in Weimar Germany. Mary's research has been supported by the Fulbright Commission, the American Friends of Marbach, and the Berlin Program for Advanced German and European Studies.

Mari Jarris is a Postdoctoral Associate at Cornell University's Department of German Studies. They received their PhD in Comparative Literature from Princeton University and German Literature from the Humboldt-Universität zu Berlin. Their research areas include Marxism, queer and feminist theory, utopianism, and nineteenth- and twentieth-century German and Russian literature. Their work has been supported by research grants from the Fulbright Commission, the German Academic Exchange Service (DAAD), American Councils, and the Coalition of Women in German.

Jörg Kreienbrock is Professor of German and Comparative Literature at Northwestern University. His research focuses on German literature from the eighteenth to the twenty-first centuries, with an emphasis on literary theory, contemporary literature, the history of science, and popular culture. Professor Kreienbrock is the author of *Kleiner. Feiner. Leichter: Nuancierungen zum Werk Robert Walsers* (2010); *Malicious Objects, Anger Management, and the Question of Modern Literature* (2012); *Das Medium der Prosa* (2020); *Sich im Weltall orientieren: Philosophieren im Kosmos 1950–1970* (2020).

Rebekah O. McMillan is Assistant Professor of History at Angelo State University in San Angelo, Texas. She received her PhD from the University of Arkansas. Her research focuses on the history of poverty and social welfare in a transnational context. She investigates the shared connections between the ideas and efforts of social reformers and poor relief schemes in Germany, Great Britain, and the United States in the late nineteenth century.

Karsten Olson is a lecturer of German in Languages and Literatures at the University of North Carolina, Asheville. He earned his PhD at the University of Minnesota and his research interests include Enlightenment journals, popular philosophy and theater, Critical Theory, as well as legal theory. His recent publications include articles on constitutional theories in the Frankfurt School, the economic theory of Franz Neumann, and the role of gender and economics in *Der Hofmeister*.

Ulrich Plass is Professor of Letters and German Studies at Wesleyan University. His scholarship addresses the history of Critical Theory, continental aesthetics, Marxism, and post-Romantic German literature. His recent publications are on Brecht's poetic rewriting of the Communist Manifesto, Adorno's labor theory of art, Marcuse's critical utopianism, and the Frankfurt School's critique of the culture industry.

Lindsay Preseau is Assistant Professor of German Studies in the Department of World Languages and Cultures at Iowa State University. She earned her PhD in Germanic Linguistics from the University of California, Berkeley. Her research lies at the intersection of sociolinguistics, applied linguistics, and language pedagogy, bringing qualitative and quantitative research on the social dimensions of language into dialogue with the ways languages are taught and legislated. Her current projects focus in particular on pedagogical representations of migrant language and on gender-inclusive and trans-affirming language practices in language education.

Matthias Rothe is Associate Professor of German and Philosophy at the University of Minnesota. He works on the interrelation between aesthetics and political economy, and on collaborative artistic practices. He has published on theater, contemporary literature, Marxism and critical theory. He recently co-edited *Brecht und das Fragment* (Verbrecher Verlag 2020) with Astrid Oesmann (Rice University) and collaboratively translated and introduced Elisabeth Hauptmann and Bertolt Brecht's *Jae Fleischhacker in Chicago* (Bloomsbury 2018) (with Phoebe von Held).

Michael Swellander is Visiting Assistant Professor of German at Skidmore College in Saratoga Springs, NY. His research interests include the history of political literature, aesthetics under censorship, journalism, and the Vormärz period. He is currently completing a book manuscript on literary responses to censorship in nineteenth-century Germany and editing a translation anthology of texts pertaining to nineteenth-century cultural journalism and the periodical landscape in Germany.

Lena Trüper is a PhD candidate in European Languages and Transcultural Studies at the University of California, Los Angeles. Her research focuses on metaphors in science and technology studies, visual studies, cybernetics, and the medical humanities. She has an MA in Art History from Goethe University Frankfurt and was a member of the DFG research group "Knowledge in the Arts" at the University of Arts in Berlin. Her articles include "Visual Natural Metaphors of Cybernetics in Arts and Popular Culture" (Transcript, 2020) and "On Ecosystems and Wired Potatoes: Art and Technology Movements in Argentina during the 1970s" (de Gruyter, 2022).

Lisa Wille is currently a postdoctoral research associate at the Institute of Linguistics and Literary Studies at the Technical University of Darmstadt, where she received her doctorate in 2019 with a dissertation on the dramatic work of *Sturm und Drang* author Heinrich Leopold Wagner (published by Königshausen & Neumann in 2021). From February to August 2022, she was a Visiting Research Scholar at Georgetown University in Washington, DC, and the University of British Columbia in Vancouver. Her research interests include eighteenth-century literature (Enlightenment, Sensibility, *Sturm und Drang*), gender studies, sociology of literature, contemporary literature, intersectionality, literature and economics, and twentieth-century literature.

Representing Social Precarity: Introduction

Ulrich Plass

"Denn die einen sind im Dunkeln
Und die andern sind im Licht.
Und man sieht nur die im Lichte
Die im Dunkeln sieht man nicht."
      Bertolt Brecht, Die Beule: Ein Dreigroschenfilm[1]

"Da ist ein Mensch drin, auch wenn es nicht so scheint. Unter den
Flicken und Fetzen bewegt sich nichts. Die Passanten gehen an dem
Haufen vorbei, als wäre er nicht da. Jeder sieht ihn, aber die Blicke
wandern sofort weiter."
      Thomas Melle, 3000 EURO[2]

I thank my two splendid and intrepid co-editors Sophie Duvernoy and Karsten Olson for their cooperation and critique in drafting and editing this introduction. The editors are thankful to the participants of the "Representations of Social Precarity" panels at the 2020 conference of the German Studies Association. Their diverse contributions inspired this introduction and this volume. For their thoughtful feedback on this volume, the editors are grateful to Benjamin Robinson and Elke Siegel.

1   Brecht, *Große kommentierte Berliner und Frankfurter Ausgabe*, vol. 19, ed. Jan Knopf et al. (Berlin und Weimar: Aufbau and Frankfurt/M: Suhrkamp, 1997), 320. ["For there's some who are in darkness / And there's others in the light. / And we see those in the light, sir / Those in darkness are out of sight."] (Bertolt Brecht, *Collected Poems*, trans. Tom Kuhn and David Constantine [New York and London: Liveright, 2018], 397).

2   "There is a human being in there, even though it doesn't seem like it. Under the rags and shreds, nothing is moving. People pass the pile as if it weren't there. Everyone sees it but their glances move on immediately" (Thomas Melle, *3000 Euro* [Reinbek bei Hamburg: Rowohlt, 2016], 7).

"Sie können sich nicht vertreten, sie müssen vertreten werden."
Karl Marx, Der achtzehnte Brumaire des Louis Bonaparte[3]

Precarity and the Challenges of Representation

The essays in this collection explore literary and filmic representations that reflect, express, probe, and interrogate histories and experiences of social precarity. "Precarity" partakes in a semantic field that includes "insecurity," "danger," "risk," "vulnerability," but also "social decline," "powerlessness," "pauperization," and "immiseration." Logically implied in the composite concept *"social* precarity" is the idea of class society, that is, of society as "an antagonistic totality" that "survives [*sich erhält*] only in and through its antagonisms and is not able to resolve them."[4] Our interest in representations of social precarity builds on an archive of scholarship concerned with the (im)possibility of representing experiences of vulnerability, marginalization, impoverishment, dispossession, and destitution as filtered through categories of social analysis such as class, gender, race, and sexuality. Crucially, the social antagonisms that shape such experiences are not only repressive and disempowering but also configure individual and collective precarity. Because these social formations tend to be fleeting and volatile, unmade as quickly as they were made, if and how they can be taken hold of as "reality" fit to be represented is a contested question. As Brecht wrote in 1931, "reality as such has slipped into the domain of the functional," and thus "the simple 'reproduction of reality' says less than ever about reality."[5]

In her critique of postcolonial and subaltern studies, Gayatri Spivak cites a conversation between Michel Foucault and Gilles Deleuze in which the latter claims "reality is what actually happens in a factory, in a school, in a barracks, in a prison, in a police station."[6] Spivak pushes back against the "positivist empiricism" at the root of calls for "concrete experience" and "what actually happens."[7] There is,

---

3   "They cannot represent themselves, they must be represented." (Karl Marx, "The Eighteenth Brumaire of Louis Bonaparte," trans. Terrell Carver, in *Marx's "Eighteenth Brumaire": (Post)modern Interpretations*, ed. Mark Cowling and James Martin [London and Sterling, VA: Pluto Press, 2002], 101).

4   Theodor W. Adorno, *Hegel: Three Studies*, trans. Shierry Weber Nicholsen (Cambridge, MA and London: MIT Press, 1994), 28.

5   Bertolt Brecht, *On Film and Radio*, ed. and trans. Marc Silberman (London: Methuen, 2000), 164.

6   Cited in Gayatri Chakravorty Spivak, *A Critique of Postcolonial Reason: Towards a History of the Vanishing Present* (Cambridge, MA and London: Harvard University Press, 1999), 255.

7   Spivak, *Postcolonial Reason*, 255. The scare quotes are Spivak's.

Spivak insists, no "pure form of consciousness" of the subaltern, and hence the project of writing a history from below to give voice to the oppressed risks replicating the "representationalist realism" espoused in Deleuze's remark. Following Spivak's rejection of the assumptions "that the oppressed can know and speak for themselves" and that "there is no representation,"[8] we suggest that critics and historians of capitalist modernity must grasp the salience of representation in two senses: "as 'speaking for,' as in politics; and representation as 're-presentation,' as in art or philosophy."[9] At the same time, we add to Spivak's critique that representation in the political sense implies a moral claim to have one's voice heard, a claim that is also expressed in the dreams, images, and myths in which the oppressed classes have, at certain historical moments, come to recognize themselves as collective subjects.[10]

The German term for political representation is *vertreten*, which is also the term Marx employs when he observes that the "peasant proprietors" in mid-nineteenth-century France were too isolated from one another, too cut off from interacting with society at large, and too immersed in the all-consuming demands of their daily labor to form a class subject capable of exercising effective political agency:

> In so far as there is merely a local interconnection amongst peasant proprietors, the similarity of their interests produces no community, no national linkage and no political organisation, they do not form a class. They are therefore incapable of asserting their class interests in their own name, whether through a parliament or constitutional convention. They cannot represent themselves, they must be represented.[11]

While the *content* of Marx's *Eighteenth Brumaire* focuses on representation in the sense of *Vertretung*, it takes the representational *form*—*Darstellung*—of a historical narrative, famous for "extravagant

---

8 Spivak, *Postcolonial Reason*, 264. Spivak attributes these assumptions specifically to a dismissal of the Marxian mode of historical interpretation, with Foucault and Deleuze serving as her two primary suspects of this rejection.

9 Spivak, *Postcolonial Reason*, 256.

10 The role of art and literature in the process of proletarian class constitution is explored, for France, in Jacques Rancière's *Proletarian Nights: The Workers' Dream in Nineteenth-Century France*, trans. John Drury (London and New York: Verso, 2012), and, for Germany, in Patrick Eiden-Offe's *Die Poesie der Klasse: Romantischer Antikapitalismus und die Erfindung des Proletariats* (Berlin: Matthes & Seitz, 2017).

11 *Marx's "Eighteenth Brumaire,"* 100–1.

imagery, withering scorn and scathing satire,"[12] but also for its theoretical reflections on the theatrical imagery of historical representation. Just as for Marx, problems of *Darstellung* and *Vertretung* stand at the center of the contributions to this volume and their attempts to understand the heterogeneity and volatility of social processes. Their scope extends from more strictly literary considerations, such as the canonical concern with realist or modernist (avant-garde, experimental, free form) types of narrative representation, to the deployments of "representation" in the political and cultural spheres, where representation pertains to questions of recognition, equality, and social justice.

Our dual understanding of "representation" as "Darstellung" (aesthetic) and "Vertretung" (political, cultural) is prompted by our volume's guiding theme of *social precarity*, a concept directly related to the rise of neoliberal governmentality over the last fifty years. A core feature of neoliberal reforms has been the redistribution of risk, removing protections from work and the commons and instead strengthening protections for financial, speculative enterprises and private property.[13] When Martin Luther King, Jr. observed in 1968 that "we all too often have socialism for the rich and rugged free enterprise capitalism for the poor,"[14] he anticipated what soon thereafter would become the core mission of neoliberal governance: introduce the principle of competition into ever more areas of life and limit the role of the state to containing the fallout from this principle by expanding the power of repressive security (the military, police, and carceral apparatus). This deliberate precarization of society by the state played a major role in helping bring about the highest level of economic inequality since the Gilded Age preceding the Great Depression. Despite being closely related to contested statistical and sociological rubrics such as "poverty wage," "social integration," "underclass," or "marginal groups," *precarity* implies an irreducibly subjective, personal, and contingent dimension; a dimension that can perhaps be rendered less marginalized and invisible if is given a distinct shape and story through artistic means. The distancing effects of artistic representation allow for experiences of precarity to emerge both in their personal and contextual specificity as well as in their everydayness.

---

12 Terrel Carver, "Imagery/Writing, Imagination/Politics: Reading Marx through the *Eighteenth Brumaire*," *Marx's Eighteenth Brumaire*, 118.

13 See e.g., Maurizio Lazzarato, "Neoliberalism in Action: Inequality, Insecurity and the Reconstitution of the Social," *Theory, Culture & Society* 26, no. 6 (2009): 109–33.

14 The quotation is from a speech given on February 23, 1968, "The Minister of the Valley," and has since circulated widely on Twitter.

We are not interested in asking whether such representations are aesthetically proper or morally justifiable, but rather in examining how they reflect and respond to social precarity through form and content; how they confirm, modify, or challenge our understanding of social precarity; and what publics they address. We contend that societies become conscious of their own inherent contradictions and challenges not only through public discourse and governmental communication but also by means of artistic form, primarily narrative and pictorial. Based on this assumption, we can ask: what ideas about precarity circulate by means of literary representation? How do literary representations reflect, reinforce, or challenge the prevalent social and cultural awareness of precarization, both today and at earlier historical junctures? How do they draw links or divisions between society's sense of precarity today and historical understandings of risk, marginalization, pauperization, or social security?

Precarity, Then and Now

With the turn of the millennium, the nouns "precariousness," "precarity," and "precariat" entered the active vocabulary of artists, activists, and journalists. The terms were intended to describe—mostly critically but also optimistically—the negativity of the neoliberal "freedoms" to which increasing numbers of the once-stable middle classes of the Global North found themselves exposed. Features of post-war social stability, such as safe employment, affordable housing, free public education, retirement security, and the right to public spaces, could no longer be taken for granted. States withdrew funding from social welfare programs at varying paces and through distinct events—in Germany, the government passed the disciplinary Hartz IV unemployment benefit reforms in 2003, while the United States, one decade earlier, had already transformed the spirit of nineteenth-century "poor laws" into the letter of welfare reform ("workfare") and crime bills under President Clinton[15]—yet these actions had the same general effect of accelerating social dislocation and atomization. This material process was propelled ideologically by a semiotic inversion, which rhetorically redefined compulsory labor as the liberation of labor from the control of legal regulations, undercutting the power of organized labor. In the US, for example, anti-union legislation is branded as protecting the "right to work," and thus decreased labor protections falsely bear the name of increased freedom.

---

15 On the links between moralizing discourse and punitive policymaking, see Melinda Cooper, *Family Values: Between Neoliberalism and the New Social Conservatism* (New York: Zone Books, 2017).

The link between social precarity and the semiotic redefinition of lived reality can also be seen in the increasing numbers of people yielding to the spell of conspiracy theories on social media. At the same time, contemporary culture imagines precarity ambivalently, that is, not only as vulnerability and insecurity but also as a gain in personal independence by being free from the traditional molds of life and work. Some of the precariat of the twenty-first century, such as freelance workers, artist entrepreneurs, and itinerant academics have their predecessors in nineteenth-century intellectuals, authors, and journalists, whose newfound freedom from aristocratic patronage and state employment cast them into precarious dependency on the "free" market. It is important, then, not to conflate the precarity of artists and the precarity of workers: the decommodified character of artistic labor is fundamentally different from wage labor. Artists work under the compulsion of their own interests, ideas, and enthusiasms; wage laborers work under the compulsion of their boss.[16]

Our volume is premised on the claim that although neoliberalism looks like a potentially catastrophic turn of capitalist modernity, it can and must be viewed as part of a larger historical pattern. With reference to Adorno and Horkheimer's concept of a "dialectic of enlightenment," this pattern can be described as a dialectic of possession and dispossession. Social inequality and precarity are not only caused by contingent political events such as wars and revolutions but are also the intrinsic byproducts of antagonistic socioeconomic processes of capitalist modernization: accumulation requires dispossession, wealth requires poverty, property requires precarity. Although its scale and scope are historically unprecedented, the expansion of "normal" capitalist "accumulation by exploitation" to neoliberal "accumulation by expropriation" and "accumulation by dispossession" are not new tools of capitalist modernization.[17] Since the Industrial Revolution, the capitalist drive to maximize profits has changed not only how people work but also how they live, think, feel, and dream. Neoliberal forms of production require an increased personal and affective commitment to one's work, blurring the line between life and labor. At the same time, early industrialization and contemporary "flexibilization" both put pressure on people to adjust their ways of living to economic demands they do not control.

---

16 Of course, artistic production includes various forms of wage labor (no film could be made without it!), but the overall distinction between artistic labor and "normal" labor holds, as Dave Beech has argued in *Art and Value: Art's Economic Exceptionalism in Classical, Neoclassical and Marxist Economics* (Chicago: Haymarket, 2016).

17 See Nancy Fraser and Rahel Jaeggi, *Capitalism: A Conversation in Critical Theory* (Cambridge: Polity, 2018), 29.

This fraught continuity of change without freedom is difficult to pin down in one cohesive historical narrative, and it has been represented in a myriad of cultural and aesthetic forms. In assembling a diverse set of representations of social precarity spanning the period from late Romanticism and the *Vormärz* to the present, our volume mirrors this formal diversity yet, at the same time, enables the reader to make sense of connections and continuities across modern German social, cultural, and literary history.

Our volume concludes with cultural production in the wake of the unilateral neoliberal break with the class compromise that guaranteed West Germany's post-war economic stability and prosperity. Sociologists Wolfgang Streek and Oliver Nachtwey describe this break as a "revolt of capital"[18] that introduced a fundamental change in politics: a rule not of people but rather a "government by markets."[19] They describe twenty-first-century Germany as a society of renewed class antagonisms. Because these antagonisms manifest themselves across a diverse spectrum of social relations and identities, they cannot be integrated into neat narratives of class conflicts occurring at the site of production. Accordingly, Nachtwey speaks of a "hidden crisis" in which downward rather than upward social mobility predominates, and which is fracturing Germany's ideological self-understanding as a "society of the middle."[20]

Nachtwey suggests that works of literature serve as "a sensitive seismograph" for social change.[21] Although works of art are formally autonomous, they are always also, as Theodor Adorno puts it, "products of social labor":[22] they are made, circulated, and consumed within the prevailing social relations of production and hence express, however obliquely, complex truths about the social world that cannot be evaluated and communicated through the quantifying methods of the social sciences. Similarities and continuities in the experience of social precarity suggest that the neat periodization between distinct kinds of capitalist societies promoted by literary and cultural historians is undercut by the relative rigidity of relations of class, property, and work—a hunch recently confirmed by economic historian Thomas Piketty, who

---

18 Wolfgang Streek, *Buying Time: The Delayed Crisis of Democratic Capitalism*, trans. Patrick Camiller (London and New York: Verso, 2014), 3.

19 Oliver Nachtwey, *Germany's Hidden Crisis: Social Decline in the Heart of Europe*, trans. David Fernbach and Loren Balhorn (London and New York: Verso, 2018), 76–81.

20 Nachtwey, *Germany's Hidden Crisis*, 129.

21 Nachtwey, *Germany's Hidden Crisis*, 2.

22 Theodor W. Adorno, *Aesthetic Theory*, trans. Robert Hullot-Kentor (London and New York: Continuum, 2002), 263.

has argued that the disproportionate increase of wealth accumulation in the hands of a small elite represents a turn to a hierarchical rentier capitalism reminiscent of the rigidly stratified societies depicted in the works of Honoré de Balzac and Jane Austen.[23]

Of course, today's world is quite different from Balzac's or Austen's, due to the "externalizing" relocation of capitalism's ugliest manifestations from the Global North to the Global South. Yet despite the gulf that separates us from the ascent of industrial capitalism, discourses on precarity from the nineteenth century to the present tend to coalesce around labor: what kind of work can a society provide for its citizens? During the *Vormärz* period, the transition from late-feudal forms of employment to "free" wage labor generated not only newly impoverished proletarians and destitute paupers but also an astonishing increase in literary productivity, especially by women.[24] Literary production became an inviting space for those excluded from the new industrial labor markets, and around 1900 the egalitarian term "cultural worker" or "art worker" [*Kunstarbeiter*] began being used as an alternative to the word "artist" to direct attention to the material conditions of artistic production.[25] Yet it would be naïve to celebrate the disenchanted production of literature—stripped of its Romantic exaltations—as an act of liberation. Today, the market dependency of literary authors either reduces them to anonymous "content providers" or subjects them to the whims of new forms of patronage, such as state or private foundation-sponsored grants and temporary appointments at universities. Against this backdrop of literature's precarious freedom, our volume sheds light on the fact that as literary history commemorates artistic achievements, it tends to forget the often precarious cultural labor of which they are made.

While there is already a significant body of scholarship, reportage, and artistic production that documents the fates of those who live on the precarious edge of society, our volume moves beyond literature's documentary and witnessing function. Instead, we probe the

---

23 Thomas Piketty, *Capital in the Twenty-First Century*, trans. Arthur Goldhammer (Cambridge, MA and London: Harvard University Press, 2014).

24 Germain Goetzinger, "Die Situation der Autorinnen und Autoren," in *Hansers Sozialgeschichte der deutschen Literatur, Band 5: Zwischen Restauration und Revolution, 1815–1848*, ed. Gert Sautermeister and Ulrich Schmid (Munich: Deutscher Taschenbuch Verlag, 1998), 38–59.

25 For instance, Lu Märten's *The Economic Situation of Artists* addresses the economics of artistic production both to provide a kind of self-help manual and to advocate for artists. Against the tendency of the capitalist specialization of labor, Märten aimed to reintegrate art into life. See *Die wirtschaftliche Lage der Künstler* (Munich: Georg Müller, 1914).

aesthetic representability of social precarity in conjunction with gendered, classed, and racialized structures of exclusion from social and political representation. Such exclusions have diverse causes and manifestations, extending from the loneliness of artistic work exacerbated by modern poverty to large-scale shifts in the global social division of labor, a division that tends to separate workers and often leads to displacement and isolation. As people's control dwindles over when, where, how, and how much they work, culture becomes an increasingly important sphere in which concerns and experiences otherwise excluded from representation are given a face and a voice. Hence, the rise of social precarity heightens the pressure on cultural representations to give meaning to lives under duress.

To account for the debilitating force that precarity and poverty exert on groups and individuals, our volume treats representations of social precarity not only as aesthetic reflections of social tensions and contradictions but also as deliberate interventions in the social discourse on marginality, poverty, and dispossession. At the same time, our contributions do not necessarily suggest that it is the ethical task of literature to represent those who cannot represent themselves, nor do they take for granted that literature and culture *can* in fact deliver politically and ethically "correct" representations. Rather, our volume explores the limits and pitfalls of literature's politics of representation, remaining mindful of the inherent dilemma that literary representations of precarity run the risk of valorizing what they challenge: that there is an inherent good to being destitute and excluded, as in Rilke's sentimental line, "Denn Armut ist ein großer Glanz aus Innen ..." ["For poverty is a great brightness from within ..."].[26]

Historicizing Social Precarity

Superficial critiques of contemporary social precarity often tell a story that starts either with the New Deal (in the US) or with Germany's (or Italy's, or France's) economic recovery after the Second World War. With reference to terms such as "neoliberalism" or "globalization," they view the current phenomenon of wealth being redistributed from the bottom to the top as an accidental imbalance of power that can be rectified by a return to post-war politics of greater income equality and moderate wealth redistribution. Critiques of neoliberal precarity tend to assert that there are smart policy solutions for mitigating

---

26 Rainer Maria Rilke, *Die Gedichte: Das Stundenbuch* (Frankfurt and Leipzig: Insel, 1986), 302.

economic inequality: progressive taxation, expanded unemployment benefits, universal health insurance, or a Green New Deal to usher in a fairer economic order. The economic arguments of such critiques, frequently inspired by reappreciations of Keynesian theory,[27] often do not go beyond regulating monopoly power,[28] advocating for consumer protections,[29] or replacing neoliberal monetarism with Modern Monetary Theory.[30] In other words, dominant liberal critiques of economic inequality remain firmly committed to the idea of the market as the most efficient allocator for distributing goods and services, provided the state engage in large-scale deficit spending and issue rules and regulations that guarantee fairness and transparency. Without wanting to downplay the timely importance of such critiques, for purposes of historicizing our present situation it is crucial to take a longer view of precarity as tied up with the evolution of capitalist societies. These societies were built on the intrinsic need for economic growth through the exploitation of labor power.

If we begin the story of modern social precarity around 1800 rather than in the mid-twentieth century, we can see that the period of prosperity after the Second World War is the exception rather than the norm of capitalist modernity. Hence, in the opening of *Capital in the Twenty-First Century*, Thomas Piketty states that "capitalism automatically generates arbitrary and unsustainable inequalities that radically undermine the meritocratic values on which democratic societies are based."[31] Although Piketty does not believe that capitalism will fail completely to sustain democratic societies, he nonetheless predicts the generation of "unsustainable inequalities" of a capitalist economy insufficiently regulated by the state. Marxist critics do not share Piketty's confidence in the regulatory abilities of the state; they tend to view state institutions as serving the interests of the capitalist class at the cost of the common good. Leaving aside the relation between the state and the economy, Piketty's story of capital from 1800 to today is not entirely at odds with Marx's, he notes, "the process by which wealth is accumulated and distributed contains powerful forces pushing toward divergence, or at any

27 An example is the enthusiastic reception of Zachary D. Carter, *The Price of Peace: Money, Democracy, and the Life of John Maynard Keynes* (New York: Penguin Random House, 2020).

28 See David Dayen, *Monopolized: Life in the Age of Corporate Power* (New York: The New Press, 2020).

29 See Zephyr Teachout, *Break 'em Up: Recovering Our Freedom from Big Ag, Big Tech, and Big Money* (New York: All Points Books, 2020).

30 See Stephanie Kelton, *The Deficit Myth: Modern Monetary Theory and the Birth of the People's Economy* (New York: Public Affairs, 2020).

31 Piketty, *Capital*, 1.

rate toward an extremely high level of inequality."[32] The "divergence" he observes is between the rate of growth (that is, "the increase in productivity, or output per hour worked"[33]) and the rate of return on capital (under "capital," Piketty subsumes "all income generating assets"[34]). Unless properly taxed and redistributed, the latter grows faster than the former: $r > g$. If left to its own devices, capitalism is a machine for producing inequality since one class of people, the owners of capital, are bound to grow ever wealthier relative to everyone else: "The entrepreneur inevitably tends to become a rentier, more and more dominant over those who own nothing but their labor. Once constituted, capital reproduces itself faster than output increases. The past devours the future."[35] Piketty tells the story of capitalist inequality with the help of numbers and graphs, and also pays attention to the artistic dimension of this story, albeit only with respect to literary depictions in the sphere of commodity exchange. Piketty's story of capital differs from Marx's in that he defines capital as "the sum total of nonhuman assets that can be owned and exchanged on some market,"[36] whereas for Marx capital is defined as the whole social mechanism of accumulation by means of exploiting labor power.

If we think of the present situation exclusively in terms of inequality, it is tempting to consider social precarity as a periodically occurring disruption of distributional fairness that can be addressed through legislation and progressive policies. Yet Marx's theory of the "general law of capitalist accumulation" provides a corrective to this reduction of social precarity to a matter of distribution. In brief, Marx's critique of political economy stipulates that because competition forces capitalists to increase the productivity of labor, the tendency is for machines ("fixed capital," "dead labor") to replace "living labor." Hence every gain in labor productivity in one company is followed by downward pressure on prices as competitors catch up and place new pressures on capitalists to force more value out of their workers ("variable capital," "living labor"). They succeed in gaining more "surplus-value" through employing more efficient tools and machinery, devising "smart" methods of surveillance and control to regulate and speed up the work process, threatening layoffs to keep wages down, or by relocating jobs elsewhere.

The allegedly new phenomenon of "jobless recoveries" harnesses gains in efficiency and productivity to use fewer workers for the

---

32 Piketty, *Capital*, 27.
33 Piketty, *Capital*, 86.
34 Erik Olin Wright, *Understanding Class* (London and New York, Verso 2015), 137.
35 Piketty, *Capital*, 571.
36 Piketty, *Capital*, 46.

accumulation of capital: "the higher the productivity of labour, the greater is the pressure of the workers on the means of employment, the more precarious therefore becomes the condition for their existence, namely the sale of their own labour-power for the increase of alien wealth, or in other words the self-valorization of capital."[37] For Marx, the capitalist mode of production is by definition a precarious one for workers, because "the worker does not employ the means of production, but the means of production employ the worker." Capitalist development tends to set a growing mass of means of production "in motion by a progressively diminishing expenditure of human power." Although Marx begins *Capital* by evoking the "wealth of societies," at its core his theory shows that capitalism produces not just inequality, but real misery. Although there are short-term fixes to this problem, the overall tendency towards immiseration is inevitable in the long run because capital accumulation requires the competitive intensification of exploiting labor power and the concomitant reduction of total (albeit not of individual) labor hours: "The fact that the means of production and the productivity of labour increase more rapidly than the productive population expresses itself, therefore, under capitalism, in the inverse form that the working population always increases more rapidly than the valorization requirements of capital."[38]

Since the working population grows at a faster rate than is needed for production, capitalism brings forth surplus populations of fluctuating sizes. To describe the phenomenon of "relative surplus populations" with the attribute "precarious" would be redundant: the concept is implied in the notion of the proletarian worker, whose existence is determined by the speed with which the demands of industrial labor consume his life force and render him superfluous: "the consumption of labour-power by capital is so rapid that the worker has already more or less completely lived himself out when he is only half-way through his life. He falls into the ranks of the surplus population, or is thrust down from a higher to a lower step in the scale."[39] Below the proletarian worker, Marx situates the "sphere of pauperism," which he divides— setting aside the "actual lumpenproletriat"—in three categories: 1. "those able to work;" 2. "orphans and pauper children;" and 3. "the demoralized, the ragged, and those unable to work, chiefly people who succumb to their incapacity for adaptation."[40]

---

37 Karl Marx, *Capital*, vol. 1, trans. Ben Fowkes (New York: Vintage Books, 1977), 798.
38 Marx, *Capital* 1, 799.
39 Marx, *Capital* 1, 795.
40 Marx, *Capital* 1, 797.

The relocation of much industrial production from the Global North to the Global South has rendered large portions of the "sphere of pauperization" invisible to middle-class Europeans and Americans. The precarity of gig workers and freelancers seems incomparably milder than the misery of slum-dwelling laborers driven from their villages. Nonetheless, there are structural similarities that make Marx's insistence on the "antagonistic character of capitalist accumulation"[41] relevant for investigating the *lived, embodied* forms of social precarity in the Global North as well as the representations of such lived forms. When Marx speaks of "people who succumb to their incapacity for adaptation," he is not talking about personal failure but an "incapacity" that results from impersonal circumstances. In contemporary capitalist societies, the capacity for adaptation always lags behind the demand for adaptation—hence the perpetual sense of being overworked and worn-out experienced by so many workers in various industries. Even though "incapacity for adaptation" does not automatically mean a fall into poverty, unemployment and less severe forms of failing to meet social expectations are stigmatized as lack of agility or willpower. Embracing flexibility and autonomy comes at the cost of an explanatory mechanism that goes beyond reflexively assigning individual responsibility to people who find themselves in exploitative circumstances. To make a long story short, it is precisely the absence of the explanatory mechanism previously provided by class theory that makes the new forms of "flexploitation" perniciously effective: in a class society where the word "class" is used only ironically and skeptically, it is predominantly the owners and managers, not the workers, who define the language through which social reality is represented. This volume therefore considers the difficult political and aesthetic question of whether literary forms of representation can constitute a counterhegemonic force against the tendency to make class invisible.

Class: Relation, not Identity

A glance at trends in sociological research over the last fifty years suggests that the challenges in understanding and addressing social precarity are compounded by the disappearance of class as an analytic category in the social sciences:

> In the work of de-representing social classes, sociology's role was at once passive and active. It was passive in the sense that,

---

41   Marx, *Capital* 1, 812.

less autonomous than it often claims to be, it gradually ceased to be interested in classes as they, in their traditional contours, came to be less represented in society. It was active in the sense that sociology makes its own contribution to the task of selecting and representing what matters socially. By ceasing to offer a representation of classes, it thus contributed to their erosion.[42]

By dismissing class analysis as obsolete, sociology and social philosophy dispensed with a critical tool for studying the socially constitutive role of power antagonisms. Instead, the discourse shifted to addressing inequality and conflict in terms of marginalization and exclusion, which implied a normalized standard of integration and inclusiveness that has since remained discursively dominant.[43] Hence, with the disappearance of class, all groups and interests that did not fit into these standards were sidelined.

The most basic definition of class is a social group constituted by shared material interests (*class* in objective terms, "in-itself") and the conscious pursuit and defense of those shared interests (*class* in self-reflexive terms, "for-itself"). It is in the *material* interest of the ruling class to appropriate as much social wealth as possible by ensuring a high rate of surplus-value extraction (Marx's basic definition of exploitation). It is in the *ideological* interest of the ruling class to conceal their material interest in exploitation as completely as possible by establishing hegemony in the field of discursive representation. Attacks on labor rights since the 1970s benefit from defining precarity in cultural and moral terms. By redefining the economic reality of precarity as cultural classism and elite arrogance, those who suffer from having their labor-power exploited are compensated for their lack of control over it by a politics of recognition and appreciation ("employee of the month"), nominal promotions (from assistant to associate manager, in rank only, without corresponding remuneration), sentimental rhetoric (praising the "dignity of labor"), and a massification of perks hitherto reserved for the managerial class (wellness, mindfulness, cultural awareness training). All these discursive interventions inform a "structure of feeling"[44] that individualizes precarity to a point where class theory is bound to look embarrassingly out of step with the popular idea that the purpose

---

42 Luc Boltanski and Ève Chapello, *The New Spirit of Capitalism*, trans. Gregory Elliott (London and New York: Verso, 2018), 391.

43 For example, a 2022 report on the rise of poverty in Germany during the previous decade stresses the socially exclusionary force of poverty: Dorothee Spannagel and Aline Zucco, *Armut grenzt aus: WSI-Verteilungsbericht 2022*. https://www.wsi.de/de/faust-detail.htm?sync_id=HBS-008464.

44 Raymond Williams, *Marxism and Literature* (Oxford and New York: Oxford University Press, 1977), 133–34.

of work is to overcome challenges through personal growth. In contrast to these powerful forms of representation, the benefit of Marx's theory is to remind us that "work" and "labor" are not individual activities, but rather occur within a compulsory, impersonal context over which workers have no control. Moreover, Marx insists that the policing and disciplining of work is an essential rather than accidental quality of the capitalist mode of production; from the (Fordist) factory, it extends into other (post-Fordist) spheres of society as well. Mindful of the distinction between essence and appearance, a Marxian historicization of precarity would understand the apparent self-determination of the "free" gig worker and freelancer as only the surface of an underlying strict routine of internalized policing, self-monitoring, and self-disciplining.

This context reveals that it is indeed crucial, when deploying and evaluating "precarity" as a critical term, to ask which dimensions of a "Prekaritätsgesellschaft"[45] can be addressed with recourse to the difficult, multi-dimensional category of class—a category that is conspicuous mostly through its absence in Piketty's account of inequality, Oliver Marchart's "post-fundamentalist" social theory, and the popular post-Marxism of Antonio Negri and Michael Hardt, who draw on metaphors of swarms, rhizomes, and networks to theorize the subjects of change as a diffuse many, "the poors" or "the multitude"[46] (but not the Marxian proletariat). The success of these and similar theories provides an additional incentive to ask: can a theory of classes and class struggle account for the spread of precarity across social and cultural strata? Can the "precariat" be meaningfully described as an emerging new class, or are its members too heterogeneous to fit into one category?

Responses to these questions depend, first, on whether one considers society to be essentially constituted by conflict and struggle, and whether class is understood in essentialist—as an identity—or in relational terms—as a non-identical, volatile social configuration, made and unmade.[47] If we grant the latter, "class" is structurally similar to

---

45 See Oliver Marchart, *Das unmögliche Objekt: Eine postfundamentalistische Theorie der Gesellschaft* (Berlin: Suhrkamp, 2013), 390–406.

46 Michael Hardt and Antonio Negri, *Multitude: War and Democracy in the Age of Empire* (Cambridge, MA: Harvard University Press, 2000). In their sequel to *Multitude*, however, they qualify the distinction between "multitude" and "crowd" or "masses" and affirm an organization of affect ("the furor of indignation") in the tradition of "the work of class struggle." (See *Commonwealth*, Cambridge, MA: Harvard University Press, 2009, 243).

47 For an exemplary constructivist account of class formation, see E.P. Thompson's *The Making of the English Working Class* (New York: Vintage Books, 1966): "class is a relationship, not a thing ... Class is defined by men as they live their own history, and, in the end, this is its only definition" (11). See also the interview with Patrick Eiden-Offe in Chapter 1 of this volume for a further elaboration on the concept of class as non-identical.

Hardt and Negri's multitude.[48] Given the dangerous rise of nationalist and nativist politics in recent years, it is crucial to retain a capacious notion of class that avoids any identitarian reduction in terms of gender, race, or nationality. The resurgence of nativism is often accompanied by claims that exclusionist, racists politics are fueled by the economic anxieties of "the working class." Moreover, such claims rest on the idea that this "working class" represents primarily white and male industrial workers: coal miners, construction workers, steel workers. Regardless of whether such cultural, racial, and pseudo-sociological attributions come from conversative or liberal commentators, they implicitly suggest that this allegedly identitarian class supports authoritarian politicians out of a sense of defeat. Due to automation, outsourcing, and, above all, "worsening overcapacity in world markets for manufactured goods,"[49] the age of labor-intensive industrial production is irretrievably past. To state the matter less abstractly, the world economy, absent exogenic shocks (wars, pandemics, natural disasters), will surely not require more industrial labor jobs in the foreseeable future, and chronic underemployment, low pay, and poor working conditions are the norm rather than the exception.[50] The challenge is thus to imagine and realize new ways of working and living beyond the old norms of regularized employment. Otherwise, in the words of Hannah Arendt, we are stuck in a world without purpose: "What we are confronted with is the prospect of a society of laborers without labor, that is, without the only activity left to them. Surely, nothing could be worse."[51]

From a mainstream liberal perspective, the dwindling demand for industrial labor is merely a decline of "opportunity" that can be addressed by retraining and education. Boosted by the pervasive propaganda of meritocracy and upward mobility, belief in the college degree as a time-tested path towards middle-class economic stability

---

48 As Patrick Greaney argues, the unrepresentability of pauperism signifies metonymically the nonidentity of the proletarian class: "Pauperism is contiguous to and interwoven with the proletariat, and it forces us to consider the nonidentity of the proletariat as a whole, the specific form of nonidentity characterized by power in its relation to impotence and in its specific form of actuality that is not only enactment" (Greaney, *Untimely Beggar: Poverty and Power from Baudelaire to Benjamin* [Minneapolis, MN and London: University of Minnesota Press, 2008] 18).

49 Aaron Benanav, *Automation and the Future of Work* (London and New York: Verso, 2020), 24.

50 Benanav, *Automation*, 55.

51 Hannah Arendt, *The Human Condition* (Chicago and London: University of Chicago Press, 2018), 5.

("Aufstieg durch Bildung") has led to devastating consequences,[52] producing an army of precariously employed college graduates who find themselves, at best, stuck in the limbo of internships and freelance work and, at worst, permanently encumbered by student debt. Under the burden of this material reality, the luminous idea of a paradoxically post-class "middle class" is growing dim. Filtered, inevitably, through the dominant cultural categories of race, gender, and sexuality, issues of social class positionality and consciousness are re-entering social discourse and the sphere of cultural and artistic production.[53]

The precarization of work has bred a new social Darwinism that requires all workers to incessantly demonstrate their sincere commitment and enthusiasm for even the lowest skilled kinds of work. Because such affective claims have traditionally been made only for positions in service and care work predominantly occupied by women (secretaries, nurses, teachers, flight attendants, etc.), historians of labor now speak of a "feminization" of all work. This transformation challenges the gendered opposition between productive male and reproductive female labor, albeit not necessarily in critical, but rather in ideological terms. While the structural scarcity of meaningful work should breed skepticism about making oneself more competitive or desirable on the job market, dominant ideologies push in the opposite direction: social media networks, HR departments, and popular media promote the illusion that our innermost needs and desires must be in harmony with our job. *Proclaim to love your work or be fired and replaced by someone who really loves the job*[54]—the more work is defined by affect and desire, the more our relation to it is framed in individualistic rather than class terms.

---

52 Silke Fokken, "Das leere Versprechen vom Aufstieg durch Bildung," *Spiegel Online*, October 22, 2018. https://www.spiegel.de/lebenundlernen/schule/deutschland-das-leere-versprechen-vom-aufstieg-durch-bildung-a-1234211.html.

53 For a recent academic study on social precarity in contemporary German literature, see Till Mischko, *Prekarität in deutschsprachigen Romane der Gegenwart* (Bern: Peter Lang, 2022).

54 "Like so many things about late capitalism, the admonishment of a thousand inspirational social media posts to 'do what you love and you'll never work a day in your life' has become folk wisdom, its truthiness presumably everlasting – stretching back to our caveperson ancestors, who I suppose really enjoyed all that mammoth hunting or whatever. Instead of 'never working,' the reality is that we work longer hours than ever, and we're expected to be available even when technically off the clock. All this creates stress, anxiety, and loneliness. The labor of love, in short, is a con" (Sarah Jaffe, *Work Won't Love You Back: How Devotion to Our Jobs Keeps Us Exploited, Exhausted, and Alone*, e-book [New York: Bold Type Books, 2021]).

If, then, the precarization and "feminization" of work are a cultural symptom of underlying material conditions, an appreciation of class critique can direct the focus onto the causal force of relations of exploitation and domination. If class is defined in such a relational way, the question of whether the precariat is a new class or rather the old proletariat in a new guise, can be posed with urgency. Marx's theory of exploitation suggests that the precariat is the latest incarnation of the proletariat, except that the relations of exploitation and domination are no longer primarily between the industrial worker and the factory owner, but rather between the high school teacher and the charter school corporation that employs her (an employer answerable primarily to its hedge fund investors rather than the public good), or the Uber driver and the company that formally is not his boss but nonetheless has as much economic and behavioral power over him as the factory owner over the worker. The teacher, perhaps a former union member, who now works in a newly privatized school, and the Uber driver who depends on supplementary income because his first job as an Amazon delivery driver pays too little to cover his monthly expenses, both belong to the precariat, regardless of whether they consciously identify as members of a class of precarious workers.

Marx's notion of the proletarian worker as a specifically modern, capitalist category is again helpful in this context. If we disregard the famous claim that the proletariat is the universal class and the subject of history, we can appreciate that Marx's origin story of capitalism underscores that the modern proletarian is the personification of social precarity. In his account of the "primitive" [*ursprünglich*] accumulation of capital, Marx proposes a model of modernization that can be studied in industrial English towns in "its classical form." Forcefully separated from the means of production, farmers, craftspeople, and workers end up with nothing to sell but their labor power to sustain their livelihoods. Capitalism's great historical innovation was the creation of a new commodity, *free* labor power, and the creation of a new market, the labor market. When Marx sarcastically described the modern proletarians as *vogelfrei* because they must "freely" sell their labor power lest they starve, he provided a prototype for modern social precarity: it is a state in which the subject is nominally free but *de facto* unfree. Hence, the "free" contract between employer and employee is in effect a relation of coercion.

Precarization: A New Idiom, a New Social Question

Over the course of the first two decades of the twenty-first century, the terms "precarity," "precarious," and "precarization" began to circulate widely, indicating both the need for a theoretically informed historical understanding at both the local and global level, and a pronounced difficulty to fulfill this need. The rise of the term "precarity" can be linked not only to the phenomenon as such but also to the contested nature of established theoretical concepts that fail to satisfactorily account for the experiences of uncertainty and vulnerability conveyed by "precarity." To name one prominent example, precarious "structures of feeling" associated with the rise of neoliberal governmentality cannot be fully accounted for by Judith Butler's influential theory of precariousness as relational "vulnerability," a condition ontologically prior to all particular occurrences of personal experience.[55] Because Butler's ruminations do not engage with class as a factor informing all social relations, their work is a valuable source for an ethics of vulnerability and for critiques of localized manifestations of precariousness, although perhaps less so for an understanding of the large-scale historical dynamics that throw populations into states of precarity.

The discourse about social precarity originated in French sociology of the 1980s, and addressed the erosion of stable social relations, which was leading to the marginalization and even exclusion of growing segments of the population from regular employment and a cohesive network of friends and family. The concern with social exclusion shifted theoretical emphasis away from inequality as the major challenge confronting advanced capitalist economies. The post-war economic stability and affluence of the "trente glorieuses" had made poverty and misery into issues that could be addressed sufficiently within a framework of inequality. The failures of Keynesian deficit spending to extend the "long boom" through the 1970s,[56] however, set the stage for asking whether capitalism would relapse into a crisis-prone generator of wealth accumulation for a small elite, or whether it was (re-)transforming into a new (old) type of cutthroat "free market" economy that could remain profitable for private corporations by reducing the tax burden needed for financing a stabilizing welfare state. Meanwhile, the dwindling resources available to the latter were moved from providing welfare and unemployment payments to building prisons to house the growing surplus populations.

The elasticity of concepts like "post-Fordist capitalism" or "neoliberal capitalism" causes more questions about capitalist continuity

---

55 Judith Butler, *The Force of Nonviolence: An Ethico-Political Bind* (London and Brooklyn: Verso, 2020), 45–6. For Butler's explicitly Levinasian ethics of precariousness, see her *Precarious Life: The Powers of Mourning and Violence* (London and New York: Verso, 2004), 128–51.

56 Robert Brenner, *The Economics of Global Turbulence: The Advanced Capitalist Economies from Long Boom to Long Downturn, 1945–2005* (London and New York: Verso, 2006), 164–86.

and discontinuity than the concepts can satisfactorily answer. "Neo-liberal" in particular has become a widely used attribute, not only in phrases such as "neoliberal economics" or "neoliberal capitalism," but also in "neoliberal culture," "neoliberal rationality," or "the neoliberal university." Pierre Bourdieu was among the first to conceptually wed neoliberalism and precarity, for instance, in a short intervention, "La précarité est aujourd'hui partout."[57] The English translation not only omits the word "néo-libérale" from the title of the volume in which this intervention was collected, it also drops the word *précarité* and renders the title as "Job Insecurity is Everywhere Now;" in the text itself, *précarité* is rendered as "casualization." These minor mistrans-lations downplay Bourdieu's insistence that how we work affects how we live: "It pervades both the conscious and the unconscious mind."[58]

When Bourdieu addresses the economic underpinnings of precari-ous work, the neoliberal world he depicts is rather reminiscent of capi-talism in its "classical form" as drawn by Marx:

> Without a doubt, the practical establishment of this [neoliberal] world of struggle would not succeed so completely without the complicity of all of the precarious arrangements that produce insecurity and of the existence of a reserve army of employees rendered docile by these social processes that make their situations precarious, as well as by the permanent threat of unemployment. This reserve army exists at all levels of the hierarchy, even at the higher levels, especially among managers. The ultimate foundation of this entire economic order placed under the sign of freedom is in effect the structural violence of unemployment, of the insecurity of job tenure and the menace of layoff that it implies. The condition of the "harmonious" functioning of the individualist micro-economic model is a mass phenomenon, the existence of a reserve army of the unemployed.[59]

Similarly, Bourdieu's colleague Robert Castel viewed the neoliberal Darwinian struggle for survival on the job market as bringing forth ever more "supernumeraries": masses of the superfluous "float-ing in a kind of social non-man's land, not integrated and perhaps

---

57 Pierre Bourdieu, *Contre-feux: Propos pour servir à la résistance contre l'invasion néo-libérale* (Paris: Raisons d'Agir, 1998), 95–101.

58 Pierre Bourdieu, *Acts of Resistance: Against the New Myths of Our Time*, trans. Richard Nice (Cambridge: Polity Press, 2000), 82.

59 Pierre Bourdieu, "The Essence of Neoliberalism," trans. Jeremy J. Shapiro, *Le Monde diplomatique*, December 1998.

unintegratable."[60] There is a tendency in Castel's and Bourdieu's the-
orizing to replace the Marxian category of class with mass, and to
universalize the experience of joining the "multitude" of the "supernumeraries:" we *all* live in fear of being rendered redundant, and hence
for falling outside the shrinking zone of social "normality." Although
the standard of normality, expressed in a term such as "Normalar-
beitsverhältnis" [normal labor relations] is instrumental in critiquing
precarity in negative terms such as decline or deterioration,[61] it is
insufficient in expressing the idea that the superfluous are not limited
to the ranks of the unemployed but include the vast numbers of underemployed and precariously employed.

Castel and Bourdieu are alarmed by the collapsing distinction
between employment and unemployment, and consequently between
work and non-work, coercion and freedom. This trend is visible in the
wage-cutting deskilling of industrial labor and new demands on managerial and service work. Thanks to new value-extracting techniques of
efficiency and flexibility, stark forms of exploitation once restricted to
the industrial proletariat can now be found in a range of professions,
especially in care, education, and service work. Precarization, Bourdieu
notes, "is part of a *mode of domination* of a new kind ... which, although
in its effects it closely resembles the wild capitalism of the early days,
is entirely unprecedented, [condensed in] the very appropriate and
expressive concept of *flexploitation*." This neologism, Bourdieu explains,
"evokes very well this rational management of insecurity" that sets up a
transnational system of competition between "the workers of the countries with the greatest social gains and the best organized union resistance ... and the workers of the socially least advanced countries, and so
breaks resistance and obtains obedience and submission."[62] *Flexploitation* is spatially facilitated by breaking down production into smaller
units (located where labor is cheapest) seamlessly interconnected by
global supply chains, which in turn enables discontinuous just-in-time
production. Increasingly, jobs require workers to change where they
work and adjust to uneven, unpredictable work hours. Moreover, it
becomes harder for workers to sustainably accommodate themselves
to these new requirements, because "flexploitation" takes command
where legal and social securities are being dismantled.

---

60 Robert Castel, *From Manual Workers to Wage Laborers: Transformation of the
    Social Question*, trans. Richard Boyd (New Brunswick and London: Transaction
    Publishers, 2003), 389.
61 Nachtwey's *Germany's Hidden Crisis* (*Die Abstiegsgesellschaft*) uses the positive
    term *Normalarbeitsverhältnis* to chart his negative diagnostic terms, such as
    Abstieg [descent] or *Niedergang* [decline].
62 Bourdieu, *Acts of Resistance*, 85.

In a similar vein, Hardt and Negri conceive of neoliberalism as domination over the management of time: due to the constant threat of unemployment, "the entire labor force becomes a reserve army, with workers constantly on call, at the disposal of the boss. Precarity might thus be conceived as a special kind of poverty, a temporal poverty, in which workers are deprived of control over their time."[63] At the same time, precarity can still be measured by conventional economic indicators: Robert Castel draws our attention to the real decline in wages due to intensified competition in a globalized labor market. He stresses the "continued deterioration of the condition of wage labor observable since the 1970s."[64]

Yet in addition to the *economic* crisis of *wage labor*, Castel believes that precarity indicates a comprehensive *social and cultural* crisis of *work*. Because all relations of employment have been rendered insecure and unstable, work can no longer provide a sense of identity. Hence, when Castel speaks of "neopauperism," he has in mind not only the unemployed or underemployed, but rather all populations for whom work has become "meaningless employment"[65] and for whom "identity through work is lost."[66] This phenomenon no longer occurs only at the margins of society but at its very center:[67]

> Just as the pauperism of the nineteenth century arose out of the heart of the dynamic of early industrialization, so too does the precariousness of labor arise from a central process .... This is more than enough to pose a 'new social question' of the same magnitude and centrality as that posed by pauperism in the first half of the nineteenth century.[68]

Pauperism is distinct from poverty because it is intrinsically related to labor and employment. Neopauperism in the twenty-first century is like nineteenth-century pauperism in that it is an essential component of the capitalist mode of production, the drive for growth and profits. Yet it does not only manifest as material immiseration but also as

---

63 Hardt and Negri, *Commonwealth*, 147.
64 Castel, *From Manual Workers to Wage Laborers*, 409.
65 Castel, *From Manual Workers to Wage Laborers*, 389.
66 Castel, *From Manual Workers to Wage Laborers*, 390.
67 Similarly, Maurizio Lazzarato describes the production of a new poverty as central to neoliberal governmentality. See his *Experimental Politics: Work, Welfare, and Creativity in the Neoliberal Age*, trans. Arianna Bove, Jeremy Gilbert, Andrew Goffey, Mark Hayward, Jason Read, and Alberto Toscano, ed. Jeremy Gilbert (Cambridge, MA and London: MIT Press, 2017), 39.
68 Castel, *From Manual Workers to Wage Laborers*, 387.

inherently contradictory affects: for instance, as being stuck in an "eternal present" without a future distinct from the present[69] or as desiring a life from which one is structurally blocked.[70] The new social question thus is concerned with the mechanisms that hold (or fail to hold) together a society that includes a growing population with dwindling prospects of materially securing their livelihoods. In addition to the rapid rise in inequality along the axis of class constitution, social precarity in the twenty-first century is uniquely characterized by a wealth divergence between generations. For those born after 1985, the post-war middle-class standard of living, including house and car ownership, is significantly less achievable than for earlier generations. Therefore, the new social question is also a generational question.[71]

"Precarization" does not necessarily mean growth in unemployment; the new social question is not primarily about who is included and excluded from the wage relation. Rather, it concerns the increased dependency of the individual on the wage alone as the worker's total income (as measured in paid sick leave, vacation time, pension insurance, etc.) is progressively reduced. The social spiral of dwindling compensation for labor power manifests as resentment towards workers who still enjoy the right to secure compensation; for instance, union workers with guaranteed pensions or public employees with paid sick leave and vacation time. At the same time, even old social-democratic rights were, as Guy Standing points out, to some degree fictitious:[72] they often required a commitment to a minimum period of employment and a gradual "earning"

---

69 See Fredric Jameson, *The Seeds of Time* (New York: Columbia University Press, 1994), 70–1.

70 What was once possible is no longer so, even as our fantasies still cling to what we feel entitled to, creating a specific kind of neoliberal affect, "cruel optimism" which Lauren Berlant delineates in its artistic precipitations: "*Cruel Optimism* depicts the work of new genres, such as the situation tragedy (in relation to melodrama and situation comedy), and an emergent aesthetics, such as in the cinema of precarity, in which attention to a pervasive contemporary social precariousness marks a relation to older traditions of neorealism, while speaking as well to the new social movements that have organized under the rubrics of "precarity" and the "precarious." These new aesthetic forms, I argue, emerge during the 1990s to register a shift in how the older state-liberal-capitalist fantasies shape adjustments to the structural pressures of crisis and loss that are wearing out the power of the good life's traditional fantasy bribe without wearing out the need for a good life" (Lauren Berlant, *Cruel Optimism* [Durham, NC: Duke University Press, 2011], 13).

71 Lisa Adkins, Melinda Cooper, and Martijn Konings, *The Asset Economy: Property Ownership and the New Logic of Inequality* (London: Polity, 2020), 68.

72 Guy Standing, "Understanding the Precariat through Labour and Work," *Development and Change* 45, no. 5 (2014): 967, fn. 5.

of benefits over time, thus forcefully "marrying" the worker to the company and hence increasing the control that capital exerts over labor. It is important, therefore, not to idealize social democracy as the golden age that preceded the current regime of neoliberalism. In both socioeconomic orders, security is not a universal right but must be earned by submission under rules of employment determined by capital rather than labor. The difference, however, lies in the worker's ability to identify with her work. Under conditions of neoliberal precarity, this is no longer possible, because the worker has been put in a position where she has become a permanent entry-level trainee, someone who is forever being asked to strive to become better, more flexible, more creative, and more innovative. Being employed has become synonymous with being under the permanent tutelage of a corporate managerial elite that demands that workers fully realize their potential at work (that is, that they actualize all their labor power) while communicating to them that giving everything is not enough: employees must both expend their full potential and, at the same time, grow it.

The flip side of what Castel describes as social disintegration is an intensified ideological integration of the worker into the corporate temple of self-improvement. One might say that as the state withdraws from its role as last guarantor of material well-being, private enterprise steps in and offers spiritual solutions, a phenomenon reminiscent of Siegfried Kracauer's description of the Weimar Republic salariat living off of cultural nourishment without being able to ameliorate either its meager compensation or its spiritual homelessness.[73] But as the COVID-19 pandemic aggravated pre-existing conditions of social isolation and mass loneliness, the "social question" has now merged with the "labor question." The "traditional" concerns about employment and compensation have become imbued with alarms over new digital forms of controlling and surveilling the workplace. The dream of working autonomously, without the constraints of a corporate office space and a boss breathing down one's neck, has turned out to be a nightmare of high-tech Taylorism invading the private sphere. Because activity monitoring now allows management to check their workers' productivity no matter where they are physically, the old topographical markers of social class—factory floor, middle-management office, corporate suite—have lost some of their representational salience. Class, one might say, is becoming a sign

---

73 See Siegfried Kracauer, *The Salaried Masses: Duty and Distraction in Weimar Germany*, trans. Quentin Hoare (London and New York: Verso, 1998).

of non-belonging, of falling through the cracks of older categories. With Guy Standing, one can understand the emerging precariat as a negatively constituted "class-in-the-making."[74] Whereas the nineteenth-century working class made gains in improving their conditions of labor, the contemporary precariat's essential experience is one of regression: its labor struggles are primarily defensive, aiming to slow down the deterioration of labor conditions. To use Standing's formula, the precariat is defined by the decreasing commodification of its labor (as measured by declining wages) and the increasing commodification of its labor power (as indicated by growing demands for flexibility).[75]

Pitfalls of the Artistic Critique

For Marx, the idea of "labor-power" designated an innate human life-capacity that can be actualized in the activity of laboring. In the capitalist production process, the human potential for labor is most fully actualized when the worker has become a mere "appendix" to the machines dominating the labor process. This is perhaps nowhere truer than in the contemporary "logistics centers," essential nodes for the global flow of goods and services: workers at these sites have their every movement dictated by machine intelligence.[76] Rather than making human workers the overseers of machines, as for instance Marx imagined it,[77] "humans are being crunched into a robot system working at a robot pace."[78] Contra Deleuze's claim in 1990, contemporary societies are as much *societies of control* as *societies of discipline*: the disciplinary power of the factory work process coexists with the business techniques described by Deleuze, such as the introjection of the factory bonus system into all layers of work.[79] In a society of control, the promises of autonomy yearned for in a society of discipline (enhanced

---

74 See Guy Standing, *The Precariat: A New Dangerous Class* (London and New York: Bloomsbury, 2011) and *A Precariat Charter: From Denizens to Citizens* (London and New York: Bloomsbury, 2014).

75 See Standing, "Understanding the Precariat through Labour and Work," 975.

76 Ceylan Yeginsu, "If Workers Slack Off, the Wristband Will Know. (And Amazon Has a Patent for It.)," *New York Times*, February 1, 2018. https://www.nytimes.com/2018/02/01/technology/amazon-wristband-tracking-privacy.html?smid=url-share.

77 Karl Marx, *Grundrisse: Foundations of the Critique of Political Economy (Rough Draft)*, trans. Martin Nicolaus (London: Penguin, 1993), 709.

78 Sarah O'Connor, "Why I Was Wrong to be Optimistic about Robots," *Financial Times*, February 8, 2021. https://www.ft.com/content/087fce16-3924-4348-8390-235b435c53b2.

79 Gilles Deleuze, "Postscript on Control Societies," *Negotiations 1972–1990*, trans. Martin Joughin (New York: Columbia University Press, 1995), 179.

mobility, control over one's time, lifelong learning) are transformed into instruments of managerial regulation and "nudging," either within the setting of a business or within the work of the individual worker, who becomes her own manager, in accordance with the ego-ideal of an "entrepreneurial self."[80]

Around the turn of the millennium, the inflationary use of the word "creativity," canonized by Richard Florida's extolling of the "creative class,"[81] served as a tacit admission that overt disciplining of workers is not required when they are driven by an internalized compulsion to actualize their labor power in the service of new, innovative products, or when new forms of work become part of the product. Just as economic wealth is precariously created through bubbles of over-valuation (e.g., the 2001 dot-com bubble and the 2008 subprime mortgage crisis, which rudely interrupted our current age of "fictitious capital"), self-realization begins to look like over-leveraging. In a parody of the classical avant-garde demand to abolish the bourgeois opposition of life and work, marshaling life into growth and productivity is celebrated as an admirable virtue: what was self-denial during the age of industrial capitalism is now self-affirmation. Creative workers (designers, illustrators, copywriters, "content providers") are mythologized as wondrous beings who draw their productivity not primarily from the skills they have acquired through training and learning, but rather from their labor power mystified as their innate spiritual, creative resource: the prototypical "human resource." Cultural producers embody the (self-destructive) fantasy of naturally occurring, limitless sources of value and hence become an important "fix" for crises of accumulation. Esther Leslie observes:

[C]ulture is the wonder stuff that gives more away than it takes. Like some fantastical oil in a Grimm fairytale, this magical substance gives and gives, generating and enhancing value, for state and private men alike. Culture is posited as a mode of value-production: for its economy-boosting and wealth-generating effects; its talent for regeneration, through raising house prices and introducing new business, which is largely service based; and its benefits as a type of moral rearmament or emotional trainer, a

---

80 "In neoliberalism ... *homo oeconomicus* is ... an entrepreneur of himself, being for himself his own capital, being for himself his own producer, being for himself the source of [his] earnings." (Michel Foucault, *The Birth of Biopolitics: Lectures at the Collège de France 1978–79*, trans. Graham Burchell [Houndmills and New York: Palgrave Macmillan, 2008], 226.)

81 Richard Florida, *The Rise of the Creative Class* (New York: Basic Books, 2002).

perspective that lies behind the "social inclusion" model, whereby culture must speak to – or down to – disenfranchised groups.[82]

Sociologically, the "creative type" culture workers are heirs to the Bohème and clash with the stereotype of the buttoned-up white-collar salaried employee, the company man of the 1950s. Yet, as Boltanski and Chiapello argue, capitalist enterprises are very capable of reabsorbing originally anti-capitalist forms of critique, and the "artistic critique" of alienation and inauthenticity (which culminated in the student revolts of 1968) was absorbed into value-generating labor by ideologically redefining the drudgery of corporate work as a succession of projects serving the higher purpose of authentic self-fulfillment.[83]

In contrast to Boltanski and Chiapello's alarm about the neoliberal neutralization of anti-capitalist critique, Isabell Lorey, in her oft-cited *State of Insecurity: Government of the Precarious*, celebrates the "self-chosen precarization" of creative workers as ushering in a new form of politics outside the established liberal order of "identity and representation." Lorey argues that the lack of class identity and hence the impossibility of political representation makes "the multiplicity of the precarious" the agent of a "radically new form of democracy."[84] With her affirmation of non-representational form, Lorey's work, which found its widest reception in the aftermath of the Occupy movement, radiates the spirit of the young millennium, when anarcho-libertarian politics and participatory, relational performance art came together in a shared embrace of grassroots, leaderless, spontaneous protest that, in its slogan, "We are the 99%," rejected the old stratifications of class politics. However, because the movement's economic demands were overshadowed by its ultimately self-defeating veneration of unorganized direct democracy, it eventually found itself diminished to an "artistic critique" of suit-wearing Wall Street bankers and ugly corporate greed. Channeling the spirit of this artistic critique, Lorey's work on precariousness heavily draws on writings from the Italian "post-operaist" (post-workerist) tradition, starting with the claim that in the age of computerized networks of knowledge, value is increasingly created not by exploited material labor but by elusive forms of immaterial productivity generated by a globally connected, fluid, non-representable "multitude."

---

82 Esther Leslie, "Add Value to Contents: The Valorization of Culture Today," in *Critique of Creativity: Precarity, Subjectivity and Resistance in the "Creative Industries,"* ed. Gerald Raunig, Gene Ray and Ulf Wuggenig (London: MayFly Books, 2011), 183.
83 See Boltansky and Chapello, *The New Spirit of Capitalism.*
84 Isabell Lorey, *State of Insecurity: Government of the Precarious,* trans. Aileen Derieg (London and New York: Verso, 2015), 100.

Lorey's description of a post-workerist "exodus" from relatively secure (perhaps even unionized) wage labor seems to exhort her readers not to spend too much time worrying about the immediate reality of social precarity and what can be done about it, and rather to appreciate that as the state increases the risk of being a person, people must get creative to make do: "In the post-Fordist conditions of precarious production, new forms of living and new social relationships are continually being developed and invented. In this sense, processes of precarization are also productive."[85] It is hardly coincidental that this and similar "progressive neoliberalist"[86] claims differ little from managerial discourse, which also celebrates novelty, inventiveness, and productivity as laudable upshots of disruption and uncertainty. The easy compatibility of these kinds of theories with corporate interests reflects a larger conundrum typical for the milieu of artists and intellectuals. On the one hand, the modern artist is by definition a precarious worker: released from aristocratic or clerical patronage, she is dependent on the market and the generosity of public and private sponsors. On the other hand, because she has had to learn how to do more with less, even a minor drop in income can have distressing consequences. The new level of social precarity brought about by neoliberal governance hits those the hardest who already lived in a state of precarity to begin with.

Significant portions of cultural production are precarious; much artistic labor is unevenly remunerated or partially unpaid, and artists in particular are expected to content themselves with non-pecuniary rewards (recognition, prestige, admiration, publicity). The labor market for cultural workers is highly fragmented and unpredictable, a fact that Lazzarato describes as the "striking ... disjunction between work and employment" in "the cultural sector."[87] Precisely this disjunction can provide the impetus for coordinating resistance against precarity, as in the "Coordination des Intermittents et Précaires," an organized movement of creative temporary and precarious workers that arose in French cities in the early 2000s and demanded access to state benefits that are normal in other industries. Such demands can be made only within an

---

85 Lorey, *State of Insecurity*, 106.
86 Nancy Fraser uses the term "progressive neoliberalism" to critique a political and cultural "configuration in which emancipation joins with marketization to undermine social protection." (Fraser, *Cannibal Capitalism* [London and New York: Verso, 2022], 69).
87 Maurizio Lazzarato, "The Misfortunes of the 'Artistic Critique' and of Cultural Employment," trans. Mary O'Neill, in *Critique of Creativity: Precarity, Subjectivity and Resistance in the "Creative Industries,"* ed. Gerald Raunig, Gene Ray and Ulf Wuggenig (London: MayFly Books, 2011), 52.

institutional framework of normality, that is, within a social consensus concerning the limits to the length of the workday, which implies that normality is premised on the ability to clearly separate work from non-work (free time, leisure, rest, etc.).

The weaker the protections of the welfare state, the more the creative class is incentivized to organize around universal demands, such as debt forgiveness or Universal Basic Income. Yet precisely because precarization blurs the boundaries between work and life, responses to precarity within the creative class tend to further individualize the politics of precarity. Whether desperately or proudly, the creative worker becomes an *Überlebenskünstler* and, with some luck, monetizes the structural contradiction of individual freedom within general unfreedom by marketing their mode of living as an example for emulation, as Sascha Lobo and Holm Friebe did with their slogan of the "digital Bohème"[88] in 2008. Fifteen years later, the disenchantment resulting from a bohemian digital lifestyle massified by means of Zoom and Slack is accompanied by growing awareness that its digital infrastructure is owned by a small number of powerful "Big Tech" monopolies that not only monitor and archive all traffic on their networks but can also censor and ban users depending on which way the winds of social normalization are blowing.

Since cognitive capitalism is still *capitalism*, it will continue to recuperate most new forms of (shared, informal, immaterial) productivity for the purposes of private value appropriation, thereby blocking any constitution of a decommodified commons, the dialectical *conditio sine qua non* for the realization of individual freedom. Lorey tries to circumvent this problem, following Virno, by focusing on what Marx described as "unproductive labor"—"unproductive" because it does not occur within the framework of a production process geared towards capital accumulation. According to Marx's theory, individual artistic work is unproductive, artistic work in the service of a for-profit corporation is not. The writer who receives an honorarium for publishing a poem in *The New Yorker* is an unproductive worker; the same writer, if Hulu or HBO employs her to write for one of their shows, becomes a productive worker. Paul Virno hones in on what Marx dismisses as an "peripheral phenomenon": work that brings about a "product that is not separable from the act of producing."[89] Marx points to services such as healing and teaching as examples. For both Virno and Lorey, service work becomes the model for cognitive and artistic forms of labor best described as

---

88 Cf. Holm Friebe and Sascha Lobo, *Wir nennen es Arbeit: Die digitale Boheme oder: Intelligentes Leben jenseits der Festanstellung* (Munich: Heyne 2008).

89 Marx, *Capital 1*, 1048.

virtuoso because they are "an activity which finds its own fulfillment (that is, its own purpose) in itself, without objectifying itself into an end product, without settling into a 'finished product.'"[90]

Understood as virtuoso performance, precarious work as theorized by Lorey collapses the distinction between labor (private) and action (public), upheld vigilantly in Hannah Arendt's concept of politics, to which both Virno and Lorey refer. Regardless of one's view of Arendt's distinction, Lorey's claim that "performative virtuoso workers automatically become political actors," because their activity occurs in "the presence of the other,"[91] cannot help but validate the neoliberal administering of risk and insecurity in the name of overcoming the ossified constraints of the oppressive, masculinist Fordist system of security. Miraculously, the vanishing of mediating factors between private and public—employers, unions, political parties—retrofits precarious workers with political agency. Even though the reality of an Arendtian public sphere conditioned on equality and freedom from necessity must remain fictitious because its prototype, ancient Athens, was based on the expropriation of labor performed by women and slaves,[92] Lorey nonetheless sees an old "form of freedom based on insecurity"[93] emerge anew, a freedom reminiscent of Arendt's recuperating an ancient concept of "freedom which is not an attribute of the will but an accessory of doing and acting."[94]

Lorey's persistent emphasis on potentiality rather than actuality (*Wirklichkeit*), on becoming rather than being ("precarization" rather than "precarity"), on emergence rather than semblance (*Schein*), on "the political" rather than "politics," on presence rather than representation, and on process rather than work, touches on a concern critical for this volume: is social precarity a theme that can be given form within the logic of an "aesthetics of the art-work" (*Werkästhetik*), or is it rather a "structure of feeling" that resists representation? If social precarity is expressed in literature and similar artforms primarily as an effect of the precarious conditions of its production, does this call for a renewed "aesthetics of production" (*Produktionsästhetik*)? Presumably, such an aesthetics of production would entail the development of new forms of

---

90 Paolo Virno, *A Grammar of the Multitude: For an Analysis of Contemporary Forms of Life*, trans. Sabella Bertoletti, James Cascaito, and Andrea Casson (Cambridge, MA: MIT Press, 2004), 52.

91 Lorey, *State of Insecurity*, 85, 84.

92 See Arendt, *The Human Condition*, 32.

93 Lorey, *State of Insecurity*, 87.

94 Hannah Arendt, "What is Freedom?," in *Between Past and Future* (New York and London: Penguin Press, 1968), 165.

collaborative and collective authorship and hence a radical break from the prevalent model of the writer as individual entrepreneur. Although constructing new forms of artistic labor might be the only way out of artistic precarity, models for collective artistic labor are utopian rather than historical. As long as even the structurally collective artform of film remains in the hands of the few (investors, producers, directors) and not the many, artistic production will remain what all capitalist production is: a "precarious system."[95]

Conclusion and Summary

Historically, the origins of modern social precarity as distinguished from medieval poverty can be traced to the emergence of a class of workers dispossessed of land and property. Compelled to sell their labor power to survive, this new class, which became known as the "proletariat" in distinction from the more general understanding of "the common people" (German, "der Pöbel," French, "le peuple"), found itself existentially exposed to the booms and busts of the expanding capitalist market. In the first chapter, Karsten Olson and literary theorist and historian Patrick Eiden-Offe explore the conceptual and economic genealogy of the proletariat by discussing the literary and theoretical representations of the *Vormärz* period which preceded its formation as a distinct social class. Before socialist and communist activists hailed it as the inevitable champion of equality and emancipation, the proletariat was a social stratum defined in the negative. Marx described it as a "buntscheckiger Haufen," a non-identical grouping which was the diffuse product of separation, dispossession, dissolution, and disintegration. The early proletariat occupied the social rift left by the destruction of the guild and estate systems, and in the negative space of its displacement and mobility, possibilities (re)emerge which were unthinkable in the presence of the organized proletariat. In their interview, Eiden-Offe argues for reading the early proletariat's radical precarity as the embodied practice of the romantic theory of a "universal progressive poetry" advocated by writers such as Ludwig Tieck and the Schlegel brothers. Based on Eiden-Offe's recuperation of a pre-Marxist "romantic anti-capitalism," the interview explores what lessons can be learned from the nineteenth-century history of proletarianization and how we can write a history of social precarity that enables us to see the confluence of global crises in an historically informed multi-perspectival fashion.

---

95 Beech, *Art and Value*, 342.

While the first chapter is centered on the theme of proletarian dis-possession, the second chapter articulates a romantic theory of precar-ious property, currency and language as developed by Adam Müller in works such as "Der poetische Besitz" ("Poetic Property;" 1806) and "Versuche einer Theorie des Geldes" ("Essays on a Theory of Money;" 1816). Müller's work is often dismissed out of hand as reactionary and uncritical, in no small part due to the searing critiques it received at the hands of Hegel, Marx, and Lukács. Jörg Kreienbrock demonstrates not only the surprising proximity of Müller's theory to these critics but also illuminates an alternative mode of ownership and property, one based not on violent dominion and occupation, but rather on acts of gratuity, grace, and charity. Müller, in his search for a Romantic "recon-ciliation of science and art," conceived of the accumulation of property (and capital) as an inherently poetic act. For instance, Müller insisted on the persistence of "werben," or the wooing of the beloved, in all acts of "erwerben": property ownership, conceived as a modality of wooing, is a continuous process of erwerben that resembles a poetic address. For Müller, the acquisition and possession of all property must be understood according to the Roman notion of *precarium* rather than *occupatio*—ownership is a lending agreement in which the lender can reclaim their property at any moment in time. Müller's idea of poetic property thus introduces an unsettling element of precarity into the economic, legal, and aesthetic aspects of society, offering an alterna-tive to what Müller referred to as the modern "republics of property," republics that by their very nature could never be anything but violent, antagonistic police states.

In the third chapter, Karsten Olson pursues a critical reading of a canonical realist novella, Annette von Droste-Hülshoff's "Die Judenbu-che" ("The Jew's Beech Tree;" 1842). Her narrator promises a glimpse into the town of B***, a fictional community representative of a world once common in Germany, now irretrievably lost. The narrator sug-gests that in order to understand the lives of the people at this time, without sliding into either "arrogant censure" or "fatuous praise," it is necessary that the reader become acquainted with the unwritten "sec-ond law" which has governed their lives for generations. This "second law" had nothing to do with the legal codes which could be found in "ancient and dusty records," and referred instead to the law of local customs, as determined by the court of public opinion and the frequent scuffles which occurred between the foresters of the landed gentry and the peasants. The narrator contends that the mid-eighteenth century, the period in which the novella is set, was a time in which "infringe-ments occurred more often, but complete unscrupulousness was rarer," thereby positioning "Die Judenbuche" as a story of historical transi-tion, as the customary minor infringements slide into a series of brutal murders. Olson reads the transition portrayed in "Die Judenbuche" in connection with Karl Marx's discussion of the natural rights of the poor, as described in the articles "Debatten über das Holzdiebstahlsgesetz" ("Debates on the Wood Theft Law;" 1842), along with Marx's later concept of "primitive accumulation." Olson argues that Droste-Hülshoff's novella provides a stark reminder, not only of the socially and economically devastating consequences of dispossession for the non-landowning rural population, but also of the limitless nature of so-called primitive accumulation.

The period following the Napoleonic wars was not only rife with political oppression but also saw an explosive growth of extreme impoverishment. *Vormärz* literature contains many depictions of poverty's hardships, but considerations of the poor's existential precarity are less common. The fourth chapter shows that the dramas of Georg Büchner form an exception by exploring the vulnerability, displacement, and hopelessness that permeate the subjectivity of the nineteenth-century German "precariat." Büchner's dramas *Dantons Tod* and *Woyzeck* do not participate in the politics of poverty, whereby depictions of poverty are integrated into a reform or revolutionary program, but rather explore subjective experiences of precarity where life is devoid of any sense of progress and yet "gets lived nonetheless."[96] Michael Swellander's chapter examines how Büchner's precarious subjects live under the all-pervasive horizon of labor as a means of survival, both within the frameworks of historical teleology and biopolitics. In *Dantons Tod*, Büchner juxtaposes the protagonists' attempts to work out politicized philosophies of history against the struggle of the nameless poor to adapt to the material conditions of revolutionary Paris: for many citizens, revolution is a new job, yet material well-being remains elusive. *Woyzeck* also portrays subjectivities shaped by an all-pervasive concept of work, but through strict bodily regulation. All experience is potential labor, and as Woyzeck says of his sleeping son: "Nothing in the world but work, even in your sleep you sweat." This chapter shows how Büchner, rather than engaging in the politics of poverty in these dramas, imagined the existential vulnerability inherent to unreliable work conditions.

In Chapter 5, Rebekah O. McMillan explores the documentary record of institutional responses to the alarming proliferation of pauperism: the Elberfeld System, the most well-known form of state-sponsored German poor relief in the nineteenth century, emerged in response to the failure of appeals to individual moral resolve to ameliorate mass

---

96 "Precarity: Commentary by Anne Allison," *Cultural Anthropology*. https://journal.culanth.org/index.php/ca/precarity-commentary-by-anne-allison.

poverty. By analyzing the System's origins and establishment, McMillan shows how the use of local poor relief volunteers to investigate the needs of the impoverished refashioned the poor through the eyes of the bourgeois middle class. Thus, the system developed alongside the stubborn belief that the hardship of the poor could be blamed on a lack of moral character. Drawing on regional archival sources from Wuppertal, North Rhine-Westphalia, and Berlin, McMillan argues that the new social dynamics at the root of the Elberfeld System influenced the management of poverty into the present moment, defining precarity through the eyes of the middle class and often compulsory and punitive social programs rather than allowing the poor to articulate their needs for themselves.

Turning to proletarian precarity in the early twentieth century, Chapter 6 focuses on Lu Märten's aesthetic and gender theory. An underrated communist-utopian thinker and writer, Märten resolutely forged a path separate from the KPD's prescriptive cultural politics and proposed an "education of desire" in the service of a new society. Specifically, Mari Jarris discusses Märten's reappropriation of the moralistic genre of the worker's autobiography in her 1909 novel *Torso: Das Buch eines Kindes* (*Torso: The Book of a Child*). The novel's first half presents the diary of an unnamed child grappling with tuberculosis and the death of her family members, and in the second half follows the child, who is now an androgynous adult Marxist named Hazar Loewen, through an assemblage of poetry, prose, drama, fairytale, and hymn. *Torso* radically upends the conventions of the worker's autobiography to imagine new ways of representing precarity: first, it depicts working-class precarity from a gendered perspective; second, it explores the implications of debility as endemic to the working class; and third, it refutes aspirations for bourgeois subjectivity and its literary expression in the confessional narrative. Jarris shows how Märten seeks to represent gendered, working-class precarity through an experimentation with form that uses the utopian potential of the fragment to express both unstable subjectivity and revolutionary new social relations.

Similar to Märten, the poet, author, and actress Emmy Hennings—most well known as one of the founders of Dada at the Cabaret Voltaire with her husband, Hugo Ball—inhabited the milieu of bohemian poverty. The seventh chapter examines Hennings' novel *Das Brandmal: Ein Tagebuch* (*The Branding: A Diary, 1920*), an autofictional work based on Hennings' experiences as a sex worker in the 1910s and told from the perspective of a young woman named Dagny. Sophie Duvernoy argues that *The Branding* is a novel about the failure to turn work into a calling, an activity that goes beyond wage labor by looking towards a metaphysical horizon. By examining the use of the word "Beruf," which originally means to be called upon (be-rufen) by God to a vocation, this contribution moves from Max Weber's discussion of "Beruf" in *The Protestant Ethic and the Spirit of Capitalism* to tracing the multiple valences of the word in Dagny's search for work. Dagny's forays into various kinds of work, including prostitution, are part of a religious quest that dovetails with a representational quest to present a narrative from a perspective that denies its own representative authority, inhabiting instead an "aesthetics of failure" (Leo Bersani). In doing so, Hennings reconfigures her lifelong commitment to Catholicism to develop a critique of capitalist labor that is both radically modernist and utterly idiosyncratic, focused on the muteness and disenfranchisement of the young female subject.

In Chapter 8, Mary Hennessy examines the terminological conflation of women and typewriters in the Weimar Republic from the perspective of the reification of capitalist social relations. Siegfried Kracauer's "Das Schreibmaschinchen" ("The Little Typewriter;" 1927) imagines an anthropomorphized, sexualized typewriter and "her" tumultuous relationship with a male narrator. While critical of reification, Kracauer's piece remains wedded to a normative understanding of the writing subject as male and frames the harassment and exploitation of women as a pleasurable experiment in commodity fetishism. Christa Anita Brück's 1930 novel *Schicksale hinter Schreibmaschinen* (*Destinies behind Typewriters*), follows Fräulein Brückner as she goes from one typing job to another—five in the course of the novel—each worse than the last. *Schicksale* offers a pointed critique of a system that saw women typists as little more than objects to be used and discarded, not unlike the typewriters at which they worked. By forcefully inserting gender into contemporary critiques of capitalism, Brück's novel offers a perspective that is notably absent from Kracauer's "Das Schreibmaschinchen" and remains undertheorized in Frankfurt School Critical Theory and in German media theory, describing women's work at the typewriter as a matter of life and death itself.

A document of the mass immiseration brought about by the impact of the Great Depression, the film *Kuhle Wampe oder Wem gehört die Welt* (*Kuhle Wampe or Who Owns the World*; 1932), a joint production by communist artists Brecht, Eisler, Ottwalt, and Dudow, revolves around the axis of a transformation in gendered work relations: while the male characters are universally unemployed, the female protagonists Gerda and Anni are employed in the advanced industrial sector of semi-automated electronics production. Chapter 9 proposes to read *Kuhle Wampe*'s reconfiguration of proletarian gender relations not as a mere inversion, but rather as a utopian wager to counter the misery of late Weimar mass unemployment through the cooperative and playful mobilization of idle labor power. Such mobilizations require as their necessary precondition, the film suggests, the work of mass organizing. At first glance, collective practices such as marching, singing, making leaflets, or participating in mass sporting events seem to merely imitate the rationalization of time, space, and motion that occurs in the factory. In such collective practices of intentional mimesis, however, the film introduces new elements of spontaneity into the coercive mechanization of life and implies that they are crucial in empowering workers to reclaim what, echoing the film's subtitle, ought to be theirs: their reproductive and sexual rights, the streets of the city, and "the world" evoked in the film's title and its penultimate scene.

Moving from *Kuhle Wampe's* playful enactment of new social relations to the coercive state socialism of East Germany, Chapter 10 considers representations of social precarity in a country where it could only be evoked by pointing to the West, to demonstrate that precariousness was specific to capitalism and had been overcome under real existing socialism. In a paternalistic society that prided itself for taking care of all its citizens, poverty and marginalization were bound to be politically scandalous; after all, this was a society that claimed to have done away with all forms of misery. What happens, however, when precarity persists and cannot be "integrated"? In the documentary films of Thomas Heise, voluntary or coerced encounters between GDR citizens and state institutions such as the "Kommunale Wohnungsverwaltung" (municipal department of housing administration) or the "Abteilung Inneres" (department of the interior) bring about either relief from precarity or heightened exposure to punitive state power. With its law against "antisocial behavior," the East German state sought to outlaw displays of social precarity. The practices and effects of moral condemnation and mass criminalization of "antisocial behavior," from which children were not spared, are recorded in Heise's films, for instance in a long sequence in *Material* that shows the aftermath of a rebellion inside a prison in the fall of 1989: while outside the prison newly empowered GDR citizens debate the possible futures of a reformed socialism, inside the penitentiary prisoners engage their guards in a debate about radical prison reform. As Rothe and Heise discuss in their conversation, the documentary foregrounding of institutions designed to regulate life in the GDR not only documents what was but also what was possible—thus, the documentation of social precarity yields images of past futures.

By the end of the nineteenth century, the health and hygiene of the working class became scientific benchmarks in the German Empire for securing its national unity by defining itself as a welfare state and colonial power. In this context, German cell biology established the bacillus as a metaphor for the unproductive laborer or supposed racial other who endangered the healthy "social organism" or *völkisch* body of the nation.

Picking up on this metaphor of the "bad cell," Barbara Albert's film *Böse Zellen* (*Free Radicals*; 2003) explores how these biopolitical couplings of nationalism and wage labor translate into the social psychology of a capitalist nation state under the pressures of twenty-first-century globalization. In Chapter 11, Lena Trüper analyses the film's biopolitical relations of health and wage labor. While the metaphor of the "bad cell" represents a strong belief in medical ideas inherited from the nineteenth century, *Böse Zellen* represents the superstitious questioning of scientific rationality as a consequence of neoliberal social precarity. Moreover, *Böse Zellen* illustrates the shift of the hygienic dispositive from the nineteenth century to the present, from identifying the "infectious" other as a "bad cell" towards identifying the whole scientific and political apparatus as the "poison" infecting the *völkisch* body, as can be witnessed in contemporary anti-vaccination conspiracy theories. Trüper argues that such metaphoric slippages are symptoms of the complex and confusing relationship between economic precarity and political fantasies about medical and scientific causes and agents.

In Chapter 12, Lisa Wille reads contemporary prose texts by Marlene Streeruwitz and Kristine Bilkau to address the situation of the educated precariat of the twenty-first century. Unlike the "classical" proletariat, the contemporary precariat is to a high degree comprised of trained and credentialed yet underemployed members of a struggling middle class. Committed to a quintessentially middle-class belief in meritocracy and equity, the promise of the powers of higher education ("Aufstieg durch Bildung") commits members of today's precariat to endless competition in a transnational marketplace. This leads to a normalizing of extraordinary duress: twenty-first-century precarians subject themselves to self-exploitation in their struggles to realize their dreams and ambitions and achieve a modicum of stability and security. This applies in particular to artists, writers, and creative workers, who are the protagonists of Streeruwitz's novel *Jessica, 30.* (2004) and Bilkau's *Die Glücklichen* (*The Fortunate*; 2015). Drawing on sociological works by Andreas Reckwitz and Oliver Nachtwey, Wille reads the two novels as offering internalized accounts of the "new social question:" Streeruwitz depicts a woman who, having completed her PhD, finds herself stuck in the permanent limbo of working on her career and her "late-modern self" in the absence of stable employment, while the "happy" couple in Bilkau's novel undergo a slow decline during which their internalized and naturalized expectations about a worry-free secure life, embodied by their parents' generation, conflict ever more with the material reality of their lives. Both novels show a growing divergence between the surface of their protagonists' lives—their normative expectations and hopes—and the material foundation necessary to realize those hopes and expectations. Psychologically, this divergence is expressed in a creeping fear of failure, an affective response to precarity that has become normalized over the last two decades and thus needs the sensorium of literary narrative to be detected.

In the thirteenth and final chapter, Lindsay Preseau discusses the instrumentalization of the "linguistic precariat" in contemporary language pedagogy. She demonstrates how two films used in language teaching, *German Class* (2019) and *Willkommen bei den Hartmanns* (*Welcome to the Hartmanns*; 2016), sanction the very exploitation of the linguistic precariat with which the student audiences are expected to engage critically. Both films legitimize the continued existence of the linguistic precariat by celebrating the "integration" of linguistically precarious characters while simultaneously affirming that their failure to adhere to monolingual and standardized language ideologies will relegate them to contingent and unskilled employment. Crucially, both films do so by appealing to neoliberal sensibilities which engage in performative inclusivity by promoting "appropriate" German as a necessary prerequisite for personal progress and "integration" while they remain mute about Germany's dark history of racial othering and colonial violence. Moreover, screening these films in pedagogical settings normalizes the use of language-learning technologies such as TalkAbroad or Duolingo which rely on the labor of the linguistic precariat and are increasingly used in German-language programs in higher education in the US. Preseau shows how these films are powerful vehicles for promoting linguistic precarity, and how such narratives have become embedded in discourses of language education more generally.

Works Cited

Adorno, Theodor. *Aesthetic Theory*. Translated by Robert Hullot-Kentor. London and New York: Continuum, 2002.

Adorno, Theodor W. *Hegel: Three Studies*. Translated by Shierry Weber Nicholsen. Cambridge, MA and London: MIT Press, 1994.

Arendt, Hannah. *Between Past and Future*. New York and London: Penguin Press, 1968.

Arendt, Hannah. *The Human Condition*. Chicago, IL and London: University of Chicago Press, 2018.

Benanav, Aaron. *Automation and the Future of Work*. London and New York: Verso, 2020.

Berlant, Lauren. *Cruel Optimism*. Durham, NC: Duke University Press, 2011.

Brecht, Bertolt. *On Film and Radio*. Edited and translated by Marc Silberman. London: Methuen, 2000.

Boltansky, Luc and Ève Chapello. *The New Spirit of Capitalism*. Translated by Gregory Elliott. London and New York: Verso, 2018.

Bourdieu, Pierre. *Acts of Resistance: Against the New Myths of Our Time*. Translated by Richard Nice. Cambridge: Polity, 2000.

Bourdieu, Pierre. "The Essence of Neoliberalism." Translated by Jeremy J. Shapiro. In *Le Monde diplomatique*, December 1998. https://mondediplo.com/1998/12/08bourdieu.

Butler, Judith. *The Force of Nonviolence: An Ethico-Political Bind*. London and New York: Verso, 2020.

Castel, Robert. *From Manual Workers to Wage Laborers: Transformation of the Social Question*. Translated by Richard Boyd. New Brunswick, NJ and London: Transaction Publishers, 2003.

Cooper, Melinda. *Family Values: Between Neoliberalism and the New Social Conservatism*. New York: Zone Books, 2017.

Cowling, Mark and James Martin. *Marx's "Eighteenth Brumaire": (Post)modern Interpretations*. London and Sterling, VA: Pluto Press, 2002.

Deleuze, Gilles. "Postscript on Control Societies." In *Negotiations 1972–1990*, translated by Martin Joughin, 177–82. New York: Columbia University Press, 1995.

Foucault, Michel. *The Birth of Biopolitics: Lectures at the Collège de France 1978–79*. Translated by Graham Burchell. Houndmills and New York: Palgrave Macmillan, 2008.

Fraser, Nancy *Cannibal Capitalism: How Our System is Devouring Democracy, Care, and the Planet – and What We Can Do about It*. London and New York: Verso, 2022.

Fraser, Nancy and Rahel Jaeggi. *Capitalism: A Conversation in Critical Theory*. Cambridge: Polity, 2018.

Greaney, Patrick. *Untimely Beggar: Poverty and Power from Baudelaire to Benjamin*. Minneapolis, MN and London: University of Minnesota Press, 2008.

Hardt, Michael and Antonio Negri. *Commonwealth*. Cambridge, MA: Harvard University Press, 2009.

Hardt, Michael and Antonio Negri. *Multitude: War and Democracy in the Age of Empire*. Cambridge, MA: Harvard University Press, 2000.

Jaffe, Sarah. *Work Won't Love You Back: How Devotion to Our Jobs Keeps Us Exploited, Exhausted, and Alone*. New York: Bold Type Books, 2021.

Kracauer, Siegfried. *The Salaried Masses: Duty and Distraction in Weimar Germany*. Translated by Quentin Hoare. London and New York: Verso, 1998.

Lazzarato, Maurizio. "The Misfortunes of the 'Artistic Critique' and of Cultural Employment." In *Critique of Creativity: Precarity, Subjectivity and Resistance in the "Creative Industries,"* edited by Gerald Raunig, Gene Ray, and Ulf Wuggenig, 41–56. London: MayFly Books, 2011.

Leslie, Esther. "Add Value to Contents: The Valorization of Culture Today." In *Critique of Creativity: Precarity, Subjectivity and Resistance in the "Creative Industries,"* edited by Gerald Raunig, Gene Ray, and Ulf Wuggenig, 183–90. London: MayFly Books, 2011.

Lorey, Isabell. *State of Insecurity: Government of the Precarious*. Translated by Aileen Derieg. London and New York: Verso, 2015.

Nachtwey, Oliver. *Germany's Hidden Crisis: Social Decline in the Heart of Europe*. Translated by David Fernbach and Loren Balhorn. London and New York: Verso, 2018.

Piketty, Thomas. *Capital in the Twenty-First Century*. Translated by Arthur Goldhammer. Cambridge, MA and London: Harvard University Press, 2014.

Rilke, Rainer Maria. *Die Gedichte*. Frankfurt and Leipzig: Insel, 1998.

Spivak, Chakravorty. *A Critique of Postcolonial Reason: Towards a History of the Vanishing Present.* Cambridge, MA and London: Harvard University Press, 1999.

Standing, Guy. "Understanding the Precariat through Labour and Work." *Development and Change* 45, no. 5 (2014): 963–80.

Streek, Wolfgang. *Buying Time: The Delayed Crisis of Democratic Capitalism.* Translated by Patrick Camiller. London and New York: Verso, 2014.

Thompson, E.P. *The Making of the English Working Class.* New York: Vintage Books, 1966.

Virno, Paolo. *A Grammar of the Multitude: For an Analysis of Contemporary Forms of Life.* Translated by Sabella Bertoletti, James Cascaito, and Andrea Casson. Cambridge, MA: MIT Press, 20.

One   Literature and the History of Precarity: An Interview with Patrick Eiden-Offe

Karsten Olson

Karsten Olson: Your previous book, *Die Poesie der Klasse* (*The Poetry of the Class: Romantic Anti-Capitalism and the Invention of the Proletariat*), which examines little-known authors and social reformers of the nineteenth century as well as machine wreckers (who are still mocked today), was very successful in the German-language world and will soon reach an international readership through translations into Spanish and English. Why was the book so successful? What is it about the *Vormärz* period that resonates with our contemporary moment?

Patrick Eiden-Offe: I could give you an easy answer and say that you have to ask readers why the book was a modest success. But I've thought about it too, of course. Especially since the question of class in literature was not a relevant topic in 2006, when I first began developing the project. To put it somewhat grandly, thought demanded to be made reality, just as reality demanded thought. After the Great Recession of 2008, it was no longer unusual for literary scholars—who are notorious for their ivory-tower interests—to think about social issues such as pauperization and proletarization. In addition, it was hard not to see a similarity between contemporary protest movements—from riots across the globe to Occupy to other public occupation movements such as the Arab Spring and Black Lives Matter—and the undisciplined oppositional movements of the *Vormärz*. Then, following Donald Trump's election in 2016, suddenly many people were able to imagine a "romantic anticapitalism" of the working class. My book's claim that we are seeing a resurgence of particular motifs from early industrial capitalism and proletarian movements of the *Vormärz* in our contemporary moment, suddenly seemed very plausible. To put it ironically: the book benefited from the crisis.

K: You suggest that there is a connection between Trump's electoral victory in 2016 and romantic anticapitalism. How should this connection be understood? To what extent are Trump and his supporters romantic anticapitalists? Should we also interpret Bernie Sanders' relative success in this light, and how should the term be understood today?

P: First, Trump's success and the initial analyses in mainstream media outlets brought up the issue of class, and the working class in particular. This topic had remained untouched for a long time, and had perhaps even become taboo. Now, the media were claiming—and I don't know whether this claim has borne out—that the "white working class" had voted Trump into the White House. So all of a sudden, class had become an important political category. And yes—"romantic anticapitalism" was used to explain this phenomenon: these people were nostalgic for an imaginary, utopian past, in which everything had been better, and in order to get it back, they were prepared to believe in a charlatan like Trump and his MAGA talk.

I think that in the end, this analysis falls short and comes to incorrect conclusions, such as the syllogism that the "working class" is *de facto* white, which is untrue, both historically and currently. But despite these incorrect assumptions, class once more became a topic of debate. Just as the Hegelian Robert Brandom says: the experience of error is also the process of producing truth. Sanders' success was—at least partially—due to a more sympathetic form of romantic anticapitalism: the memory of the good old days in which workers were respected and fought relentlessly to secure their own interests against, not alongside, these crooked billionaires. The important question, of course, is to what extent Sanders' working-class supporters were more inclusive and racially diverse than Trump's. As an outside onlooker, this seemed the case to me, and so I did have some sympathy for Bernie.

K: In your book, you provide an initial definition of the "poetics of class" using Eduard Gans, a lawyer, historian, legal philosopher, and important Hegelian, as follows: "The 'poetics' of modern life is defined by Gans through its economic precarity; 'poetry' is established through 'the concrete,' that is, the ever-present possibility of economic decline," or later in the "conflict between the poetry of the heart and the prose of circumstances." How are we to understand this form of precarity? To what extent does the modern person live in a "reality already assigned to the domain of prose"?

P: Hegel, like many other authors of the period, draws a contrast between poetry and prose in order to give a general cultural and social critique, which he delivers in a realistic, resigned tone. Prose, the prose of reality or of circumstances, stands for the new, increasingly rationalized world, or, to quote Max Weber, for the disenchanted world of modernity and of modern capitalism, in which not only economics but all of life has become calculable and predictable. There are no more surprises; our lives are programmed. Hegel would say that in principle, that's a good thing. After all, we only need to adjust to this situation, according to Hegel, and this is where the modern novel can help us, which, as a *Bildungsroman*, is nothing more than a continual retelling of how we as individuals can successfully adapt to reality. For Hegel, the modern novel—as a prose genre—represents a training ground for internalizing this new reality principle of modernity. But in the same time period, demands for reenchantment and the repoeticization of life appear; at the core, this is the program of the early Romantics. The irony is that after 1830, people such as Gans, early socialists such as Flora Tristan, Georg Weerth, and Wilhelm Weitling, and late Romantics such as Ludwig Tieck and Bettine von Arnim all realize that surprise, spontaneity, and incalculability have not died out, but are present as the precarious living conditions of the proletariat. Tristan, Weerth and the others appropriate the romantic concept of poetry and redefine it: the life of the proletariat is poetic insofar as it manifests a fundamental precarity. The proletariat literally do not know what they will live on tomorrow; they live in fear of revocation. This is a dreadful sort of poetry, of course. But when the protagonists of my book describe these desperate circumstances as a form of poetry, they are not adopting a cynical position. Quite the opposite: they believe that under these circumstances, proletarians are forced to poetically develop a new art, a new culture, a new life. Early socialism thus becomes something like the *progressive Universalpoesie* of the exploited and subjugated.

K: You write that this transformation marks the beginning of modernity; i.e., the poetry of precarity is the poetry under which we still live and suffer. Could you provide a broad description of the lost, old form of poetry, the poetry which existed before our society was completely restructured by market-based economic relations?

P: I believe that proletarization and precarization continue to be relevant terms of analysis for grasping our contemporary reality. The two Ps (we could also include pauperization as an extreme term) refer to the continual revolutionization of living circumstances such that one can never establish oneself permanently. The possibilities and tools through which people had until recently been able to negotiate their social reproduction and material existence are now defunct or "deregulated," and everyone is forced to "reorient" and "reinvent" themselves, to quote the lingo of neoliberalism. We live in a society in a paradoxical state of permanent disruption. This was also the experience of people in the *Vormärz*, but they perceived it as injurious and threw themselves into revolutionary projects. In doing so, they undoubtedly (and unwittingly) contributed to the integration of society into a market structure. But in my book, I particularly wanted to highlight "absolute" points of rupture which could not be smoothed over through the integration that followed. These are moments in which people not only lament that they are coming up short in this new capitalist society—and there was widespread misery of unimaginable proportions; reading about child labor still makes me furious—but also which challenge the entire dynamic of capitalist society. Interestingly, these are genuinely romantic moments, such as when proletarians no longer "only" demand wages for their work, but criticize the idea of wage labor as inhuman and unnatural. This is when class warfare against the employer or *Brotherr* becomes a fight for leisure, and—ultimately—for poetry. And the employer has to go because he is standing in the way. He has to go—all of my protagonists from the *Vormärz* agree on this.

K: I'd like to talk more about what, exactly, these proto-proletarians are longing for, what it is that they feel has been lost. You write a lot about the representational aspects of feudal society, and how Ludwig Tieck, for example, mourned their loss. You argue, with Tieck, that in estate society, a person was not identified solely through their work. A person couldn't be reduced to a mere function; instead, the playful, representational aspects of society were also important (a reality which was particularly visible through Carnival). The economist and philosopher Christian Garve voiced similar concerns in the late eighteenth century; according to Garve, within estate society, social divisions were based on ceremonial differentiations. Ceremonies are fundamentally performative; they illustrate differences in rank and are temporally and spatially constrained. Garve understood the newly emerging "class society" to be different: differences in class society exist only on the basis of functional relationships. You *are* an employer or an employee, it is not just a role that you play from time to time. Can you discuss this connection between work and representation (or its lack) in more depth?

P: What you've said about Garve is very interesting. Just like Tieck, he seems to have an acute sense for what was lost in the transition to a bourgeois, capitalist society, and this critique can be an irritant for us, if we accept our current bourgeois, capitalist circumstances as given. The ideological narrative of modern bourgeois society is that only in modernity did it become possible for human subjects to self-reflexively recognize that there was a critical difference between who they were and their social role; the discussion of one's "social role" only becomes relevant in capitalist modernity. Previously, in estate society, people identified completely with their social positions. This is the old narrative of differentiation within modernity, which was born out of a pre-modern soup. Tieck and Garve saw things differently: they believe that not only did there use to be a richly stratified society—and even the most hard-line modernist can't deny that estate society contained a multitude of hierarchies and particularisms—but that this stratification enabled people, even "simple," working folk, to distance themselves from their functions and roles, and reflect on these functional mechanisms. For Tieck, "representation" refers to the entire spectrum of what "vorstellen" means: to think, imagine, perform—and thus distance yourself from what is represented. By the same token, modern capitalist society dissolves the ability to achieve distance through representation for the most "numerous and poorest class." For these people, the transition to capitalism not only involves material impoverishment, but a mental and affective narrowing of life. In certain respects, Tieck, around 1800, predicts the advent of something like the *one-dimensional man*. The proletarian is now only a proletarian, nothing more. Or, more precisely: she *should* only be a proletarian. Because real proletarians didn't allow this to happen to them. They fought to retain their rights to "games, songs, jokes, and drink," as Tieck writes.

K: *The Poetry of Class* can, to a certain extent, be read as an expansion of projects advanced by theoreticians such as

E.P. Thompson, George Rudé, and other members of the New Left. Like these historians, you attempt to rescue the dignity and rationality of people who are still dismissed today, such as the aforementioned machine wreckers. Their acts of resistance are typically considered to have been pointless, or, more uncharitably, are deemed unreasonable and reactionary, resulting from a complete misunderstanding of their situation. You not only defend the machine wreckers in their historical circumstances but also claim that we can learn a lot from this form of resistance. Could you briefly explain who the machine wreckers were, how they were organized, and what their goals were? What would machine wreckers look like today?

P: The machine wreckers were the first organized group within the worker's movement who turned against the genuine capitalistic existential foundation of the working class: namely, the modern machine. Marx repeatedly claims that the working class is an "appendage" of the great machine, and thus only a functional component of the machine itself. Marx makes this claim with calculated cynicism, of course, and wants to lay bare the real cynicism of capitalist circumstances. The machine wreckers recognized that the capitalist system wanted to reduce them to a component of the machine, and protested against this vehemently, by organizing to destroy the machines themselves. The most prominent machine wreckers were the Luddites in Yorkshire at the beginning of the nineteenth century. They conspired together and moved in large groups from one weaving factory to the next at night, destroying the semi-mechanized looms which were, at the time, revolutionizing the traditional craft of weaving—that is, consuming it. They named themselves after the mythical figure of Ned Ludd, a boy who was said to have destroyed a loom and then have become the fictive leader of various groups; the Luddites signed their confessional letters "General Ludd" or "King Ludd." Through mechanization, weavers were reduced to the position of poorly-paid unskilled laborers, who could be replaced at any moment by other, cheaper, and more eager employees, and they refused to accept this. Marx and Marxist doctrine always regarded the machine wreckers with condescension, and believed that they did not understand that the machines themselves were not to blame, but the capitalist circumstances under which the machines had been introduced. The machine itself was neutral, and if used correctly, could even become an instrument of social progress. (The NRA would say, Guns don't kill people, people do.) E.P. Thompson, Eric Hobsbawm, and others have shown that the historical machine wreckers knew this already—since their daily lives were filled with hard, manual labor they knew that machines could make their lives easier—but that (drawing on their own experience, which undoubtedly brought them further than all Marxist theoreticians) none of these machines would in fact make their lives easier. Quite the opposite. In the German *Vormärz*, Weitling pointed out that one could accomplish the same amount of work with a machine in half the time—but that the workday of the average worker had doubled in length since the introduction of machines. And anyways, the machines had turned work itself, and the time one had to spend attending to them, into a living hell. Ernst Willkomm convincingly, and at length, depicts mechanized looms as torture racks, and the machines frequently lamed and mutilated workers, especially children.

The machine wreckers show us that we should be careful not to make cavalier statements about "machines" or "technology." These are always specific machines in specific circumstances, whose specific structures and contexts must be investigated—and once we do this, little capitalist technology remains that can be used for the sake of "progress." Italian Operaismo of the late 1950s theoretically took up this position again. The Operaisti showed that there can be no emancipatory use of a capitalist hell-machine such as the conveyor belt, and thus that an emancipated society would have to abolish the conveyor belt. By the way, the Operaisti theoretically came to this conclusion just as British social historians rediscovered the historic machine wreckers and historiographically recuperated them. In the 1980s, Thomas Pynchon wrote a very nice essay defending the machine wreckers with the title, "Is It O.K. To Be A Luddite?"; the answer is of course: Yes, it is!

In late-twentieth-century capitalism, the optimistic perception of technological progress, which was historically important for Marxism, has become fundamentally problematic. This naturally leads to the question of whether machine wrecking can become a relevant political practice today. I don't have an answer to this question, and I don't want to advocate for violence. But we can certainly understand the calls of contemporary climate activists to take part in new, more radical, more militant forms of activity as part of a Luddite lineage. Blockading power plants and highways and organizing disruptions becomes more effective when one can precisely pinpoint and analyze their place in the infrastructure of fossil fuel capitalism. It is doubtful that there is a progressive place for SUVs; we may, simply and undialectically, need to get rid of them, and that's what the activists are trying to do. I am quite certain that the movement will draw on the right traditions. Societal progress can sometimes (or only?) happen when one manages to move away from the capitalist ideology of progress. One of the few examples of practical machine wrecking in Germany was when ship haulers bombarded new steamboats on the Rhine with cannons, because the steamboats had put them out of a job. Today, we are once again searching for alternatives to fossil fuels, including for powering ships.

K: In his article for this volume, Jörg Kreienbrock examines Adam Müller's theory of poetic possession. Müller argues that all existing modern societies are based on the same error; namely, that they are all "republics of property." This means that even so-called democratic or enlightened republics are all based on the Roman principle of *allod*, and can understand ownership only as absolute power. Ownership requires the exclusion of all other parties—one can only possess something to the extent that others are barred from its possession. Müller then suggests a new/old form of ownership based on the Roman *precarium* or its German counterpart, *Bittleihen*. These terms understand ownership not as absolute power but as a form of petition which allows several people to exercise different rights concerning the same property. Kreienbrock describes this difference as similar to that between the verbs *erwerben* (to acquire) and *werben* (to solicit); "poetic possession" is thus understood to be a speech act which evokes "the incalculable demands of grant, gift, and grace." Does this (briefly sketched) description, along with your own knowledge of Adam Müller, reveal to you any similarities between Müller's ideas and those of Tieck and other "reactionaries" of the time, or were his theories rightly refuted by Hegel, Marx, and Lukács?

P: To be honest, I'm not that knowledgeable about Adam Müller. It's interesting, however, that not only the left Marxist tradition but also self-styled reactionaries such as Carl Schmitt, dismissed him as a reactionary. So he seems a prime candidate for recuperation—and that sounds just like what Jörg Kreienbrock is doing.

I am not familiar with Müller's concept, but we can find similar ideas in Romantics such as Tieck: if we want to formulate a truly radical critique of capitalism, we must not only debate the distribution of property, but question the concept and value of property itself. In the modern philosophy of law—particularly in Hegel—the subject status of the individual is very clearly linked to private property. This is why individuals without property, who thus have literally nothing to lose, become liminal figures in legal and subject theory—in Hegel, it is the rabble (*Pöbel*), in Fichte, the Lazzaroni (and in Marx, the *Lumpenproletariat*). The Romantics discuss other forms of subjectivity—forms that do not preserve, consolidate, and increase their identity as property, but express their true nature through dissolution and dispersion. Even Lukács couldn't hide his love for Eichendorff's *Good-For-Nothing*.

Tieck repeatedly discusses the question of what life's riches truly are, and what a rich life looks like if it does not involve amassing property. He comes to the conclusion that free time is the precondition for and realization of a truly rich life; time for oneself, and time that one can share with others. At some point, I noticed that there are few things that attest so well to this richness as Tieck's late novellas do. The people in these novellas have all the time in the world, and they share their riches with other figures through endless conversations about God, art, and the world, which constitute most of the novellas. And we can share this wealth too by taking the time to follow these endlessly meandering conversations. Arno Schmidt once summarized Tieck's philosophy of life and art as follows: "all existence is a lifelong sidestep." This form of almost systematically-enacted inefficiency only needs to be imagined and reconceived as a critique of society and capitalism.

K: You are now working together with Achim Szepanski and Frank Engster on a book project on the concept and phenomenon of overaccumulation—in the sense of over-accumulated financial capital, but also the overaccumulation of greenhouse gasses and humans in the form of a surplus proletariat. Can you say more about this project? How are you approaching the topic, and what are your sources? Do you see further resonances with the nineteenth century here, or is our current historical situation unique?

P: The book will be called *Über Über*, and we'd love to keep it that way in the English translation, with the German Umlaut, like in Motörhead. It's a joke, of course (it's reminiscent of "Hyper Hyper") but a serious one: this is about the ceaselessly tautological, and possibly also self-destructive, production of more and more, which tips over into too much: too much in the sense of accumulation, which is understood as a process of constant growth. We want to concretize and make relevant the Marxist term of overaccumulation and the crisis of overaccumulation, and measure the possible connections and overlaps of three crisis areas of overaccumulation: the overaccumulation of financial capital, the overaccumulation in carbon emissions, and human overaccumulation. Your question regarding the historical perspective in reference to the schema I proposed in *The Poetry of Class* is interesting. The phenomena of "Über Über" are all old—as old as capitalism itself—and to a certain extent, the potential crises looming in all three areas were recognized and theorized early on. Yet these three crises have worsened dramatically in the past three decades, and they are interwoven and mutually reinforce each other in new ways—these three forms of overaccumulation are accumulating on top of one another, so to speak.

This also gives us a means of writing a history of capitalism: firstly, as a history of recurring events, repetitions, and revivals—for example, in the concept of money as a "means of circulation," the "period of circulation," and the concept of the "cyclical crisis": these belong to the functional mechanisms of the system itself, which reproduces itself beyond and even by means of crises. Then there are "crisis of implementation," in which a new accumulative regime, a new form of capital value, establishes and stabilizes itself. And thirdly, the history of capitalism proceeds by linear development following an immanent teleology: a systems logic that will paradoxically culminate in the collapse of the system. The difficulty lies in distinguishing between these three different types of crises. Theories of collapse are perhaps so discredited because historically, there have always been people—"prophets of doom," as they were called—who believed that a cyclical crisis or a crisis of implementation heralded the end of the system. This doesn't, however, preclude the possibility of a total collapse, or that this possibility may not someday be realized. It remains unclear what a final implosion will look like, though if you look around the world today, you can get a sense of how it might happen. That's what we want to look at in our book; methodologically, it's a bricolage which puts together conceptual history, especially in the Marxist tradition, the remainders of reality haunting these terms, and weak, but tenacious revolutionary fantasies. Even in dark times, we must not turn our backs on poetry.

Works Cited

Brandom, Robert. *A Spirit of Trust: A Reading of Hegel's Phenomenology*. Cambridge, MA: Harvard University Press, 2019.

Eiden-Offe, Patrick. *Die Poesie der Klasse. Romantischer Antikapitalismus und die Erfindung des Proletariats*. Berlin: Matthes & Seitz, 2020.

Gans, Eduard. *Rückblicke auf Personen und Zustände*. Edited by Norbert Waszek. Stuttgart: Frommann-Holzboog, 2007.

Garve, Christian. "Betrachtung einiger Verschiedenheiten in den Werken der ältesten und neuern Schriftsteller, besonders der Dichter." In *Gesammelte Werke*, 1, edited by Kurt Wölfel, 116–90. Hildesheim: Olms, 1985.

Hegel, Georg Wilhelm Friedrich. *Werke in zwanzig Bänden. Vorlesungen über die Ästhetik*, vol. 15, edited by Eva Moldenhauer and Karl Markus Michel. Frankfurt: Suhrkamp, 1970.

Hobsbawm, E.J. "The Machine Breakers." *Past & Present* 1 (1952): 57–70. http://www.jstor.org/stable/649989.

Lukács, György. "Joseph von Eichendorff." In *German Realists in the Nineteenth Century*. Translated by Jeremy Gaines and Paul Keast, edited by Rodney Livingstone, 50–68. Cambridge, MA: MIT Press, 1993.

Marx, Karl and Friedrich Engels. "Manifest der Kommunistischen Partei." In *Werke*, edited by Hildegard Scheibler, 459–93. Berlin: Dietz, 1990.

Müller, Adam. "Der poetische Besitz." In *Kritische Ausgabe*, vol. 2, edited by Walter Schroder and Werner Siebert, 261–2. Neuwied and Berlin: Luchterhand, 1967.

Rudé, George F.E. *The Crowd in the French Revolution*. Westport, CT: Greenwood Press, 1986.

Schmidt, Arno. "'Fünfzehn.' Vom Wunderkind der Sinnlosigkeit." In *Bargfelder Ausgabe. Werkgruppe 1*, 2, edited by Jan Philipp Reemtsma et al., 285–332. Zurich: Haffmans, 1992.

Thompson, E.P. *The Making of the English Working Class*. London: Penguin, 2013.

Tieck, Ludwig. "Der junge Tischlermeister: Novelle in sieben Abschnitten." In *Schriften: in zwölf Bänden*, edited by Uwe Schweikert, 9–418. Frankfurt: Deutscher Klassiker Verlag, 1988.

Weber, Max. "Science as Vocation." In *The Vocation Lectures*, edited by David Owen and Tracy B. Strong. Translated by Rodney Livingstone, 1–31. Indianapolis, IN: Hackett, 2004.

Weitling, Wilhelm. *Garantien der Harmonie und Freiheit*. Stuttgart: Reclam, 1974.

Two   Precarious Property: Adam Müller's Theory of Poetic Possession

Jörg Kreienbrock

Introduction

From January 1808 to April 1809, Adam Müller and Heinrich von Kleist edited the journal *Phöbus. Ein Journal für die Kunst* (*Phöbus. A Journal for the Arts*). In the introduction to volume 7, "Philosophische und Kritische Miszellen" ("Philosophical and Critical Miscellanea"), Müller compares the journal to a marketplace. "Build up your market!" one of the participants in a fictional conversation exclaims and continues: "lug your philosophical, critical and news wares together, as many as you possess."[1] The marketplace of the *Phöbus* is a space where various critical and philosophical commodities accumulate and are traded according to the participant's assets [*Vermögen*].[2] Philosophy and criticism are

---

1   Adam Müller, "Einleitung zu den philosophischen und kritischen Miszellen," *Kritische Ausgabe*, vol. 1, ed. Walter Schroeder, Werner Siebert. (Neuwied: Luchterhand, 1967), 507: "Baut euren Markt auf!"; "schleppt philosophische, kritische und Zeitungs-Waaren zusammen, so viel ihr vermögt."

2   It is not without irony that after only twelve volumes the publication of the journal as well as the cooperation between Kleist and Müller ended because of financial difficulties. Cf. Knittel: "Ab dem 7. Stück, im Dezember 1808 mit 46 Seiten Umfang erschienen, verlegt auf Betreiben Adam Müllers die Walther'sche Hofbuchhandlung in Dresden den in tiefen finanziellen Schwierigkeiten steckenden *Phöbus* … Als Kleist im Frühjahr 1809 die Schlussabrechungen sieht, kommt es zum Zerwürfnis zwischen ihm und Müller, da letzterer ohne Wissen Kleists Walther bei der Überlassung des Journals große finanzielle Zugeständnisse gemacht hat." [After the seventh volume, which appeared in December of 1808 with a length of 46 pages, the deeply financially troubled *Phöbus* was published by the Walther court publisher of Dresden at the prompting of Adam Müller … When Kleist saw the final accounts in 1809, it led to a rift between him and Müller, since the latter had, without Kleist's knowledge, made great financial

treated like goods. One of the ideas circulating in this metaphorical marketplace is Müller's own theory of poetic property, as outlined in the fourth piece of the "Philosophical and Critical Miscellanea" entitled "The Poetic Possession" (*Der poetische Besitz*). This essay interprets the theory of a specifically poetic form of precarious appropriation as it relates to: 1. Müller's general philosophy of circulation; and 2. the Roman law institute of the *precarium*. Müller's notion of precarious property tries to overcome what Hegel in his *Ästhetik* analyzes as the "conflict between the poetry of the heart and the opposing prose of the conditions of existence."[3] He calls for a caring, affective poetry of relations, which includes both subjects and objects, human beings and things, capable of mediating poetry and prose, imagination and reality.

Following Hegel's and Marx's scathing critiques of Müller, Georg Lukács labels Müller's romantic economy as fundamentally reactionary. In an essay on Joseph von Eichendorff published in *German Realists of the Nineteenth Century* (*Deutsche Realisten des 19. Jahrhunderts*) he writes: "Thus, their exposure of the contradictions of the capitalist division of labour turns into an uncritical glorification of the social conditions which existed at a time when this division of labour was still unknown. This is at the root of the Romantic enthusiasm for the Middle Ages."[4] Jochen Marquardt comes to a similar conclusion: "Even

---

concessions to Walther when giving him the journal.] Anton Philipp Knittel, "Phöbus: Ein Journal für die Kunst," in *Kleist-Handbuch: Leben – Werk – Wirkung*, edited by Ingo Breuer (Stuttgart, Weimar: Metzler, 2013), 166.

3   Georg Wilhelm Friedrich Hegel, *Werke in zwanzig Bänden*, vol. 15: *Vorlesungen über die Ästhetik*, ed. Eva Moldenhauer, Karl Markus Michel (Frankfurt: Suhrkamp, 1970), 393: "Konflikt zwischen der Poesie des Herzens und der entgegenstehenden Prosa der Verhältnisse."

4   Georg Lukács, "Joseph von Eichendorff," *German Realists in the Nineteenth Century*, trans. Jeremy Gaines and Paul Keast, ed. Rodney Livingstone (Cambridge, MA: MIT Press, 1993), 63. Georg Lukács, "Joseph von Eichendorff," in Lukács, *Deutsche Realisten des 19. Jahrhunderts* (Bern: Francke, 1951), 60: "So schlägt die Aufdeckung der Widersprüche der kapitalistischen Arbeitsteilung um in eine unkritische Verherrlichung jener Gesellschaftzustände, die diese Arbeitsteilung noch nicht gekannt haben; hier ist die Quelle der Schwärmerei für das Mittelalter." In *Capital*, vol. 3, Marx rejected Müller's romantic national economy. His comment on Müller's theory of debt reads as follows: "It would be impossible to drivel out a more hair-raising absurdity than this in so few lines. Not to mention the comic confusion of worker with capitalist, the value of labour-power with interest on capital, etc. – the receipt of compound interest is simply explained by saying that capital is lent out and then brings in compound interest. Our Müller's procedure is characteristic of the Romantics in every detail. Its content is formed out of everyday prejudices, skimmed from the most superficial appearance of things. This false and trivial content is then supposedly 'elevated' and rendered poetic by a mystifying mode of expression." Karl Marx, *Capital*, vol. 3, trans. David Fernbach (London: Penguin, 1991), 522.

though the ideologue Adam Heinrich Müller was a critic of capitalism from the right, in the end he had to become an apologist for it, since he considered it useful—in a historically contingent sense–to humanize capitalism through a state concept linked to estate feudalism."[5] But, contrary to these critiques, Müller's reverence for medieval feudalism represents more than merely the wish to humanize the current capitalist exchange economy; nor is his representation based on an uncritical or nostalgic affirmation of a pre-Capitalist past, but is instead guided by the careful analysis of non-exclusive forms of property relations, such as the fiefdom. Richard T. Gray notes that "Müller holds the distinction of being one of the nineteenth-century German intellectuals who has come to be interpreted both as a proto-fascist political thinker and as a proto-Marxist economic theoretician."[6] For example, Müller anticipates Karl Marx's analysis of feudal modes of production in the section on "Pre-capitalist Economic Formations" of the *Foundations* and in chapter 47 of the first volume of *Capital*, something already indicated by Hannah Arendt in the 1932 essay "Adam Müller-Renaissance?,"[7] in which she defends Müller against the fascist appropriation by Othmar Spann and his circle, a line of argumentation which prompted Joseph Vogl to ask: "Are they [romantic critics of capitalism, J.K.] indebted to a flight into a (feudal) past, or a present of absolute modernity? Are their societal concepts pre- or rather anti-capitalist, or must one recognize in them a capitalism *avant la lettre*?"[8] Following Vogl's question,

---

5   Jochen Marquardt, "Die Vermittlung zwischen Ökonomie und Poesie: Adam Müllers Analyse der Französischen Revolution und deren Anwendung auf seine ästhetische Theorie," *Deutsche Romantik und Französische Revolution* (Wrocław: Wydawnictwo Uniwersytetu Wrocławskiego, 1990), 178: "Der Ideologe Adam Heinrich Müller freilich mußte, obgleich Kritiker des Kapitalismus von rechts, letztlich als dessen Apologet wirken, indem er es – geschichtlich bedingt – überhaupt für nützlich hielt, ihn durch eine am ständischen Feudalismus orientierte Staatsauffassung zu vermenschlichen."

6   Richard Gray, "Hypersign, Hypermoney, Hypermarket: Adam Müller's Theory of Money and Romantic Semiotics," *New Literary History* 31, no. 2 (2000): 298.

7   Hannah Arendt, "Adam Müller-Renaissance?," in *Reflections on Literature and Culture*, ed. Susannah Young-Ah Gottlieb (Stanford, CA: Stanford University Press 2007), 38–45.

8   Joseph Vogl, "Romantische Oekonomie: Regierung und Regulation um 1800," in *Marianne – Germania: Deutsch-französischer Kulturtransfer im europäischen Kontext*, vol. 2, ed. Étienne François (Leipzig: Leipziger Universitätsverlag, 1998), 471. "Sind sie der Flucht in eine (feudale) Vergangenheit oder einer Gegenwart unbedingter Modernität verpflichtet? Sind ihre Gesellschaftskonzepte prä- bzw. anti-kapitalistisch, oder muß man in ihnen einen Kapitalismus *avant la lettre* erkennen?" Cf. Ethel Matala de Mazza, *Der verfasste Körper: Zum Projekt einer organischen Gemeinschaft* (Freiburg: Rombach, 1999); Reinhard Saller, *Schöne Ökonomie: Die poetische Reflexion der Ökonomie in frühromantischer Literatur* (Würzburg: Königshausen & Neumann, 2007).

this essay attempts to elucidate Müller's peculiar political economy situated precariously between *feudal past* and *unconditional modernity*, proto-fascism and proto-Marxism.

Poetic Property

In "Der poetische Besitz," Müller points to a peculiar proximity of the German verbs *werben* and *erwerben*. He finishes the short text with an address to the reader:

> Mark my words carefully, and don't shy away from my strange language! – Your love for every good in the world is based on the fact that you court [wirbst] the love of this good in return, and that it will thus become part of you to an ever larger degree. You will not extort anything, not even the poorest, meanest thing, but through courtship [werben] you will indeed win it, and this is the meaning of that lovely word, 'to acquire' [*erwerben*].

> [Merke auf, was ich jetzt sagen werde, und scheue nicht vor dem seltsamen Ausdruck! – Deine Liebe zu jedem Gute der Welt ruht darin, daß du um die Gegenliebe solches Gutes wirbst, und selbige dir in immer vollerem Maaße zu Theil wird. Erzwingen wirst du nichts, auch das ärmste, geringste nicht, aber wohl durch werben gewinnen, und das ist die Bedeutung des schönen Wortes erwerben.][9]

Grimms Wörterbuch makes the proximity, if not identity, of *werben* and *erwerben* clear. In the entry on "werben" one reads: "to court (something), through effort to acquire (something)" [(etw.) werben (etw.) (durch bemühung) erwerben].[10] And in the entry "erwerben" Grimm underscores the "unusual linguistic relation" [merkwürdigen Wortverhältnisse] between *werben* and *erwerben* and notes an "exchange of the concepts," which is to be understood as, "verti, versari, conversari in negotiari, tractare, parare, transform so to speak into trade, to negotiate."[11]

In this linguistic proximity, Müller believed to have discovered a process of reciprocity in the act of acquisition itself. He calls for a

---

9   Adam Müller, "Der poetische Besitz," in *Kritische Ausgabe*, vol. 2, ed. Walter Schroeder and Werner Siebert (Neuwied: Luchterhand, 1967), 261.

10   Jacob and Wilhelm Grimm, *Deutsches Wörterbuch*, ed. Berlin-Brandenburgische Akademie der Wissenschaften Berlin (Stuttgart: Hirzel, 1961) 29, 153.

11   Grimm, *Deutsches Wörterbuch*, 3, 1060.

loving wooing and courtship of the good one wants to own, instead of a forceful and potentially violent act of appropriation. True ownership is based on a loving relationship between owner and property. For Immanuel Kant, in contradistinction, the "concept of possession" [Begriff des Habens] is inextricably connected to the idea of having something "under my control (in potestate mea positum esse)[12] [in meiner Gewalt]."[13] Erwerb, according to the *Metaphysik der Sitten* (*Metaphysics of Morals*) means "taking control of it (occupatio)."[14] Kant writes: "That is mine which I bring under my control (in accordance with the law of outer freedom) which, as an object of my choice, is something that I have the capacity to use (in accordance with the postulate of practical reason); and which, finally, I will to be mine (in conformity with the Idea of a possible united will)."[15] Daniel Loick comments: "For this reason, jurisprudence defines the right of ownership as a classical right of domination to this day."[16] It is Müller's project to replace this forceful, if not violent, dominion over the object, in which the "juridical subjects all over the world act without being bound by a reciprocal obligation"[17] with a doctrine of property based on mutuality, interdependence, and reciprocity. For Müller, possession, in order to be useful, must be emancipated from the notion of dominion, and instead be thought of in terms of a "poetry of the heart" [Poesie des Herzens]. Counterexamples to the idea of domination can be found in the concepts of the Roman *usus fructus* or the Germanic *Nießbrauch*, which instead of violent occupation are based on acts of gratuity, grace, and charity. *Usus fructus* is based on the right of the owner of a property to forgo use, and instead grant this right to another party. It is this temporally constrained renunciation of the right of possession, what Werner Hamacher calls the "release of ownership" [Freigabe des Eigentums],[18] which is central to Müller's

---

12 Immanuel Kant, *The Metaphysics of Morals: Introduction, Translation, and Notes by Mary Gregor* (Cambridge: Cambridge University Press, 1991), 75.

13 Immanuel Kant, *Kants Werke: Akademie-Textausgabe*, vol. 5: *Die Metaphysik der Sitten* (Berlin: de Gruyter, 1968), 362.

14 Kant, *The Metaphysics of Morals*, 81; Kant, *Die Metaphysik der Sitten*, 369.

15 Kant, *The Metaphysics of Morals*, 80; Kant, *Die Metaphysik der Sitten*, 368. Cf. Richard Tuck, *Natural Right Theories: Their Origins and Development* (Cambridge: Cambridge University Press, 1979); Daniel Loick, *Der Missbrauch des Eigentums* (Berlin: August Verlag, 2016), 102–7.

16 Loick, *Der Missbrauch des Eigentums*, 103: "Die Rechtswissenschaft definiert darum bis heute das Eigentumsrecht als klassisches Herrschaftsrecht."

17 Loick, *Der Missbrauch des Eigentums*, 103: "Rechtssubjekte über die Welt disponieren, ohne an eine reziproke Verpflichtung gebunden zu sein."

18 Werner Hamacher, "The One Right No One Ever Has," *Sprachgerechtigkeit* (Frankfurt: Fischer, 2018), 357.

conceptualization of poetic property, as a precarious relation of love [*Liebe*] and requited love [*Gegenliebe*].

What this renunciation or right also recognizes is the possibility that one's loving appeal [*erwerben*] might go unanswered; after all, *Gegenliebe* is not guaranteed. Hence, the possibility of failure, rejection, and abandonment cannot be eliminated from the logic of poetic appropriation. In this sense, poetic ownership follows the incalculable demands of grant, gift, and grace. Poetic property is located outside of a symmetrical exchange economy of give and take. The reciprocity of *Liebe* and *Gegenliebe* transcends and undermines any logic of a purely mathematical calculation. This incalculability has far-reaching implications; if the taking possession of property is a poetic act—based on speech acts like address, plea, and appeal, thereby exposing the *werben* in *erwerben*—then this necessarily also implies different notions of economy, exchange, and circulation. Ownership is no longer the result of a single act of occupation, but rather a continuous process of renewal and actualization. Müller writes:

> But though you may continue to love the acquired good, it also possible to lose it, and the thought of this loss, the thousand ways in which it could be lost, must keep your eyes open: every day in which your ownership is still granted, must appear to you like a new acquisition, like a new gift. You must tend to your possession with the beautiful care of love, like a mother for her child, and not with the common anxiety of fear, like the jailor guarding his prisoners.

> [Aber sollst du das erworbene Gut fort lieben, so mußt du es auch verlieren können, und der Gedanke, wie auf tausend Wegen es verloren gehen möchte, muß deine Augen offen erhalten: jeden Tag, an welchem sein Besitz dir noch vergönnt wird, muß es dir wie ein neuer Erwerb, wie ein neues Geschenk erscheinen. Mit der schönen Sorge der Liebe, wie die Mutter ihr Kind, nicht mit der gemeinen Sorge der Angst, wie der Kerkermeister seinen Gefangenen, pflegst du deinen Besitz.][19]

Müller differentiates between two different types of *Sorge*, which can either be translated as care or as anxiety. Müller differentiates caring for the object like a mother for her child from the anxious will of the jailer. While beautiful care [*schöne Sorge*] is concerned with the

---

19 Müller, "Der poetische Besitz," 261.

well-being, integrity, and development of the object, common anxiety [*gemeine Sorge*] confines it, separates it from circulation and use.

The right to acquire and possess property, according to Müller, who in "Der poetische Besitz" generalizes and radicalizes non-possessive notions of property like *usus fructus* and *Nießbrauch*, cannot be conceived without the idea of abandoning this right. Hence, ownership is precarious, acquisition and loss coincide. A loving owner renounces their right to forcefully rule over, control, and hold on to their property. To love a good means being willing to give it up and let someone else enjoy it. Again, Müller uses the metaphor of kinship. The way a mother cares for her child, a true owner cares for their property. This care is not possessive or jealous. It does not stem from the fear of loss, but rather cherishes and recognizes that which is possessed as a gift, a gift which can be revoked at any moment. Loving care for property acknowledges the fact that all property is precarious. It is not a stable state but an uncertain relation of continuous appropriation.

Precarious Possessions

In Justinian's *Digest*, one finds the following definition of the Roman law institute of the *precarium*:

> A *precarium* is what is conceded in use to a petitioner in response to prayers for however long, while the grantor agrees. This type of liberality comes *ex iure gentium*, and differs from a *donatio* where who gives, gives in such a way that he does not receive it back: who gives a *precarium* gives in such a way that he will receive it back, when he wishes to take the *precarium* back to himself.[20]

The *precarium* introduces a notion of property and use that differs from that of possession. Precarious goods can be used but not owned, since they can always revert back to the original granting party. Therefore,

---

20 Wendy Davies and Paul Fouracre, *Property and Power in the Middle Ages* (Cambridge: Cambridge University Press, 2002), 45. Similar definitions can be found in Ulpian's *Institutes*. Cf. Borkowski: "Precarium is what is conceded to one who asks for it for his use for as long as the person who made the concessions suffers it ... And it differs from a gift in that someone who makes a gift does it on terms of not getting it back, whereas someone who makes a concession by precarium gives it back expecting to get it back when he chooses to dissolve the precarium." (J.A. Borkowski, *Borkowski's Textbook on Roman Law*, 5th edn, ed. Paul du Plessis [Oxford: Oxford University Press, 2015], 316). Cf. Jan Dirk Harke, *Precarium: Besitzvertrag im römischen Recht* (Berlin: Duncker & Humblot, 2016).

the *precarium* is, in Walter Benjamin's sense, "a good that cannot be a possession."[21] Giving and receiving a *precarium* is based on acts of "generosity" [*Freigiebigkeit*],[22] as Paul Sokolowsky points out. It is a free gift without any obligations. But the *precarium* is not a gift, as Justinian and other jurists point out, since it can be taken back at any time. The right of the client to use an object or a piece of land remains precarious, it can be suspended at any moment by the patron. The renunciation of the right of ownership by the patron is not final. They do not give up their right of ownership but their right of use. They concede their right without giving it up completely. This contract *ex iure gentium*, as von Savigny notes, is between "patron and client a sort of family relation, like a father's to his children, no proper obligation, no contract, could be recognised."[23] In this sense, the *precarium* resembles a *peculium*, something a *filius familias* can receive from his father, which he can use but not own. Children under Roman law were barred from legal ownership, since all ownership was restricted to the *pater familias*. The *precarium* is located in a precarious zone at the limits of codified law, outside of the *iure gentium*, but within the "limits of social recognition" [*Schranken sozialer Anerkennung*].[24]

Similarly, Müller's conceptualization of property locates the grounds of private property in social relations, like those of family or feudal dominion. He attempts to envision a model of reciprocal interdependence that is not based exclusively on juridical categories but is regulated by concrete social circumstances. The remarkable ambiguity of the *precarium* as a law of concession and prayer within the statutes of Roman property law has often been noted; for example, Moritz Stubenrauch's comment to the Austrian General Civil Code [*Allgemeine Bürgerliche Gesetzbuch*] from 1811 states: "Some citizens recognize in the same [*precarium*, J.K.] an unnamed contract. Others do not even recognize it as a legal transaction, but rather only as a special qualification to the

---

21 Walter Benjamin, "Notes toward a Work on the Category of Justice," in *The Messianic Reduction: Walter Benjamin and the Shape of Time*, trans. Peter Fenves (Stanford, CA: Stanford University Press, 2011), 257.

22 Paul Sokolowsky, *Die Philosophie im Privatrecht*, vol. 2 (Halle: Niemeyer, 1907), 81.

23 Friedrich Carl von Savigny, *Possession in the Civil Law*, trans. Erskine Perry (London and Calcutta: Thacker & Co, 1888) 202. Cf. Sokolowsky: "Sehr bezeichnend sprechen die späteren römischen Juristen hier von einem Besitz, welcher durchaus rechtmäßig sei, dessen Autorität sich in den Schranken sozialer Anerkennung behaupte, nicht aber bis zur Verteidigung durch ein ordentliches judicium, durch eine dingliche Klage hinanreiche – justa quidem possession, sed quae non pergat ad judicii vigorem." Sokolowsky, *Die Philosophie im Privatrecht*, 81.

24 Sokolowsky, *Die Philosophie im Privatrecht*, 81.

type of ownership."[25] It remains unclear whether the *precarium* must be considered to be an implicit contract without explicit codification or whether it is situated outside the realm of codified law. Although Müller does not mention the Roman *precarium* directly, he refers in the *Essays towards a Theory of Money* [*Versuche einer Theorie des Geldes*] to a medieval distinction between two types of property: *feod* and *allod*.[26] He writes:

> All of the institutions of the Middle Ages testify to the fact that in this time, two types of property were recognized: the Feod and the Allod, unlimited property and property based on good faith. The Feod was given priority in every instance, in accordance with all history and legal precedents, a priority ordained by God and the natural order of things; the Allod grew out of the economical usufruct[27] of the Feod, and was limited and bounded in all aspects by the Feod.

> [Die Institutionen des Mittelalters bezeugen alle, daß man in jenen Zeiten zwey Hauptgattungen des Eigenthums anerkannte, das Feod und Allod, unbeschränktes und auf Treu und Glauben überlassenes Eigenthum. Das Feod hat nach aller Geschichte und allen Rechtsansichten jener Zeit die Priorität, die ihm von wegen Gott und der Natur der Ding an allen Orten zukommt; das Allod kennt man nur als erwachsend aus dem sparsamen Nießbrauch des Feod, und von allen Seiten bedingt und beschränkt durch dieses.][28]

The Franconian/Middle Latin term *allod*—combining the words *all* and *od*, *full* and *property*—is often translated as "Eigengut" or "Vollgut." In contradistinction, the possession of a *feod* is conditional. It is "property based on good faith" [auf Treu und Glauben überlassenes Eigenthum] and can always be recalled. In the Middle Ages *feodal possession* is based

---

25 Moritz Stubenrauch, *Das Allgemeine Bürgerliche Gesetzbuch vom 1. Juni 1811*, vol. 3 (Vienna: Friedrich Mann, 1858), 168: "Einige Civilisten sehen in demselben einen ungenannten Contract. Andere betrachten dasselbe nicht einmal als ein Rechtsgeschäft, sondern nur als eine besondere Qualification des Besitzes."
26 The relation of the Roman *precarium* to the medieval institutions of feod and allod is complicated. Cf. Ernst Levy, "Vom Precarium zur germanischen Landleihe," *Zeitschrift der Savigny-Stiftung für Rechtsgeschichte: Romanistische Abteilung*, 66 (1948): 1–30.
27 The legal right to use and enjoy the fruits or profits of something belonging to another; can refer to leasing, or any other form of conditional property.
28 Adam Müller, *Versuche einer Theorie des Geldes* (Jena: Gustav Fischer, 1922), 23.

on "terms based on the services to be rendered" [*Bedingungen dafür zu leistender Dienste*] and is always threatened by its "eventual reversion" [*eventuellen Heimfall*].[29] According to Müller's reconstruction, the idea of personal property as *allod* grew out of feudal *usufruct*.

The re-discovery of a Germanic idea of property right in the forms of *allod* and *feod* exemplifies Müller's anti-Napoleonic resentment, a resentment which is also visible in Jacob Grimm's *Von der Poesie im Recht* (*Of the Poetry in Law*) and Friedrich Carl von Savigny's *Vom Beruf unserer Zeit für Gesetzgebung und Rechtswissenschaft* (*Of the Vocation of our Age for Legislation and Jurisprudence*), both of which call for an investigation into the historical origins and transformations of German law. For Grimm and von Savigny, law is based in the concrete living spirit [*Volksgeist*] of the people, not in an abstract codification like the *Code Napoléon*. According to Müller in *The Elements of Statecraft*, German medieval property law is based on a "Theory of the Character of all Goods."[30] It represents the "the true, living nature of property." Against the "Roman school," the Germanic Middle Ages developed personal, for example, feudal, models of property.[31] "Fiefdoms, majorats," Müller writes, "are only reactions against Roman influence."[32] What Müller and others recognize in the Middle Ages is a feudal society not governed by the law of unconditional private property, but one at least partially characterized by a notion of possession that is communal, for example, based on sharing and mutuality. Modernity, according to Müller, is defined by the slow replacement of the *feod* by *allod*, communal property by private property. Against "despotism over things,"[33] which Müller, as well as Marx in the *Critique of Hegel's Philosophy of Right*, locates within the tradition of Roman law, Müller envisions a medieval and feudal notion of property based on the idea of a commonwealth against what Michael Hardt and Antonio Negri would refer to as a *republic of property*. In their recent book *Commonwealth*, Hardt and Negri revive the notion of the commons for contemporary emancipatory politics. "What is central for our purposes here," Hardt and Negri write, "is that the concept of property and the defense of property remain the foundation of every modern political constitution. This is the sense in which the

---

29 Müller, *Versuche einer Theorie des Geldes*, 23.
30 Müller, *Die Elemente der Staatskunst*, vol. 1 (Berlin: Sander, 1809), 240: "wahre lebendige Natur des Eigenthums."
31 Müller, *Die Elemente der Staatskunst*, 236.
32 Müller, *Die Elemente der Staatskunst*, 238: "Lehen, Majorate sind eigentlich bloße Reactionen gegen den römischen Einfluß."
33 Karl Marx, "Zur Kritik der Hegelschen Rechtsphilosophie," *Marx-Engels-Werke*, vol. 1 (Berlin: Dietz, 1981), 315.

republic, from the great bourgeois revolutions to today, is a republic of property."[34] The concept of the commons employed by Hardt, Negri, and others usually denotes material and immaterial resources which can be used by all members of a community. The classical medieval example is that of the *Allmende*, which represents the common ownership of land of a village. Daniel Loick observes: "The commons make private annexation, i.e., the exploitations, of social products impossible, and thereby also the connected forms of injustice, dysfunction and alienation." Commons foster "non-selfish coordination and cooperation" and are not based on an abstract law but actualize "affective-habitual resources" in concrete environments.[35]

According to Müller, this circulation of property between the members of the community does not transform objects into commodities but rather leaves them in a state of permanent precarity, that is, they can be used but never fully owned. Müller's discussion of communal property focuses on the possibility of use without possession. The relation between fief and vassal is concrete and personal, not abstract and economical as in the symmetrical exchange of commodities. Commons are based on *Treu* and *Glauben* (good faith), as Müller notes, and medieval society is structured by "networks of reciprocal favors."[36] If one accepts property as a form of *feod*, Müller claims, there is a possibility to overcome the separations of modern capitalism and a return to a pre-stabilized harmony based on the principles of reciprocity and circulation, which prohibit accumulation of property by the individual. Wealth, he writes, "doesn't exist in the things themselves, and cannot be held onto by holding onto the things."[37] Müller believed that, despite the emancipatory rhetoric, the property laws developed during the French Revolution, due in part to their roots in Roman law, remained nevertheless a republic of property, and as such represented a tyranny over both the people and things subjected to them.

---

34 Michael Hardt and Antonio Negri, *Commonwealth* (Cambridge, MA: Harvard University Press, 2011), 15.

35 Loick, *Der Missbrauch des Eigentums*, 129: "Die Commons verunmöglichen private Aneignung des gesellschaftlichen Produzierten, d.i. Ausbeutung, und die damit zusammenhängenden Formen von Ungerechtigkeit, Dysfunktionalität und Entfremdung"; "nicht-egoistische Koordination und Kooperation"; "affektiv-habituelle."

36 Niklas Luhmann, "Inklusion und Exklusion," *Soziologische Aufklärung* (Opladen: Westdeutscher Verlag, 1995), 133: "Netzwerke des wechselseitigen Gunsterweises."

37 Müller, *Die Elemente der Staatskunst*, 348: "liegt nicht in den bloßen Sachen, er läßt sich nicht festhalten, indem man die Sachen festhält."

Following his principle of mutual reciprocity, Müller calls for a conceptualization of private property law that connects Roman property and German feudal law: "true private law will require the confluence of the vital elements of Roman and feudal law with each other." He argues that true private property rights would recognize the living "character of things."[38] Like the Roman *precarium*, rights of private property should be situated on the threshold of codified law. Müller is no revolutionary and does not call for an abolishment of private property. Instead, his romantic medievalism imagines a (modern?) feudal society, one in which concrete, reciprocal social relations still exist and have not been universally replaced by the law of private property, commodification and exchange. For Müller, as for Marx, private property is a principle that does not bring about association but dissociation and strife. The "Preservation of Property,"[39] which John Locke defines in the *Second Treatise of Government* as central to modern state power, must necessarily lead to a state of permanent civil war, according to Müller. All societies based on the principle of private property therefore must necessarily resemble police states, since the right to private property pits one individual against the other. The right to property is a right of dissociation and separation, not of association and community. In *Essays Towards a Theory of Money*, Müller writes: "If there is only private property, and all property exists separated around each isolated proprietor, then the government, no matter how liberal and well-meaning it may be, can only achieve its purpose of protecting private property and property owners through an iron band of force."[40] The "Roman legal terms concerning the exclusive rule of private property ... turn state power into a force of categorical despotism."[41] Hence, it was a fundamental error of the French revolutionaries to subsume the "despotic concept of private property under human rights."[42] The republic

---

38 Müller, *Die Elemente der Staatskunst*, 239: "In dem wahren Privat-Rechte werden also römische und feudalistische Elemente lebendig miteinander verknüpft werden müssen"; "Persönlichkeit der Sachen."

39 John Locke, *Second Treatise of Government*, ed. Mark Goldie (Oxford: Oxford University Press, 2016), 63.

40 Müller, *Versuche einer Theorie des Geldes*, 24: "Gibt es nur Privateigenthum, steht alles Eigenthum abgesondert für sich um den isolirten Eigenthümer her, so kann die Regierung, wie liberal und wohlmeinend sie auch sey, ihre Bestimmung, Eigenthum und Eigenthümer zu schützen, nur durch Zwang, durch ein eisernes Band erreichen."

41 Müller, *Versuche einer Theorie des Geldes*, 25: "Römische Rechtsbegriffe von der Alleinherrschaft des Privateigenthums ... constituiren die Staatsgewalt zum unbedingten Despotismus."

42 Müller, *Die Elemente der Staatskunst*, 229: "Begriff des despotischen Eigenthums unter die Menschenrechte."

of property is therefore not a republic of reciprocity and mutuality, as imagined by Müller in "Der poetische Besitz" and the "Twelve Speeches on Eloquence" [*Zwölf Reden über die Beredsamkeit*], but is rather a tyrannical police state, where the disputes of isolated property owners can only be mediated by force.

Bittleihen

While there is no immediate translation of *precarium* into English, German historians of law often use the term *Bittleihe* to render the peculiar structure of this legal concept. The word *Bittleihe*, combining the acts of *bitten*, pledging, asking, and *leihen*, giving or lending, affords to recognize the *precarium* as a kind of speech act, something one can acquire only having made a pledge or petition. Isidore of Seville in his *Etymologiae* gives the following definition: "A *precarium* is when a creditor, having been petitioned with a prayer, allows a debtor to take *fructus* from the *possessio* of a *fundus* ceded to him."[43] A *precarium* is the result of a *preces*, a prayer in which the debtor appeals to the creditor and pleads for a loan. Similar to the process of *Erwerben*, a *precarium* is a rhetorical, if not a poetic act of *Werben*. As discussed in the section on poetic property, for Müller, all true possession is built on poetic acts of acquisition. Courting property is an imminently linguistic process, one which is characterized by acts of calling, wishing, and luring: "You love that which you have acquired through effort and artful skill, because you have had to anticipate it, recognize it, wish for it, and attract it."[44] What is unusual about this is that, while under Roman law a human debtor addresses a human creditor, Müller imagines a direct, romantic address to the inanimate piece of property itself. In this romantic overture to the inanimate, Müller's theory of property is not dissimilar to discussions of the function of the apostrophe within poetry; Barbara Johnson emphasizes that in lyric poetry the apostrophe "involves the direct address to an absent, dead, or inanimate being by a first-person speaker,"[45] and Jonathan Culler states in *Theory of the Lyric*: "The function of apostrophe would be to posit a potentially responsive or at least attentive universe, to which one has a relation."[46] Müller's

---

43 Davies and Fouracre, *Property and Power in the Middle Ages*, 45.

44 Müller, "Der poetische Besitz," 261: "Was du erworben hast mit Mühe und biegsamer Kunst, das liebst du, weil du es hast kommen sehn, weil du es erkannt, gewünscht, gerufen, gelockt hat werden müssen."

45 Barbara Johnson, "Apostrophe, Animation, Abortion," *English Literary History* 59 (1991): 141–65, 185.

46 Jonathan Culler, *Theory of the Lyric* (Cambridge, MA and London: Harvard University Press, 2015), 216.

notion of poetic property takes into account this idea of a responsive or attentive universe, for example, a relation between subject and object that is not based on domination but rather resembles the structure of rhetoric, which Müller defines as a "dialogue" [*Wechselrede*].[47] Müller discusses the speech acts of pleading, pledging, and praying in the "Twelve Speeches on Eloquence" [*Zwölf Reden über die Beredsamkeit*], a lecture series he held in Vienna in May and June 1812. Here, he identifies "the dialogue as source of eloquence in general."[48] This theory of the relation between speaker and listener is based on Müller's foundational "Doctrine of Opposites" [*Lehre vom Gegensatze*], in which he claims that "speaker and listener ... stand in a relationship of continuous interaction."[49]

Müller views this reciprocity between speaker and listener as a fundamentally Republican quality:

> That is why eloquence flourishes in republics, not only because everyone is permitted to speak, but rather because everyone is accustomed from early on to speak within the free disposition of the republic and into their neighbor's ear, and because whoever wishes to lead must learn to listen and understand many different, particular things, tolerate them, and be responsible to so many.[50]

In order to rule one needs to obey. The spoken language of the republic is not one of legislation or execution but of a common sharing. All participants of the Republican communication share a "freie Gesinnung" (free disposition). Friedrich Balke argues that this disposition is in part the result of renouncing one's own subjectivity: "Müller's formulation for the new, 'higher rhetoric' reads: 'protestation against the self,' that

---

47 Müller, "Zwölf Reden über die Beredsamkeit," *Kritische Ausgabe*, vol. 1, ed. Walter Schroeder and Werner Siebert (Neuwied: Luchterhand, 1967), 341.
48 Müller, "Zwölf Reden über die Beredsamkeit," 322: "das Gespräch als Quelle der Beredsamkeit überhaupt."
49 Müller, "Lehre vom Gegensatze," *Kritische Ausgabe*, vol. 1, ed. Walter Schroeder and Werner Siebert (Neuwied: Luchterhand, 1967), 215: "Redner und Hörer ... stehen in dem Verhältnisse durchgängiger Wechselwirkung."
50 Müller, "Zwölf Reden über die Beredsamkeit," 334: "Darum gedeiht in Republiken die Beredsamkeit, nicht bloß, weil jedem mitzureden erlaubt ist, sondern weil jeder frühe gewöhnt wird einzugehn in die freie Gesinnung, in das Ohr des Nachbars, weil, wer herrschen will, so vieles Unabhängige, so viel eigentümliche Weise zu hören und zu empfinden, neben sich dulden muß und so vielen gehorchen muß."

is, the suspension of the principle of self-preservation, the principle at the root of all modern philosophy."[51] According to Müller, it is only through suspending one's own position that the speaker can simultaneously hear themself, as well as the other: "the art of listening results from free dominion over this sense, in the ability to hear the meaning of others and simultaneously of oneself."[52] Rhetoric is "the art of hearing yourself like a third party, with protestation, with opposition, with another disposition, not merely with another ear, but rather almost with another heart than one's own."[53] For Müller, this specific form of oral rhetoric, which founds a particular social order of mutual listeners, has been lost. The decline of oratory is not a specifically German problem, although Müller directs his most intense attacks against "the instrument of the German language,"[54] but is directly connected to a particular conception of economy. The decline of the spoken and the rise of the written word goes hand in hand with the rise of money. According to Müller, it was the printing press, which made it possible to preserve the "bad, false and meaningless,"[55] replacing living speech. Analogously, money stands in for something absent:

> It was as with money relations: when one could manage by oneself, one paid others with the power of one's own hands and services, one paid one's contemporaries with one's person: one only used gold and silver when people were distant or absent, or for the future. – Gold and silver have the same relation to the living deed as the written word does to the living word.

---

51 Friedrich Balke, "Die 'Zirkulation des Staates': Adam Müller und die Medien der politischen Steuerung um 1800," *Kontingenz und Steuerung: Literatur als Gesellschaftsexperiment 1750–1830*, ed. Torsten Hahn, Erich Kleinschmidt, and Nicolas Pethes (Würzburg: Königshausen & Neumann, 2004), 458: "Müllers Formel für die neue, die 'höhere Rhetorik' lautet: 'Protestation gegen sich selbst', also Suspension des Prinzips der Selbsterhaltung, das aller neuzeitlichen Philosophie zugrunde liegt."
52 Müller, "Zwölf Reden über die Beredsamkeit," 335: "Die Kunst zu hören besteht also in der freien Herrschaft, die man über diesen Sinn erhält, in der Fähigkeit, im Sinn des andern und doch zugleich sich selbst zu hören."
53 Müller, "Zwölf Reden über die Beredsamkeit," 334: "die Kunst, sich anzuhören wie ein Dritter, mit Protestation, mit Opposition, mit anderen Gesinnungen, nicht bloß mit einem andern Ohr, sondern fast mit einem andern Herzen als dem seinigen."
54 Müller, "Zwölf Reden über die Beredsamkeit," 322: "das Instrument der deutschen Sprache."
55 Müller, "Zwölf Reden über die Beredsamkeit," 328: "Schlechte, Falsche und Unbedeutende."

[Es war wie mit den Geldverhältnissen: wo man mit sich erreichen konnte, da vergalt man einander mit der Kraft seiner Hände und mit Diensten, man zahlte dem Gegenwärtigen und Zeitgenossen mit der Person: nur für die Entfernten, für die Abwesenden, für die Zukunft bediente man sich des Goldes und Silbers. – Gold und Silber verhält sich zur lebendigen Tat grade wie die Schrift sich zu dem lebendigen Worte verhält.][56]

While in this theory of oratory Müller criticizes the influence of money, in other parts of his oeuvre, especially in the *Essays Concerning a New Theory of Money* [*Versuche einer neuen Theorie des Geldes*], he praises the circulation of money as that medium which initiates a true sociability. The force of commodities like that of language and of faith are capable of founding and sustaining a community: "The power of goods, which is sought by everyone in order to be included with everyone, the power of the word or of belief, in which many or all members of civil society unite: both powers are only manifestations of the desire of everyone to be included in the totality."[57] The accelerated circulation of money and commodities prohibits one's attachment to property. It counteracts the negative tendencies of a "vice grip" [*krampfiges Festhalten*] on particular goods. Just as in the reciprocal relationship of *Liebe* and *Gegenliebe*, here the owner is able to let go of their property. Ownership has no permanence but remains precarious in the permanent circulation of capital. Müller also identifies the proximity of *Werben* and *Erwerben* in

---

56 Müller, "Zwölf Reden über die Beredsamkeit," 327.

57 Müller, *Versuche einer Theorie des Geldes*, 31: "Die Macht der Waare, die um des Beyanderseyns Willen mit Allen von Allen gesucht wird, die Macht des Wortes oder des Glaubens, worin sich viele oder alle Mitglieder der bürgerlichen Gesellschaft vereinigen: beyde Mächte sind nur Offenbarungen des Bedürfnisses aller bey einander zu seyn."

See Breithaupt: "Adam Müller, the so-called economist of the Romantics, rationalizes money as the very essence of community since money functions as a form of communication understood and accepted by everyone. Müller compares this ability of money to function as a medium that unites a people with the mediating force of poetry" (Fritz Breithaupt, "The Ego-Effect of Money" in *Rereading Romanticism*, ed. Martha Helfer [Amsterdam and Atlanta: Rodopi, 2000], 253). See Jochen Marquardt, "Die Vermittlung zwischen Ökonomie und Poesie: Adam Müllers Analyse der Französischen Revolution und deren Anwendung auf seine ästhetische Theorie," *Deutsche Romantik und Französische Revolution* (Wrocław: Wydawnictwo Uniwersytetu Wrocławskiego, 1990). See also Jochen Marquardt, *"Vermittelnde Geschichte": Zum Verhältnis von ästhetischer Theorie und historischem Denken bei Adam Heinrich Müller* (Stuttgart: Verlag Hans-Dieter Heinz, 1993).

the orator's relationship to language. In a strict sense, the speaker and, by extension the poet, does not possess a language. It is not a property over which they could rule freely. Instead, it is a good that remains precarious. It is a gift that cannot be kept by asserting but instead by renouncing one's right to property. Like the *precarium*, language can be understood as a good that can be used without being fully owned. The relation of the poet to language is therefore of an essential precarity. Each poetic speech act is a *Bittleihe*, an address not only to the listener but to language itself. It is a plea for the gift of language. Poetic language is the language of a precarious "release" [*Freigabe*] (Hamacher) or "generosity" [*Freigiebigkeit*] (Sokolowsky), renouncing the right and will to property and simultaneously calling for a community of possessionless poets. In other words, in the precarious poetic act of pledging and granting temporary possession, the principal non-givenness of all possessions appears. The language of poetry, which cannot be taken and owned like an object, is based on the idea of a generous address to an Other. Hence, in poetry, the human being appears as a "a being pleading for language" [*um Sprache bittende(s) Wesen*].[58] It is a language of pre-predicative speech acts like "die Bitte, das Gebet, de[r] Wunsch"[59] [the request, the prayer, the wish]. This gratuity is not a one-time act of grace but is instead a continuous process of give and take that points to what Hamacher calls *Sprachgerechtigkeit*: "Language-justice, conversational-justice would be the unregulated, unnormed and therefore human beginning of all 'civil' and 'political' justice."[60] In this sense, Müller's idea of poetic property must be understood as a plea for a notion of a just language based on poetic acts of *Werben* and *Erwerben*. Its irreducible precarity resists an immediate appropriation and application for political ends. Instead, to cite Hegel, it points towards the utopia of a "Poesie des Herzens," able to undermine the "Prosa der Verhältnisse." This utopia is a non-place in the literal sense of the word. It predates any political or socioeconomic order, resembling a "sanctuary" [*Freistätte*],[61] an open and precarious space of free and unregulated discourse. Here, justice is inaugurated through poetic acts of addressing, calling, and courting the Other.

---

58 Hamacher, "Vom Recht, Rechte nicht zu gebrauchen: Menschenrechte und Urteilsstruktur," 89.

59 Hamacher, "Vom Recht, Rechte nicht zu gebrauchen," 88.

60 Hamacher, "Kein Schweigeasyl – Bestechlichkeit ist keine Hoffnung (Celan)," *Sprachgerechtigkeit*, 335: "Sprach-Gerechtigkeit, Gesprächs-Gerechtigkeit wäre der unreglementierte, unnormierte und darum menschliche Anfang jeder 'bürgerlichen' und jeder 'politischen' Gerechtigkeit."

61 Hamacher, "Freistätte – Zum Recht auf Forschung und Bildung," *Sprachgerechtigkeit*, 286.

Works Cited

Arendt, Hannah. "Adam Müller-Renaissance?" In *Reflections on Literature and Culture*, edited by Susannah Young-Ah Gottlieb, 38–45. Stanford, CA: Stanford University Press, 2007.

Balke, Friedrich. "Die 'Zirkulation des Staates': Adam Müller und die Medien der politischen Steuerung um 1800." In *Kontingenz und Steuerung: Literatur als Gesellschaftsexperiment 1750–1830*, edited by Torsten Hahn, Erich Kleinschmidt, and Nicolas Pethes, 123–46. Würzburg: Königshausen & Neumann, 2004.

Benjamin, Walter. "Notes toward a Work on the Category of Justice." In *The Messianic Reduction: Walter Benjamin and the Shape of Time*, translated by Peter Fenves, 257–8. Stanford, CA: Stanford University Press, 2011.

Borkowski, J.A., and Paul J. Du Plessis. *Borkowski's Textbook on Roman Law*, 5th edn. Edited by Paul du Plessis. Oxford: Oxford University Press, 2015.

Breithaupt, Fritz. "The Ego-Effect of Money." In *Rereading Romanticism*, edited by Martha Helfer, 227–58. Amsterdam and Atlanta, GA: Rodopi, 2000.

Culler, Jonathan. *Theory of the Lyric*. Cambridge, MA and London: Harvard University Press, 2015.

Davies, Wendy, and Paul Fouracre. *Property and Power in the Middle Ages*. Cambridge: Cambridge University Press, 2002.

Gray, Richard. "Hypersign, Hypermoney, Hypermarket: Adam Müller's Theory of Money and Romantic Semiotics." *New Literary History* 31, no. 2 (2000): 295–314.

Grimm, Jacob and Wilhelm Grimm. *Deutsches Wörterbuch*. Edited by Berlin-Brandenburgische Akademie der Wissenschaften Berlin. Stuttgart: Hirzel, 1961.

Hamacher, Werner. "Vom Recht, Rechte nicht zu gebrauchen: Menschenrechte und Urteilsstruktur." In *Sprachgerechtigkeit*, 93–126. Frankfurt: Fischer, 2018.

Hamacher, Werner. "Kein Schweigeasyl – Bestechlichkeit ist keine Hoffnung (Celan)." In *Sprachgerechtigkeit*, 323–36. Frankfurt: Fischer, 2018.

Hamacher, Werner. "The One Right No One Ever Has." In *Sprachgerechtigkeit*, 336–62. Frankfurt: Fischer, 2018.

Hamacher, Werner. "Freistätte – Zum Recht auf Forschung und Bildung." In *Sprachgerechtigkeit*, 283–322. Frankfurt: Fischer, 2018.

Hardt, Michael and Antonio Negri. *Commonwealth*. Cambridge, MA: Harvard University Press, 2011.

Harke, Jan Dirk. *Precarium: Besitzvertrag im römischen Recht*. Berlin: Duncker & Humblot, 2016.

Hegel, Georg Wilhelm Friedrich. *Werke in zwanzig Bänden: Vorlesungen über die Ästhetik*, vol. 15, edited by Eva Moldenhauer and Karl Markus Michel. Frankfurt: Suhrkamp, 1970.

Johnson, Barbara. "Apostrophe, Animation, Abortion." *English Literary History* 59 (1991): 141–65.

Kant, Immanuel. *Kants Werke: Akademie-Textausgabe*, vol. 5: *Die Metaphysik der Sitten*. Berlin: de Gruyter, 1968.

Kant, Immanuel. *The Metaphysics of Morals: Introduction, Translation, and Notes by Mary Gregor*. Cambridge: Cambridge University Press, 1991.

Knittel, Anton Philipp. "Phöbus: Ein Journal für die Kunst." In *Kleist-Handbuch: Leben – Werk – Wirkung*, 166, edited by Ingo Breuer, 162–6. Stuttgart and Weimar: Metzler, 2013.

Levy, Ernst. "Vom Precarium zur germanischen Landleihe." *Zeitschrift der Savigny-Stiftung für Rechtsgeschichte: Romanistische Abteilung* 66 (1948): 1–30.

Locke, John. *Second Treatise of Government*. Edited by Mark Goldie. Oxford: Oxford University Press, 2016.

Loick, Daniel. *Der Missbrauch des Eigentums*. Berlin: August Verlag, 2016.

Luhmann, Niklas. "Inklusion und Exklusion." In *Soziologische Aufklärung*, Vol 6, edited by Niklas Luhmann, 237–67. Opladen: Westdeutscher Verlag, 1995.

Lukács, György. "Joseph von Eichendorff." In *Deutsche Realisten des 19. Jahrhunderts*, 49–65. Bern: Francke, 1951.

Lukács, György. "Joseph von Eichendorff." In *German Realists in the Nineteenth Century*. Translated by Jeremy Gaines and Paul Keast, edited by Rodney Livingstone, 50–69. Cambridge, MA: MIT Press, 1993.

Marquardt, Jochen. "Die Vermittlung zwischen Ökonomie und Poesie: Adam Müllers Analyse der Französischen Revolution und deren Anwendung auf seine ästhetische Theorie." In *Deutsche Romantik und Französische Revolution*, edited by Gerard Kozielik, 169–79. Wrocław: Wydawnictwo Uniwersytetu Wrocławskiego, 1990.

Marquardt, Jochen. *"Vermittelnde Geschichte": Zum Verhältnis von ästhetischer Theorie und historischem Denken bei Adam Heinrich Müller*. Stuttgart: Verlag Hans-Dieter Heinz, 1993.

Marx, Karl. *Capital, Volume 3*. Translated by David Fernbach. London: Penguin, 1991.

Marx, Karl. "Zur Kritik der Hegelschen Rechtsphilosophie." In *Marx-Engels-Werke*, 44 volumes. vol. 1/2, 201–336. Berlin: Dietz, 1956–2018.

Matala de Mazza, Ethel. *Der verfasste Körper: Zum Projekt einer organischen Gemeinschaft*. Freiburg: Rombach, 1999.

Müller, Adam. "Der poetische Besitz." In *Kritische Ausgabe*, vol. 2, edited by Walter Schroeder and Werner Siebert, 261–2. Neuwied: Luchterhand, 1967.

Müller, Adam. *Die Elemente der Staatskunst*, vol. 1. Berlin: Sander, 1809.

Müller, Adam. "Einleitung zu den philosophischen und kritischen Miszellen." In *Kritische Ausgabe*, vol. 1, edited by Walter Schroeder and Werner Siebert, 505–7. Neuwied: Luchterhand, 1967.

Müller, Adam. "Lehre vom Gegensatze." In *Kritische Ausgabe*, vol. 1, 195–248, edited by Walter Schroeder and Werner Siebert. Neuwied: Luchterhand, 1967.

Müller, Adam. *Versuche einer Theorie des Geldes*. Jena: Gustav Fischer, 1922.

Müller, Adam. "Zwölf Reden über die Beredsamkeit." In *Kritische Ausgabe*, vol. 1, edited by Walter Schroeder and Werner Siebert, 293–451. Neuwied, Berlin: Luchterhand, 1967.

Saller, Reinhard. *Schöne Ökonomie: Die poetische Reflexion der Ökonomie in frühromantischer Literatur*. Würzburg: Königshausen & Neumann, 2007.

Savigny, Friedrich Carl von. *Possession in the Civil Law*. Translated by Erskine Perry. London and Calcutta: Thacker & Co., 1888.

Sokolowsky, Paul. *Die Philosophie im Privatrecht*, vol. 2. Halle: Niemeyer, 1907.

Stubenrauch, Moritz. *Das Allgemeine Bürgerliche Gesetzbuch vom 1. Juni 1811*, vol. 3. Vienna: Friedrich Mann, 1858.

Tuck, Richard. *Natural Right Theories: Their Origins and Development*. Cambridge: Cambridge University Press, 1979.

Vogl, Joseph. "Romantische Oekonomie: Regierung und Regulation um 1800." In *Marianne – Germania: Deutsch-französischer Kulturtransfer im europäischen Kontext*, vol. 2, edited by Étienne François, 417–89. Leipzig: Leipziger Universitätsverlag, 1998.

Three   Die Judenbuche and the Rights of the Poor

Karsten Olson

Annette von Droste-Hülshoff's novella, *Die Judenbuche* (*The Jew's Beech*), published in 1842, is a crime novel characterized by a narrative overdetermination, an overdetermination which creates unresolvable ambiguity. The main character, Friedrich Mergel, is doubled in the wan apparition Johannes Niemand (literally, Johannes Nobody), the presumed illegitimate son of his uncle Simon. Presumed, but never explained. The only evidence of Johannes' origin is his likeness to Friedrich, and the horror expressed by Friedrich's mother upon first encountering him. When Johannes dies at the end of the novella, or rather, what the reader learns is Friedrich masquerading as Johannes, he is found hanged in the titular Jew's Beech [*Judenbuche*], and it is never divulged if his death is to be attributed to murder or suicide. All that is stated is that Friedrich/Johannes is thrown into the carrion pit, and not buried in the church cemetery. In other words, the only thing which is certain is his guilt. When Friedrich is discovered hanged in the Jew's Beech, his discovery echoes the visitations of his father's ghost, which had appeared to locals as a "swollen blue face peeping through the branches"[1]–even though his father did not hang. In reality, Hermann Mergel died freezing to death in the same woods which would eventually witness the deaths of his son Friedrich, the usurer Aaron, and the forester Brandis. Like his son's, Hermann's death remains unexplained. Instead of providing a single, definitive answer, three potential answers are suggested simultaneously and without any obvious preference. It is possible Hermann froze due to his own

---

1   Annette von Droste-Hülshoff, *The Jew's Beech* (Richmond: Alma Books Ltd, 1958), trans. Lionel Thomas and Doris Thomas 26; Droste-Hülshoff, *Die Judenbuche*, 19: "geschwollenes blaues Gesicht durch die Zweige lauschen."

drunken incompetence, or perhaps it was the inadvertent negligence of Margret misinterpreting his calls for help for the wind, or possibly Hermann died as the result of a plot against her abusive husband by Margret and her brothers. This overstuffing with signification penetrates down to the level of the temporal markers beginning each new section. In addition to the numerical calendar date, the age of the protagonist, the day of religious observance, and the current state of the natural world are all layered one on top of the other, with no effort made to distinguish between them or create a hierarchy. Each is potentially significant, each is a clue, each is loaded with portent.

The result of this symbolic overcharging is a story whose meaning has remained elusive for centuries. Or rather, *The Jew's Beech* has acted as a cipher into which vastly different purposes and intents have been read. *The Jew's Beech* has been read by turns as a proto-naturalist text, readings which highlight the detailed descriptions of both the natural world surrounding the fictitious village of B*** and the daily lives of its inhabitants. Or *The Jew's Beech* is interpreted as a paradigmatic Biedermeier text, a reactionary apology for the patriarchal rule of the aristocracy, written by one of its own. Or perhaps, in order to account for the supernatural, unnerving elements of the narrative, *The Jew's Beech* must be read as a Gothic crime novel. It is not the intent of this chapter to find the correct reading to *The Jew's Beech*. The irreducibility of Annette von Droste-Hülshoff's work is not sleight of hand. One of the issues the book seeks to address is the fundamental inaccessibility of the past. The past is not one, nor is it knowable. There is no such thing as "the way it really was,"[2] to quote Walter Benjamin's lampooning of the "historian's task," as defined by Leopold von Ranke. Instead there is only a contradictory, multi-perspectival morass, a multitude of the way things *might* have been. The central questions one must ask are therefore, which pasts are shown, how are they explained, and to what end? In other words, what is the futurity of these potential pasts? This chapter will focus on the discussions of law and criminality contained within *The Jew's Beech* as a means of assessing its utilization of the past. Droste-Hülshoff's criminal analysis will be brought into conversation with Karl Marx's articles pertaining to wood-theft legislation, also published in 1842. This is done with the intent of showing that both writers perform a kind of "romantic anticapitalism," as described by Patrick Eiden-Offe in *Poesie der Klasse*, that is, a retelling of the past which

---

2   Walter Benjamin, "On the Concept of History," *Walter Benjamin: Selected Writings*, ed. Howard Eiland and Michael William Jennings (Cambridge, MA: Harvard University Press, 2006), vol. 4, 391.

shows its (plural) lost possibilities and forgotten promises, in the hopes of creating "a social history with a sense of possibilities."[3]

A Picture of Life among the Hills of Westphalia

The Jew's Beech begins by granting a scant two clauses to the would-be protagonist, Friedrich Mergel: "Born in 1738, Friedrich Mergel was the only son of a small farmer or freeholder of the humbler kind in the village of B***."[4] Year of birth and social standing. No further information is provided. Rather than expanding on this description, the narrative veers off sharply, with Friedrich Mergel not returning for another four pages. Instead, the true central figures of the story are introduced; the town of B***, its inhabitants, and the surrounding woods. The reader's perspective is that of a hypothetical "traveler" entering the village from afar, breaching the "picturesque beauty of its situation in a green forest glen among an imposing range of hills remarkable for their historical associations,"[5] surveying the "smokey and poorly constructed buildings" of its residents. The historical allusion is explained by the subtitle of the section: the green forest which surrounds B*** is the Teutoburg Forest, connecting the town and its population to the mythical origins of the Germanic peoples. By crossing this wooded threshold, the reader has entered into "one of those remote areas without industry, commerce or main roads," a place "where a strange face still created a sensation and a journey of a hundred miles made even a man of rank the local Ulysses."[6] In a gesture definitive for Droste-Hülshoff, the ancient pedigree of the Battle of the Teutoburg Forest is overlaid with that of Ulysses, layering one symbolic value on top of the other in order to leave no doubt: this is a region untouched by the march of time, with the passage of time here represented by industry, commerce, and roads. The imposing forests and hills are therefore less important as a spatial barrier than as a temporal one, preserving

---

3   Patrick Eiden-Offe, *Die Poesie der Klasse Romantischer Antikapitalismus und die Erfindung des Proletariats* (Berlin: Matthes & Seitz, 2020), 33.

4   Droste-Hülshoff, *The Jew's Beech*, 11; Droste-Hülshoff, *Die Judenbuche*, 11: "Friedrich Mergel, geboren 1738, war der einzige Sohn eines sogenannten Halbmeiers oder Grundeigentümers geringerer Klasse im Dorfe B."

5   Droste-Hülshoff, *The Jew's Beech*, 11; Droste-Hülshoff, *Die Judenbuche*, 11: "malerische Schönheit seiner Lage in der grünen Waldschlucht eines bedeutenden und geschichtlich merkwürdigen Gebirges."

6   Droste-Hülshoff, *The Jew's Beech*, 11; Droste-Hülshoff, *Die Judenbuche*, 11: "einer jener abgeschlossenen Erdwinkel ohne Fabriken und Handel, ohne Heerstraßen … wo noch ein fremdes Gesicht Aufsehen erregte und eine Reise von dreißig Meilen selbst den Vornehmeren zum Ulysses seiner Gegend machte."

within them "a place once common in Germany, and with all the faults and virtues, all the eccentricity and narrow-mindedness that can only flourish under such conditions."[7]

Within the first two pages, there are at least three temporalities at play: there is the modern moment, the 1842 date of publication; there is the calendar year of the events that are about to unfold, 1738; and there is the third temporality, a timeless, ancient time, a time "before." The narration repeatedly assures the reader that the place they are about to enter is a different world. Not only do the events "within" conclude in 1789 (a convenient shorthand for the threshold to modernity), but even within this time frame, B*** lags behind its surroundings, a relic of another age. The continual stressing of the relative time in which the events occur does not merely serve to provide an evocative setting for a mystery. The narrator needs to impress on the audience the difficulty of traversing this historical threshold. After describing the geographical and temporal location of B***, the narrator warns: "It is difficult to view that time impartially, for since its passing either arrogant censure or fatuous praise have been bestowed on it, while the witness who has first-hand experience is blinded by too many familiar memories and the later generation is not capable of comprehending it."[8] Similarly, the ominous poem which precedes the narration challenges:

> Where is the hand so fraught with gentle art
> That tangled skein of narrow mind my part,
> So steadfast that trembling it may throw
> The stone upon a wretched creature's woe?[9]
> [Wo ist die Hand so zart, daß ohne Irren
> Sie sondern mag beschränkten Hirnes Wirren,
> So fest, daß ohne Zittern sie den Stein
> Mag schleudern auf ein arm verkümmert Sein?][10]

---

7   Droste-Hülshoff, *The Jew's Beech*, 12; Droste-Hülshoff, *Die Judenbuche*, 11: "ein Fleck, wie es deren sonst so viele in Deutschland gab, mit all den Mängeln und Tugenden, all der Originalität und Beschränktheit, wie sie nur in solchen Zuständen gedeihen."

8   Droste-Hülshoff, *The Jew's Beech*, 12; Droste-Hülshoff, *Die Judenbuche*, 12: "Es ist schwer, jene Zeit unparteiisch ins Auge zu fassen; sie ist seit ihrem Verschwinden entweder hochmütig getadelt oder albern gelobt worden, da den, der sie erlebte, zu viel teure Erinnerungen blenden und der Spätergeborene sie nicht begreift."

9   Droste-Hülshoff, *The Jew's Beech*, 11.

10 Droste-Hülshoff, *Die Judenbuche*, 11.

The reader, and all those "born in light" are asked to withhold judgment, to "lay scales aside."[11] In isolation, this poem could be read as a generic warning about the impossibility of accessing the past, of generational change. However, the careful demarcation of a "lost" world which surrounds this poem makes it clear that a very specific historiographical problem is being addressed. The difficulty in traversing this particular threshold is what Reinhart Koselleck describes as the "Janus face" of political and social concepts. According to this theory, all such terms have two meanings, one which faces backwards towards antiquity and another which faces forward towards modernity, and it is impossible to understand terms from the pre-modern in their original context without an act of historical translation. This is the foundation of conceptual history which, as a discipline, charts the radical changes that concepts underwent as a result of the "industrial and political" revolutions of the eighteenth and nineteenth centuries.[12] In other words, when the narrator of *The Jew's Beech* urges the reader to withhold judgment, and to instead try to understand the events within the context of the world in which they took place, what is demanded of the reader is a work of translation, of reconstructing forgotten meanings and social relations.

In the Shadow of Sovereign Violence

The practical implications of this temporal and conceptual gulf are most visible in the laws and sense of legality which existed within the town of B***. Following another abrupt shift, the narrator continues: "As a result of primitive and often inadequate legislature [*Gesetzen*], the ideas of the inhabitants as to right and wrong had become somewhat confused, or rather beside the official legal system there had grown up a second law based on public opinion, usage and superannuation arising from neglect."[13] Within this passage, the narrator models the critical posture previously endorsed: the initial, somewhat reactionary assertion of the immorality of the populace is, if not entirely rescinded,

---

11 Droste-Hülshoff, *The Jew's Beech*, 11.
12 Reinhart Koselleck, "Richtlinien für das Lexikon politisch-sozialer Begriffe der Neuzeit," *Archiv für Begriffsgeschichte*, vol. 11 (Bonn: Bouvier Verlag, 1967), 82.
13 Droste-Hülshoff, *The Jew's Beech*, 11; Droste-Hülshoff, *Die Judenbuche*, 11–12: "Unter höchst einfachen und häufig unzulänglichen Gesetzen waren die Begriffe der Einwohner von Recht und Unrecht einigermaßen in Verwirrung geraten, oder vielmehr, es hatte sich neben dem gesetzlichen ein zweites Recht gebildet, ein Recht der öffentlichen Meinung, der Gewohnheit und der durch Vernachlässigung entstandenen Verjährung."

modified. It is not that the population of B*** is lawless or barbaric, but rather, in the absence of the institutions which would actively enforce a written legal codex, they operate in accordance with self-imposed norms, negotiating amongst themselves a social order deemed to be more or less just by those who participate in it. What is being described here, and what the spatial and temporal distance to the outside world has preserved, is perhaps best understood through the lens of *sovereign violence* as developed by Michel Foucault in *Discipline and Punish*. *Discipline and Punish* is best known for the concept of *panopticism*, which argues that modern subjectivity was created as a system of external and internal supervision and control, a micro economy of correction within the individual which would allow for maximum efficiency and productivity at the macro level. In order to demonstrate what was truly new about panopticism, Foucault devotes nearly as much space to establishing the rules and internal logic of the *preceding* regime of power (to which the lost world of B*** would belong), namely sovereign violence, in order to understand both how it functioned and why it eventually failed.

The theoretical enemy for Foucault is an all-too-convenient narrative of progress, which proposes that society collectively moved away from the "barbarity" of sovereign violence towards "gentler" forms of punishment in the name of rationality and an increased sense of "humanity." The problem with this historical narrative is twofold: first, it obscures the violence and barbarity latent in modern systems of coercion and punishment. But second, it neglects the inefficiencies (and thereby, unintentional freedoms) which had existed under the traditional system of sovereign violence. As a specific case study, the horrific execution and torture of the would-be regicide Robert-François Damiens stands metonymically at the beginning of the book, representing both the ideals and failings of the old order. As to the ideals to which this system aspired, one first reads with horror the tortures of hell which were to be visited on the body of Damiens. Quickly, however, horror slides into dark comedy as the demonic vision is confronted with the mundane difficulties of the material world. The specially-fashioned tongs intended to rip the flesh from his body only succeed in a (no doubt uncomfortable) pinching, and the horses tasked with "drawing" the body into quarters eventually faint from the exertion.[14] In the end, Damiens *is* destroyed in a grisly fashion, but it is impossible to overlook the flaws of the proceedings; *both* are representative for legality and criminal justice as it existed in the pre-capitalist

---

14   Michel Foucault, *Discipline & Punish*, trans. Alan Sheridan (New York: Random House, 1995), 3.

world. First, punishment is visited on the body of the perpetrator, the person of Damien. As a regicide and therefore the worst kind of criminal imaginable, Damien's body must be absolutely annihilated. The atrocity of crime is an assault on the body of the sovereign, and must be met in kind.[15] Punishment is a form of duel, "the physical confrontation between the sovereign and the condemned man," and as such is an opportunity to display the incredible asymmetry of power between the sovereign and the common people in all of its horrific glory.[16] The reestablishment of this asymmetry is the purpose of sovereign violence, which functions as an economy of terror, and not one of example or legal precedent.[17]

But the sloppy realization of Damien's execution stands symbolically for another aspect of sovereign violence, namely its inefficiencies as a system of social control. Sovereign violence is a blinding light, a demonstration of the overwhelming force of the sovereign. Criminals, by contrast, "could remain in the shade; they received light only from that portion of power that was conceded to them, or from the reflection of it that for a moment they carried." The wild excesses of sovereign violence also betray weakness. The sovereign as embodied in the king and his representatives is not an all-knowing, all-seeing power. "[I]n the absence of continual supervision," sovereign violence can only maintain control indirectly through awe and terror.[18] This negative space which surrounds sovereign violence is described by Benedict Anderson in his discussion of dynastic realms in *Imagined Communities*. Dynastic realms are defined by a "high center" and "porous borders," governing bodies in which "sovereignties faded imperceptibly into one another."[19] This stands in stark contrast with modern states whose sovereignty "is fully, flatly, and evenly operative over each square centimeter of a legally demarcated territory." This second law is the law of the panopticon, the law of modernity, and not coincidentally, it is also the law of a society which has been completely penetrated by the rationalizing force of capitalism. Anderson notes that this gave dynastic realms the surprising ability to "sustain their rule of immensely heterogeneous, and often not even contiguous, populations for long periods of time."[20] Of course, the implication is that this "rule" was of an entirely different kind. The day-to-day reality of those

---

15   Foucault, *Discipline & Punish*, 56.
16   Foucault, *Discipline & Punish*, 73.
17   Foucault, *Discipline & Punish*, 49.
18   Foucault, *Discipline & Punish*, 187.
19   Benedict Anderson, *Imagined Communities: Reflections on the Origin and Spread of Nationalism* (London and New York: Verso, 2016), 19.
20   Anderson, *Imagined Communities*, 19.

living in the dark regions, those areas far from the "high centers" of sovereign violence (such as the population inhabiting the fictive town of B***) operated under the confines of only marginally restricted self-rule. This is the "neglect" referred to by the narrator of *The Jew's Beech* when describing the legal code. The blinding light of sovereign violence was always accompanied by the relative autonomy of local peasantry who lived in the darkness surrounding it, enjoying a freedom which proved unacceptable as modern society began to demand discipline and absolute obedience in its armies, factories, and schools. It was this neglect which enabled and, furthermore, necessitated the formation of a "second law," and it is this "second law" which is both the historical context and the moral baseline against which the legal infractions presented in *The Jew's Beech* are to be measured.

Law as Battleground

This "second law," established in the absence of sovereign interference, the law of custom, was a site of contestation. "Public opinion and usage," was experienced differently by two distinct groups within B***: the "landowners" [Gutsbesitzer] on the one hand and the "peasants" [Untergebene] on the other. The landowners acted as *de facto* magistrates, who "punished or rewarded in accordance with motives which were honest for the most part." The peasants in turn "acted as seemed feasible and compatible with a somewhat elastic interpretation of what could be reconciled with conscience."[21] In other words, both peasants and landowners acted in accordance with their own material interests, testing the limits of what social convention would allow. All inhabitants of B*** operated within a shared gray zone of behavior deemed socially acceptable by "public opinion," "and it only occurred sometimes to the loser in a law-suit to consult the ancient and dusty records."[22] What this meant in practice is that certain forms of illegality were common and, to a large extent, socially acceptable. As such, criminality, understood in the modern sense as a violation of the letter of the law, did *not* represent a state of lawlessness in B*** and did not necessarily constitute a breach of social norms. Instead, criminality in this sense existed as one form of possible social interaction among many, and was therefore regulated

---

21 Droste-Hülshoff, *The Jew's Beech*, 12; Droste-Hülshoff, *Die Judenbuche*, 12: "der Untergebene tat, was ihm ausführbar und mit einem etwas weiten Gewissen verträglich schien."
22 Droste-Hülshoff, *The Jew's Beech*, 12; Droste-Hülshoff, *Die Judenbuche*, 12: "und nur dem Verlierenden fiel es zuweilen ein, in alten staubigten Urkunden nachzuschlagen."

by the same publicly-negotiated standards. The narrator refers humorously and euphemistically to the town's peasants as being "restless and enterprising," as well as "stiff-necked, wily and spirited." Simply put, these were people who committed crimes constantly, and "violation of the forest and game laws was the order of the day." As crime belonged within the realm of public discourse, only ceremonial effort would be made to conceal its occurrence. On the one hand, forest raids occurred primarily at night, but on the other, their sheer scale foreclosed any possibility of their remaining secret. These raids are described as involving a convoy of forty carts, along with every single able-bodied man in the village. The procession was led by a "seventy-year-old headman," who did so with "as much conscious pride as he displayed taking his seat in the court-room,"[23] and when these criminals returned the next morning their faces "glowed like bronze"[24] in the morning light. In both roles, as leader of a band of thieves and as member of the local court, the village elder serves a public function, representing the interests of his fellow peasant citizens.

The question then becomes: how does a society lacking strong authoritative oversight and clear legal precedent function? If crime, even as understood by the more lax, customary measures of the "second law," is rampant, how are cases argued, disputes settled? The answer is violence. But it was a particular, regulated form of violence, one which was itself subject to social and moral restrictions. The reader learns that in the town of B*** and its surrounding forests, brawls and skirmishes took place often. The heroic cast of the robber band setting off into the dark forest is no accident; they are an army marching off to do battle with a rival force, that of the foresters, a proxy army hired by the owners of the forest. "[T]he timber was carefully patrolled, but less by lawful means than by continually renewed attempts to overcome violence and cunning with the same weapons,"[25] with the loser in such clashes forced to "console himself as best he could for a broken head."[26] The previously-described peasant army was marred by the occasional "bandaged head" upon their return, but they could take solace in the

---

23 Droste-Hülshoff, *The Jew's Beech*, 14; Droste-Hülshoff, *Die Judenbuche*, 13: "mit gleich stolzem Bewußtsein anführte, wie er seinen Sitz in der Gerichtsstube einnahm."

24 Droste-Hülshoff, *The Jew's Beech*, 15.

25 Droste-Hülshoff, *The Jew's Beech*, 14; Droste-Hülshoff, *Die Judenbuche*, 12: "ward allerdings scharf über die Forsten gewacht, aber weniger auf gesetzlichem Wege als in stets erneuten Versuchen, Gewalt und List mit gleichen Waffen zu überbieten."

26 Droste-Hülshoff, *The Jew's Beech*, 13; Droste-Hülshoff, *Die Judenbuche*, 12: "sich jeder selbst seines zerschlagenen Kopfes zu trösten."

fact that the foresters had fared much worse, as they were "carried out of the woods battered, bruised, blinded by snuff and unable to perform their duties for some time."[27] The humorous tone of this passage indicates two important aspects of these confrontations: first, the clear bias towards the peasants shows the alignment of public opinion and, second, none of these historical conflicts, which serve as the prelude to the novella, are particularly serious. While the foresters would undoubtedly prefer *not* to have been blinded with snuff and beaten, no examples of permanent harm are given. One is reminded of the accounts of peasant revolts provided by E.P. Thompson in which peasants would seize a mill or bakery of a proprietor judged to be greedy, sell the goods for what they deemed to be a fair market price, and then give the resulting proceeds back to the owner. These actions would only escalate to physical violence, such as beating the owner or burning down the building, in cases of repeat offenses against the perceived public good.[28] What both the historical examples provided by Thompson, as well as those fictitious events modeled by Droste-Hülshoff in her novel demonstrate are crimes by way of political action. They show a restrained attempt by the lower orders of society to correct a perceived injustice, whether that injustice is the generation of profit from the sales of bread or grain, or an inequitable access to wood.

In this introduction to the region, the reader is told that the society of B*** was one in which "legal form mattered less, the spirit was adhered to more strictly, infringements occurred more often, but complete unscrupulousness was rarer."[29] *The Jew's Beech* is a story which charts the inversion of this reality, eventually ending in a world in which greater law and order have been purchased at the cost of increased immorality. This is presented as a general maxim of morality and not coincidence, for "a person who acts according to his convictions, however imperfect they may be, can never perish entirely, whereas nothing destroys the soul more surely than an appeal to external legal forms in contradiction to one's inner sense of justice."[30] The autonomy afforded

---

27 Droste-Hülshoff, *The Jew's Beech*, 15; Droste-Hülshoff, *Die Judenbuche*, 13; "aus dem Walde getragen wurden, zerschlagen, mit Schnupftabak geblendet und für einige Zeit unfähig, ihrem Berufe nachzukommen."

28 E.P. Thompson, "The Moral Economy of the English Crowd in the Eighteenth Century," *Past & Present* 50 (1971): 113.

29 Droste-Hülshoff, *The Jew's Beech*, 13; Droste-Hülshoff, *Die Judenbuche*, 12: "daß die Form schwächer, der Kern fester, Vergehen häufiger, Gewissenlosigkeit seltener waren."

30 Droste-Hülshoff, *The Jew's Beech*, 13; Droste-Hülshoff, *Die Judenbuche*, 12: "Denn wer nach seiner Überzeugung handelt, und sei sie noch so mangelhaft, kann nie ganz zugrunde gehen, wogegen nichts seelentötender wirkt, als gegen das innere Rechtsgefühl das äußere Recht in Anspruch nehmen."

by the darkness surrounding sovereign violence has dissolved, and in its place has emerged a new, brutal reality.

The Universal(izing) Rights of the Poor

Within this introduction to the legal practices of B***, three truths are presented simultaneously. First, in the absence of formal courts, disputes were settled through ritualized battles between the peasants and the proxies of the landowners, the foresters. Second, that in these skirmishes "the advantage usually lay with the peasants,"[31] a fact which is borne out by all of the examples provided. And finally, that this "advantage" of the peasants over the landlords corresponded with a more just world, one in which "complete unscrupulousness was rarer." The narrator's conviction in the intrinsic justice of this state of affairs closely parallels the conclusions of another work from 1842, namely Karl Marx's series of articles published under the title "Proceedings of the Sixth Rhine Province Assembly: Debates on the Law on Thefts of Wood." As the title suggests, in these articles, Marx is commenting on the regional assembly's deliberations concerning a restructuring of the laws concerning wood theft. At the heart of these debates is the question of what constitutes "theft," as well as the nature of property itself. One of Marx's primary critiques is that the assembly, operating exclusively in their own self interest (that of the landowning classes), have falsely labeled theft what can at best be described as "pilfering" and, through this semantic sleight of hand, have converted "a citizen into a thief."[32] The problem is an (intentional) lack of conceptual precision. The new laws expand the term "theft" to include the customary practice of collecting dead branches by reducing theft to merely "[t]he appropriation of wood from someone else."[33]

In order to highlight the inadequacy of this form of argumentation, Marx gives two counterexamples which he believes constitute *real* theft: the stealing of already felled lumber and the cutting down of green trees. The problem in the first instance is that one is stealing not only the material of the wood but also the labor invested by the owner into removing it from its naturally occurring state, that is, to use the language of later Marx, the surplus value which transforms it from a mere wood into a commodity. The second example does not correspond as neatly

---

31 Droste-Hülshoff, *The Jew's Beech*, 14.
32 Karl Marx, "Proceedings of the Sixth Rhein Province Assembly," *Collected Works of Karl Marx, Frederick Engels*, vol. 1, trans. Richard Dixon (London: Lawrence and Wishart, 1975), 225.
33 Marx, "Proceedings of the Sixth Rhein," 226.

with later Marxist theory. In the "Debates," Marx writes, "In order to appropriate growing timber, it has to be separated from its organic association. Since this is an obvious outrage against the tree, it is therefore an obvious outrage against the owner of the tree."[34] There is a slippage here which is worth noting. This argument relies first on an idea of the indivisibility of the natural organism of the tree, a oneness which blurs into a second "organic" unity, that between the tree and its proprietor. This assertion seems at odds not only with later Marx but also in relation to other statements contained within these articles. For example, Marx asserts that one of the dangers not recognized by the assembly and the landowning class is that, by falsely conflating pilfering with theft, they risk revealing the illegal nature character of property itself: "If every violation of property without distinction, without a more exact definition, is termed theft, will not all private property be theft? By my private ownership do I not exclude every other person from this ownership? Do I not thereby violate his right of ownership?"[35] At stake here is, what is the basis of the first property claim? What legitimizes absolute, exclusionary ownership? In other words, what justification can possibly naturalize the relationship between property owner and property?

The contradiction between these statements is only apparent. In asserting the organic oneness of property/proprietor, Marx, like the narrator of *The Jew's Beech*, is attempting to reconstruct a vanishing legal order, something Marx refers to interchangeably as the "supreme penal code of the sixteenth century," the "leges barbarorum" or "Germanic law."[36] The reason for Marx's interest in the old model of ownership is due to the fact that this organic understanding of property brought with it unintended consequences and privileges for the non-owner. If what the proprietor owns is the rights to the tree in the sense of its natural unity, the vitality of its green wood, what is implicitly excluded from ownership is everything which ceases to be part of this living entity. As soon as a branch dies and falls to the ground, it can no longer be said to belong to either the tree or its owner. As a result, "[t]he gatherer of fallen wood only carries out a sentence already pronounced by the very nature of the property."[37] This is what Marx refers to as the "indeterminate" nature of medieval property rights: "every medieval form of right, and therefore of property also, was in every respect hybrid, dualistic, split into two;" the two parts were described as "a private right of the owner and a private right of the non-owner."[38]

34 Marx, "Proceedings of the Sixth Rhein," 226.
35 Marx, "Proceedings of the Sixth Rhein," 228.
36 Marx, "Proceedings of the Sixth Rhein," 226.
37 Marx, "Proceedings of the Sixth Rhein," 227.
38 Marx, "Proceedings of the Sixth Rhein," 233.

Just as the wealth of the proprietor finds its "natural" corollary in the organic unity of the tree, the poor sense their "kinship" with the "dry, snapped twigs and branches separated from organic life," matter which as a category constitute the *"alms of nature."*[39] Marx contends that it was the "fluid essence" of medieval property, that is, the "mixture of private and public right," which was stripped away in the modernizing and rationalizing of legal procedures: "For the purpose of legislation, such ambiguous forms could be grasped only by understanding, and understanding is not only one-sided, but has the essential function of making the world one-sided."[40] As would later be explored by Theodor Adorno, Walter Benjamin, and others, Marx is arguing here that the essentializing nature of understanding and conceptualization is not incidental to the process, but is rather its constitutive action. The significance of this within a legal context is that any attempt at a universal legal code will *also* necessarily lead to law produced from a single perspective, instantly destroying the hybridity and fluidity inherent in the "second law."

Marx is not a reactionary advocating a return to the medieval order, and the description of understanding as the process of "confining each of the contents of the world in a stable definiteness" is not a condemnation. On the contrary, it is this essentializing process which "brings out the manifold diversity of the world, for the world would not be many-sided without the many one-sidednesses." The problem is rather *which* perspective is universalized to the legal perspective per se. Just as the narrator of *The Jew's Beech* saw greater justice in a situation in which the interests of the poor tended to dominate when legality became fraught, Marx argued that the customary rights of the poor have an inherent proximity to universal justice. Marx takes this principle a step further, arguing that it is *only* the customary rights of the poor that can be universalized into law, and indeed in this case "custom is the *anticipation* of a legal right."[41] The reasoning supporting this claim is murky, but the basic outline can be described as follows: the form of the law is its "universality and necessity," and it is against this baseline that the "customary rights" of both the aristocracy and poor are compared. The so-called "customary rights" of the aristocracy are found to be no such thing, but rather "customary wrongs," "formations of lawlessness." This is because the "customary rights" of the aristocracy are by nature exclusionary, and as such, privileges rather than necessities. They are fundamentally *not* universalizable because they operate on the basis of

---

39 Marx, "Proceedings of the Sixth Rhein," 234.
40 Marx, "Proceedings of the Sixth Rhein," 233.
41 Marx, "Proceedings of the Sixth Rhein," 231.

exclusion, granting access to some and not to others, and it is a logical impossibility to universally grant exclusionary status. They are privileges and not rights because rather than being necessary to those who possess them, they are only *"menus plaisirs,"* which garnish a legal system already heavily weighted in their favor.

By contrast, the "customary rights" of the poor, such as the right to glean, the right to scavenge firewood, the right to gather berries, traditional rights which have "been permitted by the owners *since time immemorial,"* are all examples of the right to survival. "Up to now the *existence of the poor class itself* has been *a mere custom* of civil society, a custom which has not found an appropriate place in the conscious organization of the state."[42] In essence, Marx performs here a realignment of Kant's categorical imperative. Marx agrees with the Kantian assertion that one should act such that one's actions could become universal law. The issue is that Kant uses this dictum to justify the existing bourgeois order, for example, by claiming that theft is everywhere and at all times morally wrong, because one would not wish to live in a world in which everyone stole. Marx, by contrast, would argue that it is impossible to universalize actions which deny the right of existence to other human beings. To label gleaning or the collection of firewood "theft" is to condemn those who participate in these actions to death. Marx is not advocating a state of lawlessness, but rather believes that "[t]he wise legislator" will work to prevent crime, not through the slavish application of an existing legal code, but through raising up the poor class such that it has "the *real possibility* of enjoying its rights."[43] By concretizing property rights from the perspective of the landowning classes, the conditions of existence of the poor, which had hitherto only been permissible as a result of customary rights, are destroyed. Marx's attentiveness to the destruction of customary rights in the debates on wood theft are a tentative first sketch of what he would later refer to as "ursprüngliche Akkumulation," normally translated as "primitive accumulation" but better understood as the original/originary moment of accumulation. This is the moment in which the double freedom of the proletariat is established: "Free workers, in the double sense that they neither form part of the means of production themselves, as would be the case with slaves, serfs, etc., nor do they own the means of production, as would be the case of the self-employed. The free workers are therefore free from, unencumbered by, any means of production of their own."[44] The utopian moment which

---

42 Marx, "Proceedings of the Sixth Rhein," 234.
43 Marx, "Proceedings of the Sixth Rhein," 235.
44 Karl Marx, *Capital: A Critique of Political Economy,* vol. 1, trans. Ben Fowkes (London: Penguin, 1990), 874.

is lost is the possibility of solidifying the law, not from the perspective of the propertied, but the propertyless, potentially creating a morally rational legal framework based on the universal needs of the disenfranchised.

The Changing Face of Crime in B***

The Jew's Beech is a book of transition, a crime novel whose central mystery is source of the escalation in scale and brutality of crime in B***. It is a story which begins with comical, contained scuffles between the townsfolk and the foresters, and culminates in multiple grisly murders. Somehow, B*** has moved from frequent minor "infringements" to instances of complete "unscrupulousness." In order to determine why and how the crimes of B*** are changing, it is necessary to provide a brief overview of those crimes. In terms of theft, there are the aforementioned forest raids by the townsfolk. The audience never learns exactly what is stolen on such nights, if the theft is limited merely to fallen brush and therefore represented a contestation along the lines of customary rights, or if they also included "green wood." Given the scale of these operations and number of carts, it seems likely that the townspeople were indeed also cutting down healthy trees. Nevertheless, these raids are placed in sharp contrast with a new kind of wood theft as perpetrated by the so-called "Blue-Smocks," [*Blaukittel*], a clandestine group known only by their (purported) dress. Where the raids of the townspeople were carried out as an open secret, no character ever admits to any knowledge of the Blue-Smocks' actions or members. Despite a lack of specifics regarding the nature of the town raids, there is also a clear sense that the methods of the Blue-Smocks are new. The Blue-Smocks participate in a completely unsustainable form of clear cutting, showing no interest in either the niceties of customary rights nor in the survival of the forest itself. The county clerk laments a recent raid: "The scoundrels ruin everything ... if only they'd spare the young wood, but to cut oak saplings no thicker than my arm, not big enough for oars even! It's as though they liked doing harm to others as much as making a profit!"[45] Another scene of destruction created by the Blue-Smocks is rendered in gory detail "... only recently the axe had

---

45 Droste-Hülshoff, *The Jew's Beech*, 55; Droste-Hülshoff, *Die Judenbuche*, 34: "Die Schandbuben ... ruinieren alles; wenn sie noch Rücksicht nähmen auf das junge Holz, aber Eichenstämmchen wie mein Arm dick, wo nicht einmal eine Ruderstange drin steckt! Es ist, als ob ihnen andrer Leute Schaden ebenso lieb wäre wie ihr Profit!"

raged here pitilessly. Everywhere tree stumps projected, many several feet above the ground, just as they could be cut most conveniently by somebody in a hurry ... a beech in full leaf lay right across the path, its branches stretching high above, its foliage, still fresh, trembling in the night wind."[46] The reader is confronted with the still-warm corpse of a beech tree, prefiguring the eventual murder of the forester Brandis, who likewise is felled by an ax of the Blue-Smocks. The narrator echoes the clerk's horror at the wasteful excesses of the Blue-Smocks, with little details such as the height of the tree stumps indicating a new form of wanton destruction. These are no longer townsfolk gathering resources necessary for survival, from woods upon which their very existence depends. Instead, the Blue-Smocks are a "swarm of pine looper caterpillars" which lay "waste to the countryside,"[47] with no regard for any living thing.

This change in the practice of wood theft was experienced as a "rude jolt" to the previously "slumbering laws."[48] The actions of the Blue-Smocks are described repeatedly as "intolerable," again in implicit contrast to the large-scale theft which had preceded them. In response, the landowners greatly increase both the foresters and the number of patrols sweeping the forests, measures which prove completely ineffective. Gone are the days in which the townspeople would meet the landowners' proxies in open combat, contesting who had what rights over the surrounding forests. The Blue-Smocks are ghosts leaving destruction in their wake, constantly evading any direct detection (beyond sound, as noted by Vance Byrd in "Der holzgerechte Jäger").[49] The foresters and the Blue-Smocks are "always changing places like the sun and the moon, in possession of the terrain and never meeting."[50] No one in the novella has any doubt that the Blue-Smocks remain elusive through employing spies, and it is speculated that these spies are not limited to the townspeople, but

---

46 Droste-Hülshoff, *The Jew's Beech*, 34; Droste-Hülshoff, *Die Judenbuche*, 23: "vor kurzem die Axt unbarmherzig gewütet hatte. Überall ragten Baumstümpfe hervor, manche mehrere Fuß über der Erde, wie sie gerade in der Eile am bequemsten zu durchschneiden gewesen waren; die verpönte Arbeit mußte unversehens unterbrochen worden sein, denn eine Buche lag quer über dem Pfad, in vollem Laube, ihre Zweige hoch über sich streckend und im Nachtwinde mit den noch frischen Blättern zitternd."
47 Droste-Hülshoff, *The Jew's Beech*, 45.
48 Droste-Hülshoff, *The Jew's Beech*, 44.
49 Vance Byrd, "Der holzgerechte Jäger: Forester Fictions and Annette von Droste-Hülshoff's *Die Judenbuche*," *The Germanic Review* 89, no. 4 (2014): 362.
50 Droste-Hülshoff, *The Jew's Beech*, 47; Droste-Hülshoff, *Die Judenbuche*, 30: "wie Sonne und Mond, immer abwechselnd im Besitz des Terrains und nie zusammentreffend."

that the foresters themselves have been compromised. But despite general suspicion, and even direct accusations towards both Friedrich and his uncle Simon, no one is ever directly revealed to be working in service of the Blue-Smocks. Just how much the situation has changed from the old town raids is revealed when Friedrich, after Brandis insults him and his mother, intentionally misleads the head forester away from his colleagues and towards the Blue-Smocks. The outcome of this single, direct interaction between the foresters and Blue-Smocks plays out very differently from those which had come before. Instead of throwing snuff in his eyes, Brandis is struck down with a single blow from an ax and discarded with the rest of the forest waste.

A similar escalation and transformation of violent practices can be observed in the violence directed towards the town's Jewish usurer, Aaron. In a passage which was rightly granted much scrutiny by Byrd,[51] a young Friedrich is asked by his mother Margret, "Fritz … are you going to be good now and make me happy, or are you going to be wicked and tell lies or drink and steal?"[52] Friedrich does not provide a direct answer, but rather responds "Hülsmeyer steals, Mother." When his mother denies the accusation, Friedrich provides two concrete examples in which Hülsmeyer has stolen: first from Aaron, beating him and stealing sixpence, and again by stealing wood from the forest, according to Brandis. Upon learning the circumstances of the thefts, Margret dismisses both instances on the same grounds: "Hülsmeyer is a respectable man, one of us,"[53] while Aaron is a Jew and Brandis is a forester, thereby excluding both from the "us" of the townsfolk. It seems hardly coincidental that the two figures against whom the traditional values of the town are arrayed are the same two figures who later die as a result of Friedrich's actions, through misdirection in the case of Brandis and through the direct murder of Aaron. So while this moment is often heralded as an example of a pervasive antisemitism in *The Jew's Beech*, such a reading neglects both the narrative consequences of this interaction, and more importantly, the clear hypocrisy of Margret's plea.[54] Margret begging Friedrich not to "tell lies or drink and steal" is

---

51 Byrd, "Der holzgerechte Jäger," 345.
52 Droste-Hülshoff, *The Jew's Beech,* 24; Droste-Hülshoff, *Die Judenbuche,* 18: "Fritzchen … willst du jetzt auch fromm sein, daß ich Freude an dir habe, oder willst du unartig sein und lügen, oder saufen und stehlen?"
53 Droste-Hülshoff, *The Jew's Beech,* 24.
54 A particularly drastic reading is provided by Martha Helfer in "Reading Blood: Annette von Droste-Hülshoff's *The Jews' Beech Tree,*" *The Word Unheard: Legacies of Anti-Semitism in German Literature and Culture* (Evanston: Northwestern University Press, 2011). In the chapter "Reading Blood: Annette von

thinly veiled language asking him not to be like his father Hermann, who was well known for drinking and beating both of his wives. Violence against women is both prevalent and invisible in the town of B***, belonging to what Slavoj Žižek would refer to as "objective violence." Unlike "subjective violence," which is experienced by society as a "perturbation of the 'normal,' peaceful state of things," objective violence is "the often catastrophic consequences of the smooth functioning of our economic and political systems," in other words, the latent violence of the status quo.[55]

Violence against both women and Jews is presented within *The Jew's Beech* as something which is so normal that it hardly warrants mentioning. And yet mentioned it is. In a ghastly image, we see Hermann's first wife flee his house covered in blood one week after their marriage, only to die shortly thereafter. In the wake of this violence, Margret claims that only women who are "stupid or worthless" are beaten by their husbands, and defiantly marries the widower Hermann, to her detriment. The reader must once again watch as a bloodied woman leaves Hermann's house, this time in order to dig frantically for herbs in the garden, the implication being that Margret is looking for an herbal remedy to pregnancy, and is likely a victim of rape. Likewise, later in the novella the gaiety of a town wedding is punctuated by the disconsolate tears of the bride to be, who is to be married off to "an ill-humored old man whom she was supposed to love into the bargain,"[56] again implying a life of servitude and nonconsensual sex. Even the semi-heroic, semi-comical adventures of the town wood raids are blemished only by the fear of the women left behind, who "start up in [their] sleep" at the sound of every "shot and feeble cry," while "no one else took any notice."[57] And while Margret *tells* us that violence against Aaron is fine because he is a Jew and therefore not part of the community, the altercation between Hülsmeyer and Aaron has clearly left a strong impression on Friedrich, who has a hard time reconciling it with any

---

Droste-Hülshoff's *The Jews' Beech Tree*," she argues that the Mergel family must be read as the threat of the hidden, secret Jew, and the corruptive influence eating at the heart of the town of B***, and that the "anti-Semitism permeating the novella is so subtle and complex that it has eluded critical attention for over one hundred and fifty years" (111). While the chapter provides many interesting details and has a wonderful attention to the language of the novella, it has a decidedly flattening effect on the interpretive possibilities of *The Jew's Beech*, reducing the story to little more than a dog-whistle intended for fellow anti-semites.

55 Slavoj Žižek, *Violence: Six Sideways Reflections* (New York: St Martin's, 2008), 2.
56 Droste-Hülshoff, *The Jew's Beech*, 74.
57 Droste-Hülshoff, *The Jew's Beech*, 15.

form of morality. Similarly, when Aaron is heckled and tormented by the wedding party while attempting to collect his debts from a now adult Friedrich, the acts are portrayed with the same flat affect used to describe the plight of the bride. The violence against both women and Jews in B*** is frequent, unsettling, and carefully documented by the narrator. However, the primary function of this objective violence and persecution is to act as a baseline in order to highlight instances of a new, "subjective violence," the transition from mass wood pilfering of the villagers, the beatings of foresters and casual antisemitic violence, to the devastating clear-cutting of the Blue-Smocks and the murder of Aaron and Brandis. The result is a "A Picture of Life among the Hills of Westphalia," one which both mourns the loss of greater equality and self-determination of the inhabitants of B***, while falling short of creating a regressive utopia, a longing for a return to simpler times.

The Precarization of the Villagers of B***

The flash-forward at the end of the novella provides a stark image of B*** at the dawn of modernity. Friedrich's uncle Simon "had died long ago, but not before he had become completely impoverished through lawsuits and debtors whom he could not sue ... He had finally eaten the bread of a beggar and died on a pile of straw in a shed which was not his own."[58] Margret and her possessions had gone "to rack and ruin," and the "the village people had soon tired of helping, for it is natural to Man to abandon those who are actually the most helpless,"[59] causing Friedrich to lament: "All gone, all dead!" The Brede Wood, the scene of Friedrich's father's death, Brandis and Aaron's murders, his own eventual murder or suicide, has been annihilated. Friedrich, when asked why he took the long way around the former woods, responds "people told me the wood had been felled, and that now there are so many cross-paths, so I was afraid I wouldn't get out again."[60] While this is clearly an obfuscation of his real reasons for avoiding the wood (fear of the titular Jew's Beech), the destruction of the Brede Woods is confirmed when the son of Brandis marches through it, his cap "well

---

58 Droste-Hülshoff, *The Jew's Beech*, 93; Droste-Hülshoff, *Die Judenbuche*, 55: "war lange tot, aber zuvor noch ganz verarmt, durch Prozesse und böse Schuldner, die er nicht gerichtlich belangen durfte ... Er hatte zuletzt Bettelbrod gegessen und war in einem fremden Schuppen auf dem Stroh gestorben."

59 Droste-Hülshoff, *The Jew's Beech*, 94; Droste-Hülshoff, *Die Judenbuche*, 55: "Die Leute im Dorf waren es bald müde geworden, ihr beizustehen ... wie es denn die Art der Menschen ist, gerade die Hilflosesten zu verlassen."

60 Droste-Hülshoff, *The Jew's Beech*, 100.

heated by the sun," eventually taking shade under the Jew's Beech for the simple fact that "all around there was no tree."[61] The reader is told that, after the murder of Brandis, the Blue-Smocks disappeared forever, never raiding the woods again.[62] Nevertheless, the protective cocoon which had sheltered this community from the march of time has evaporated, exposing B*** to the full force of modernity. What has happened?

One possible explanation is to return to the case studies provided by Marx in part eight of *Capital Volume I*, "So-Called Primitive Accumulation." In example after example, Marx details how the aforementioned hybridity, indeterminacy of property under feudal laws, a system which relied on overlapping rights and customs shared by the property "owner" as well as the "non-owners," was collapsed into simple, exclusionary property rights. Ownership came to be defined through exclusion: you own that to which no one else has access. The age-old question as to what rights the poor have to firewood, fallen grain, berries, and fairly priced bread is answered succinctly in the negative: they have no rights. Returning to the language of the "Debates on the Law on Thefts of Wood," the "mere customs" which had been the basis of the very "existence of the poor class itself" have been destroyed. Retrospectively, it would be argued that such destruction was part of a larger rational if not divine plan, freeing the labor necessary to fuel

---

61 Droste-Hülshoff, *The Jew's Beech*, 104.
62 The origin and nature of the Blue-Smocks is also worthy of consideration at this juncture, particularly in connection with Friedrich's twenty-eight-year absence. If one believes the narration that the Blue-Smocks are indeed a primarily external force, almost entirely distinct from the local wood thieves, then the only evidence as to their origin is their connection with the river, which is both their means of escape and conveyance of the stolen goods. Although the river is unnamed, it is likely either the Weser or a fictitious river similar to it, emptying into the North Sea. As discussed by Byrd, the largest consumers of wood at this time would be the British and Dutch mercantile empires ("Der holzgerechte Jäger," 350), and of course geographically, the Dutch would be in the best position to mount raids this deep into German territory. It is therefore not without significance that Friedrich's years of slavery occur first at the hands of the Ottoman Empire, the generic placeholder for Eastern barbarity … and then in the custody of a Dutch trade ship. What is remarkable about this transition is how seamless it is for the dejected Friedrich. "He did not have a much better time of it on the [Dutch] ship" (98) [Auf dem Schiffe war es ihm nicht viel besser gegangen (57)] on which "the rope's end ruled as harshly as the Turkish whip" (99) [das Schiffstau regierte ebenso streng wie die türkische Peitsche (57)]. What is being created here is what Patrick Eiden-Offe refers to as an instance of "white slavery," in which German authors bring labor under early capitalism into direct comparison with literal slavery in the Americas or the Middle East in order to highlight how dire the plight of the new working class was (*Die Poesie der Klasse*, 208).

the Industrial Revolution which was on the horizon and which would lead to greater prosperity for all. But such revisionist histories neglect the reality that thousands simply died once their right to existence was removed. It is telling that upon his return, Friedrich interacts only with four named figures: the baron, his wife, the son of Brandis the forester, and the Hülsmeyer family. While little is known about the Hülsmeyers, all three of the other figures belong to the beneficiaries of the new propertied order. The destruction of the old way of life was foretold in the first page of the novella, which described B*** as "a place once common in Germany," but now presumably vanished, and with it "all the faults and virtues, all the eccentricity and narrow-mindedness that can only flourish under such conditions."[63] This destruction was not overseen by the secretive Blue-Smocks or the Jewish usurers, but rather by the goodly lord and his family, who remain beneficent and charitable as they remove the material foundation upon which the town of B*** is based. And lest the modern reader rest too easy, imagining that the time of primitive accumulation is over, believing that we have fully transitioned into a society of employers and employees with codified rights for each party, it is important to remember that Marx saw primitive accumulation as a process without end. "The capitalist-relation presupposes a complete separation between workers and the ownership of the conditions for the realization of their labor. As soon as capitalist production stands on its own feet, it not only maintains this separation, but reproduces it on a continually extending scale."[64]

The question must therefore be, which of the poor's current rights are, in fact, "mere custom," the result of an unspoken, uncodified common sense? The collecting of fallen wood once seemed an absolute right of the poor, the "alms of nature" which they had been guaranteed since time immemorial. Today, after an intervening two centuries of violence, there is a new common sense, one which dictates the absolute sanctity of private property, private property understood as the absolute exclusion of all other claims to a plot of land. *Of course* it is illegal to first trespass onto land which is not one's own, and then, heaven forbid to take something from that land which belongs absolutely to the landholder! In most areas in the United States the owner would be within their rights to defend the former "alms of nature" with lethal force. Where the new lines of separation between workers and the "realization of their labor" will be drawn is impossible to say, but certain recent developments in the United States, such as hedge funds purchasing vast numbers of single-family homes, the Supreme Court mandating that those poor

---

63 Droste-Hülshoff, *The Jew's Beech*, 12.
64 Marx, *Capital I*, 874.

who are unable to leave their state of residence carry their children to term, or the evermore contentious water rights in the Southwest which favor pistachio farmers over municipal centers, may give some indication. It is unclear if we will ever find ourselves in the (admittedly somewhat lazily-imagined) consumerist-dystopia portrayed by Mel Brook's in his 1987 film *Spaceballs*, in which the air necessary to breathe is sold to us by *Perri-Air*. But the fact that we still breathe for free should be viewed strictly as a technical and not moral limitation.

Works Cited

Anderson, Benedict. *Imagined Communities: Reflections on the Origin and Spread of Nationalism*. London and New York: Verso, 2016.

Benjamin, Walter. "On the Concept of History." In *Walter Benjamin: Selected Writings*, vol. 4, edited by Howard Eiland and Michael William Jennings, 389–401. Cambridge, MA: Harvard University Press, 2006.

Byrd, Vance. "Der holzgerechte Jäger: Forester Fictions and Annette von Droste-Hülshoff's *Die Judenbuche*." *The Germanic Review* 89, no. 4 (2014): 345–64.

Droste-Hülshoff, Annette von. *The Jew's Beech*. Translated by Lionel Thomas and Doris Thomas. Richmond: Alma Books, Ltd., 1958.

Droste-Hülshoff, Annette von. "Die Judenbuche." In *Sämtliche Werke*, vol. 2, edited by Bodo Plachta and Winfried Woesler, 11–62. Frankfurt: Deutscher Klassiker Verlag, 2003.

Eiden-Offe, Patrick. *Die Poesie der Klasse. Romantischer Antikapitalismus und die Erfindung des Proletariats*. Berlin: Matthes & Seitz, 2020.

Foucault, Michel. *Discipline & Punish*. Translated by Alan Sheridan. New York: Random House, 1995.

Helfer, Martha B. "Reading Blood: Annette von Droste-Hülshoff's *The Jews' Beech Tree*." In *The Word Unheard: Legacies of Anti-Semitism in German Literature and Culture*. Evanston, IL: Northwestern University Press, 2011.

Koselleck, Reinhart. "Richtlinien für das Lexikon politisch-sozialer Begriffe der Neuzeit." In *Archiv für Begriffsgeschichte*, vol. 11, edited by Erich Rothacker, 81–99. Bonn: Bouvier Verlag, 1967.

Marx, Karl. *Capital: A Critique of Political Economy*, vol. 1. Translated by Ben Fowkes. London, England: Penguin, 1990.

Marx, Karl. "Proceedings of the Sixth Rhein Province Assembly: Debates on the Law on Thefts of Wood." In *Collected Works of Karl Marx, Frederick Engels*, vol. 1, translated by Richard Dixon, 224–65. London: Lawrence and Wishart, 1975.

Thompson, E.P. "The Moral Economy of the English Crowd in the Eighteenth Century." *Past & Present* 50 (1971): 76–136. http://www.jstor.org/stable/650244.

Žižek, Slavoj. *Violence: Six Sideways Reflections*. New York: St Martin's, 2008.

Four We Poor People: The Personal
Experience of Precariousness in
Dantons Tod and *Woyzeck*

Michael Swellander

Georg Büchner's plays *Danton's Death* (*Dantons Tod*; 1835) and *Woyzeck* (1836) are groundbreaking for depicting poverty as an individual and isolating experience. The characters' differing existential dilemmas, intensified by poverty, show how poverty can act as a barrier to political solidarity, rather than as a political rallying point. Bringing these subjective and relational qualities of poverty to light is Büchner's political intervention in the literary representation of poverty. His plays show complicated, contradictory experiences of poverty, as opposed to the sympathetic depictions promoting political reform that became common in the *Vormärz*. To this point, I argue that Büchner's plays can be productively discussed in terms of "precariousness." Precariousness— the feeling of insecure contingency upon which one's life and livelihood nonetheless depends—is at once shared across classes and experienced as irreducibly personal. As Oliver Marchart writes, precariousness, rather than being a quantitatively determinable sociological status, might be best characterized as a series of questions one worriedly asks oneself about the future: will I make enough money to pay rent this month? Will my contract be renewed? Such questions, Marchart writes, "which touch the innermost form of our subjectivity, make it clear that processes of precarization cannot be illustrated through the quantitative methods of the social sciences alone."[1] The subjective quality of precariousness and its resistance to representation via quantitative sociological approaches make this experience personal and unique depending

---

1   Oliver Marchart, *Die Prekarisierungsgesellschaft: Prekäre Proteste: Politik und Ökonomie im Zeichen der Prekarisierung* (Bielefeld: transcript Verlag, 2013), 10–11. All English translations of German texts are my own, except when otherwise noted.

on one's circumstances, which individually affects one's relationship to time, agency, and one's own body. Judith Butler has argued that social precariousness or "vulnerability" is *not* a subjective state, but an objective, universal feature of "our interdependent lives," an assertion fundamental to their critique of individuality and central to the politics of non-violence they have articulated.[2] While this statement is true from an ethical viewpoint, this is not the perspective provided by Büchner's plays, which instead focus on immediate, personal experiences of precariousness. The conflicts that arise between his characters due to their contradictory subjective experiences of precariousness are fundamental to his understanding of the experience of social vulnerability. Scholars have observed that the thematization of politics in Büchner's plays cannot be reduced to a political program, indeed the politics of Büchner's characters contradict one another; nevertheless, the "immanent contradictory nature" of the experience of poverty has not been as thoroughly explored.[3]

Büchner, I argue, was aware that the precarious feeling attached to material deprivation is difficult to translate into an essential condition for a new political subject. Neilson and Rossiter, similarly, have shown precariousness to be difficult to politicize because it is the norm under capitalism, rather than the exception; to end precarity, one might just have to end capitalism.[4] Consequently, I argue further that Büchner also saw the individual experience of wrestling with this feeling as a barrier for liberal political programs. And yet, Büchner's contradictions do not culminate in political nihilism. Büchner's choice to spotlight the social disintegration of the *citoyens* in *Dantons Tod* and the psychic and social destruction of Woyzeck is in and of itself political, implicitly criticizing the reformist politics of his time and gesturing toward a future, as-yet unarticulated political understanding, one which could incorporate the contradictions in his dramas. By foregrounding the poor figures of *Dantons Tod* and *Woyzeck*, while simultaneously refusing to simplify or idealize their plight, it may be possible to lay the foundation for a politics which goes beyond the idealism against which Büchner warned.

Burghard Dedner distinguishes Büchner's writing from most liberal, *Vormärz*-era "Pauperism literature," which saw new levels of mass poverty as part of a historical and economic "transition crisis," one which would eventually be solved by the same industrialization which was its cause.[5] Büchner, argues Dedner, belonged to a minority of intellectuals,

---

2   Judith Butler, *The Force of Non-Violence* (London and New York: Verso, 2020), 39.
3   Gerhard Knapp, *Georg Büchner* (Stuttgart: Metzler, 2000), 101.
4   Brett Neilson and Ned Rossiter, "Precarity as a Political Concept, or Fordism as Exception," *Theory, Culture & Society* 25, nos 7–8 (2008): 51–72, 52.
5   Burghard Dedner, *Georg Büchner: Woyzeck* (Stuttgart: Reclam, 2000), 189.

including Friedrich Engels, who saw mass poverty as an inescapable, structural side effect of industrialization. However, after publishing the revolutionary pamphlet *The Hessian Messenger* (*Der hessische Landbote*) in 1834, a pamphlet which demanded the violent uprising of Hessen's poor to overcome economic exploitation ("Peace to the peasants! War on the palaces!"[6]), Büchner proposes no solutions to poverty in his writings. From then on, aside from reiterating in his letters that it was the poor and uneducated, not the "liberal" and "absolutist" ideologues, who were the only revolutionary class in society, Büchner dedicates his writing to exploring the experience of poverty without attempting to articulate specific political programs through it. Unlike roughly contemporaneous literary discussions of poverty, such as Bettina von Arnim's *This Book Belongs to the King* (*Dies Buch gehört dem König, 1843*) or the outpouring of poetry and journalism demanding reform of the work conditions of Silesian weavers, Büchner takes no overt moral stance on poverty in his literary work. Arnim's descriptions of poverty, for example, are motivated by the specific need to reform the Berlin *Armendirektion*, which administered, to her mind, insufficient relief to the poor, who appeared to those better-off onlookers as potentially beyond aid: "you may say: 'it's not going to help,' I say: 'it will indeed' ...."[7] While many politically engaged authors of the 1830s and 1840s "expected a change of the social 'evils' coming from the side of the property owners, the rich, whose consumption should be 'softened' and 'shaken up' through detailed descriptions of misery," Büchner wanted to show the complex subjectivity of the poor in his literary writing, without moralizing or politicizing their plight outright.[8]

Büchner's approach to showing poverty differs in three major ways from that of the reformist *Vormärz* writers discussed above. First, Büchner favored direct intervention among the poor of Hesse, rather than appeals to local administration for reform. Second, he wanted to show poverty in a manner that eschewed sympathy, both between the characters on the stage as well as between the audience and those characters. Third, Büchner's literary writing depicts different levels of poverty, which prove to have very different influences on the characters

---

6   Georg Büchner, *Complete Plays, Lenz and Other Writings* (London: Penguin Books Kindle Edition, 1993), 167; Büchner, *Sämtliche Werke*, vols. 1 and 2, ed. Henri Poschmann and Marie Poschmann (Frankfurt: Deutscher Klassiker Verlag, 2006), vol. 2: 400: "Friede den Hütten! Krieg den Palästen!"

7   Bettina von Arnim, *Werke und Briefe*, vol. 3 (Frankfurt: Deutscher Klassiker Verlag, 1995), 330.

8   Lutz Kroneberg and Rolf Schloesser, eds. *Weber-Revolte 1844: Der schlesische Weberaufstand im Spiegel der zeitgenössischen Publizistik und Literatur* (Cologne: Informationspresse, C.W. Leske, 1979), 24.

experiencing them. *Der hessische Landbote*, Büchner's only explicitly political text, does not advocate social change via reform, which would require appeals to the morality of the rich, but rather addresses the poor directly, entirely circumventing the closed communication systems of official institutions.[9] Büchner's goal with his pamphlet was political agitation, not sympathy. His disinterest in sympathetic depictions continues into his first play, *Dantons Tod*, which depicts the Reign of Terror. Büchner writes in a letter to his family that *Dantons Tod* has no moral ambition. Rather than appealing to his public's sympathy, Büchner pursued a historiographical realism effectively outside morality: "The writer is no preacher of morality, he invents and creates characters, he makes past ages live again, and people can learn just as well from that as from the study of history and from their observation of what happens around them in real life."[10] The figures in his plays transgress the moral and political standards of both their and Büchner's times. Finally, Büchner did not treat poverty as a monolith, but acknowledged in his writings the different levels of poverty one could experience. To this point, Dedner notes two definitions of poverty [*Armuth*] in the 1817 Brockhaus *Conversations-Lexikon*: a poor person is one who "supports himself through honest work, but despite exerting his power and industry cannot earn as much as he requires for himself and his dependents"; but poor people are also those who, according to the second definition, "have shelter nowhere and sleep in caves, in the streets, in fields, in stalls and in forest cabins."[11] These two different manifestations and experiences of poverty—one of "treading water" and the other of destitution and improvised shelter—both feature in Büchner's plays and are not reducible to a singular experience or political significance of poverty.

Central to Büchner's realism was his effort to show the centrifugal effects of the experience of poverty. The individual experiences of economic precariousness—the sense of insecurity inseparable from their poverty—were more likely to dissolve solidarity than to provide a touchstone of common experience. In the following sections, I will show

---

9 A move not dissimilar to the concept of the "counter public," or *Gegenöffentlichkeit* as explored by Sigrid Weigel in *Flugschriftenliteratur 1848 in Berlin: Geschichte und Öffentlichkeit einer volkstümlichen Gattung* (Stuttgart: Metzler Verlag, 1979), 8–9.

10 Büchner, *Complete Plays*, 202; Büchner, *Sämtliche Werke*, vol. 2: 410: "Der Dichter ist kein Lehrer der Moral, er erfindet und schafft Gestalten, er macht vergangene Zeiten wieder aufleben, und Leute mögen daraus lernen, so gut, wie aus dem Studium der Geschichte und der Beobachtung dessen, was im menschlichen Leben um sie herum vorgeht."

11 Dedner, *Georg Büchner: Woyzeck*, 192.

how different aspects of precariousness present themselves in Büchner's plays, namely in the shifting personal and political allegiances of Büchner's characters, the tension between economic determinism and characters' sense of personal agency, their relationship to time, and the isolating quality of precariousness that Büchner develops in his plays.

One feature of precariousness that makes it productive for discussing Büchner is what we might call its liminality, or its effect of making individuals feel as if they existed in between social groups. As Robert Castel has written, precarity sets a subject trembling between "zones" of durable social integration and relative social isolation or disaffiliation.[12] Büchner's poorest characters exist in this precarious "in-between" place, an experience which makes them adaptable to various bad situations and, in the case of *Woyzeck*, motivates the title character to work in a frenzy as he seeks opportunities to make ends meet. Precariousness also makes Büchner's characters less likely to hold firm political or moral positions. We see this form of precariousness in scene I.2 of *Dantons Tod*, the longest of the play's so-called street scenes depicting everyday public life during the Reign of Terror. The scene begins with Simon and his wife in a physical and verbal fight over the latter's apparent encouragement of their daughter to work as a prostitute. Simon's wife justifies her daughter's prostitution through the threat of the family's economic descent. Simon's pants, as well as the schnapps he drinks, come from his daughter's earnings: "Would you have a single pair of trousers to put on if 'er young gentlemen didn't take theirs off? You old brandy barrel, do you want to die of thirst if her little trickle runs dry?"[13] Simon, who at the beginning of this scene threatened to stab his wife to death over the state of his daughter, can accept and encourage her prostitution by the end of the scene and continues to enjoy his pants and schnapps, asking his wife to lead him to the corner where their daughter solicits.[14]

In *Woyzeck*, precariousness encourages the title character's frenetic activity as he tries to keep his head above water financially. Woyzeck, as a soldier, belongs to a *border group* [*Grenzgruppe*], as Thomas Nipperdey calls members of this profession in the early nineteenth century,

---

12 Robert Castel, *From Manual Workers to Wage Laborers: Transformation of the Social Question*, trans. and ed. Richard Boyd (Piscataway, NJ: Transaction Publishers, 2003), xvi.

13 Büchner, *Complete Plays*, 9; *Sämtliche Werke*, vol. 1: 18: "Hättest du nur ein Paar Hosen hinaufzuziehen, wenn die jungen Herren die Hosen nicht bei ihr heruntließen? Du Branntweinfaß, willst du verdursten, wenn das Brünnlein zu laufen aufhört, he?"

14 Büchner, *Sämtliche Werke*, vol. 1: 21.

between the middle class and the underclasses.[15] Making Woyzeck feverishly busy with work was one of the biggest liberties Büchner took in adapting the historical Christian Woyzeck's biography, who was abjectly poor and no longer a soldier at the time he murdered Johanna Christiane Woost. The effect of this change is that the existence of Büchner's Woyzeck is entirely dedicated to the pursuit of money as a matter of life and death. As one of his employers, the captain, puts it: "you rush through the world like an open razor, you'll cut us to ribbons; you're running as if you had a regiment of Cossacks to shave, all in a quarter of an hour, and were due to be hanged after the very last hair."[16] Woyzeck's breathless activity and economic desperation make him distrustful of philosophical abstraction and promote in him a moral relativism, as he tells the captain in an earlier scene: "If you don't have no money. Morality don't get much of a look in when our sort gets made."[17] Büchner sets his dramas squarely between social classes and animates them through the precariousness of his characters, who worry constantly about sinking further into poverty. The poor in Büchner's plays are not merely motivated by their poverty, but by the worry that they could become poorer, making them adaptable and opportunistic in their politics and morality.

Economic Determinism and Individual Agency

While *Dantons Tod* and *Woyzeck* invoke, in different ways, a sense of economic determinism as tragic fate, both plays contain passages that work against such a reading. In *Dantons Tod*, economic determinism is lampooned as an excuse for poor characters' refusal to take responsibility for their actions. Scene I.2 of *Dantons Tod* develops a complex view of the agency of Paris' poor and their relationship to the revolution. As the fight between Simon and his wife proceeds, they address each other in a complicated mix of registers, employing neoclassical and biblical vocabulary as well as colloquial pejoratives. In a comic style reminiscent of Shakespeare and the French Romantics,[18] Simon

---

15 Thomas Nipperdey, *Deutsche Geschichte 1800–1866: Bürgerwelt und starker Staat* (Munich: C.H. Beck, 1984), 220.

16 Büchner, *Complete Plays*, 123; *Sämtliche Werke*, vol. 1: 160: "Er (Woyzeck) läuft ja wie ein offnes Rasiermesser durch die Welt, man schneidt sich an Ihm. Er läuft, als hätt Er ein Regiment Kosack zu rasiern und würde gehenkt über dem letzten Haar nach einer Viertelstunde."

17 Büchner, *Complete Plays*, 119; *Sämtliche Werke*, vol. 1: 155: "Wer kein Geld hat. Da setz einmal seinsgleichen auf die Moral in die Welt."

18 Knapp, *Georg Büchner*, 107.

freely imitates the neoclassical rhetoric of the revolution's major players while being fall-down drunk: "Romans, hand me a knife! *He sinks
to the ground.*"[19] Simon's drunken appeal to his fellow "Romans" and
blind faith in the revolution make his wife feel betrayed, calling him
"Judas."[20] This scene simultaneously highlights the self-conscious
theatricality of the revolution and the failure of the Parisian poor to
leverage material well-being by adopting it. Immediately juxtaposed to
this rhetorical complex is the effort of a nearby *citoyen* to simplify and
politicize the daughter's behavior. The daughter is not responsible for
her prostitution, he insists, but is rather compelled by hunger: "What
has she done? Nothing! It's her hunger what whores and begs."[21] The
rest of the scene seems to happen in spite of Simon and his wife, rather
than in response to them: several *citoyens* hold speeches on the necessity to kill the "velvet-handed" layabouts who benefitted from the first
wave of the revolution but who have subsequently assumed the roles
of the aristocrats who were killed; a young man is almost hanged on
suspicion of being one of these privileged men; and Robespierre invites
the crowd that has formed to the Jacobin Club. The scene ends with
Simon and his wife left alone and reconciling with a dubious appeal to
the blamelessness the *citoyen* had suggested earlier for Simon's daughter: "Porcia, can you ever forgive me? Did I truly hit you? 'Twas not my
hand, 'twas not my arm, my madness did it."[22] Again, we see the comic
incongruity of adapting a concept of economic, and in this case psychological, determinism to account for an individual domestic fight. The
economic determinism described by the *citoyen* gives Simon a model
of causality whereby he can relieve himself of blame for attacking his
wife, which at once undermines the validity of the *citoyen*'s model by
agreeing with it. The political solidarity achieved through the common
experience of poverty is at once shown triumphantly mobilizing the
people of Paris and lampooned as the movement's participants bungle
its rhetoric and confuse its concepts.

Alfons Glück has argued that poverty is to *Woyzeck* what fate is to
classical tragedy, with economic determinism acting as a kind of irre-
sistible conveyor belt carrying Woyzeck and his family to their horrific

---

19 Büchner, *Complete Plays*, 9; *Sämtliche Werke*, vol. 1: 17: "Gebt mir ein Messer,
    Römer! *Er sinkt um.*"
20 Büchner, *Sämtliche Werke*, I:18.
21 Büchner, *Complete Plays*, 9; *Sämtliche Werke*, vol. 1: 18: "[W]as tat sie? Nichts! Ihr
    Hunger hurt und bettelt."
22 Büchner, *Complete Plays*, 12; *Sämtliche Werke*, vol. 1: 121: "Ha, kannst du mir
    vergeben, Porcia? Schlug ich dich? Das war nicht meine Hand, war nicht mein
    Arm, mein Wahnsinn tat es."

end.[23] Despite the apparent inevitability of Woyzeck's end due to his poverty, he is shown struggling against it through his constant work to feed Marie and his young son, creating a tension between his actions and the statements he utters to his captain with finality, "poor, that's what I am."[24] Despite material conditions determining nearly all facts of their lives, Büchner's characters do not live as if their outcomes were predetermined. Büchner's poorest characters are subject to material circumstance and exploited by characters of greater means, but there are moments suggesting they are not mere sheep for the slaughter, as Martin Wagner has shown in his reading of *Woyzeck*. Woyzeck's subservience and tragic fate have been handily metaphorized in the play's frequent comparisons of him to animals: he is compared variously to a horse, a cat, and a dog at different points in the play. Wagner has shown, however, with reference to Judith Butler's writing on interpellation, the inherent ambivalence of such comparisons, problematizing interpretations of *Woyzeck* as a social drama where Woyzeck is completely deprived of agency.[25] Woyzeck, on the one hand, is compared to an animal—a "beast" or a "dog"—and his subservience is therefore expected, but in accepting the appellation, Wagner notes, Woyzeck also has creative freedom. He can serve his "masters"—the captain, the doctor—like a dog, but he can also disobey like a dog, as when he urinates in the alley outside the professor's laboratory, wasting a potential scientific specimen.[26] In this scene, the doctor reproves Woyzeck for urinating outside, "like a dog." Woyzeck's response is more matter-of-fact than apologetic: "But, Doctor, when it's a call of nature!"[27] Woyzeck's response is in part provided by his designation as a dog, which is simultaneously subservient to its master, but which cannot be kept from disobeying when "nature calls." Woyzeck does not, and cannot, fully refuse participating in the doctor's experiments, but by denying the doctor a specimen he "tests" a form of resistance.[28] Rather than describing Woyzeck as being without agency, it is more accurate to describe him as clinging to the agency he does have, even in settings where he is subservient.

---

23   Alfons Glück, "Der 'Ökonomische Tod': Armut und Arbeit in Georg Büchners *Woyzeck*," *Georg-Büchner Jahrbuch* 4 (1984): 167–226, 169.
24   Büchner, *Complete Plays*, 119; *Sämtliche Werke*, vol. 1: 56: "Ich bin ein armer Kerl."
25   Martin Wagner, "Büchner und Butler: Das Pferde-Narrativ in den Woyzeck-Entwürfen und die Handlungsfähigkeit des postsouveränen Subjekts," *Monatshefte* 104, no. 4 (2012): 477–88, 483.
26   Wagner, "Büchner und Butler," 481.
27   Büchner, *Complete Plays*, 121; *Sämtliche Werke*, vol. 1: 160: "Aber Herr Doctor, wenn einem die Natur kommt."
28   Wagner, "Büchner und Butler," 477.

Precarious Time

Precariousness also affects the perception of time, which we can observe throughout *Dantons Tod* and *Woyzeck*. Nipperdey writes in a passage describing nineteenth-century economic precariousness that demoralized German workers lived in a perpetual present of work and could not plan their future: "Uncertainty, the dwindling prospect that something might be worth it, and shifting economic conditions led to living in the moment, squandered earnings, less planning for the future, and less upward striving, motivation to work, and discipline."[29] Nipperdey's description of nineteenth-century precariousness resonates with Armstrong's elaboration of Büchner's temporal metaphor from *Der hessische Landbote* that the life of Hessian farmers is "a long workday." This metaphor, writes Armstrong, illustrates the "absoluteness" and "permanence" of work in the lives of Hessian farmers (and by extension the poor characters in Büchner's plays).[30] Work dominates their time and their existence is defined by their labor function. The long workday of Büchner's *Landbote*, understood in the context of the economic insecurity Nipperdey describes, is sealed off from the past and future: the unreliability of work to provide for the basic necessities of workers makes the past irrelevant and the future unimaginable. Responding to the insecurity of modern jobs, Bourdieu writes that the elimination of the future through precarious work affects the worker's ability to resist, because one simply loses hope in the future, being unable see one's place in it: "by making the future uncertain, [casualization] prevents all rational anticipation and, in particular, the basic belief and hope in the future that one needs in order to rebel, especially collectively, against present conditions, even the most intolerable."[31] Büchner shows two forms of experiencing the precarious present in *Dantons Tod* and *Woyzeck*: in *Dantons Tod*, the poor characters momentarily distract themselves from their present plight with political executions they believe will culminate in a better future, and in *Woyzeck* the titular character is imprisoned in a perpetual present defined by work.

Harro Müller has shown how the spectacle of the guillotine in *Dantons Tod* distracts the people from their hunger and the future, offering them a dark communion of "heads instead of bread, blood instead of

29 Nipperdey, *Deutsche Geschichte*, 226.
30 William Bruce Armstrong, "Arbeit und Muße in den Werken Georg Büchners," *Text + Kritik* 1981, 63–98, 68.
31 Pierre Bourdieu, *Acts of Resistance: Against the New Myths of Our Time*, trans. Richard Nice (Cambridge: Polity Press, 1998), 82.

wine."[32] Similarly, the temporarily displacing references to antiquity (*Römer*) and the constant address of revolutionaries to each other as "Bürger" (*citoyen*), which itself carries ancient Roman resonances, distract the poor from the urgency of their plight by substituting it with the ideal of timeless, self-historicizing republic. We see this disjunction of temporalities in the first appearance of Robespierre, who enters just as a young man has escaped lynching. "What's going on here, citizens?" he asks in the present tense. The *citoyen* responds with a future-tense challenge to Robespierre: "It's about time something *was* going on!" In other words, what is all this killing in the name of the revolution adding up to? The urgency of the present, where there has been no opportunity to plan the future, grips the citizens in this scene and breaks through the suspension of such temporalities offered by Robespierre's polite address of "Bürger," with its echoes of the Roman Republic. The solution to the hunger crisis of the present is the distraction of the *citoyens* with a promise of the future enabled, supposedly, by the guillotine. Another *citoyen* interjects with a plea for food, but cannibalistically substitutes nourishment itself with aristocrats, the apparent cause of their hunger: "Our wives and kids are screaming for bread, we want to feed them on the flesh of aristocrats."[33] Patrick Fortmann relates this link of hunger and violence, which is present throughout the play, to the recurring spectacle of the guillotine which attempts to soothe the pain of the stomach by stimulating the eyes.[34] The futurity of this desire for the "flesh of aristocrats" lies in the metonymic quality of the guillotine, whereby, "the moment is not captured, cannot be temporalized, but instead further moments, further beheadings are demanded."[35] This futurity is underscored by the odd shift to the participle form of "totgeschlagen" by the group of *citoyens* in the scene, which is uttered as an imperative but carries the sense of the future perfect: "Beaten to death" exclaims a *citoyen*, "whoever can eat and write!" This is followed by a collective cry of, "Beaten to death, beaten to death!"[36] It is as though by referring to an already completed future action, the crowd is actualizing an ideal revolutionary future that allows them to leave their present hunger unaddressed even longer.

---

32 Harro Müller, *Taubenfüße und Adlerkralle: Essays zu Nietzsche, Adorno, Kluge, Büchner und Grabbe* (Bielefeld: Aisthesis, 2016), 174.

33 Büchner, *Collected Plays*, 25; *Sämtliche Werke*, vol. 1: 20: "Unsere Weiber und Kinder schreien nach Brot, wir wollen sie mit Aristokratenfleisch füttern."

34 Patrick Fortmann, *Autopsie von Revolution und Restauration: Georg Büchner und die politische Imagination* (Freiburg: Rombach Verlag, 2013), 214.

35 Müller, *Taubenfüße und Adlerkrallen*, 175. My translation.

36 Büchner, *Complete Plays*, 10. Büchner, *Sämtliche Werke*, vol. 1: 19: "Totgeschlagen wer essen und schreiben kann!" "Totgeschlage, totgeschlage!"

The character Woyzeck, as opposed to the crowds in *Dantons Tod*, is contained in a perpetual present, where each moment prolongs his attempt to earn a living. We can see Woyzeck's hurried sense of time in the play's shaving scene, observed from the outside by the captain and framed in Armstrong's binary of "work" and "leisure:"

> OFFICER: Steady, Woyzeck, steady; one thing after another. You're making me quite giddy. What on earth am I to do with the spare ten minutes if you finish too early today? Woyzeck, just think, you've still got a good thirty years to live, thirty years! That's 360 months, not to mention the days, the hours, the minutes! What are you going to do with all this vast expanse of time? Pace it, Woyzeck, pace it!
> WOYZECK: Yessir!
> [HAUPTMANN: Langsam, Woyzeck, langsam; eins nach dem andern; Er macht mich ganz schwindlich. Was soll ich dann mit den Minuten anfangen, die Er heut zu früh fertig wird? Woyzeck, bedenk' Er, Er hat noch seine schöne dreißig Jahr zu leben, dreißig Jahr! Macht 360 Monate, und Tage, Stunden, Minuten! Was will Er denn mit der ungeheuren Zeit all anfangen? Teil Er sich ein, Woyzeck.
> WOZYECK: Ja wohl, Herr Hauptmann.][37]

The captain, who throughout the play holds forth on moral philosophy, dreads the extra ten minutes Woyzeck would leave him by finishing his barbering early. His life, to use Armstrong's metaphor, is "a long Sunday,"[38] which the captain knows as a "vast expanse of time" he must fill with activity to avoid existential despair. "Activity, Woyzeck," he admonishes, "activity!"[39] Woyzeck, of course, does not lack things to do. In addition to shaving the captain, he is an *Einsteher* (an older soldier who is paid to serve in the stead of a younger conscript), a test subject for the doctor, and cuts disciplinary rods in the woods with Andres. The difference between the captain's sense of time, regimented into "days, hours, minutes," and Woyzeck's, is that, for the latter, each moment must facilitate an activity that provides him money. For the captain, his main concern with time is to occupy his mind to distract himself from a vacant sense of "eternity": "I get really frightened for the

---

37 Büchner, *Complete Plays*, 119. Büchner, *Sämtliche Werke*, vol. 1: 154.
38 Armstrong, "Arbeit und Muße," 68.
39 Büchner, *Complete Plays*, 119. Büchner, *Sämtliche Werke*, vol. 1: 155: "Beschäftigung, Woyzeck, Beschäftigung!"

world when I think of eternity."[40] Woyzeck also becomes possessed by a sense of eternity later in the play, but it is an obsession bound up with his murderous jealousy of Marie and the drum major rather than an abstract existential concern from which he distracts himself in his day-to-day thoughts. Wozyeck overhears Marie shout "Immer zu!" while she is dancing with the drum major, which can be translated as "Don't stop!" For Woyzeck, however, this expression of delight comes to stand for relentless (*immer*) internal pressure and strife (the forward tendency of *zu*). In Büchner's depiction, the ceaseless activity of Woyzeck's daily life of making ends meet bleeds over into a psychological disturbance that propels his murder of Marie at the end of the play, during which he repeats the phrase again: "Can I hear it there too?." Woyzeck says in scene 16, "Does the wind say it too? Will I go on hearing it over and over: stab, stab, stab her dead?"[41]

The Isolating Quality of Precariousness

Contemporary discussions of precariousness have shown how, perhaps counterintuitively, economic precariousness isolates those experiencing it from one another, even while the feeling of precariousness is held in common by so many across many different classes. The isolating quality of precariousness derives from what Marchart has called its "relationality." Unlike poverty, as noted above, precariousness cannot be quantifiably measured and identified, but emerges subjectively and in relational configurations. Marchart writes, "Precarity can never be absolute, but rather is always only relational, that is, it is defined against the current standards and norms of gainful employment." Precarious-ness can only be defined against normative standards of security: if the norm for employment includes health insurance and a long-term contract, people whose jobs lack these features feel more vulnerable. Such norms are not just societal, but personal, which means that the feeling of precariousness is not limited to a particular class, like the uninsured, but is experienced across social classes. Marchart remarks that, although precarity's effects may be most clearly visible in those

---

40 Büchner, *Complete Plays*, 119. Büchner, *Sämtliche Werke*, vol. 1: 154–5: "Es wird mir ganz angst um die Welt, wenn ich an die Ewigkeit denke."
41 Büchner, *Complete Plays*, 129; *Sämtliche Werke*, vol. 1: 164: "Hör ich's da auch? Sagt's der Wind auch? Hör ich's immer, immer zu, stich tot, tot." This statement derives, in a modified form, from Clarus' report on Johann Christian Woyzeck, who allegedly heard the words "immer drauf, immer drauf!" as he lay in bed. See Dedner, *Georg Büchner: Woyzeck*, 56.

without work, precariousness is also experienced by the employed who see themselves surrounded by a "reserve army" of insecure workers ready to take their positions.[42] In a regime of insecurity, where precarity and not stability is the norm, all workers feel vulnerable in their positions to some extent. This general sense of precariousness can make one's insecurity seem irreducibly personal and unique, rather than a widely shared experience.

Büchner shows this isolating quality of the precariousness' relational quality in his plays. His poor characters identify differences in their situations that prevent solidarity, dismiss each other's feelings of precariousness, or simply do not recognize themselves in each other's struggle. We see this isolating quality of precariousness in *Dantons Tod* when *citoyens* dismiss each other's politics and material needs. In II.6, Simon patriotically admonishes the *citoyens* with whom he is going to arrest Danton, "Forward, citizens! You will render great service to your country!" to which one of them replies, "I wish the country'd render some service to us! For all the 'oles we've made in other people's bodies, not a single 'ole has gone from our own trousers!"[43] The *citoyen* criticizes not only Simon's patriotism here, implied in his unenthusiastic echo of Simon's statement, but aligns the revolution with work. While the effort to build a fatherland may have been done out of political idealism, it was also done with the expectation of repayment, implied by the verb "verdienen." The *citoyen* has killed, putting holes in other people, on behalf of the fatherland, and thereby earned (*sich verdient machen*) a pair of new pants. If the fatherland would "earn" the *citoyen*, it would procure the pants or else risk defaulting, which would spell the guillotining of the National Convention. Büchner shows in this scene that the outcome of the revolution depends not on the politics of Robespierrean virtue (*Tugend*) or Dantonist pleasure (*Genuß*), but, in this instance, on the satisfaction of basic material needs. Rather than formulate the material needs of the poor into a political program, however, Büchner shows such needs to be individually determined and resistant to politicization, as when another *citoyen* responds to the need for decent clothes with the ironic question, "Do you want your flies sewn up then?" to which all the onstage characters laugh.[44] The *citoyen*'s concern about his clothing is exploited by his compatriot for a joke about his virility,

42 Marchart, *Prekarisierungsgesellschaft*, 12–13.
43 Büchner, *Complete Plays*, 39; *Sämtliche Werke*, vol. 1: 50: "Vorwärts Bürger, ihr werdet euch um das Vaterland verdient machen!" "Ich wollte das Vaterland machte sich um uns verdient; über all den Löchern, die wir in andrer Leute Körper machen, ist noch kein einziges in unsern Hosen zugegangen."
44 Büchner, *Sämtliche Werke*, vol. 1: 50: "Willst du, daß dir dein Hosenlatz zuginge?"

suggesting that if he fixes the holes in his pants he should sew closed the fly as well. Büchner first presented ragged pants as a synecdoche for the ailing poor, but with the above joke they are depoliticized, changed into a personal problem of the *citoyen*, rather than indicative of a general concern. The joke at once creates a collective around itself, integrating those who laugh, while simultaneously frustrating solidarity around the *citoyen*'s sense of precariousness and need for adequate clothing.

As suggested by the verb "verdienen" in the passage above, characters in *Dantons Tod* and *Woyzeck* compare various experiences to work. In *Dantons Tod*, Simon's wife defends her daughter's prostitution by insisting that the body is a set of tools, with each appendage, including the sex organs, being equally practical for earning a living: "We work with all the rest of our body, why not with that bit as well?"[45] In *Woyzeck*, the body is not only instrumentalized, but commodified. For Marie and Woyzeck, who struggle throughout the play just to stay afloat economically, even their bodies are referred to as potential goods that could be pawned or, in Woyzeck's case, sold for medical experimentation. When a neighbor, Margreth, chides Marie over having eyes for the handsome drum major, Marie retorts with a violent reference to her neighbor's poverty: "Take your own [eyes] to the yid and get 'em polished, perhaps they'll shine too and someone could flog 'em for a couple of buttons."[46] Marie's reference to a Jewish buyer of jewel-like eyes foreshadows scene 20, where Woyzeck buys his murder weapon from a Jewish merchant, who commodifies even death, offering Woyzeck, his troubled client, "a nice economical death."[47] Woyzeck buys a knife from the merchant with two pennies, which is the infamous price the doctor pays him for his urine, "2 groschen a day."[48] These instances point to lives of economic struggle, but Marie and Woyzeck experience these struggles in different ways and along gendered lines. Woyzeck sees himself and his lot of "poor souls" as doomed, caught in an inescapable system of exploitation that dominates every moment of life, even in sleep. When Woyzeck sees his son lying asleep with sweat on his brow, he remarks, "nothing in the world but work, even in your sleep you sweat. That's us, that is: the bloody poor!"[49] Woyzeck foresees the

---

45 Büchner, *Complete Plays*, 9; *Sämtliche Werke*, vol. 1: 18: "Wir arbeiten mit allen Gliedern, warum denn nicht auch damit?"

46 Büchner, *Complete Plays*, 114; *Sämtliche Werke*, vol. 1: 148: "Und wenn! Trag Sie Ihr Auge zum Jud und laß Sie sie putze, vielleicht glänze sie noch, daß man sie für zwei Knöpf verkaufe könnt."

47 Büchner, *Complete Plays*, 131; *Sämtliche Werke*, vol. 1: 166.

48 Büchner, *Sämtliche Werke*, vol. 1: 157: "arme Kerle."

49 Büchner, *Complete Plays*, 118; *Sämtliche Werke*, vol. 1: 156: "Alles Arbeit unter der Sonn, sogar Schweiß im Schlaf. Wir arme Leut!"

same life for his son that he has lived, whereas Marie harbors fantasies of transcending the economic class into which she was born, primarily through marriage or a sexual relationship with the drum major. These different experiences and expectations of their impoverishment are examples of Büchner's understanding that precariousness is a deeply individual experience, one which resists being translated into a political category.

Two of the most salient moments in *Woyzeck* showing precariousness' subjective qualities are when Woyzeck and Marie, independently of each other, lament their poverty, both at an individual and at a collective level. In a discussion of morality conducted as Woyzeck is shaving his captain, Woyzeck says:

> WOYZECK: We poor people. Money, you see, sir, it's the money. If you don't have no money. Morality don't get much of a look in when our sort gets made. We're flesh and blood after all. Us lot just don't have a chance in this world or the next; if we ever got to heaven I reckon we'd have to help with the thunder.
> [WOYZECK: Wir arme Leut. Sehn Sie, Herr Hauptmann, Geld, Geld. Wer kein Geld hat. Da setzt einmal einer seinesgleichen auf die Moral in die Welt. Man hat auch sein Fleisch und Blut. Unseins ist doch einmal unselig in der und der andern Welt, ich glaub' wenn wir in Himmel kämen, so müßten wir donnern helfen.][50]

Woyzeck takes a subversive view of morality in this passage, suggesting that it is determined by economics ("money, money") and the philosophical opportunities it affords, in this case the opportunity to consider morality detached from the needs of "flesh and blood," shelter, and nourishment. Woyzeck also creates a dichotomy here between an impoverished "we" ("Wir arme Leut," "unseins") and an implied second-person plural including the captain. This is not a dichotomy born of animosity on Woyzeck's part, but an instance of empathy with those who suffer similarly or more than he does, as we also see in scene 8, where he reflects on the suffering of his child.[51]

Despite the sense of a shared fate ("... if we ever got to heaven I reckon we'd have to help with the thunder"), a look at Marie's soliloquy shows that expressions of collective identification—"wir arme Leut," "unseins"—do not always contribute to political solidarity between those invoking them. In scene 8, Marie has just put her child

50 Büchner, *Complete Plays*, 119; *Sämtliche Werke*, vol. 1: 155–6. Translation modified.
51 Knapp, *Georg Büchner*, 201–2.

to bed and looks at herself in a broken mirror wearing an earring the drum major has given her. Woyzeck's statement to the captain echoes in Marie's soliloquy:

> MARIE: [Looks in the mirror again.] Bet you that's gold! Our sort don't 'ave much, a dump like this and a broken bit of mirror – but me mouth's just as red as them grand madames' with their bloody great mirrors and their fancy gents what kiss their 'ands; a poor woman, that's what I am.
> [MARIE: *Spiegelt sich wieder*. S'ist gewiß Gold! Unsereins hat nur ein Eckchen in der Welt und ein Stückchen Spiegel und doch hab ich ein so rote Mund als die großen Madamen mit ihren Spiegeln von oben bis unten und ihren schönen Herrn, die ihnen die Hand küssen; ich bin nur ein arm Weibsbild.][52]

Here we see another dichotomy, this time gendered, between the poor ("unsereins") and rich ("die großen Madamen"). Rather than cleaving the two groups apart with unassailable difference like Woyzeck does, however, Marie imagines herself crossing over into the boudoirs of the grandes dames when she wears an earring of real gold. Marie indulges in a fantasy of hypergamy to which Woyzeck has no access, evidenced by the definitive line Woyzeck delivers to the captain: "But poor, that's what I am."[53] In both scenes, Woyzeck and Marie refer to collectivities of the poor without fully including the other based on notions of social mobility influenced by their gender. In presenting the two poorest characters in the play this way, Büchner suggests internal struggles among the poor that would stand in the way of political collectivization.

Finally, the importance of economic precariousness for Büchner's depiction of the characters above is underscored by the beggar scene in *Dantons Tod* (II.2), which features presumably one of the poorest characters in Büchner's *oeuvre*. The beggar, by reaching a social nadir, seems to have achieved unlikely material and psychological stability. He is, counterintuitively, regarded as a kind of aristocrat because his poverty has allowed him to divorce himself from the world of work. In the scene, he asks a group of gentlemen and ladies for money, and they reproach him for appearing soft and well-fed, insufficiently downtrodden to deserve their pity. Upon handing the beggar coins, the second gentleman exclaims: "He's got hands like velvet. What

---

52   Büchner, *Complete Plays*, 118; *Sämtliche Werke*, vol. 1: 153.
53   Büchner, *Sämtliche Werke*, vol. 1: 156: "Ich bin ein armer Kerl."

confounded cheek!"[54] The scene is remarkable for how it uses the politically charged vocabulary of an earlier street scene I.2, in which a *citoyen* introduces the metaphor of "velvet hands" (*Samthände*) as a betraying feature of the rich, whom the people must kill (*totschlagen*) to free themselves from exploitation and hunger: "you have ragged jackets, and they have warm overcoats; your fists are calloused, and their hands are velvet ... ergo, they're rats and must be destroyed."[55] The parallel between the two scenes continues with the beggar's inquiry about the provenance of the gentleman's coat ("How did you come by your coat, sir?"), another identifying feature of the rich enumerated earlier by the *citoyen*, to which the gentleman replies, "Work!" and offers the beggar a coat like it if he will come work for him.[56] Rather than take the gentleman up on his offer, the beggar interrogates the purpose of work: "Why did you work, sir?"[57] When the gentleman responds that he worked in order to possess the coat, the beggar, jester-like (the gentleman had previously referred to him as a *Narr*), interrogates his values, pointing out the unnecessary worry he had expended on behalf of a pleasure, a "Genuß." "A blackguard," namely himself, "does the same" ("Ein Lumpen tut's auch"); the beggar proposes an alternative to the model for acquiring pleasure than suffering (*sich quälen*) for it: "The sun shines warm out here in the street, and life's so easy."[58] The beggar expresses himself in a manner Patrick Fortmann compares to the ancient cynics,[59] insisting that pleasure is to be had for free in the street if one looks for it. The beggar's proposal may seem glib, but by presenting it in terms identical with the previous scene, Büchner makes this short exchange a critical reframing of the earlier mob scene. The beggar is coded as aristocratic, and the gentlemen are coded as workers, flipping the work/privilege dichotomy that motivated the previous conflict. The beggar scene complicates Büchner's concept of the people, and especially of the poor, making it more internally differentiated than the already complicated duality often ascribed to it of shortsightedness

---

54 Büchner, *Complete Plays*, 31; *Sämtliche Werke*, vol. 1: 42: "Er hat eine Hand wie Samt. Das ist unverschämt."
55 Büchner, *Complete Plays*, 10; Büchner, *Sämtliche Werke*, vol. 1: 18: "ihr habt Löcher in den Jacken und sie haben warme Röcke, ihr habt Schwielen in den Fäusten und sie haben Samthände ... ergo sie sind Spitzbuben und man muß sie totschlagen."
56 Büchner, *Sämtliche Werke*, vol. 1: 42.
57 Büchner, *Complete Plays*, 31; *Sämtliche Werke*, vol. 1: 42: "Warum habt Ihr gearbeitet?"
58 Büchner, *Complete Plays*, 31; *Sämtliche Werke*, vol. 1: 42: "Die Sonne scheint warm an das Eck und das geht ganz leicht."
59 Fortmann, *Autopsie von Revolution und Restauration*, 285.

combined with exclusive revolutionary potential.[60] There is no sign of the beggar's alignment with revolutionary politics of the poor *citoyens*, much less the Jacobins, but rather in his resignation and criticism of the gentleman's idealism, he resembles the melancholic disenchantment of Georges Danton. The scene raises the question of whether the beggar could be integrated into the revolutionary people at all, or whether he, like the other "velvet-handed" aristocrats, would need to die to make way for the republic.

Büchner's presentation of poverty as an experience frustrating political solidarity does not culminate in political nihilism for the plays discussed here. In the case of *Woyzeck*, Büchner's taking the experience of such a wretched figure as Woyzeck out of the margins of society and history and putting it at the center of his drama is inherently political. Büchner's plays, however, avoid sympathy and identification, both between the characters themselves and between the audience and the characters. The political contribution of these plays remains anticipatory, and any future politics that would integrate their figures could not afford to idealize them but must take them with all their contradictions. Heiner Müller's 1985 acceptance speech for the Georg Büchner Prize forebodingly described the consummation of Woyzeck's political and social implications, likening it to a messianic "resurrection" of Woyzeck from the forgotten grave of a dog: "Woyzeck lives where the dog is buried, the dog's name: Woyzeck. We are waiting for his resurrection with fear and/or hope that the dog will return as a wolf."[61] Müller's return of the left-for-dead dog as wolf can be read as expanding on the political potential Elias Canetti saw in Büchner's literary writing, which he praised for keeping its most marginal characters "intact." This intactness provides a sign of the figure that may, through resurrection (*Auferstehung*) or perhaps through an uprising (*Aufstand*), shape our future.

Canetti's own acceptance speech for the Georg Büchner Prize in 1972 refers to Büchner's poetic and political contribution as "the discovery of the small" [*das Geringe*]. Büchner's "discovery" of *das Geringe* for literature—which connotes the invisibly small, marginalized, as well as, metaphorically, the lowest social classes—is remarkable for how it does not interfere with the figure by way of a rescuing pity (*Erbarmen*). Rather, this desire for mercy, while implicitly present, is hidden

---

60 Theo Buck, *"Riß in der Schöpfung": Büchner-Studien* (Aachen: Rimbaud Verlag, 2000), 15.
61 Heiner Müller, *Explosion of a Memory*, edited and translated by Carl Weber, 106 (New York: PAJ, 1989). German: Heiner Müller, *Werke*, vol. 8 (Frankfurt: Suhrkamp, 2005), 282–3.

in Büchner's texts so that his subjects may be shown wholly (*intakt*) without moral impositions by their author:

> This discovery presupposes pity, but only if this pity remains hidden, if it is silent, if it does not speak, only then does the small remain intact. The poet who flaunts their feelings, who inflates what is small with his pity, defiles and destroys it. Woyzeck is hounded by the words and voices of others, yet remains untouched by the author. To this day, no one else has come close to Büchner's reverence for the small.

> [Diese Entdeckung setzt Erbarmen voraus, aber nur wenn dieses Erbarmen verborgen bleibt, wenn es stumm ist, wenn es sich nicht ausspricht, ist das Geringe intakt. Der Dichter, der sich mit seinen Gefühlen spreizt, der das Geringe mit seinem Erbarmen öffentlich aufbläst, verunreinigt und zerstört es. Von Stimmen und von den Worten der Anderen ist Woyzeck gehetzt, doch vom Dichter ist er unberührt geblieben. In dieser Keuschheit fürs Geringe ist bis zum heutigen Tage niemand mit Büchner zu vergleichen.][62]

The Christian moral connotations of Canetti's description (*Erbarmen, Keuschheit*) distantly echo Büchner's account of the dramatist who, god-like, creates (*erschaffen*) history anew in its own likeness, without presuming to alter what is already given.[63] Büchner's withholding of explicit pity, his preservation of the contradictions and "obscene language" (as Büchner described the bawdy dialogue of *Dantons Tod* in a letter to his parents) that animate his characters resembles a form of poetic chastity and purity honoring history: "[the dramatist's] play must be neither more moral nor more immoral than history itself."[64] Büchner's poetic and political intervention in the literary representation of poverty was to preserve its subjective, differentiated experience among his characters, who, though finding themselves at odds in the plots of Büchner's plays, had to be so represented for their precarious existence to remain fully "intact." It was through Büchner's withholding of overt sympathy that he could show figures who Müller believed all should hope for, or fear.

---

62 Elias Canetti, "Rede zur Verleihung des Büchner-Preises 1972," in *Büchner-Preis-Reden 1972–1983*, vol. 2, ed. Herbert Heckman (Stuttgart: Reclam Verlag, 1984), 30.
63 Büchner, *Sämtliche Werke*, vol. 2: 410.
64 Büchner, *Complete Plays*, 201; Büchner, *Sämtliche Werke*, vol. 2: 410: "darf nicht sittlicher noch unsittlicher sein, als die Geschichte selbst."

Works Cited

Armstrong, William Bruce. "Arbeit und Muße in den Werken Georg Büchners." *Text + Kritik* (1981): 63–98.

Arnim, Bettina von. *Werke und Briefe*, vol. 3. Frankfurt: Deutscher Klassiker Verlag, 1995.

Buck, Theo. *"Riß in der Schöpfung": Büchner-Studien.* Aachen: Rimbaud, 2000.

Bourdieu, Pierre. *Acts of Resistance: Against the New Myths of Our Time.* Translated by Richard Nice. Cambridge: Polity, 1998.

Büchner, Georg. *Complete Plays, Lenz and Other Writings.* London: Penguin Books Kindle Edition, 1993.

Büchner, Georg. *Sämtliche Werke*, vols. 1 and 2. Edited by Henri Poschmann and Marie Poschmann. Frankfurt: Deutscher Klassiker Verlag, 2006.

Butler, Judith. *The Force of Non-Violence.* London and New York: Verso, 2020.

Canetti, Elias. "Rede zur Verleihung des Büchner-Preises 1972." *Büchner-Preis-Reden 1972–1983*, vol. 2. Edited by Herbert Heckman. Stuttgart: Reclam, 1984.

Castel, Robert. *From Manual Workers to Wage Laborers: Transformation of the Social Question.* Translated and edited by Richard Boyd. Piscataway, NJ: Transaction Publishers, 2003.

Dedner, Burghard. *Georg Büchner: Woyzeck.* Stuttgart: Reclam, 2000.

Fortmann, Patrick. *Autopsie von Revolution und Restauration: Georg Büchner und die politische Imagination.* Freiburg: Rombach, 2013.

Glück, Alfons. "Der 'Ökonomische Tod': Armut und Arbeit in Georg Büchners *Woyzeck.*" *Georg-Büchner Jahrbuch* 4 (1984): 167–226.

Knapp, Gerhard. *Georg Büchner.* Stuttgart: Metzler, 2000.

Kroneberg, Lutz and Rolf Schloesser, eds. *Weber-Revolte 1844. Der schlesische Weberaufstand im Spiegel der zeitgenössischen Publizistik und Literatur.* Cologne: Informationspresse, C.W. Leske, 1979.

Marchart, Oliver. *Die Prekarisierungsgesellschaft: Prekäre Proteste. Politik und Ökonomie im Zeichen der Prekarisierung.* Bielefeld: Transcript, 2013.

Müller, Harro. *Taubenfüße und Adlerkrallen: Essays zu Nietzsche, Adorno, Kluge, Büchner und Grabbe.* Bielefeld: Aisthesis, 2016.

Müller, Heiner. *Explosion of a Memory: Writings.* Translated by Carl Weber. New York: PAJ Publications, 1989.

Müller, Heiner. *Werke*, vol. 8. Frankfurt: Suhrkamp, 2005.

Neilson, Brett and Ned Rossiter. "Precarity as a Political Concept, or Fordism as Exception." *Theory, Culture & Society* 25, nos. 7–8 (2008): 51–72.

Nipperdey, Thomas. *Deutsche Geschichte 1800–1866: Bürgerwelt und starker Staat.* Munich: C.H. Beck, 1984.

Wagner, Martin. "Büchner und Butler: Das Pferde-Narrativ in den Woyzeck-Entwürfen und die Handlungsfähigkeit des postsouveränen Subjekts." *Monatshefte* 104, no. 4 (2012): 477–88.

Weigel, Sigrid. *Flugschriftenliteratur 1848 in Berlin: Geschichte und Öffentlichkeit einer volkstümlichen Gattung.* Stuttgart: Metzler, 1979.

Five   Hilfe von Mensch zu Mensch:
Social Precarity and the
Elberfeld System

Rebekah O. McMillan

In 1843, the German Brockhaus encyclopedia included an entry describing a new phenomenon within the age-old problem of poverty. Titled *"pauperismus,"* the entry described the "much discussed" development sweeping through industrialized countries of Europe, including the German states. The lexicon defined it as:

> a condition where a numerous class of people can secure through the most strenuous work at most the most minimal subsidies (and cannot even be certain of this), a class whose members are– even before they are born–doomed for their entire lives to such a condition, a class that has no prospects of improvement and that, in fact, sinks deeper and deeper into lethargy and brutality.[1]

While the word was not wholly new it took on new meaning. Originally the term pauper referred to someone who was in need of charity. By the 1750s there began a change that connected pauper to mean those who had fallen under the care of the state, meaning they were unable to support themselves. However, by the nineteenth century, pauper and pauperism "became more and more abstract and more pejorative" and had "slipped into public discourse in sentences reeking of condemnation and moral superiority."[2]

---

1   "Pauperismus," in *Brockhaus Conversations-Lexikon der Gegenwart* (Leipzig, 1840), vol. 4, 65.
2   Lynn Hollen Lees, *The Solidarities of Strangers: The English Poor Laws and the People, 1700–1948* (Cambridge: Cambridge University Press, 1998), 40.

The lexicon articulated the condition as a new type of poverty caused by a changing nature of work and society that was unlike the more traditional culprits of old age and illness. The depression of wages prohibited workers from providing life's necessities for themselves and their families. The term specifies that even strenuous work, implying long hours or multiple jobs, would not ensure protection from poverty. Pauperism's reach extended to the womb, indicating that groups of people were plunged into poverty before they were born with little possibility of improvement. Because work provided no security against this new type of poverty, it was feared by nineteenth-century thinkers that pauperism would naturally lead to degeneration amongst the masses into idleness, drunkenness, and other "animalistic" vices.[3]

The inclusion of pauperism in the encyclopedia was representative of a growing unease spreading across industrialized Europe, and a fear for the future of society. Pauperism lay at the heart of what was known to contemporaries as the *soziale Frage* (Social Question). In the wake of the Napoleonic wars, Germany underwent a social and economic transformation that saw a rate of population growth that exceeded the growth in the absorptive capacity of new industrial labor. Coupled with a highly unequal distribution of wealth and the separation of the rural population from their old usage rights of common property [*Gemeinheitsteilung*], poverty became more widely spread and took on a new quality of destitution: hunger and low life expectancies were common characteristics of pauperism.[4] This crisis was not only economic but also social and cultural, for it challenged the Enlightenment assumption that through their use of reason alone individuals could advance in society as long as rights of property and commerce were secured. The failure of both civil society and the state to prevent the rise of pauperism provided fertile conditions for the emergence of a new proletarian class consciousness that began to reshape how individuals viewed themselves in relation to society, the state, and capitalist markets.[5]

---

3   "Pauperismus," 65–74.
4   For relevant statistical data, see *Sozialgeschichtliches Arbeitsbuch, Band 1: Materialien zur Statistik des deutschen Bundes 1815–1870*, ed. Wolfram Fischer, Jochen Krengel and Jutta Wietog (Munich: C. H. Beck, 1982).
5   For a canonical account of this dynamic, see Werner Conze, "Vom 'Pöbel' zum 'Proletariat': Sozialgeschichtliche Voraussetzungen für den Sozialismus in Deutschland," *Vierteljahrsschrift für Sozial- und Wirtschaftsgeschichte* 41, no. 4 (1954): 333–64.

Industrial workers were tied to the economy in ways they had never been before. When fluctuations in the market occurred, the individual's existence was thrown into jeopardy. Poverty was a paradox for liberals who were forced to reconcile their adherence to laissez-faire principles with the reality that it produced unequal results. In an account on the effects of pauperism in Leipzig, one writer stated that "society and private property is threatened by the growing encroachments of poverty," and that society would "soon recognize that much crime is only the consequence of too great of poverty and that many become criminals only after he lacked the funds to satisfy the hunger of his family."[6] As a result of these consequences, a developing threat to the social order began consuming the minds of political, religious, educational, and business leaders. The mass group of paupers was seen as constituting a volatile presence that could become unruly at a moment's notice and was seen as endangering the social peace.

Concerns over the lower classes were an ever-present problem to nineteenth-century social commentators and thinkers. Most of them understood the Social Question as an unsettling product of modernity, with one German social reformer calling it "the riddle of mankind."[7] The world was changing at a rapid pace, and this rapidity had dire consequences for those who lacked the means and ability to adapt to it quickly. The political and economic ideas that legitimated the new socio-political order of the nineteenth century were associated with the Enlightenment notion of steady social progress, rooted in advances in science and technology. Pauperization challenged the assumption that the moral individual by itself had the capacity to keep up with, and adjust to, the historical forces of progress, and attention was being directed at the wealthy and their responsibility to reduce the growing divergence between the rich and the poor. The economist Friedrich Bülau noted in 1834:

In our time, a sudden anxiety has spread among the rich, and they would like to safeguard themselves at any price against the danger they fear from the growing misery of the poor. If they were to take the most natural measures and make it easier for the poor to lift themselves up through their own efforts to a higher level of physical and spiritual welfare, this would help both them

---

6 Anonymous, *Die Armuth und die Mittel ihr entgegen zu wirken* (Leipzig: Wigand, 1844).

7 "Die Armenpflege – eine praktische Lösung der sozialen Frage,"*Armendirektorium/Magistrat der Stadt Berlin*, Armendirektion: Konferenzen deutscher Armenpflege 1879–1883. A Rep 003-01. Nr. 634, 41. Landesarchiv Berlin.

and the whole of society. But they are merely trying to look after themselves at the cost of the poor, and they believe that they have removed the danger when they have used new restrictions to entrench themselves against the working classes, consequently intensifying the cause of the danger.[8]

Bülau was critical of the initial reaction of the wealthy to the rise of pauperism. Rather than seeking to pass restrictive and repressive legislation or attempting to rid society of the poor's presence through something like immigration, those in power "should first explore whether a more remunerative sphere of activity might not open up."[9]

The Social Question, in sum, was the product of industrial development, population growth, the lifting of medieval limits on occupational freedom, and the ineffectiveness of European governments to handle the fallout of the revolutionary transformation from feudalism to capitalism. Concerns over riots, unrest in industrial cities, the growing appeal of socialism, and worries over health and disease, encouraged nineteenth-century social reformers, intellectuals, church leaders, members of the bourgeoisie, and political actors to find solutions to society's ills while continuing to normalize and valorize the inherent traits of the upper and middle classes as standards by which to judge society. As the term pauperism came to widen the conception of poverty within a society, it was the expectation that an advanced and civilized nation could ameliorate the suffering of the poor and destitute. If the suffering was a product of modernity, then modern advances could also fix it.

The Elberfeld System

It was within the context of this great transformation that the Elberfeld System, the most notable form of state-sponsored German poor relief in the nineteenth century, came into existence. The Elberfeld System operated under the conviction that it was only through an intimate, individualized knowledge of both the condition of the poor individual as well as the circumstances responsible for this destitution that the societal problem of poverty could be solved within a community. To this end, the Elberfeld System utilized local poor relief volunteers, recruited from the middle and upper classes, to investigate the needs of the impoverished, with the additional goal of building relationships

---

8   Friedrich Bülau, *Der Staat und die Industrie: Beiträge zur Gewerbspolitik und Armen-polizei* (Leipzig: Göschen, 1834), 25.

9   Bülau, *Der Staat und die Industrie*, 55.

between those officials and the poor to ensure relief was deserved and appropriate. This framework of the Elberfeld System is reflected in its key operating phrase: *Hilfe von Mensch zu Mensch* (help from person to person).[10] However, these officials did more than just investigate requests for need. Through their building of personal relationships with the poor, the officials were expected to exercise oversight and control over the poor to ensure their proper conduct and reduce the giving of undeserving aid.[11] The process of building relationships between the poor and their socioeconomic betters and then allowing those betters to determine the worthiness of a relief petitioner enabled the condition of poverty to be defined in their image rather than allowing the poor themselves to dictate the causes or conditions of their situation.

The Elberfeld System was understood by its practitioners and admirers as an enlightened form of charity and reflected two prominent contemporary modes of thought. First, the system embodied classical liberal principles of individual sovereignty. Notions of autonomy transformed the responsibility placed on individuals in that they were accountable for their conduct to fellow humans and to God. This marked a shift away from more communal notions prevalent in the pre-industrial era that was dominated by church charity. These ideas had a tremendous influence on the perceptions toward poverty in that the idea of work reflected one's self-worth. Additionally, the idea of the autonomous individual allowed the indigent to be understood as having become poor as a direct consequence of unwise life choices. Since the individual was now in control of their own fate and their actions were to determine this fate, the individual was expected to take charge of their conduct.

The second principle that the Elberfeld System reflected was that of Hegelian idealism, which asserted a collective responsibility for the common good of society. Hegel argued that the world is best understood through active engagement rather than passive contemplation. This active engagement produces an understanding of the world based upon observation and reason. Hegel, for example, saw the changes brought by early industrialization in Britain and the French Revolution and asserted that through engaging with the impact of these events his native Germany could pursue a different approach to change through

---

10 *Städtische Armenverwaltung Elberfeld. Jahres Bericht für das Rechnungsjahr 1909 (April 1, 1909–März 31, 1910)*, BR 007 NR. 43028 Armenverwaltung Elberfeld 1910–1926, Landesarchiv Nord-Rhein Westfalen.

11 Victor Böhmert, *Das Armenwesen in 77 deutschen Städten* (Dresden: Armenstatistisches Bureau des Deutschen Vereins für Armenpflege und Wohltätigkeit, 1886), 74.

the active pursuits of social elites and the state.[12] Since individual sovereignty left little room for poverty being a consequence of circumstances out of the individual's control, idealism helped those bourgeois social reformers committed to laissez-faire practices to find a way to rationalize increased interference with the consequences of an unrestricted market's fluctuations. By focusing on individual intervention, intervention required due to the perceived inadequacy of the poor individuals in question, the Elberfeld System was therefore able to offer structural poor aid without undermining the fundamental suppositions of a liberal economy.

Deserving Versus Undeserving Poor

Traditional views of poverty, held since the Middle Ages, understood the condition to operate in a dichotomy between the deserving and the undeserving poor. The deserving poor were those individuals who had fallen upon hard times due to factors beyond their control, typically those related to the natural progressions of life such as old age, disability, or sickness. These conditions were treated communally through provisions being given directly to those in need by the wealthy or through church distributions.[13] One of the earliest German examples is the building of the social settlement called the Fuggerei in Augsburg by Jakob Fugger in 1516. The settlement comprised fifty-two houses of 106 apartments along with communal squares and a church. Inhabitants came and went through a gate making it a small community within the city of Augsburg. As a settlement for the deserving poor within the community, this meant that most inhabitants were the elderly, widows, the disabled, and orphans. Rent was extremely low, equivalent to the worth of the widow's mite in the Synoptic Gospels,[14] but residents were also expected to say three prayers a day (the Lord's Prayer, Hail Mary, and the Apostles' Creed) for Jakob Fugger and the Fugger family.[15] The existence of the

---

12 Georg Friedrich Hegel, trans. T.M. Knox, *The Philosophy of Right* (Oxford: Oxford University Press, 1967), 123–54.
13 Sebastian Schmidt, "The Economy of Love: Welfare and Poor Relief in Catholic Territories of the Holy Roman Empire (1500 to 1800)," *Poverty and Welfare in Modern German History*, ed. Lutz Raphael (New York: Berghahn Books, 2017), 23–7.
14 See Mark 12:41–44, Luke 21:1–4.
15 Martin Kluger, *The Fugger Dynasty: The German Medici in and around Augsburg: History and Places of Interest*, trans. Christa Herzer (Augsburg: Context Verlag, 2008).

deserving poor within society was accepted as a reality and little was done to prevent their existence as their management was maintained on a communal level.

By contrast, the undeserving poor were understood to be those individuals impoverished as a result of their own actions; in other words, those deemed capable of work who chose not to. This group was ineligible for any kind of relief, given that their condition was due to their own flawed nature—furthermore, it was believed that giving the undeserving poor relief would only encourage their behavior and lead to the belief that social relief was a right. Rather than supply financial aid, it was seen as the community's responsibility to institutionalize the undeserving poor in an attempt to reform their behavior and return them to proper conduct. These institutions, such as poorhouses or workhouses, were supposed to be so unappealing that they would incentivize the poor to avoid them at all costs.

The categorization between deserving and undeserving poor enabled a clear delineation between who was justified in receiving aid and who should be punished or reformed, helping to distinguish how and what kind of relief was to be administered. While the deserving poor were considered a natural occurrence, the undeserving poor were a source of significant concern to the upper and middle classes. It was generally held that the numbers of the undeserving poor should be kept at a minimum, and their treatment should be so harsh so as to dissuade other members of the lower classes from choosing a similar path. It was believed that the undeserving poor weakened the fabric of society and, if left unchecked, that their presence could fester like a disease. Yet as pauperism gripped European society the delineation between these groups became blurred and the traditional approaches to managing poverty no longer proved effective. Paupers also became synonymous with the term *die Eigentumlosen*, people without possessions.[16] This characteristic feature also indicated their potential for disrupting the social order. Being a people without possessions, the poverty-stricken had nothing to lose by rising up and demanding better conditions or, worse, leading the nation into a revolution. To stave off disaster the other groups in society responded by constructing ways to manage the developing Social Question.

---

16 Carl Jantke and Dietrich Hilger, *Die Eigentumslosen. Der deutsche Pauperismus und die Emanzipationskrise in Darstellungen und Deutungen der zeitgenössischen Literatur* (Munich: Karl Alber Verlag, 1965), 256–65.

Historical Context of the Elberfeld System

Elberfeld's history during the early years of industrialization played an important role in the development of the poor relief system that bore the city's name. By the late eighteenth century, Elberfeld's place in the Wupper valley in the Rhineland region experienced an economic boom, thanks to a thriving textile industry specializing in the dyeing of fabric, where new demands on land and resources grew significantly.[17] There was also significant population growth as factory jobs drew workers to the city. Estimates place Elberfeld's population around 50,000 by the 1850s and it was evident that the Wupper valley was a place of significant urban character and a noticeably stratified class structure.[18] As industrialization flourished, however, so too did this new form of poverty, influenced by the inherent instability of wage labor. This rapid increase and changing nature of poverty did not go unnoticed to the city's inhabitants. As early as 1788 the regional weekly newspaper, *Bergische Magazin,* was one of the first to consider the new social problem as it sought to locate the source of this new type of "misery." The publication's contributors emphasized the practices of waste and carelessness as the root causes of the poor's condition.[19] As the discussion continued, however, there seemed to be a greater awareness that this new type of poverty was related to the unequal accumulation of wealth in the hands of the bourgeoisie and that if something was not done then the poor's condition would continue to deteriorate.[20]

One of the most important transformations for the Rhineland writ large, and Elberfeld in particular, was its experience in relation to the French Revolution and its status as an occupied territory during the early years of the nineteenth century. The French presence brought to end the last remnants of the feudal relationships that still existed,

---

17 Wilhelm Langewiesche, *Beschreibung und Geschichte dieser Doppelstadt des Wupperthals nebst besonderer Darstellung ihrer Industrie, einem Überblick der Bergischen Landesgeschichte* .... (Barmen: W. Langewiesche, 1863), 243–4. J.F. Knapp, *Geschichte, Statistik und Topographie der Städte Elberfeld und Barmen im Wupperthale: Mit Bezugnahme auf die Stadt Solingen und einige Städte des Kreises Lennep* (Iserlohn and Barmen: Wilh. Langewiesche, 1835), 187, 197–8. Vincent Paul Sonderland, *Die Geschichte von Barmen im Wupperthale* (Eberfeld: Büschler, 1821), 117–18, 120–1.

18 Herbert Kisch, *From Domestic Manufacture to Industrial Revolution: The Case of the Rhineland Textile Districts* (Oxford: Oxford University Press, 1989), 137–8.

19 *Bergisches Magazin*, IX. Stück, 1. Nov. 1788, S. 68. *Bergisches Magazin*, X. Stück, 5. Nov 1788, S. 73. As cited in Barbara Lube, "Mythos und Wirklichkeit des Elberfelder Systems," in *Gründerzeit: Versuch einer Grenzbestimmung in Wuppertal*, ed. Karl-Hermann Beeck (Cologne: Rheinland-Verlag, 1984), 158–9.

20 *Bergisches Magazin*, XXXVI. Stück, May 9, 1789, 283. As cited in Lube, "Mythos und Wirklichkeit des Elberfelder Systems," 159.

destroyed the required payments of tithes, broke up monastic lands, and spread ideas of liberty and equality.[21] The Rhineland's relationship to its French occupiers and the larger motivations of the French Revolution were paramount for future political, economic, and social developments. Friedrich Engels, a native of Elberfeld and the son of one of the city's most prominent manufacturers, argued that "the Rhineland was ahead of the remaining German lands, revolutionized by the French because of its industry, and ahead of the other German industrial districts (Saxony and Silesia) because of its French revolution."[22]

The sphere of poor relief was one of the areas radically transformed by French occupation. As new markets opened, sales expanded, employment skyrocketed, and wages increased as new entrepreneurs were drawn to the region. There was also an increased presence of a growing middle class in municipal government affairs, thanks in part to the spread of revolutionary principles. For example, the Prussian Municipal Ordinance of 1808 enabled urban self-government and instituted some liberal reforms by allowing property-owning males the right to vote and to have a say in civic administration. This included transferring the responsibility of poor relief from church hands to local officials, stating, "The entire care for the poor, then, will be entrusted to the hands of the citizenry, their sense of community, and the charity of the inhabitants of the city."[23] The Municipal Ordinance, aided by the pressures of revolutionary ideas, formally introduced the relationship between civic responsibility and poor relief. Poor relief, which had for centuries been dominated by religious principles and institutions, was transformed into a realm of political action, something which citizens could shape through direct participation. The citizens of Elberfeld now had the right, and obligation, to participate and craft a bourgeoisie sphere of poor relief organized under public supervision.

The shift to state-sponsored relief was short-lived, however, due to the pressures of the French Continental System and the stresses created

---

21 T.C.W. Blanning, *The French Revolution in Germany: Occupation and Resistance in the Rhineland, 1792–1802* (Oxford: Clarendon Press, 1983), 63–7.

22 Friedrich Engels, "Die deutsche Reichsverfassungskampagne," in *Marx-Engels-Werke*, vol. 7 (Berlin: Dietz, 1960), 117.

23 *Sammlung der für die Königlichen Preußischen Staaten erschienenen Gesetze und Verordnungen von 1806 bis zum 27sten Oktober 1810* (Berlin, 1822; (reprint. Bad Feilnbach, 1985), 324–7, 330–3, 342–50. *German History in Documents and Images*, German Historical Institute, Washington, DC. www.germanhistorydocs.ghi-dc.org.

by the wars to liberate Europe from Napoleonic control, wars which were then followed by a series of crises in 1816 that included an industrial depression, a poor harvest, and a smallpox outbreak. As a result of these varied hardships, Elberfeld residents began to notice an uptick in begging and demanded that civic authorities crack down on indiscriminate begging by enforcing the punishment of a three- to six-month prison sentence, particularly for those beggars in locales where public welfare measures were in place. Eventually citizens' willingness to donate to the public relief funds decreased to such a degree that, when met with rising expenditures for operation, the poor relief institutions in the city were forced to close. Yet the newly established relationship between citizen responsibility and poor relief did not weaken. The words "civic virtue" and "citizenship" had become important signifiers expressing "a new sense of self" reflecting "a new willingness to take responsibility" for poor relief and over time this relationship was "defended" and "expanded."[24]

Over the next half century, the city of Elberfeld would vacillate between church and public relief efforts for the poor. The church was reluctant to give civic authorities total control, first because they wished to keep a strong Christian connection in the giving of aid, and second because they benefited directly from the indiscriminate almsgiving from the city's wealthy. Elberfeld struggled through economic downturns in the 1820s and into the 1830s producing rising unemployment, high food prices, and increased taxes. Finally, in 1840, due to inadequate solutions to a growing problem, the church formally relinquished control of poor aid and a communal system of poor relief regulated by the municipal government was established the next year, in 1841; a system which would be an important precursor to the Elberfeld System's founding in 1853.[25] This reorganization would also prove fleeting due to inadequacies within its organizational method, insufficient funding, and the ever-increasing need for support among residents. The apparent inadequacies of the new system led to widespread critique; in 1848, an anonymously written article in the Elberfeld newspaper criticized the civic control of poor relief, claiming it had become "much more expensive" and urged a return to ecclesiastical hands.[26] Critics claimed that there were insufficient guardians to

---

24   Lube, "Mythos und Wirklichkeit des Elberfelder Systems," 160–1.
25   *Armenordnungen 1841–1849*, RII 51, Stadtarchiv Wuppertal.
26   "Brief der Witwe Budde an Oberbürgermeister von Carnap," in *Historische Texte aus dem Wupperthale: Quellen zur Sozialgeschichte des 19. Jahrhunderts* ed. Karl-Hermann Beeck and Tânia Ünlüdağ (Wuppertal: Born Verlag, 1989), 423.

effectively monitor the poor, and those who did serve largely neglected their duties, thereby causing the increase of both "pauperism" and civic "expenditure[s]."[27]

The Hamburg Example

The disappointment of the 1841 reorganization efforts signaled an important moment in the trajectory of civic based poor relief for the city of Elberfeld. While it was widely recognized that there was both a need for more poor relief, given the continued increase in numbers and demand, and a desire amongst the city's middle- and upper-class residents to aid in this process, the search for a more ideologically and structurally effective framework continued. A suitable framework would come from a set of reforms begun in the commercial center of Hamburg in the late eighteenth century. These reforms were largely the work of Johann Georg Büsch, who sought to respond to the economic and social challenges created when laissez-faire practices turned Hamburg into a "beggars' metropolis."[28] He believed that poor relief needed to be redirected away from almsgiving and indiscriminate relief into a more well-organized structure that put those in need to work. This was not to be a private endeavor but a greater communal responsibility.

For Hamburg's reorganization efforts, Büsch posited several important features that would be heavily influential for the Elberfeld System. Büsch's first reform vision supported the idea that poor relief should be a civic obligation taken on specifically by those of the middle class who had previously been left out of civic responsibility but were now able to take part in shaping local government, further demonstrating the Enlightenment's impact on civic policy through the blending of civic engagement, individualism, and republican political ideals. Serving as a poor guardian was a natural first step on the civic career ladder, one which would ideally foster a sense of civic pride and deeper commitment of those involved to republican institutions. Elberfeld would adopt this by recruiting the vast majority of its poor guardians from this social class.

---

27 Local Government Report, *First Annual Report* (1871–1872), "The Poor Law System of Elberfeld," report by Andrew Doyle, Esq., 1872, in British Parliamentary Papers, C. 516, Parliamentary Archives, London, iii–iv.
28 Johann Georg Büsch, "Allgemeine Winke zur Verbesserung des Armenwesens," *Zwei kleine Schriften* (1786), n.p.; Mary Lindemann, *Patriots and Paupers: Hamburg 1712–1830* (Oxford: Oxford University Press, 1990), 96.

Second, Büsch believed that, in order to solve its underlying causes rather than treat its symptoms, poor relief needed to be individualized. He advocated for the role of *Armenpfleger*, or poor guardian, to oversee and know the personal situation of the poor in order to adequately treat their condition. He also advocated for the division of the city's population into districts, believing it was the best way to manage the large numbers of a city's inhabitants. According to Büsch, "larger cities fostered anonymity ... Lack of knowledge, lack of oversight, and lack of contact were the greatest obstacles to a good poor relief."[29] The idea of individualized and regionalized poor relief would prove the most influential to the Elberfeld System and to those systems which Elberfeld would inspire.

Büsch believed that investment in a more efficient poor relief system by individuals dedicating their time, knowledge, and especially resources was the best way to ensure poverty was dealt with properly. This conviction led to Büsch's third axiom of poor relief; he was vehemently opposed to the idea of imposing a poor tax on the city's citizens, arguing that it fundamentally separated citizen accountability to the system and allowed individuals to be blissfully ignorant of what was going on. Furthermore, Büsch feared that a poor tax would provide the middle and upper classes with a false sense of satisfying their civic duties to the poor, convincing them that nothing else needed to be done when taxes were "solving the problem." By contrast, if individuals were personally invested in the system's daily performance and overall outcome, it would be impossible to complacently criticize the ineffectiveness of the local government. Instead they would know the challenges of poor aid firsthand, prompting them to seek practical solutions. This notion of civic responsibility had already been introduced within Elberfeld thanks to earlier French occupation and so its leaders in the late 1840s were ready to resume the connection between poor relief and responsibilities of citizenship.

The final feature of Büsch's reforms that were influential for Elberfeld's later plans dealt with building rapport between the impoverished and the larger community. Büsch argued that it was more effective to achieve and maintain trust with the poor rather than to create a relationship based on discipline and punishment. The workhouse, for example, damaged the possibility of trust because it lumped all types of the impoverished together, no matter the causes of that poverty, and further made it nearly impossible to determine what those causes had been. By contrast, individualized poor relief and participation by citizens as poor guardians would build this essential trust between pauper

---

29 Lindemann, *Patriots and Paupers*, 114.

and caretaker, and "the aid afforded him would be more effective, the advice more pertinent, and the disciplining and educational means more opportune."[30]

The Structure of the Elberfeld System

The official reorganization of Elberfeld's poor relief plan took effect in 1853, thanks to the work of three bourgeois industrialists and bankers, Daniel von der Heydt, Gustav Schlieper, and David Peters. The specifics of the system were laid out in the *Armenordnung*, or General Poor Law, in July 1852, which enabled the establishment of a formal Poor Law Administration, the *Städtische Armenverwaltung*. This body included a president, four members of the town council, and four typically wealthy and distinguished citizens. The four citizens were appointed to their positions for three years and would retire by rotation, always leaving at least three citizen members with extensive knowledge and experience of how the system worked. Below the *Armenverwaltung* was the backbone of the Elberfeld System, the *Armenvorsteher* or *Bezirksvorsteher*, district overseers, and *Armenpfleger*, poor guardians. These positions were unpaid but compulsory for citizens of Elberfeld. Every male citizen who was eligible to vote [*stimmfähig*] was required to serve as a guardian or overseer.[31] If an individual refused to serve, they thereby forfeited their right to vote in municipal affairs for three to six years and paid a higher rate in taxes, although there were several valid excuses that would exempt some citizens, such as ill health, affairs that would require long or frequent absence from the city, being over the age of sixty, or holding another public office.[32] This compulsory feature was not new or unique to the Elberfeld System. Most German towns required their citizens to work in the service of poor relief. What was unique to the Elberfeld System was its emphasis on individualized relationships with the poor, a change which significantly intensified the demands placed on citizen workers while also increasing the power they had over determining the condition of poverty.[33] Additionally, by connecting citizenship as the prerequisite to serving as a poor guardian, this overwhelmingly

---

30 Johann Georg Büsch, "Vorschläge zur Verbesserung des Hamburgischen Armenwesens 1786," cited in Lindemann, 115.

31 *Neue Armenordnung für die Gemeinde Elberfeld, beschlossen in der Gemeinderaths Sitzung vom 9 Juli 1852*, Landesarchiv Nordrhein-Westfalen.

32 W. Walter Edwards, *The Poor Law Experiment at Elberfeld*, 679.

33 E.P. Hennock, *The Origin of the Welfare State in England and Germany, 1850–1914: Social Policies Compared* (Cambridge: Cambridge University Press, 2007), 54.

precluded the poor themselves from serving in this role. This meant that service as a guardian was imbued with much more than just a qualifier of voting, it meant that service was for those who held a social status higher than the poor and within that social status the ability to judge the actions of those who were in need.

The compulsory component of the German poor relief system made it a responsibility of citizenship, and therefore viewed by those individuals as a great honor. Supporters of the Elberfeld System argued that this was reflected in the continued service of its citizens even after they had served their required three-year terms. For example, in 1898 there were over eighty-six individuals listed as having served over twenty-five years or more as a poor visitor. By 1903, the fiftieth anniversary of the system, the number had increased to 110.[34] The continued years of dedication of those serving twenty-five or fifty years was testament, according to its admirers, to how the System benefited not just the impoverished but also its more well-to-do citizens. For champions of the System, it was the experience as guardians that instilled within them an understanding of civic responsibility and reflected the Elberfeld System's key philosophy that it took constant individualized knowledge of the poor's condition to effectively reduce its presence within a community. In 1898, the president of the poor administration, Ewald Aders, quipped to a group of visitors: "In order to find out how the Poor Law administration is looked upon in Elberfeld, you have only to ask a citizen if he is a visitor; he will answer either that he is, or that he has been, or he will blush with the consciousness that he has not had that honor conferred upon him."[35]

The appointment process of poor guardians was one marked by a uniquely "liberal spirit" in which a citizen's religion or politics did not weigh in their ability to serve. The only factor was a willingness to perform the role believed to be in possession by all of Elberfeld's citizens, meaning those who fit the socioeconomic qualifier of voting.[36] The body of poor guardians came from Elberfeld's professional business

---

34 *Städtische Armenverwaltung Elberfeld: Jahres-Bericht für das Rechnungsjahr 1888–89.* W. Grisewood and A.F. Hanewinkel, *Jubilee Celebrations of the Elberfeld Poor Law* (1903), 6.

35 W. Grisewood and A.F. Hanewinkel, *The Elberfeld System of Poor Law Relief* (Liverpool: D. Marples & Co, 1898), 10.

36 *Städtische Armenverwaltung nach Einführung des Elberfelder Systems: Liste von Personen, die von der städtischen Armenverwaltung zu Elberfeld für das Amt eines Armenpflegers vorgeschlagen wurden und ein Bericht über die Tätigkeit des Elberfelder Frauenvereins innerhalb der Armenpflege.* March 7, 1884, RII 101, Stadtarchiv Wuppertal.

classes, white-collar workers, and master craftsmen. The neighboring town of Barmen in 1870 made a list of its poor guardians that included their occupations. The most prevalent occupation was that of merchant [*Kaufmann*], followed by carpenter [*Schreiner*], teacher [*Lehrer*], and ribbon weaver [*Bandwirker*].[37] The reliance on recruiting guardians from these professional classes continued as the Elberfeld System spread beyond the Rhine region. In 1903, Dresden, which had adopted the System in 1880, had 795 poor relief officials, of which 25 percent came from artisans and tradesmen, another 20 percent from commercial occupations, and 8 percent from industrial entrepreneurs and manufactures. The diversity of occupational backgrounds held by guardians demonstrates the allure that this position afforded to those who could use the position as a reflection of their social superiority and power over the poor.[38]

The Petitioners

Within the Elberfeld System's organization, any person who found themselves destitute or without work had the right to apply for relief. Their income had to be less than what could suffice for the "absolute necessaries of life" [*das unabweislich Notwendige*]. This designation was determined per family based on the cost of living related to family size, wages, as well as housing, food, and clothing costs.[39] Requests for relief were made directly to the assigned district guardian and in turn the guardian was required "at once [to] inquire personally and carefully into the circumstances of the case."[40] This investigation was to be one in which the guardian probed the character of the petitioner [*Hülfesuchenden*]. It was described as "an examination so close and searching, so absolutely inquisitorial, that no man who could possibly escape from it

---

37 *Verzeichnis des Personals der städtischen Armenverwaltung, Einteilung der offenen Armenpflege in 22 Bezirke und 264 Quartiere und örtliche Begrenzung derselben; Angabe der Armenärzte und deren Distrikte sowie Bezeichnung der Bezirksversammlungslokale* 1870, RII 8, Stadtarchiv Wuppertal.

38 Wolfgang Hofmann, "Aufgaben und Struktur der kommunalen Selbstverwaltung in der Zeit der Hochindustrialisierung," in *Deutsche Verwaltungsgeschichte*, vol. 3, ed. Kurt G.A. Jeserich, Hans Pohl and Georg-Christoph von Unruth (Stuttgart: Deutsche Verlags-Anstalt, 1984), 618.

39 *Städtische Armenverwaltung. Elberfeld. Instruction für die Bezirksvorsteher und Armenpfleger* vom 4 Januar 1861, cit. in Böhmert, *Das Armenwesen in 77 deutschen Städten*, 73.

40 A. Lammers, "The Town of Elberfeld," in *Das Armenwesen und die Armengesetzgebung in Europäischen Staaten*, ed. A. Emminghaus (Berlin: Herbig, 1870), 98–9.

would submit to it."[41] Questions included basic biographical information: name, age, place of birth, how long they had lived in Elberfeld,
and if they had lived somewhere else and for how long (important for
the settlement/residency qualification), if they were married, had any
children and how many, and if these children were of school or working
age. The physical health of the petitioner and his family was recorded
along with whether he and his family members were living a "moral
and honest life," a designation left to the guardian to determine.[42]
In order for a person seeking aid to receive help, it was necessary to
prove that he could not exist without it. This required the guardian to
determine not only the condition of the poor but also to ascertain the
presumed causes of this poverty. In a description of this investigation
it was noted that it was "not a merely nominal or superficial inquiry
in which the applicant has no difficulty in palming off some plausible
story of distress and the cause of it, but is what it professes to be, a
strict investigation into the circumstances of the man's life and present
position."[43]

Once the guardian determined that a petitioner was indeed worthy of relief, an evaluation which was, again, at the sole discretion of
the poor guardian, the petitioner's case was brought to the next district meeting where the guardians would share their findings. Cases
were decided on a simple majority vote by the district guardians and
the overseer. Relief, especially that of money or food, was given on a
week-by-week basis in Elberfeld. If petitioners received material goods
such as furniture or clothing, the guardian was required to check from
time to time to ensure the pauper had not pawned the items for cash.
What this clearly indicates is that the Elberfeld System operated under
the assumption that the poor could not be implicitly trusted and that
their condition could cause them to slip into the practices of pauperism
at any moment. Any changes, however minor, in the condition of the
application were to be noted by guardians and the poor were considered to be under "constant surveillance."[44]

Petitioners were encouraged to find work within the region's textile
industry. If there was no work to be had, which was noted to be rare,
then the city would provide employment.[45] If there were a large number of unemployed petitioning for relief, the city would create a public

41 Doyle, "The Poor Law System of Elberfeld," xv.
42 Doyle, "The Poor Law System of Elberfeld," xvi.
43 Instruction für die Bezirksvorsteher und Armenpfleger, cit. in Böhmert, Das Armen-
    wesen in 77 deutschen Städten, 73.
44 Doyle, "The Poor Law System of Elberfeld," xvi–xvii.
45 Doyle, "The Poor Law System of Elberfeld," xvii.

work project, usually in the form of the improvement of a road or bridge. The wages of all relief recipients were tracked in a wages book [*Verdienstbuch*] which required their employer to record their daily earnings and notify their guardian of any instances of idleness or poor conduct. These records were reviewed by the poor guardian and could be grounds for their removal from receiving aid if their actions were deemed undeserving.[46] Additionally, if the recipient's actions were considered undeserving, if they pawned their relief items for cash, or if they suffered from pauperism as a result of idleness or drunkenness, their guardians would report these actions to the municipal police. There were strict consequences for this type of behavior, the minimum of which was a loss of relief from the poor administration, while the maximum penalty was one-month imprisonment.[47]

Implementation and Adoption

When the city's leaders put forth the plan detailing the radical restructuring of their poor relief plan in 1852, the response from Elberfeld's bourgeoisie was overwhelming skeptical. While there was widespread agreement that reform was necessary, the proposed plan was characterized as "utopian" and "impracticable."[48] However, these hesitations evaporated following the success of the System's implementation using the new criteria and investigative process. The success was "proven" by newly implemented statistical models. In fact, these statistical figures became the most influential measure to evaluate the effectiveness of the System. It was on the basis of statistical analysis showing decreasing costs to the city as well as the numbers of those labeled paupers which facilitated the System's spread to other German cities. Given that the number of paupers, on the whole, steadily decreased in the time since the System's application, this was seen as testament to the fact that the methods and administration of the Elberfeld System worked and were therefore worthy of emulation. The reduction of expenditures was of particular appeal, since one of the problems of the old system was so-called indiscriminate giving and therefore uncontrollable costs. As is seen in Table 1, there was a significant reduction in the numbers of those requesting aid in the first year of application. By the mid-1860s the proportion of the population requesting relief remained steady at about 2 percent.

---

46 Böhmert, *Das Armenwesen in 77 deutschen Städten*, 49–70.
47 Doyle, "The Poor Law System of Elberfeld," xvii–xviii.
48 Doyle, "The Poor Law System of Elberfeld," xviii.

Table 5.1 Average Number of Paupers in Elberfeld and Expenditures[49]

Year	Population	Number of Paupers	Expenditure (Thalers)
1852	50,364	4000	59,548
1853* New System adopted	50,418	1460	25,606
1866	64,963	1370	24,842
1867	65,321	1496	27,182
1868	67,000	1408	25,559
1869	71,000	1062	25,739

To give these statistics their proper context, a degree of interpretation is required. First, it is important to remember that these numbers reflect only those individuals actively requesting aid, and second, only those individuals who qualified as "worthy" under the new classification system. This meant that many individuals who were in need may not fit the new classification and would not be eligible under the Elberfeld System. Therefore, the numbers do not account for actual conditions of the poor yet they were used as a tangible selling point for the System. The tactic of using statistical modeling as proof for the effectiveness of a program by showing its reducing numbers remains a common practice for welfare states today, omitting the outliers that fail to fit the narrative of success or failure. Another important interpretation comes when looking at the relationship between the number of paupers in relation to the expenditures. If one assumes the number aided drops to the same degree as the number of those classified as poor, then the cost per person aided would actually represent an increase from the previous model. For example, in 1852 the individual cost per recipient was at about 15 thalers. Between 1866 and 1868 the individual cost remained about 18 thalers but it jumped to 24 thalers in 1869. This is surprising as it would seem reducing the individual expenditures would be a great

---

49 *Städtische Armenverwaltung nach Einführung des Elberfelder Systems: Städtische Armenverwaltung in Elberfeld. Drei Quartal-Berichte (umfassend die Monate Januar-September) des Jahres 1853*, RII 96, Stadtarchiv Wuppertal; *Städtische Armenverwaltung nach Einführung des Elberfelder Systems: Städtische Armenverwaltung Elberfeld. Verhandlungen der Hauptversammlungen der Städtischen Armenverwaltung Januar 14, 1867–Januar 30, 1868 mit den Jahresberichten für 1866 und 1867*, RII 99, Stadtarchiv Wuppertal, and Doyle, "The Poor Law System of Elberfeld," xxi–xxii.

selling point of the System. Rather what these numbers indicate is that it was less about individual costs and more that the recipients had been proven worthy of relief under the careful investigative process central to the Elberfeld System. While numbers can be helpful for general observations, they only tell one part of the overall story.

From 1853 to 1914, most German cities adopted the Elberfeld System as their poor relief management plan. Out of two hundred major German cities, only thirty had not adopted the Elberfeld System and its organization principles in some way or another by the outbreak of the First World War. Leading German social reformer Emil Münsterberg emphasized this development when speaking at the fiftieth anniversary celebration of the System, claiming that there was "no greater" poor relief system within Germany and that no large German city had either not introduced its principles or "at least approached the question of its introduction."[50] The penetration of the Elberfeld System is all the more remarkable as it occurred within highly regional relief systems governed at the state level. Despite states' autonomy, it was the effective strategy, careful resource use, and diligent supervision of the poor that prompted many cities to accept the program. The Elberfeld System "was so successful that relief officials and social reformers came to see it as the embodiment of the very idea of rational, yet compassionate, assistance, and reformers would often debate whether the reorganization of relief in a specific city truly embodied the principles of the Elberfeld System."[51]

Forms of Resistance

While much focus in this work has been given to the inception and structure of the Elberfeld System, as well as the reasons for why upper- and middle-class individuals were drawn to the System, little has been said regarding how the poor themselves responded to these new approaches and the inquisition into their lives. This gap is true for any narrative on the history of poverty and welfare, as it deals with those outside the realms of power who leave little record of their experiences. Given that the Elberfeld System operated as a function of the state, it made it difficult for the poor to find ways to easily resist or show their discontentment. The System intentionally kept them outside the means to define poverty for themselves. Additionally, it relegated the poor into

---

50 Emil Münsterberg, *Das Elberfelder System* (Leipzig: Dunker and Humbolt, 1903), 44.

51 Larry Frohman, *Poor Relief and Welfare in Germany from the Reformation to World War I* (New York: Cambridge University Press, 2008), 96.

Table 5.2 Adoption of the Elberfeld Poor Relief System in Various Towns, 1853–1911[52]

Year	City	Year	City
1853	Elberfeld	1880	Leipzig, Dresden, Mühlheim
1862–3	Barmen, Krefeld, Duisburg, Halberstadt	1881	Kassel, Rostock, Bremerhaven
1864	Essen	1882	Magdeburg, Potsdam, Stralsund
1865	Altona	1883	Frankfurt, Fulda, Zwickau
1867	Ruhrort	1884	Gotha, Halle
1868	Hagen	1885	Posen, Greifswald
1870	Neuwied	1888	Cologne
1871	Kiel	1889	Aachen, Bielefeld
1874	Dortmund	1893	Hamburg, Erfurth
1875	Elbing, Stuttgart, Bremen	1895	Mainz, Münster, Breslau
1876	Siegen, Darmstadt	1898	Mannheim, Danzig
1877	Düsseldorf, Oldenburg, Naumburg	1911	Lübeck
1878	Königsberg, Landsberg, Hanau		

fitting a definition of poverty defined by their overseers who used the values attributed to their socioeconomic position as a tool of power.

The most obvious way for the poor to demonstrate their agency was through supporting working-class associations and socialist political parties, which experienced a steady growth in Germany during the latter half of the nineteenth century. This support, however, often did not immediately change the day-to-day reality of those in poverty, particularly those under the exacting investigation and constant oversight of the Elberfeld System. Within this system, the only direct avenue of response for the poor was to lodge formal complaints with the municipal government or poor law authorities if they believed their guardian had not properly evaluated their claims for relief. One such claim, made by Herr Pütz, asserted that the investigations to determine his eligibility for relief were carried out incorrectly, and were inadequate in their

---

52 George Steinmetz, *Regulating the Social: The Welfare State and Local Politics in Imperial Germany* (Princeton, NJ: Princeton University Press, 1993), 97. Frohman, *Poor Relief and Welfare in Germany*, 159.

investigation of his poverty and relied on information from people Pütz claimed were his enemies. This complaint was made to the *Regierungspräsident* in Düsseldorf, after Pütz's initial claim had been rejected by both the Poor Law Administration and the mayor of Elberfeld. The bureaucratic slog and paper trail required to lodge a complaint disproportionately damaged the petitioner. The wronged party not only had to have the time and effort to lodge such a complaint, which required the petitioner supplementing additional documentation but also to face an uncertain amount of time before another formal decision was made. Pütz sent his initial request in September 1915, but by December the situation had still not been resolved, leaving him without aid for an extended period of time.[53]

While the outcome of complaints like that of Herr Pütz was not recorded, it can be assumed that more often than not the complaints were dismissed, presumably on the grounds of either insufficient evidence or the higher authority choosing to support a local authority's decision. Additionally, a constant questioning of a poor guardian's decisions would not have incurred good will on the part of the citizen-volunteers who fulfilled these roles. Had their judgment been constantly questioned, it might have encouraged them to refuse to serve or undermine the whole System's structure. Even as the Elberfeld System, and other localized relief methods, underwent a process of professionalization in the early twentieth century, the knowledge and training of the of social workers engendered an expertise that would not be easily overlooked. This encouraged higher civic authorities to defer to their decisions.

Legacy of the Elberfeld System

The Elberfeld System leaves a multifaceted legacy within Germany as well as in the formation of modern welfare states. As the System spread throughout Germany in the late nineteenth century, it also garnered the attention of British and American social reformers who used its guiding principles as the basis for the expansive private relief association known as the Charity Organization Society. This organization became the bedrock for responding to social perceptions around poverty and asserting solutions to tackle the same challenges British and American reformers saw plaguing their societies just as prevalent in Germany. Through the ubiquity of this organization, the Elberfeld System and its organizing

---

53 BR 0007 Nr. 43028: *Armenverwaltung Elberfeld 1910–1926*, 305–6, Landesarchiv Nordrhein-Westfalen.

principles had a profound impact on centralized poor relief efforts in the twentieth century, namely the rise of professionalized social work as a function of the state, one which broke localities into manageable districts, assigned professional social workers a set number of cases to investigate, and used their analyses to determine the worthiness of the petitioner. The rise of professionalized social work took the place of the volunteer *Armenpfleger*. However, the concerns over delineating between the deserving and undeserving poor as well as the values and judgment placed over the poor dictated by those middle- and upper-class poor guardians did not disappear. Rather, they were incorporated into the framework of state-based professionalized social work.

Even within welfare state functions today, there remains a constant fear over the threat of the undeserving poor receiving help. Their perceived presence within society is used as a justification to scale back or eliminate aid to the impoverished. The threat of the undeserving poor receiving help is central to American views of poverty and the American welfare state, if its minimal programs could be qualified as such. Stereotypes of welfare queens, made famous in 1974 by the Cadillac-driving and identity-shifting Linda Taylor, pervade the minds of those who view the welfare state as being rife with fraud and corruption.[54] Taylor was accused of carrying out the greatest case of welfare fraud, swindling over $150,000 in taxpayer funds from welfare programs in one year. Not only was this an exaggeration of her fraudulent welfare crimes (estimated to be approximately $40,000 over many years), the pernicious stereotype of the dishonest, scheming, and self-enriching welfare recipient became a central message in Ronald Reagan's 1976 presidential campaign and an issue he would continue to raise throughout his two terms in office. This stereotype became the justification for the belief that poor relief programs bring far more damage than relief. For Reagan, and those who have continued to hold this position, it was the lack of oversight and investigation into the lives of someone like Linda Taylor that enabled the fraud to take place. The means-tested features of contemporary welfare programs were not enough to prevent Taylor from swindling funds. Therefore, the programs themselves must be eliminated, as they seemed to breed corruption.

Likewise, the accusation launched against Taylor for being undeserving came, in part, from her proximity to items deemed "luxurious." A long-held idea about poverty is that the impoverished are precluded from possessing or enjoying any niceties of life, as if all they can request

---

54 Josh Levin, *The Queen: The Forgotten Life behind an American Myth* (New York: Little, Brown and Company, 2019).

are the bare necessities to live and nothing beyond. Possessing any conveniences, according to this logic, indicates the undeserving condition of the petitioner. For example, under the Elberfeld System, if a member of the petitioner's family was buried using public funds and the family followed the poor-house hearse in a coach, then it is believed that it "prove[s] that the relations of the deceased were able to spend money, and prove that they had obtained the use of hearse under false pretenses."[55] The poor are viewed with an air of continual suspicion, almost as a form of punishment for being poor and in need of aid.

Additionally, the behavior of those seeking relief is continuously examined and evaluated to determine their worthiness. Similarly to their nineteenth-century counterparts, critics of the welfare state today claim that the poor have fallen into their position as a result of poor life choices, rarely recognizing the place that unfettered capitalistic practices hold in creating this condition. Any relief that is provided should be kept to an extreme minimum so as to not encourage a dependence upon public relief efforts. These same fears held today just as they were in the nineteenth century are the basis for means-tested programs, central to current welfare state operations. Individuals must prove certain qualifiers, based upon a formula to determine worthiness, to receive help and then continuously open their lives to investigation to guarantee additional help. This is seen, for example, in Germany's unemployment program, Hartz IV, which was created in 2005 under the motivation to narrow who could claim welfare benefits. Hartz IV operates under the agreement that individuals who qualify for assistance must meet regularly with a job center advisor, prove they are looking for work, or join a job skills training program. If an applicant refuses to do so, their payments can be "sanctioned," meaning withheld or limited until they resume these activities; the rules are even more complex for individuals under the age of thirty-five. This determination is largely made at the discretion of the advisor but is supposed to operate as a form of pressure to keep the unemployed from relying too much on benefits. However, a recent study by the organization *Sanktionsfrei* argues that this tactic does more harm than good, specifically in its psychological impact, in helping to remove those in need from welfare rolls.[56] There is, however, an added dimension to the critiques of Hartz IV, coming largely from groups on the German political right, such as *Alternative für Deutschland*. Germany has, for well over several decades, been a place that many refugees and asylum seekers have sought out due to

---

55 Doyle, "The Poor Law System of Elberfeld," xvi–xvii.
56 Ben Knight, "Germany's Welfare Experiment: Sanction-free 'basic security,'" *Deutsche Welle*, December 8, 2018. https://p.dw.com/p/39eZh.

its social and economic stability. Opponents to this practice claim that Germany has turned into a migrant's welfare oasis, causing a host of unintended issues, including rising costs and abusing programs, given that German law allows for asylum seekers to claim welfare benefits. The rising cost enables welfare state critics to couch their resistance to the programs not on their worthiness but rather that funds are being used to aid non-Germans, and in turn that their status makes them undeserving of such relief.[57] This argument, too, ignores true conditions of need for those who are impoverished, and puts that designation into the hands of those outside of poverty.

Another example of means-tested programs, coming from the American context, is through the proving of work requirements to justify providing health insurance benefits through Medicaid. In June 2018, Arkansas became the first US state to require beneficiaries to prove their number of hours worked to continue receiving benefits. The initiative targeted "nondisabled, working-age, low-income adults" who are individuals believed to be, by welfare critics, the most prone to be undeserving of relief since they are able to work and may choose not to.[58] Beneficiaries lose access to health care, including prescription drugs, if they do not report their working hours. Always cushioned in a rhetoric that emphasizes helping the poor, Arkansas Governor Asa Hutchinson claimed, "This is not about punishing anyone … It's to help them to move out of poverty and up the economic ladder." By November 2018 over 12,000 people were removed from receiving benefits. Most of the stories that have emerged from those who lost coverage demonstrate that it is not from being unwilling to submit their working hours or from not working, but due to the poor implementation of the program, the inflexibility of the system, and the available reporting methods.[59] Arkansas is not alone in adding features to better "know" the poor in helping to determine the worthiness of receiving welfare benefits. Tennessee, Florida, Wisconsin, and Maine are just a few states that have, within the past several years, passed a drug-testing requirement to receive benefits from programs such as Supplemental Nutrition

---

57 "Germany: Welfare Payments to Foreigners Nearly Double over 12 Years," *Deutsche Welle*, December 27, 2019. https://p.dw.com/p/3VNnm.

58 Benjamin Hardy, "First, Get a Job: Arkansas's Medicaid Work Requirements Begin," *Arkansas Times*, June 14, 2018. https://arktimes.com/news/cover-stories/2018/06/14/first-get-a-job.

59 Benjamin Hardy, "Locked out of Medicaid: Arkansas's Work Requirement Strips Insurance from Thousands of Working People," *Arkansas Times*, November 19, 2018. https://arktimes.com/news/cover-stories/2018/11/19/locked-out-of-medicaid-2.

Assistance Program, Temporary Assistance for Needy Families, and Women, Infants and Children, all to determine the worthiness of the poor. While these initiatives have proven to be either a waste of taxpayer money or created dire circumstances by removing people in need from health care and access to food, they garnered enough support to pass through state legislatures as a means of investigating the condition of the poor and make judgments on their status through those results.[60]

The Elberfeld System illuminates how those in power sought to respond to the changing nature of poverty in the late nineteenth century through municipal relief efforts. Ultimately, this chapter argues that those initiatives were fundamental in helping form modern welfare systems. In turn, many of those same ideas continued to influence the way poverty is understood today. While the exact structure and operation of the Elberfeld System has faded from the role of poor relief in today's welfare state operation, its legacy remains by allowing poverty to be defined by those who distribute and police aid rather than the poor themselves.

Works Cited

Armenordnungen 1841–1849, RII 51, Stadtarchiv Wuppertal.
Armenverwaltung Elberfeld 1910–1926. BR 0007 Nr. 43028 104–22; 305–6; 308–9; 311–12. Landesarchiv Nordrhein-Westfalen.
Armenordnung für die Stadt Elberfeld und Geschäftsordnung für die städtische Armenverwaltung daselbst vom 9. Juli 1852. Wiedergeprüft am 4. Januar 1861, am 21. November 1876 und am 2. Dezember 1890, Artikel 4, RII 90, Stadtarchiv Wuppertal.
Beeck, Karl-Hermann and Tânia Ünlüdağ, eds. *Historische Texte aus dem Wupperthale: Quellen zur Sozialgeschichte des 19. Jahrhunderts*. Wuppertal: Born Verlag, 1989.
Bergisches Magazin, IX. Stück, Nov. 1, 1788, p. 68.
Bergisches Magazin, X. Stück, Nov. 5, 1788, p. 73.
Bergisches Magazin, XXXVI. Stück, May 9, 1789, p. 283.
Blanning, T.C.W. *The French Revolution in Germany: Occupation and Resistance in the Rhineland, 1792–1802*. New York: Clarendon Press, 1983.
Böhmert, Victor. *Das Armenwesen in 77 deutschen Städten*. Dresden: Selbstverlag des armenstatistischen Bureaus des Deutschen Vereins für Armenpflege und Wohltätigkeit, 1886.
Bülau, Friedrich, *Der Staat und die Industrie. Beiträge zur Gewerbspolitik und Armenpolizei*. Leipzig: Göschen, 1834.

---

60 Darlena Cunha, "Why Drug Testing Welfare Recipients is a Waste of Taxpayer Money," *Time Magazine*, August 15, 2014). http://time.com/3117361/welfare-recipients-drug-testing/.

Büsch, Johann Georg. "Allgemeine Winke zur Verbesserung des Armenwesens." *Zwei kleine Schriften*. 1786: n.p.

Conze, Werner. "Vom 'Pöbel' zum 'Proletariat': Sozialgeschichtliche Voraussetzungen für den Sozialismus in Deutschland." *Vierteljahrsschrift für Sozial- und Wirtschaftsgeschichte* 41, no. 4 (1954): 333–64.

Cunha, Darlena. "Why Drug Testing Welfare Recipients Is a Waste of Taxpayer Money." *Time Magazine*, August 15, 2014. http://time.com/3117361/welfare-recipients-drug-testing/.

"Die Armenpflege—eine praktische Lösung der sozialen Frage." *Armendirektorium/ Magistrat der Stadt Berlin, Armendirektion: Konferenzen deutscher Armenpflege 1879–1883*. A Rep 003-01. Nr. 634, 41–5. Landesarchiv Berlin.

Die Armuth und die Mittel ihr entgegen zu wirken. Leipzig: Otto Wigand, 1844

Doyle, Andrew. "The Poor Law System of Elberfeld." Local Government Report, *First Annual Report* (1871–1872). British Parliamentary Papers, 1872 [C. 516].

Edwards, Walter W. "Poor Law Experiment at Elberfeld." *Contemporary Review* 52 (1878): 675–93.

Emminghaus, A., ed. *Das Armenwesen und die Armengesetzgebung in europäischen Staaten*. Berlin: Herbig, 1870.

Engels, Friedrich. "Die deutsche Reichsverfassungskampagne." In *Marx-Engels-Werke*, vol. 7, 9–107. Berlin: Dietz, 1960.

Fischer, Wolfram, Jochen Krengel, and Jutta Wietog, eds. *Sozialgeschichtliches Arbeitsbuch, Band 1: Materialien zur Statistik des deutschen Bundes 1815–1870*. Munich: C. H. Beck, 1982.

Frohman, Larry. *Poor Relief and Welfare in Germany from the Reformation to World War I*. Cambridge: Cambridge University Press, 2008.

Grisewood, W. and A.F. Hanewinkel. *The Elberfeld System of Poor Law Relief*. Liverpool: D. Marples & Co., 1898.

Grisewood, W. and A.F. Hanewinkel. *Jubilee Celebrations of the Elberfeld Poor Law*, Liverpool: D. Marples & Co., 1903.

Hardy, Benjamin. "First, Get a Job: Arkansas's Medicaid Work Requirements Begin." *Arkansas Times*, June 14, 2018. https://arktimes.com/news/cover-stories/2018/06/14/first-get-a-job

Hardy, Benjamin. "Locked out of Medicaid: Arkansas's Work Requirement Strips Insurance from Thousands of Working People." *Arkansas Times*, November 19, 2018. https://arktimes.com/news/cover-stories/2018/11/19/locked-out-of-medicaid-2.

Hegel, Georg Friedrich. *The Philosophy of Right*. Translated by T.M. Knox. Oxford: Oxford University Press, 1967.

Hennock, E.P. *The Origin of the Welfare State in England and Germany, 1850–1914*. Cambridge: Cambridge University Press, 2007.

Hofmann, Wolfgang. "Aufgaben und Struktur der kommunalen Selbstverwaltung in der Zeit der Hochindustrialisierung." In *Deutsche Verwaltungsgeschichte*, vol. 3, edited by Kurt G.A. Jeserich, Hans Pohl, and Georg-Christoph von Unruth, 578–642. Stuttgart: Deutsche Verlags-Anstalt, 1984.

Jantke, Carl and Dietrich Hilger, eds. *Die Eigentumslosen: Der deutsche Pauperismus und die Emanzipationskrise in Darstellungen und Deutungen der zeitgenössischen Literatur*. Freiburg and Munich: Karl Alber Verlag, 1965.

Kisch, Herbert. *From Domestic Manufacture to Industrial Revolution: The Case of the Rhineland Textile Districts*. Oxford: Oxford University Press, 1989.

Kluger, Martin. *The Fugger Dynasty: The German Medici in and around Augsburg: History and Places of Interest*. Translated by Christa Herzer. Augsburg: Context Verlag, 2008.

Knapp, J.F. *Geschichte, Statistik und Topographie der Städte Elberfeld und Barmen im Wupperthale: Mit Bezugnahme auf die Stadt Solingen und einige Städte des Kreises Lennep*. Iserlohn/Barmen: Wilh. Langewiesche, 1835.

Knight, Ben. "Germany's Welfare Experiment: Sanction-free 'basic security.'" *Deutsche Welle*, December 8, 2018. https://p.dw.com/p/39eZh

Lammers, A. "The Town of Elberfeld." In *Das Armenwesen und die Armengesetzgebung in europäischen Staaten*, edited by A. Emminghaus, 89–98. Berlin: Herbig, 1870.

Langewiesche, Wilhelm. *Beschreibung und Geschichte dieser Doppelstadt des Wupperthals nebst besonderer Darstellung ihrer Industrie, einem Überblick der Bergischen Landesgeschichte ...* Iserlohn and Barmen: Wilh. Langewiesche, 1863.

Lees, Lynn Hollen, *The Solidarities of Strangers: The English Poor Laws and the People, 1700–1948*. Cambridge: Cambridge University Press, 1998.

Levin, Josh. *The Queen: The Forgotten Life behind an American Myth*. New York: Little, Brown and Company, 2019.

Lindemann, Mary. *Patriots and Paupers: Hamburg 1712–1830*. Oxford: Oxford University Press, 1990.

Lube, Barbara. "Mythos und Wirklichkeit des Elberfelder Systems." In *Gründerzeit: Versuch einer Grenzbestimmung in Wuppertal*, edited by Karl-Hermann Beeck, 158–84. Köln: Rheinland-Verlag, 1984.

Münsterberg, Emil. *Elberfelder System*. Berlin: Duncker & Humblot, 1903.

Neue Armenordnung für die Gemeinde Elberfeld, beschlossen in der Gemeinderaths-Sitzung vom 9 Juli 1852. Armenanstalt zu Elberfeld Bd. 6 1852–1865, 10. BR 0007 Nr. 1668. Landesarchiv Nordrhein-Westfalen.

"Pauperismus." In *Brockhaus' Conversations-Lexikon der Gegenwart*, vol. 4, ed. Carl August Espe. Leipzig: Brockhaus, 1840, 65–47.

Sammlung der für die Königlichen Preußischen Staaten erschienenen Gesetze und Verordnungen von 1806 bis zum 27sten Oktober 1810. Decker: Berlin, 1822.

Schmidt, Sebastian. "The Economy of Love: Welfare and Poor Relief in Catholic Territories of the Holy Roman Empire (1500 to 1800)." In *Poverty and Welfare in Modern German History*, edited by Lutz Raphael, 23–48. New York: Berghahn Books, 2017.

Städtische Armenverwaltung nach Einführung des Elberfelder Systems: Städtische Armenverwaltung in Elberfeld. Drei Quartal-Berichte (umfassend die Monate Januar–September) des Jahres 1853, RII 96, Stadtarchiv Wuppertal.

Städtische Armenverwaltung nach Einführung des Elberfelder Systems: Städtische Armenverwaltung in Elberfeld. Drei Quartal-Berichte (umfassend die Monate Januar–September) des Jahres 1853, RII 96, Stadtarchiv Wuppertal.

Städtische Armenverwaltung nach Einführung des Elberfelder Systems: Städtische Armenverwaltung Elberfeld. Verhandlungen der Hauptversammlungen der Städtischen Armenverwaltung Januar 14, 1867–Januar 30, 1868 mit den Jahresberichten für 1866 und 1867, RII 99, Stadtarchiv Wuppertal.

Städtische Armenverwaltung Elberfeld. Jahres-Bericht für das Rechnungsjahr 1888–89.

Städtische Armenverwaltung nach Einführung des Elberfelder Systems: Liste von Personen, die von der städtischen Armenverwaltung zu Elberfeld für das Amt eines Armenpflegers vorgeschlagen wurden und ein Bericht über die Tätigkeit des Elberfelder Frauenvereins innerhalb der Armenpflege. March 7, 1884, RII 101, Stadtarchiv Wuppertal.

Sonderland, Vincent Paul. *Die Geschichte von Barmen im Wupperthale.* Eberfeld: Büschler, 1821.

Steinmetz, George. *Regulating the Social: The Welfare State and Local Politics in Imperial Germany.* Princeton, NJ: Princeton University Press, 1993.

Verzeichnis des Personals der städtischen Armenverwaltung, Einteilung der offenen Armenpflege in 22 Bezirke und 264 Quartiere und örtliche Begrenzung derselben; Angabe der Armenärzte und deren Distrikte sowie Bezeichnung der Bezirksversammlungslokale, 1870, RII 8, Stadtarchiv Wuppertal.

Six Precarity and Form: Lu Märten's Intervention in the Worker's Autobiography

Mari Jarris

Writing in the Social Democratic women's journal *Die Gleichheit* [*Equality*] in 1912, Clara Zetkin reflects on a worker's play published three years earlier: "It offers a piece of proletarian reality that makes the hardship and ruin of the entire exploited class come alive within the fates of individuals, but also their rebirth into a pure, powerful humanity through their thinking and acting for others in preparation for the act of liberation."[1] The author of this celebrated one-act drama, *The Miners* (*Bergarbeiter*, 1909), was Lu Märten (1879–1970), a socialist author who would later become known for her contributions to the debates on Marxist aesthetics in the early 1920s. With this reception by Zetkin and other contemporaries within the Social Democratic Party (SPD), Märten's reputation as a "proletarian author" was sealed.

In the same year, Märten published her first novel, *Torso: The Book of a Child* [*Torso. Das Buch eines Kindes*, 1909], which was praised by critics as a worker's autobiography. *Torso* paid homage to this best-selling genre by telling the story of a proletarian girl's illness and displacement followed by her political radicalization.[2] Furthermore, it was based

I am grateful to the editors of this volume, in particular, to Sophie Duvernoy, for her careful editing of this chapter. I would also like to thank the Coalition of Women in German, the Fulbright Commission, and the German Academic Exchange Service (DAAD) for funding my archival research on Lu Märten at the International Institute of Social History in Amsterdam.

1   All translations are mine. Clara Zetkin, "Ein Arbeiterdrama," in *Die Gleichheit*, Beilage "Für unsere Mütter und Hausfrauen," no. 16 (1912): 61.
2   Birgit A. Jensen, "Bawdy Bodies or Moral Agency? The Struggle for Identity in Working-Class Autobiographies of Imperial Germany," *Biography* 28, no. 4 (2005): 544.

on autobiographical details: like her protagonist, Märten had lost all of her family members and had been diagnosed with terminal kidney disease when she wrote *Torso* in her late twenties.[3] Yet the novel departs dramatically from genre conventions. While *Torso*'s first half provides a first-person account of proletarian life, the second half of the novel upends the conventions of the worker's autobiography through radical formal experimentation, moving from odes to "Personality" to symbolist drama and scenes from a fairytale.

In the early twentieth century, workers' life writings were expected to portray the hardships of proletarian life for the benefit of a bourgeois readership. The demand for "authenticity" in these accounts often translated into a formulaic plot that chronicled the protagonists' exploitation and victimization, culminating in their self-determination within the class struggle.[4] Workers' autobiographies typically took the form of a confessional or epic narrative.[5] The public's desire for first-person accounts of working-class life was purportedly philanthropic, and undoubtedly voyeuristic. As August Bebel informs readers in his 1909 preface to the influential autobiography of the Austrian factory worker and women's activist Adelheid Popp: "For the upper strata of society, this is a completely new world that opens up before their eyes, but it is a world of misery, of hardship, of moral and spiritual atrophy, that makes you ask yourself in horror, how can this be possible in our society, so proud of its Christianity and civilization?"[6] Märten begins *Torso* by meeting her readers' expectations of proletarian life, depicting it as a struggle with eviction, untreated illness, and starvation wages. However, she soon departs from this narrative to offer a critique of mythologized proletarian identity, bourgeois notions of subjectivity, and the gendered assumptions that underlie them.

---

3   Chryssoula Kambas, *Die Werkstatt als Utopie: Lu Märtens literarische Arbeit und Formästhetik seit 1900* (Tübingen: Niemeyer, 1988), 14.

4   In a representative passage connecting individual struggles with the collective fate of the proletariat, Moritz William Theodor Bromme concludes his autobiography, *Lebensgeschichte eines modernen Fabrikarbeiters* (*The Life History of a Modern Factory Worker*, 1905) by insisting that he does not see himself as a martyr despite the hardship he has gone through, because he knows he has hundreds of thousands of "comrades in suffering" (*Leidensgenossen*) who have endured as much as or more than him. Moritz William Theodor Bromme, *Lebensgeschichte eines modernen Fabrikarbeiters*, ed. Paul Göhre (Jena: Eugen Diedrichs, 1905), 368; Kambas, *Die Werkstatt als Utopie*, 51.

5   Sabine Hake, *The Proletarian Dream: Socialism, Culture, and Emotion in Germany, 1863–1933* (Berlin and Boston: De Gruyter, 2017), 143.

6   August Bebel, "Ein Geleitwort," in Adelheid Popp, *Die Jugendgeschichte einer Arbeiterin von ihr selbst erzählt* (Munich: Ernst Reinhardt, 1909), 3.

Torso's move to an assemblage of modernist forms foreshadows the Marxist aesthetic theory of "classless forms" that Märten would develop in the 1920s as a democratic alternative to the Communist Party's (KPD) top-down, content-driven cultural politics.[7] By undermining the formal and ideological conventions of the worker's autobiography, Märten sought to depict the contradictions of embodied working-class precarity without resorting to the mythologies of the proletariat dominant in her time. In place of the masculine revolutionary at the center of the typical worker's autobiography, Märten offers the reader an incomplete torso assembled from various literary forms, while demanding that new aesthetic and social relations emerge from this provocation.

Torso is roughly divided into two parts: it begins as the diary of an unnamed child grappling with the death of her family members and her own illness; then the novel follows the grown protagonist, now a Marxist named Hazar Loewen intent on writing a book, through an assemblage of poetry, prose, drama, fairytale, and hymn. An enthusiastic review in a daily newspaper comments on this rupture:

> When you read the first part, you're profoundly happy to have discovered this accomplished work of art, this rich, mature, pure book. But Lu Märten was not content with merely writing the absorbing, wonderfully lively story of a 'child.' ... She wanted more, not to give us just anything, but to disperse herself, gather herself, search for herself, discover herself, in order to overcome herself!"[8]

By shifting from chronological, first-person narration to a polyperspectival, nonlinear narrative, Märten seeks to create new literary forms that represent precarity as an experience of fragmented subjectivity. The novel's lack of resolution and the protagonist's inability to fully align herself with normative scripts is accompanied by suggestions of queer and classless alternatives in the fleeting polyamorous relationships

---

7   Märten is best known for her debate on Marxist aesthetics and bourgeois heritage with Gertrud Alexander, the cultural editor of *Die Rote Fahne,* and her ethnographic study of aesthetic forms emerging from it, *Wesen und Veränderung der Formen/Künste* (*Essence and Transformation of the Forms/Arts,* 1924). In this work, she offers her theory of "classless forms" as a stage beyond the "pure forms" of bourgeois art. Lu Märten, *Wesen und Veränderung der Formen/Künste. Resultate historisch-materialistischer Untersuchungen* (Frankfurt: Taifun Verlag, 1924), 209.

8   J. Friedberg, *R. Piper & Co Pamphlet Containing Reviews of Torso,* 1909, Lu Märten Papers, Folder 120, International Institute of Social History, Amsterdam, the Netherlands.

and enactment of genre-crossing forms. *Torso* did not affirm proletarian identity by adopting bourgeois notions of masculine agency, as was typical of the worker's autobiography, but instead presented the instability of gendered, working-class precarity as a challenge to literary form itself.

This chapter argues that *Torso* upends the conventions of the worker's autobiography to imagine new ways of representing precarity: first, it depicts working-class precarity from a distinctly gendered perspective; second, it posits debility as endemic to the working class; and third, it rejects aspirations for bourgeois subjectivity and its literary realization in the confessional narrative. Märten presents social relations beyond marriage, monogamy, and the biological family as necessarily implicated in the project of revolutionizing aesthetic form. Transforming both social and aesthetic relations necessitates the rejection of gender and genre conventions to allow for the emergence of non-normative alternatives. *Torso* formally enacts these changes by departing from a linear narrative structured by "straight time" and depicting the fracturing of the narrative voice as the work moves between prose, poetry, and drama. Märten not only offers the fragment—or the torso—as a more accurate rendering of gendered, working-class precarity than the alleged wholeness of bourgeois subjectivity, but also suggests that it contains a utopian potential to evoke new aesthetic forms to accompany the revolutionized sociality. As *Torso's* protagonist observes: "Shattering a form to arrive at its content and finding a new form for the content—that is art."[9]

Shattering the Form of the Worker's Autobiography

Märten's journalism and art criticism had already appeared in a range of publications including *Die Zeit, Die Hilfe, Die Gleichheit,* and *Arbeiterinnen-Zeitung* when she wrote *Torso* and *Bergarbeiter*. Märten's ensuing reputation as a proletarian author was not hindered by the fact that she did not, strictly speaking, come from a working-class background, but rather from impoverished and declassed nobility.[10] Her contemporaries received both *Bergarbeiter* and *Torso* as autobiographical works and they were revived in the 1970s and 1980s in the German Democratic Republic (GDR) for their "enormous documentary value

---

9 Lu Märten, *Torso. Das Buch eines Kindes* (Munich: R. Piper & Co., 1909), 206.
10 Ursula Münchow, *Frühe deutsche Arbeiterautobiographie*, Literatur und Gesellschaft (Berlin: Akademie-Verlag, 1973), 46; Kambas, *Die Werkstatt als Utopie*, 9.

due to their authentic character."[11] Though contemporary scholars have distanced themselves from the GDR reception of *Torso*, they have continued to interpret the novel primarily through Märten's biography.[12]

Workers' autobiographies in the early twentieth century typically told stories of personal struggle, upward mobility, or revolutionary awakening. While authors such as Carl Fischer and Gustav Hänfling did not present their life writings in a single political framework, others, including Moritz William Theodor Bromme, Adelheid Popp, Wenzel Holek, and Franz Rehbein chronicled the emergence of their class consciousness and commitment to the SPD. These autobiographies, which were strongly informed by their editors' expectations and interventions, sought to provide an unmediated glimpse into the "reality" of proletarian suffering. As Paul Göhre, SPD member and editor of numerous workers' autobiographies, announces in his introduction to Bromme's *Lebensgeschichte eines modernen Fabrikarbeiters* [*The Life Story of a Modern Factory Worker*, 1905], his aim is to offer a "general knowledge of the real life of today's proletariat, penned by the proletarians themselves."[13]

Frank Trommler has observed that "proletarian literature at the beginning of the century was increasingly characterized by this mythologization of the proletariat as an autonomous historical force, as the embodiment of a natural humanity that must only be awakened."[14] In *Torso*, Märten only initially conforms to this expectation of the worker's

---

11   Münchow, *Frühe deutsche Arbeiterautobiographie*, 7.

12   Kambas, author of the only monograph on Märten to date, argues, "With *Torso* Märten wrote her autobiography," while Sonja Dehning qualifies *Torso* as a "fictional autobiography." Kambas, *Die Werkstatt als Utopie*, 55 and Sonja Dehning, *Tanz der Feder. Künstlerische Produktivität in Romanen von Autorinnen um 1900* (Würzburg: Königshausen & Neumann, 2000), 188. The parallels between *Torso* and Märten's own childhood are undeniable: the protagonist's siblings bear the same names as her own, with the exception of her younger brother Hermann, who appears as "Erman." The deaths in the novel mirror her own loss of her family members. However, the existing autobiographical interpretations of *Torso* minimize its formal experimentation and often fill in the gaps with details from Märten's own life rather than exploring the literary function of the ambiguity they produce.

13   Paul Göhre, "Zur Einleitung," in *Lebensgeschichte eines modernen Fabrikarbeiters*, by Moritz William Theodor Bromme (Jena: Eugen Diedrichs, 1905), [emphasis in original]. Göhre solicited and edited many of the major workers' autobiographies, including Fischer's *Denkwürdigkeiten und Erinnerung eines Arbeiters* (1903), Bromme's *Lebensgeschichte eines modernen Fabrikarbeiters* (1905), and Wenzel Holek's *Lebensgang eines deutsch-tschechischen Handarbeiters* (Jena: Eugen Diedrichs, 1909).

14   Frank Trommler, *Sozialistische Literatur in Deutschland. Ein historischer Überblick* (Stuttgart: Kröner, 1976), 240.

autobiography, which is limited to the "representation of the worker in his relationship to the class struggle, to work, to his coworkers, to his family."[15] Following the genre conventions in the first part of *Torso*, Märten chronicles the childhood of a proletarian girl through a series of diary entries. The protagonist depicts her politicization through her initial contact with the Land Reform Movement and radicalization with her discovery of the "dialectic, sharp as glass—the *discerning, scathing, militant* principle."[16] However, her contact with Marxism does not culminate in enthusiastic party membership or an affirmation of her political agency. She remains on the fringes of society, and increasingly distances herself from normative political and social institutions in her search for adequate aesthetic and relational forms.

Märten's departure from the "great, swelling immediacy" demanded of the proletarian author unsettled the prominent art critic Wilhelm Hausenstein. In his review of *Torso*, he admits: "The book has wonderfully visual language, but the cultivation of rhetorical beauty becomes pretentious." The novel's second half causes him to regretfully observe "one would like to ask the author … to continue the trajectory along which the first part of the book proceeds so animatedly: the trajectory of a simple epic."[17] In both her fiction and her major work of aesthetic theory, *Wesen und Veränderung der Formen/Künste* [*Essence and Transformation of the Forms/Arts*, 1924], Märten rejected genre conventions as well as the entangled ideological investments of socialist party politics. In *Torso*, her unorthodox approach to genre is apparent in its resonance with Expressionist prose and Symbolist drama through the protagonist's fragmentary consciousness; the slippage between reality, dream, fantasy, and hallucination; and the personification of Consciousness, Delusion, and Personality in the dramatic episodes. Märten "shatters the form" of the workers' autobiography by depicting the precarity of working-class life through a fragmentary and experimental literary form, producing a work that puzzled and provoked her readers. Within the narrative, the protagonist repeatedly reflects on the dialectics of

---

15   Münchow, *Frühe deutsche Arbeiterautobiographie*, 12.
16   Märten, *Torso*, 89 [emphasis in original].
17   In his review of Märten's one-act play, *Bergarbeiter*, Hausenstein explains what he understands to be the task of the proletarian author: "It is very difficult to capture proletarian life poetically without elevating, stylizing, or constructing it … The poet of the proletariat must create with great, swelling immediacy, without an aesthetic consciousness. One imagines him to be primitive – but absolutely spot on." Wilhelm Hausenstein, "Aus einer Besprechung in der 'Münchner Post,'" in *R. Piper & Co Pamphlet Containing Reviews of Torso*, 3, Folder 115, Lu Märten Papers, International Institute of Social History, Amsterdam, the Netherlands; Hausenstein, "Bergarbeiter. Schauspiel in einem Akte von Lu Märten," in *Der Kampf*, Lu Märten Papers.

form and content as the driving force behind artistic production: "there is no other justification for form than content. And the content that cannot be forced into existing forms must find a new one."[18] In *Torso*, Märten traces the dialectical movement of precarity from its disruption of subjective and narrative stability to its intimation of utopian social and aesthetic relations.

Gender in the Worker's Autobiography

In her comprehensive study of workers' life writings, Sabine Hake considers the challenges of reading these texts today:

> Is their main purpose to promote social reform or socialist mobilization? Are they modeled on bourgeois narratives of individual advancement or directed toward a collectivist view of society? Can this kind of writing be likened to a therapeutic process through which a clear sense of self is acquired or restored? Or do the writers merely produce the performances of subjectivity considered necessary for admission to the bourgeois public sphere?[19]

These questions highlight the extent to which Märten rejected the terms of the genre. Rather, she formulated more fundamental objections to the notions of subjectivity, identity, and form undergirding the worker's autobiography. She does not frame her novel as inspiration for proletarian women, in contrast to Popp's *Jugendgeschichte einer Arbeiterin* [*The Autobiography of a Working Woman*, 1909], which was published in the same year as *Torso*.[20] In place of agitational appeals, Märten portrays the dissolution of subjectivity as well as its constitutive structures: the social conventions of marriage, linear time, and masculine productivity. She represents the fracturing effects of precarity, portraying the "incomplete individuality" of proletarian women and the latent emancipatory

---

18 Märten, *Torso*, 175.
19 Hake, *The Proletarian Dream*, 145.
20 Adelheid Popp concludes her autobiography by stating her intentions for its publication: "When I sensed the need to write about how I became a socialist, it was driven solely by the wish to bring courage to the countless women workers who thirst for activity with a heart full of longing, but are scared away again and again, because they do not believe themselves capable of achieving something. Just as socialism transformed me and gave me strength, it can do the same for others" (Popp, *Die Jugendgeschichte Einer Arbeiterin*, 104).

potential of this fragmented consciousness as an alternative to gendered bourgeois subjectivity.

The worker's autobiography was a product of the tension between individual and collective notions of subjectivity, which often played out in the negotiations between the editor and author. In his introduction to Carl Fischer's *Denkwürdigkeiten und Erinnerungen eines Arbeiters (Memories and Reminiscences of a Worker*, 1903), Göhre argues that this work deserves a place alongside the autobiographies of distinguished historical figures. "A man of the people is not among them," he maintains. "A life account of his world is missing: the world of the people, in which the subject is much less individuality, and much more a partial manifestation of the great masses."[21] As Hake has observed, working-class men were able to establish their individuality and distinguish themselves from the bourgeois notion of "the anonymous masses"— often espoused by the editors themselves—by performing their masculinity, which was itself perceived as a form of self-determination. In Fischer's case, this manifests in a homosociality that includes quips about exchanging a daughter for a day of work and outbursts of profanity that win him the respect of his foreman.[22]

This masculine assertion of individuality, however, was not available to women authors.[23] Instead, women could choose between distancing themselves from what Bebel refers to as the "moral and intellectual atrophy" of the working class by adopting bourgeois norms of chaste femininity—as Ottilie Baader did in *Ein Steiniger Weg. Lebenserinnerungen einer Sozialistin [A Stony Path: Memories of a Socialist]*—or setting aside questions of sexuality and gender specificity like Popp.[24] *Torso* takes a different path by depicting a protagonist who is chronically ill and thus has a fraught relationship to her body, is uninterested in marriage or children, and has an androgynous gender identity.

Märten does not attempt to assemble a recognizable whole from the fragments of bourgeois individuality that are afforded to working-class women. On the contrary, she places the experience of working-class women at the center of her narrative in order to explore the ways in which their precarious position troubles gender and class identities. *Torso's* protagonist does not suddenly acquire class consciousness through

21   Paul Göhre, "Vorwort," in *Denkwürdigkeiten und Erinnerungen eines Arbeiters*, by Carl Fischer, vol. 2: Leben und Wissen (Leipzig: Eugen Diedrichs, 1903), iv.

22   Fischer, *Denkwürdigkeiten und Erinnerungen eines Arbeiters*, 124; 282.

23   Hake, *The Proletarian Dream*, 152.

24   Bebel, "Ein Geleitwort," 17; Jensen, "Bawdy Bodies or Moral Agency?," 550, 554; Katharina Gerstenberger, *Truth to Tell: German Women's Autobiographies and Turn-of-the-Century Culture* (Ann Arbor, MI: University of Michigan Press, 2000), 107.

her contact with the SPD or abstract notions of capitalist exploitation. Rather, her political and artistic practices are transformed by witnessing working-class women:

> [T]he concept of the worker initially did not conjure a particular understanding of a work pace or a wage rate for me, but rather at once and self-evidently a countless number of incomplete and incompletely existing individuals. I saw – determined by my early readings – first and foremost women from among the masses as the least conscious and most exploited part of the working class ...

> Then it was the plight of women that left its mark on me through all of my own suffering, and for a long time turned my nights into agony; yes, it was this, which lured the first, now forgotten songs from my soul.

> [[U]nter dem Begriff Arbeiter erstand mir zunächst nicht irgendwelche Vorstellung eines Arbeitstempos oder einer Lohnhöhe, sondern zugleich und selbstverständlich eine Unzählichkeit von unvollkommenen und unvollkommen existierenden Individuen. Ich sah, bestimmt durch meine erste Lektüre, vor allem die Frauen als den in der Masse unbewußtesten und ausgenütztesten Teil der Arbeiterschaft.

> Dann war es die Not der Frauen, die mich unter allen eigenen Schmerzen seinen Augenblick verließ, und die meine Nächte lange Zeit zu einer Pein machte; ja, sie war es, die mir die ersten, nun vergessenen Lieder aus der Seele lockte.][25]

The protagonist's first creative impulses emerge from a sense of helplessness at the suffering of working-class women, a group to which she belongs. Her poetry is "lured" out by this lived experience rather than consciously curated as the product of deliberate authorship.[26] Although the protagonist suggests that Marxism provided her with a framework for understanding the exploitation of working-class women, this revelation is not tied to party politics. Instead, the

---

25 Märten, *Torso*, 70–1.
26 The reference to the protagonist's "first, now forgotten songs (*Lieder*)" recalls the title of Märten's first published poetry collection, *Meine Liedsprachen* (1906).

structural oppression of proletarian women catalyzes her artistic practice, in which she attempts to find adequate forms for expressing such
fragmented individuality, as well as the revolutionary potential of this
marginalized perspective.

The protagonist takes up the Romantic and Marxist understanding
of the division of labor as the division of the individual, while reframing it in explicitly gendered and aesthetic terms. Märten references this
critique, developed by both John Ruskin and Karl Marx, throughout
her writings. As Ruskin argued, "[i]t is not, truly speaking, the labour
that is divided, but the men:—Divided into mere segments of men—
broken into small fragments and crumbs of life."[27] Ruskin's solution to
this fragmentation through the combined "labor of the head, the heart,
and the hand" appears repeatedly in Märten, who similarly evokes the
ideal of medieval craft production.[28] *Torso* only alludes to this utopian
synthesis, which remains outside of the bounds of the novel. Head,
heart, and hand remain disconnected from one another, a fact that limits the working class to specific forms of manual labor, and is reflected
in the fracturing of consciousness and narrative perspective in the novel's second half.

While Ruskin and Marx, as well as most authors of workers'
autobiographies, assume that this division occurs in the factory and
the fragmented individuals are men, Märten explores how the gendered division of labor contributes to the even greater precarity of
working-class women. At the same time, the exclusion of women from
certain professions and areas of the labor market, including artistic production, grants them a greater distance from the rigidity of commodified labor. As Märten later argues in *Die Künstlerin* [*The Woman Artist*,
1919], women's unwaged reproductive labor is both an unequal burden
that prevents their "differentiation" within capitalism, and a relational
model that, if generalized, would permit the emergence of collectiv-
ist forms such as "social motherliness" (*soziale Mütterlichkeit*) divorced
from biological notions of the family.[29] According to Märten, the solution to the gendered distinction between public and private spheres
does not lie in the defense of family life against the market, but rather

27 John Ruskin, *The Stones of Venice*, vol. 2 (London: Smith, Elder and Co., 1873),
    165.
28 Lu Märten, "Die künstlerischen Momente der Arbeit in alter und neuer Zeit
    (1903)," in *Formen für den Alltag. Schriften, Aufsätze, Vorträge*, ed. Rainhard May
    (Dresden: Verlag der Kunst, 1982), 10.
29 Lu Märten, *Die Künstlerin*, ed. Chryssoula Kambas (Bielefeld: Aisthesis, 2001),
    106–7, 32.

in the complete socialization of the private sphere through collective childrearing and living, which will necessarily give rise to new forms of intimacy and experiences of gender.[30]

Debility and the Working Class

Märten makes a further intervention in the genre by substituting the typical narrative of the non-disabled, male worker with that of a debilitated child and young adult excluded from both wage labor and conventional gender scripts. Due to her illness, *Torso's* protagonist is unable to attend school regularly, work in a factory like her brothers, or engage in paid labor or unpaid reproductive labor along with her sister and mother. Märten's expansion of the worker's autobiography beyond the factory or agricultural worker to include non-normative gendered and embodied experiences reflects a broader understanding of proletarian precarity. Precarity is not only a product of insufficient wages, dangerous working conditions, and workplace injuries, but also the gendered and often racialized experience of what Lauren Berlant calls "slow death" or the "condition of being worn out by the activity of reproducing life": the physical and mental exhaustion of entire populations within capitalism.[31] For those barely getting by, such as Märten's young protagonist, living is already dying: "In the nights and through the pain I always ask myself: how will this life and my life go—and must I really use up all of my energy in suffering?"[32]

Building on Berlant's notion of slow death, Jasbir Puar employs the term "debility" to describe experiences of precarity that do not fall within the binary of disabled or non-disabled. In contrast to "disablement," Puar maintains, debilitation "foregrounds the slow wearing down of populations instead of the event of becoming disabled." Without a distinct before and after, debility cannot be represented in a clear narrative arc. In *Torso*, Märten's depiction of debility illustrates the limits of the epic and confessional narratives typical of workers' autobiographies by dwelling on the "normal" or mundane

---

30 Märten identifies Lily Braun's model of the *Einküchenhaus* or "single-kitchen house" as an example of a collective housing project with a centralized kitchen designed to relieve women from housework. During her time in the Land Reform movement, Märten served as a spokesperson for the *Einküchenhaus*. See Kambas, *Die Werkstatt als Utopie*, 30–1.

31 Lauren Berlant, *Cruel Optimism* (Durham, NC: Duke University Press, 2011), 100.

32 Märten, *Torso*, 39.

costs of capitalism that resist closed narrative forms.[33] The story of a working-class child unable to work cannot be resolved through self-realization in labor, political practice, or the subordination to "straight time" that would otherwise dictate her transition to married life and motherhood.[34]

The protagonist's inability to produce value is framed as a constitutive component of precarity, as the counterpoint to her brother Walter's compensated labor. In this way, Märten posits the protagonist's everyday experience of debility as a necessary supplement to the image of the revolutionary proletariat embodied by the male wage laborer: the political imagination must extend beyond factory walls and labor organizations to those excluded from capitalist forms of production. Far from glorifying the marginalized perspective of her protagonist, Märten confronts the reader with the contradictions of this expanded image of the working class. The protagonist reflects on the frustration and shame conjured by her need to represent her experience, which eventually causes her to depart from the confessional mode:

> I've been thinking I'll have to earn money soon and haven't learned how to—didn't go to school and have always been sick. Now I want to learn a trade, but there's no money for it and Walter doesn't want me to, because I'm sick and he wants to do everything himself. So we often have long, intense fights, and there's nothing I can do. I read everything you're supposed to read, but I don't know what to do with it. I want to write books myself, but I'll never be able to do it and no one can know about it.

> [Ich denke, daß ich bald Geld verdienen müßte und habe nichts dazu gelernt – und keine Schule gehabt und immer krank gewesen. Jetzt möchte ich etwas lernen, aber es ist kein Geld dafür, und Walter will es nicht, weil ich krank bin und will alles allein schaffen. Dann zanken wir uns oft solange und heftig, und ich kann nichts tun. Ich lese alles, was man lesen sollte, ich weiß aber nicht, was ich einmal damit tun soll. Ich möchte selber Bücher schreiben, aber das werde ich wohl nie können, und von dem da soll niemand wissen.][35]

---

33 Jasbir K. Puar, *The Right to Maim: Debility, Capacity, Disability* (Durham, NC: Duke University Press, 2017), xiii–xiv.

34 José Esteban Muñoz, *Cruising Utopia: The Then and There of Queer Futurity* (New York: New York University Press, 2009), 22.

35 Märten, *Torso*, 23.

Torso's first part, "Childhood," begins as the protagonist lies awake at night, reflecting on her illness, her wavering belief in God, and her compulsion to write a diary. The protagonist tells her story in real time, in simple, childlike language, cultivating a sense of immediacy. She witnesses her brothers receive insufficient wages, her mother sell their belongings in a futile attempt to pay off their mounting debt, and her sister maintain the household by day and sew clothing for wealthy patrons by night. The only form of activity she can engage in is writing. Yet instead of serving as an outlet for self-realization, as is implied by the autobiographical form, the self-conscious act of writing is portrayed as a shameful indulgence that "no one can know about."[36]

Throughout the novel, the protagonist reflects on the effect of the illness and death in her family on her writing: "During the day I write secretly in this book. Secretly, because it's not what I want to write, only what always *comes back to me, so that I have to hold onto it.*"[37] The need to stay silent so as not to disturb her dying father, her helplessness when observing her siblings and mother labor while unable to work or attend school herself, and of course, the pain that confines her to bed are not sources for romanticized narratives of suffering, but obstacles that limit her art to representing that pain. The gaps between diary entries reproduce the disruption of the protagonist's illness for the reader. After an indeterminate pause, the narrator picks up her pen again: "The fact that I'm just sneaking back to my book now, and only hesitantly, is because it wasn't always possible to utter a word from all of the screams and all of the pain."[38] The protagonist frequently imagines the dialogue with her reader taking place not in written, but in oral form—as if the reader can hear her words and screams—contributing to the illusion that this is not a stylized fictional text, but a document allowing direct access to her thoughts as they come to her.

The protagonist's single attempt to monetize her work by selling riddles to a newspaper meets with further disillusionment: "When I have no choice but to be sick, I invent various [riddles] and, recently, I sent them to a newspaper to earn some money, because it wouldn't have been worth it otherwise. The newspaper printed them too, but they didn't give me any money for them. I won't do anything like that anymore."[39] Motivated by the need to earn money as much as by the desire to write, the protagonist interprets her inability to commodify her work as further confirmation that she lacks artistic potential. The

---

36 Märten, *Torso*, 23.
37 Märten, *Torso*, 1 [emphasis in original].
38 Märten, *Torso*, 40.
39 Märten, *Torso*, 37.

literary forms that are available to the protagonist are the short forms of riddles, plays, fairytales, and poetry. These forms—largely associated with "low" culture—come to constitute the novel as a whole. In the first half, the protagonist repeatedly alludes to the stigmatization of short forms as well those that fall outside of a sober realism. She recounts her suppression of fantasy during her childhood storytelling: "When we used to be sick a lot as children, I always had to tell stories at night. But I was always somewhat ashamed and just told stories about everyday incidents; I couldn't say what I really wanted, because it was so strange [*fremd*]."[40] The protagonist is unable to create a heroic narrative out of her poverty and illness: this condition only contributes to her compulsion to discipline her imagination as an irresponsible flight from reality.

When the protagonist attempts to write a short story, she finds herself slipping into fantasy and composes a fairytale that she eventually destroys in frustration. She tells the story of a woman with a passion for music who is forced to give up playing the violin after she marries because her husband cannot accept this distraction from her domestic duties. This sacrifice leads to the woman's illness and death, at which point the narrator loses control over the story and it begins to tell itself: "That's what I wanted to portray, and I did it, but it didn't really work the way I wanted and ultimately turned into a fairytale, because the woman's violin started to play itself after she was long dead. But it wasn't supposed to be a fairytale." Just as the violin began to play after the woman's death, the protagonist's story unfolds on its own accord. The protagonist experiences this slippage into fairytale—a form of folk art that, as a collective and traditionally oral form, is particularly resistant to monetization—as a reckless indulgence at odds with the pragmatic demands of the market. Consequently, the protagonist recounts: "Then I burned everything up again, because I know too little about what really goes on between people."[41] The protagonist's illness prevents her from gathering experiences for her stories or even from transforming her diary into a legible autobiography. At the same time, she initially rejects fantasy as mere escapism, leaving her with no options to develop her work. Märten's challenge to the generic bounds of the worker's autobiography plays out in the protagonist's struggle with form in the novel's first half. Unable to mold her life into the teleological narrative of the mythologized proletarian, the protagonist embodies the fractured subjectivity that fall outside of this genre and identity. In its second half, *Torso* pursues the forms that could adequately render this experience of precarity.

---

40 Märten, *Torso*, 23.
41 Märten, *Torso*, 24.

Queer Relationality Beyond the Subject

Märten's temporary adoption of the confessional mode in the first half of *Torso* only heightens the reader's disorientation in the second half of the novel when this structure falls away. While the subtitle, *The Book of a Child*, determines the reader's expectations for the diary (*Tagebuch*) of its first half, the fragmentary and suggestive figure of the title, *Torso*, is centered in its second half. The confessional narrative is displaced by the fractured and depersonalized appearance of contrasting literary forms in which the protagonist's perspective is merely one of many. This shift is both a further fragmentation and affirmation of the protagonist's identity: amidst the multiplicity of forms and perspectives, the protagonist is finally given a name: Hazar Loewen. This deliberately exoticized name combines the gender-neutral, Arabic first name meaning "vigilant" and "nightingale" with a variation on Märten's mother's surname, "von Loeben," transformed into "lion" and stripped of its class signifier.[42] Hazar's outsider status is emphasized by this uncritical allusion to a racial "other," nonhuman animals, and ambiguous gender identity. The formal rupture in the novel is accompanied by Hazar's departure from normative relational forms: following the death of her biological family, she leaves the prospect of married life behind and moves between polyamorous relationships. The episodic scenes of the second half are presented as a misaligned composite of continually shifting genres and perspectives, ultimately producing the image of a torso.

The diary's chronological narration is interjected with pauses reflecting the interruptions caused by the protagonist's illness or family members' deaths. This realist technique serves to further enhance the impression of linear time. Yet following her mother's death, which comes after the passing of her father, older brother, and sister, Hazar's usual stream of consciousness is replaced by incomplete, repetitive phrases and gaps:

> I may still speak – because I am still alive. Once upon a time there
> was a scream. – My mother is dead – and I am still alive! –
> Once upon a time there was a scream. –
> Once upon a time there was a long night – I did not want to rest
> in my restless happiness – all the bells were ringing in me – all
> the homecoming bells – Going home –
> The morning awoke so grey – I stared constantly at a letter,
> "Mother is so sick, – the worst is coming – – –"

---

42 Kambas, *Die Werkstatt als Utopie*, 9.

I saw the lie. – I stared lifelessly – – there stood Fred Angele in the door – the way he looked – he had braced himself as if for a crime – that's how he came to me. – Then I screamed the question at him – the little word – – –
Then he just nodded like that – – –
– – – – –

[Ich darf noch reden – denn ich lebe ja noch. – Es war einmal ein Schrei. – Meine Mutter ist tot – und ich lebe noch! – Es war einmal ein Schrei. –
Es war einmal eine lange Nacht – da wollt' ich nicht zur Ruhe vor ruhelosem Glück – da läuteten alle Glocken in mir – alle Heimatglocken – Nachhausekommen. –
Der Morgen weckte so grau – ich starrte immer auf einen Brief, die "Mutter sei so krank, – das Schlimmste sei nahe – – –"
Ich wußte die Lüge. – Ich starrte ohne Leben – – da stand Fred Angele in der Tür – wie sah der aus – der hatte sich gepackt wie zu einer Tat – so kam er auf mich zu. – Da schrie ich ihm die Frage entgegen – das kleine Wort – – –
Da nickte er nur so – – –
– – – – –][43]

When Hazar learns of her mother's death, she is in the hospital recovering from an operation to address the episodes of pain that frequently confine her to bed and had been diagnosed as terminal. The "homecoming bells" are quickly silenced when she realizes that her childhood home no longer exists. Presented as a reconstruction of the initial shock, the fragmentary thoughts and em dashes mirror the experience of trauma and the fracturing of the protagonist's consciousness. Although she "may still speak," her voice is no longer a continuous thread that carries the narrative, nor the intentional expression of her interiority.

Märten evokes the genre of the fairytale through the recurring phrase, "Es war einmal ein Schrei." Recalling the sound of the violin that plays on after the woman's death, the disembodied scream marks the transition from the exploration of authorship as constitutive of the self in the novel's first half to the polyperspectival narration of the second half. The scream does not emerge directly from Hazar and, detached from the individual, it begins a new story in which Hazar's voice is one among many. At the same time, the scream serves as a hyperbolic rebellion against the desire for proletarian writing "without an aesthetic consciousness" demanded by readers of workers' autobiographies.[44] Taken

---

43   Märten, *Torso*, 136.
44   Hausenstein, "Bergarbeiter. Schauspiel in einem Akte von Lu Märten," 3, Lu Märten Papers.

to its extreme, trauma without stylization is merely unintelligible and even unwritable. It is not pure experience, but rather a reminder of the contradictions of the demand for authenticity.

When Hazar's character is salvaged from death, her first-person perspective is sidelined as she is also not fully alive or restored to coherent subjecthood: "Ich starrte ohne Leben," she recalls. She continues to eschew convention rather than attempting to recreate the stability of the family. After her childhood attempts to suppress her imagination, she now embraces fantasy as an alternative to regulatory (hetero)normative structures. Her choice to escape into art represents the alternative path to the protagonist of her fairytale, who gave up her music to save her marriage. As Hazar's fiancé, Fred Angele, observes, "[t]he decisive factor in your life is creation, not being together or uniting with me."[45] When he attempts to protect her from the news of her mother's death, the casual, even dismissive language of her recollections clashes with the gravity of the event, suggesting Hazar's growing disengagement from the relationship. Definite articles replace pronouns ("wie sah der aus") and vague filler words supplant adjectives ("Da nickte er nur so"). Fred Angele's paternalism in withholding the truth—which she perceives as lying—is characteristic of his normalizing and normative function in the narrative. The fragmentation of Hazar's consciousness announced in this passage is finalized with the death of her last remaining sibling, unmooring her completely from her biological family. Fred Angele repeatedly attempts to drag her out of her fantasies into the practicalities of everyday life. "Why do you want to have a routine (*Alltag*), which everyone merely tolerates?" Hazar inquires. "But Fred Angele doesn't know about me, doesn't understand my language. Flesh remains flesh, and word only word. Day is day, and night remains night. Nothing is solved."[46] Hazar increasingly distances herself from her fiancé, and the relationship eventually dissolves.

With the loss of her normative grounding, Hazar's character becomes more diffuse, moving between genres and intimate constellations. Two fantastical figures suddenly appear: Nysos, recalling the Greek god of ecstasy, suffering, madness, wine, dance, and festivity (in German: "Dionysos") and "the dancer Eli."[47] The fantasy world they occupy together contrasts starkly with the life that Hazar shares with Fred Angele. While Hazar's life with her fiancé is chronicled in abrupt, repetitive, and often incomplete sentences—"I drag myself along"; "Sometimes I can't go

45 Märten, *Torso*, 154.
46 Märten, *Torso*, 239.
47 Märten, *Torso*, 174.

on"; "Uphill and downhill"—the episodes with Nysos and Eli are rendered in ornate, stylized language.[48] After drinking wine from Nysos's
hands following their first encounter, Hazar ceases to drive away the
fantasies that she had suppressed throughout her childhood: "I feel a
new rhythm inside of me … I am so restless and reveling in this agitation and burden—this plentitude—I serve all unfamiliar creation, all
unfamiliar souls (*allen fremden Seelen*)."[49] Hazar's embrace of fantasy is
framed as an erotic encounter with something beyond herself, an excess
that breaks down the final boundaries of her own subjectivity.

Märten rejects aspirations for a unified self, countering the larger
project of workers' autobiographies to "[produce] knowledge about the
worker's soul."[50] In *Torso*, the myth of individual interiority is replaced
with a subjectivity that is fundamentally relational, a mosaic assembled
by multiple voices or "souls." "Fred Angele appears so foreign [*fremd*],"
Hazar reflects, "The many souls frightened him away."[51] Although this
plurality proves incompatible with monogamous marriage, it allows
for new existential and narrative possibilities. The "fremde Seelen" in
the dream sequences and the dramatic episodes with Nysos and Eli
function as a *Verfremdungseffekt* that underscores the constructedness of
the confessional form and its underlying assumptions about individuality and interiority. Desire is a lack that points beyond the self toward
the unknown, driving Hazar's search for relational and aesthetic forms
emerging from this instability.

Hazar's encounter with Nysos and Eli serves as a turning point in
the novel, after which it takes on an increasingly fragmentary form.
They appear in a dreamlike interlude dividing the novel's two parts.
All but the first page of this passage was struck from the 1908 manuscript of *Torso* by Märten's editor at Piper Verlag—undoubtedly due to
its eroticism—but the episode nevertheless made its way into the final
publication.[52] The scene opens with an anthropomorphic description

---

48 Märten, *Torso*, 239.
49 Märten, *Torso*, 177.
50 Hake, *The Proletarian Dream*, 140–41.
51 Märten, *Torso*, 179.
52 Sexual content was unusual for workers' autobiographies, although men
    were granted more leeway than women. The most open descriptions of sexual
    encounters—including attempted rape, seduction by a fourteen-year old girl,
    and *coitus interruptus* as a means of birth control—can be found in Bromme's
    autobiography, causing the editor, Göhre, to warn the readers not to let the
    book fall in the hands of children. Göhre, "Zur Einleitung," xii; Bromme, *Leb-
    ensgeschichte eines modernen Fabrikarbeiters*, 217, 218, 225; Lu Märten, "Torso. Das
    Buch eines Kindes (Manuscript)" (1908), Lu Märten Papers, Folder 120, Interna-
    tional Institute of Social History, Amsterdam, the Netherlands.

of the autumn sun "[shouting over] the forest with radiant exultation," evoking the setting of a fairytale. During their night together in the forest, Hazar first declines Eli's outstretched hands before going to Nysos. After Hazar and Nysos sleep together, she notes her lack of concern for Fred Angele, reflecting, "Then I was in a secure and blissfully forgetful rapture [*Ergriffenheit*] with you." Yet Nysos is immediately thrown into a panic by the thought of his own fiancée. Hazar perceives his panic as a regression to normative scripts: "But you had forgotten me and my path in this moment, you were not the devoutly smiling heir of the great connoisseurs of beauty, who justify all new forms, you were the heir of an old world of prescriptions and promises."[53] The ambivalent status of this episode—which is dismissed as a "delusion" by Fred Angele and presented as a dream—frames Hazar's desire to generate new aesthetic forms along with the creation of alternative social forms. Although Nysos proves to be too entrenched in the conventions of the "old world" to accompany her further, Eli offers to continue with Hazar: "Give me your hand for a wordlessly beautiful dream. From now on – – –."[54]

Hazar later finds the harmony she could not achieve with Fred Angele or Nysos and Eli with a sculptor, Lonza, and his former lover, Lisa. When Lisa approaches Hazar, Hazar invites her to join the relationship: "Then came a strange time between the three of us. With festival of roses and light, under which lies and truth slept in equal standing. Lisa celebrated beauty—for Lonza's sake—und celebrated me. Dangerous games. The unspoken, the enigmatic." These idyllic relations only last for a moment, however: "And now festival and light are extinguished, and Lisa is sick with doubt."[55] Lisa, like Nysos, remains attached to monogamy as a form of stability. She is unfulfilled by this new arrangement, in which she is both feminized and marginalized in relation to the negligent and masculinized Lonza and androgynous Hazar. While the latter two are concerned primarily with their art, and view sensuality as an extension of their creative projects, Lisa seeks a form of intimacy beyond their abstract investment in beauty. The relationship ends and when Lisa reappears, the genre has shifted from prose to drama. In the chapter "Scene on a Stage"—as well as in the increasingly frequent episodes presented as a script with stage directions—Hazar's account is decentered, as the genre no longer demands the privileging of a single perspective.

53 Märten, *Torso*, 184.
54 Märten, *Torso*, 185.
55 Märten, *Torso*, 225.

Lisa: … Do you remember that night with us when you lay on white roses and we celebrated your beauty? …

Lisa (slowly): It happened that we came together again at that same hour, everything was so strangely similar to that night – only you had left. Then it happened, a child came from this night – conceived by a longing that was not for me – – – the child grew a little – and looked like you – Hazar.

Hazar (has let go of Lisa and is leaning on the wall, hardly audible): So it wanted to be – – –

(Pause)

(Silently): How old is the child, so that this could be seen to be true?

Lisa: Two years old.

Hazar: Where is it?

Lisa: Dead.

– – – – –

[Lisa: … Weißt du noch die Nacht, als du bei uns auf weißen Rosen lagst und wir deine Schönheit als Fest hatten? …

Lisa (langsam): Es geschah, daß wir zueinanderkamen, zu einer gleichen Stunde, alles war so seltsam ähnlich jener Nacht – nur du warst fortgegangen. Da geschah es, daß aus dieser Nacht ein Kind wurde – gezeugt aus einer Sehnsucht, die nicht mir galt – – – das Kind wuchs ein wenig – und sah aus, wie du – Hazar.

Hazar: (hat Lisa losgelassen und sich an die Wand gelehnt, kaum hörbar): Also das wollte sein – – –

(Pause.)

(Tonlos): Wie alt ist das Kind, daß dies wahr zu sehen wäre?

Lisa: Diese zwei Jahre alt.

Hazar: Wo ist es?

Lisa: Tot.

– – – – –][56]

In contrast with the earlier episodes, in which Lisa's perspective is mediated by Hazar's perception of the events, this dramatic dialogue disrupts her first-person narration. At the same time, it offers another form of immediacy: without Hazar's retrospective narrativization, the dialogue lacks a clear interpretative framework. The characters' body language detailed by the stage directions—Hazar stroking Lisa's hair as she tells her that she once loved her, then letting go and backing

---

56 Märten, *Torso*, 292–3.

away—emphasizes the fragility of the scene, the interpretive possibility introduced by physical proximity, tone, and staging.[57] Finally, the extravagant symbolism—the bed of white roses, the child born out of the desire for an absent person, its premature death—is further dramatized by the laconic speech that concludes with the total absence of language.

The queer relations between Hazar, Lisa, and Lonza hint at alternatives to marriage, heterosexuality, and individualized artistic production, yet the death of their child reveals that the persistence of these new forms cannot depend on the reproductive reflexes of the "old world."[58] The fate of the collectively-conceived child in *Torso* suggests a more fundamental challenge to reproductive futurity, to the behaviors and desires that reproduce heteronormativity, the family, gender, and genre.[59] The impossibility of this relationship and the child resulting from it serves as a reminder of the need for a greater transformation of collective practices beyond isolated acts of intimacy.

Conclusion: Suggestive Forms

In *Torso*, Märten undermines the formal conventions of the worker's autobiography through a disorienting movement between narrative perspectives and genres. She expands the depiction of working-class precarity to include non-normative gendered and embodied experiences, challenging the stability of bourgeois subjectivity and its corresponding genre conventions. The narrative closure offered by the worker's autobiography that culminates in the assertion of masculine subjectivity or identification with the party precludes the utopian potential of the fragment. This destruction of form is therefore the first step toward what Märten would later develop into her theory of classless forms: aesthetic forms that overcome the division between art, craft, and manual and machine labor, as well as bourgeois genre distinctions.[60] Interjected between odes to "Personality" and "the Conscious Human," reflections on the function and possibilities of art tie

---

57 Märten, *Torso*, 291–2.
58 Märten, *Torso*, 184.
59 The fate of the collective child would continue to serve as a dramatic allegory for the production and reproduction of socialism from Sergei Tretiakov's *Khochu rebenka!* (*I Want a Baby!*, 1926), to Bertolt Brecht's *Der kaukasischer Kreidekreis* (*The Caucasian Chalk Circle*, 1944–5).
60 Lu Märten, *Wesen und Veränderung der Formen und Künste*, 209.

the protagonist's aesthetic aspirations to the formal experimentation found in the novel:

> Shattering a form to arrive at its content and finding a new form for the content – that is art.
>
> That is why we speak of images and aims when we proclaim the way; that is why we do not disdain images and utopias – may they be called Christianity or socialism – for they are all traces and paths, and no one provides their last form or framework – they can only conceptualize it.
>
> The ingenious artwork, however, remains a torso.
>
> For: Where is the form for everything and the final thing that can be suffered and thought? Where is the scream that would have to be screamed? – And because there is no such thing, the strongest things are compelled to the suggestive forms that point beyond themselves – to the symbol – to the message of the splinters that testify to the earthquake – all of the force goes into the part. For you yourself and that which you must depict is a torso – a symbol that allows for thought behind and beyond it. A limb, of which the body knows, a path, whose aim it can conceptualize – a silence, that will make it scream. – Art.
>
> [Eine Form zertrümmern, um zu ihrem Inhalt zu gelangen und für den Inhalt neue Form finden – das ist Kunst.
>
> Darum reden wir von Bildern und Zielen, wenn wir vom Wege verkünden; darum verachte man nicht Bilder und Utopien – mögen sie nun Christentum oder Sozialismus heißen – denn sie sind allesamt Spuren und Wege, und niemand gibt seine letzte Form und Hülle – er kann sie nur denken.
>
> Das geniale Kunstwerk aber bleibt noch Torso.
>
> Denn: Wo ist die Form für das Alles und das Letzte, was gelitten und gedacht sein kann? Wo ist der Schrei, der geschrien werden müßte? – Und weil es solches nicht gibt, drängt alles Stärkste zur andeutenden, über sich hinausweisenden Form – zum Symbol – zur Botschaft der Splitter, die vom Erdbeben zeugen – geht alle Wucht zu einem Teil. So bist du selbst und was du zeigen mußt ein Torso – Symbol, was hinter und vor sich denken läßt. Ein Glied, von dem [d]er Körper weiß, ein Weg, dessen Ziel er denken kann. – Ein Schweigen, das ihn schreien machen wird. – Kunst.][61]

---

61 Märten, *Torso*, 206.

The unresolved tension between the fragment and the whole, silence and the scream, reality and fantasy, constitutes the precarity that Märten seeks to capture in *Torso*: the in-between that renders assimilation undesirable and utopia necessary yet still unattainable. While the workers' autobiographies of the early twentieth century contributed to the mythological construction of the "proletariat as an autonomous historical force," Märten confronts this fantasy with symbols, splinters, torsos, and limbs whose absences are the closest approximation to utopian relations.[62] Completed in the same year as Rilke's "Archaischer Torso Apollos" ("Archaic Torso of Apollo," 1908), Märten's *Torso* is not a monument to the timelessness of art, but to its radical historicity, not a celebration of virility, but an acknowledgment of the contradictions of gendered embodiment and queer desire. Märten pursues the suggestiveness of the fragment without attempting to make it whole. She offers the figure of the torso to catalyze the imaginative work of generating new forms of production, relationality, and, ultimately, a new Marxist aesthetic.

Works Cited

Bebel, August. "Ein Geleitwort." In *Die Jugendgeschichte einer Arbeiterin von ihr selbst erzählt*, edited by Adelheid Popp, 3–5. Munich: Ernst Reinhardt, 1909.

Berlant, Lauren. *Cruel Optimism*. Durham, NC: Duke University Press, 2011.

Bromme, Moritz William Theodor. *Lebensgeschichte eines modernen Fabrikarbeiters*. Edited by Paul Göhre. Jena: Eugen Diedrichs, 1905.

Dehning, Sonja. *Tanz Der Feder. Künstlerische Produktivität in Romanen von Autorinnen um 1900*. Würzburg: Königshausen & Neumann, 2000.

Fischer, Carl. *Denkwürdigkeiten und Erinnerungen eines Arbeiters*. Jena: Eugen Diedrichs, 1903.

Friedberg, J. "Aus einem Artikel der 'Neuen Badischen Landeszeitung'." In *R. Piper & Co Pamphlet Containing Reviews of Torso*, 1909. Folder 115, Lu Märten Papers, International Institute of Social History, Amsterdam, the Netherlands.

Gerstenberger, Katharina. *Truth to Tell: German Women's Autobiographies and Turn-of-the-Century Culture*. Ann Arbor, MI: University of Michigan Press, 2000.

Göhre, Paul. "Vorwort." *Denkwürdigkeiten und Erinnerungen eines Arbeiters, Volume 2: Leben und Wissen*, by Carl Fischer, 4–12. Leipzig: Eugen Diedrichs, 1903.

Göhre, Paul. "Zur Einleitung." *Lebensgeschichte eines modernen Fabrikarbeiters*, edited by Moritz William Theodor Bromme, 5–12. Jena and Leipzig: Eugen Diedrichs, 1905.

Hake, Sabine. *The Proletarian Dream: Socialism, Culture, and Emotion in Germany, 1863–1933*. Berlin and Boston: De Gruyter, 2017.

Hausenstein, Wilhelm. "Aus einer Besprechung in der 'Münchner Post.'" In *R. Piper & Co Pamphlet Containing Reviews of Torso*, 1909. Folder 115, Lu Märten Papers, International Institute of Social History, Amsterdam, the Netherlands.

---

62   Trommler, *Sozialistische Literatur in Deutschland*, 240.

Hausenstein, Wilhelm. "Bergarbeiter. Schauspiel in einem Akte von Lu Märten." In *Der Kampf*. Folder 115, Lu Märten Papers, International Institute of Social History, Amsterdam, the Netherlands.

Jensen, Birgit A. "Bawdy Bodies or Moral Agency? The Struggle for Identity in Working-Class Autobiographies of Imperial Germany." *Biography* 28, no. 4 (2005): 534–57.

Kambas, Chryssoula. *Die Werkstatt als Utopie. Lu Märtens literarische Arbeit und Formästhetik seit 1900*. Tübingen: Niemeyer, 1988.

Märten, Lu. *Die Künstlerin*. Edited by Chryssoula Kambas. Berlin: Aisthesis Verlag, 2001.

Märten, Lu. "Die künstlerischen Momente der Arbeit in alter und neuer Zeit (1903)." In *Formen für den Alltag. Schriften, Aufsätze, Vorträge*, edited by Rainhard May, 9–14. Dresden: Verlag der Kunst, 1982.

Märten, Lu. *Torso. Das Buch eines Kindes*. Berlin: R. Piper & Co., 1909.

Märten, Lu. *Torso. Das Buch eines Kindes (Manuscript)*. 1908. Folder 120, Lu Märten Papers, International Institute of Social History, Amsterdam, the Netherlands.

Märten, Lu. *Wesen und Veränderung der Formen/ Künste. Resultate historisch-materialistischer Untersuchungen*. Frankfurt: Taifun Verlag, 1924.

Münchow, Ursula. *Frühe deutsche Arbeiterautobiographie*. Berlin: Akademie-Verlag, 1973.

Muñoz, José Esteban. *Cruising Utopia: The Then and There of Queer Futurity*. New York: New York Unit Press, 2009.

Popp, Adelheid. *Die Jugendgeschichte einer Arbeiterin*. Berlin: J.H.W. Dietz, 1922.

Puar, Jasbir K. *The Right to Maim: Debility, Capacity, Disability*. Durham, NC: Duke University Press, 2017.

Ruskin, John. *The Stones of Venice*. London: Smith, Elder and Co., 1873.

Trommler, Frank. *Sozialistische Literatur in Deutschland. Ein historischer Überblick*. Stuttgart: Kröner, 1976.

Zetkin, Clara. "Ein Arbeiterdrama." In *Die Gleichheit*, Supplement, "Für unsere Mütter und Hausfrauen," no. 16 (1912): 61.

Seven

In Search of a Divine Calling, or Lunch: Unproductive Labor in Emmy Hennings' *Das Brandmal*

Sophie Duvernoy

> *How can I say so hopelessly that I have no calling. I'm here, after all. Here. Becoming aware of my life, feeling myself here, in this space, holding myself, keeping myself: that's already a calling.*
>
> [*Wie kann ich nur so hoffnungslos sagen, ich gehe ohne Beruf. Ich bin doch da. Bin da. Daß ich bewußt werde meines Lebens, mich hier empfinde, im Raume fühle, mich fasse, behalte, das ist Beruf.*][1]

Das Brandmal. Ein Tagebuch [*The Branding: A Diary*], published by poet and actress Emmy Hennings in 1920, is an unusual text in modernist literature: a fictionalized first-person account of the author's own experiences as a prostitute in the 1910s. It is likely the only literary work in this period written about prostitution by someone who practiced the trade herself.[2] The novel follows an elusive figure, a former actress whom we come to know as Dagny, as she arrives penniless in Cologne, works odd jobs and then as a prostitute, finds work as an actress again, and finally catches a life-threatening fever in Budapest. The first-person

---

1 Emmy Hennings, *Das Brandmal, Das Ewige Lied* (Göttingen: Wallstein Verlag, 2017), 70. Thereafter referred to as *DB*. All English translations of *DB* included in this chapter are my own. As of March 2022, a translation of *DB* is available: see Emmy Hennings, *The Branding: A Diary*, edited, translated, and with an introduction by Katharina Rout (Peterborough, ON: Broadview Press, 2022).

2 For an overview of the Expressionist fascination with prostitution, see Christiane Schönfeld, *Dialektik und Utopie: Die Prostituierte im deutschen Expressionismus* (Würzburg: Königshausen und Neumann, 1996). Schönfeld argues that the prostitute occupies a privileged place in Expressionist literature as the ambiguous figure *par excellence*, embodying the "différance" of the virgin and whore that "represents unreadability itself." Schönfeld, 155.

narrative is told in a fragmented, meandering style, and is inflected with Dagny's religious musings, which the work unfolds in the manner of a confession.[3] The story ends neither with Dagny's destruction nor salvation, but shows how she is chewed up by various jobs over the course of her peregrinations. Thus Dagny finishes the novel in much the same dissolute, impoverished state with which she began.

This chapter argues that *Das Brandmal* (*DB*) thematizes radical withdrawal as a means of making the author and narrator's precarity apparent. By this, I mean that Hennings practices what Leo Bersani and Ulysse Dutoit have called an "aesthetic of failure," which "engage[s] in sacrificial or crippling moves" to claim, "*My work is without authority.*"[4] This aesthetic of failure allows Hennings to use her own powerlessness as a fundamental condition for bearing witness to her life as a marginalized, poor woman around 1910. Simultaneously, an aesthetic of failure makes apparent the actual impossibility of bearing witness adequately to such a life. This interpretation brings *DB* into conversation with other modernist texts about poverty which, as Patrick Greaney has argued, "'double' the appearance of poverty by intertwining 'linguistic poverty' with 'socioeconomic poverty.'"[5] Poverty can only be represented through the failure of representation. *DB*, in turn, emphasizes the specific impoverishment of testimony from a gendered perspective. Dagny, as a poor woman, holds an aesthetic of failure and lack of authority to be a fundamental condition of her own existence. Rather than succumbing to silence, however, *DB* performs a double movement, using a position of negativity and withdrawal to nonetheless unfold its story.

The double movement within *DB* is mirrored by the doubling of Dagny and Hennings herself. Hennings' own life was just as precarious as that of her protagonist, Dagny. Born in 1885, Hennings was hollowed out by her morphine addiction and bohemian lifestyle by 1920, at the age of thirty-five. She was a poor, self-educated woman from a working-class background who moved among artists from the bourgeoisie and middle class. Though she was affiliated with the Cabaret

---

3   See Mirjam Berg, "Writing the Inner Strife: Emmy Hennings's *Das Brandmal. Ein Tagebuch* (1920)." Manuscript for publication in *Women in German Expressionism: Gender, Sexuality, Activism*, ed. Anke Finger and Julie Schoults, forthcoming from University of Michigan Press, shared with me by courtesy of Mirjam Berg.

4   Leo Bersani and Ulysse Dutoit, *Arts of Impoverishment: Beckett, Rothko, Resnais* (Cambridge, MA: Harvard University Press, 1993), 1, 3–4. My thanks to Patrick Greaney, whose comments on the initial version of this paper and book *Untimely Beggar: Poverty and Power from Baudelaire to Benjamin* (Minneapolis, MN: University of Minnesota Press, 2008), were great sources of help and inspiration. The citation of Bersani comes from Greaney's insightful discussion of poverty and withdrawal as forms of power in the nineteenth century.

5   Greaney, *Untimely Beggar*, xv.

Simplicissimus in Munich and was a founding member of the Cabaret Voltaire in Zurich, her work was eyed suspiciously by members of the avant-garde, and she was frequently dismissed as a hysterical hussy by the (primarily male) artists who surrounded her.[6] Yet Hennings deliberately wielded her precarity in her own cabaret performances and writing. In a seminal study of Hennings' life and work, Nicola Behrmann cites a 1912 review in *B.Z. am Mittag* that shows just how discomfiting Hennings could be: she was "little *Emmy Hennings*, half saint, half Apache girl of Montmartre, who compresses the dangerous attraction of life as an outcast into short, wild scenes."[7] It could be uncomfortable to watch Hennings perform: she was unafraid to bare her pain and weakness, staging a grotesque interplay of desire and decay. By making her own exclusion and lack of power visible, Hennings played with her role as a helpless woman to shock and move her audience, and produced work that defies clear interpretation. Behrmann interprets this as Dadaist radicalism *avant la lettre*: "She represented: nothing."[8] The conscious choice to use crippling gestures and withdraw from representational possibilities permeates Hennings' work from this period.

Dagny's aesthetic of failure is unfolded on two different levels: in the novel's narrative strategy and its plot. Dagny is both a "bad artist"—one who cannot achieve the artistic authority to tell her story—and a "bad subject": someone "who [has] failed to internalize the gospel of work."[9] Yet her withdrawal from work is not motivated by politics but religion.[10] This fascination with religion makes Hennings a "bad

---

6   See Ruth Hemus, *Dada's Women* (New Haven, CT: Yale University Press, 2009), 36. Hennings took many lovers (Ferdinand Hardekopf, Johannes R. Becher, and Erich Mühsam among them), and her contemporaries often were more interested in her sexual availability than her work. Even in posthumous reception, Hennings has long been relegated to the sidelines of Dada as Hugo Ball's partner and muse.

7   Nicola Behrmann, *Geburt der Avantgarde - Emmy Hennings* (Göttingen: Wallstein Verlag, 2018), 147. Emphasis in the original; my translation.

8   Behrmann, *Geburt der Avantgarde*, 13; my translation.

9   I am taking the term "bad subjects" from the Marxist feminist theorist Kathi Weeks, who uses it to describe those "who failed to internalize the gospel of work – a history of 'bad subjects' who resist and may even escape interpellation." See Kathi Weeks, *The Problem with Work: Feminism, Marxism, Antiwork Politics, and Postwork Imaginaries* (Durham, NC and London: Duke University Press, 2011), 79.

10 Hennings is not the only Expressionist to voice a deep interest in spirituality, but is more committed to Catholic doctrine than many of her contemporaries, who explored spirituality and world religion more syncretically.

See Alexander Nebrig, "Expressionismus, Neue Sachlichkeit," in *Handbuch Literatur und Religion*, ed. Daniel Weidner (Stuttgart: J.B. Metzler, 2016), 181–5. Nebrig notes that in Expressionist literature, a desire for transcendence typically goes hand in hand with internal dissolution.

modernist": her work expresses a deep devotion to Catholicism that appears, from our contemporary perspective, to be at odds with her radical choice of topics. Modernist social critique often uses secular or Marxist language and ideas to envision alternatives. But in *DB*, Hennings explores earthly precarity in relation to transcendental precarity. She believes that God, though invisible and inconstant, is present in modernity. Her critique of representation and work may share sympathies with a socialist discourse of alienation, but looks instead to a utopian Christian horizon which can imagine a life fulfilled through its link to the divine.

In place of alienated wage labor, Dagny dreams of pursuing an activity in the service of God—a *Beruf*. Beruf, which means "calling" and goes far beyond "work" or "labor," is a form of fulfilled activity that links one's earthly life to God. Yet while Dagny continually appeals to God throughout the novel, she never receives the answer she longs for. Thus, the novel is suffused with a repeated lament: I am without a calling [*Ich bin ohne Beruf*]. Her search for work, and her various questions about labor, are part of a search for God. All her forays into work, including prostitution, are part of a religious quest that lead her to reject regular wage labor in favor of an alternative economy that is at times surreal, at times transcendent. The ultimate outcome of these reflections is that Dagny attempts to turn her own existence—the only thing which cannot be rendered abstract—into her *Beruf*. The rest of the novel, I argue, is a poetic attempt to grapple with this realization and imagine its consequences—both in terms of the economic exchanges it implies, and in terms of the subjective burden it carries.

A Diary of Failure

Any discussion of *DB* must begin by acknowledging the complex entanglement in which the narrator places herself: she is a subject beyond society and beyond language who is attempting to write a diary, an intimate account of her own day-to-day life. From the very beginning, the narrator establishes representational withdrawal as a fundamental condition of the novel and her life. She announces: "I want to begin in the name of the Nameless, even though I feel so far from it. Precisely for this reason: in its name. The Nameless is the first and final cause of my being" (*DB*, 9). She invokes the name of a divinity beyond—or without—a name, beginning with a condition of representative impossibility. Not only does this divinity have no name, but it is impossibly far away, completely out of reach. Her own existence is built on a chasm between herself and this God, while her own consciousness is deeply discontinuous: "But in truth I can no longer understand, hold, grasp. It's as if everything were dissolving" (*DB*, 9).

How can she write a diary under these conditions? Neither the narrating subject, nor the purported object of the novel (her day-to-day life), exhibit internal continuity. External continuity also does not exist: "It took such a long time until one day, I finally admitted to myself: I am a person without definition (*ich bin ein ungeordneter Mensch*)" (*DB*, 9). The narrator's use of "ungeordnet" is unusual; though it might simply mean "chaotic," it is an adjective more readily applied to objects rather than people. It suggests that she cannot be organized or ordered, readily placed within a social system and into a recognizable role. The narrator can neither be represented personally nor socially because of her fragmented consciousness and lack of personal agency.

The narrator now delivers the *coup de grâce*: "I am a woman. I suspend control: the question of 'why' and 'whence.' I admit only the 'how.'" The sentences in this paragraph are discontinuous; they float together, touching but separate (*DB*, 9). Yet the way in which the third sentence gently touches off the second knits together the entire unit of utterances. Being a woman, in this instance, means having a fragmented consciousness which cannot understand ("why" and "whence"), but only experience ("how"). The choppy sentences perform this gesture linguistically by existing as separated utterances. The first page of the novel thus performs multiple crippling gestures that set up the narrative as a series of failures. Not only does the narrator have no internal continuity, but even if she were to overcome this obstacle, she remains unable to offer the reader causal connections, or an account that links together events into a comprehensible sequence. Furthermore, it is suggested that an immutable condition of the narrator's existence—her gender—is at the root of this impossibility. Yet she ends this invocational passage by stating, "now I'm searching again ...." The diary consciously sets up its goal: finding a path from this fundamental condition of negativity to confront the impossibility of expression.

Finding a Calling

We do not learn much about Dagny in the first pages except that she is a woman, has no money, worked last as an actress, and is now without a calling. *DB* thus suggests that the narrator's two quests—to recuperate a sense of herself and find a calling—are intertwined. The narrator returns repeatedly to the question of her calling, and makes it key to her own self-determination. Once yet another temporary job has run its course, she laments:

> I'm without a calling once more. To think that I began to reflect on my calling so early – already as a child – ... and now I'm without one.

[So bin ich denn wieder ohne Beruf. Wenn ich bedenke, daß ich schon so früh an meinen Beruf zu denken begann – schon als kleines Kind dachte ich daran – ... und jetzt habe ich doch keinen Beruf.]

(DB, 67)

A calling has always been central to Dagny's understanding of her own life, and yet it continues to elude her. For someone who survives only on odd jobs and acting gigs, the serious tone of this statement—that she began "to reflect on [her] calling as a child"—seems almost comical. Yet *Beruf* refers to more than a job: it is an entire trajectory that can guide and shape one's life. Although Dagny is aware that she is "a person without definition," a calling can offer her an external measure of order, placing her in a context in which her actions can achieve purpose and she can regain some measure of continuity.

Beruf is a central term of Max Weber's seminal work, *The Protestant Ethic and the Spirit of Capitalism*, published fifteen years before *DB*. In his text, Weber argues that the word achieved initial importance through Luther's Bible translation, in which it means to be called on by God to do holy work. To have a *Beruf* is to have a calling bestowed upon oneself from a higher authority. It is a demand upon body and spirit to train, hone, and existentially prepare oneself for a particular activity in the world.[11] Luther, however, did not fully renew the concept, but rather maintained the "traditionalist view" that the exact calling chosen was unimportant; what was important was that one *felt* called to this divinely-ordained path through lifelong devotion to one's station.[12]

The Calvinists transformed the concept of calling to justify capitalist self-determination, Weber's famous argument goes. A calling became more closely linked to the practicalities of work, and less tied to the idea of a divine path. Kathi Weeks has summarized this transformation as follows: in industrial modernity, "one should set oneself to a lifetime of 'organized worldly labour' *as if* (and not, as we will see, precisely *because*) one were called to it by God."[13] In the move from *because* to *as if*, Weeks summarizes the pivotal turn in Weberian *Geschichtsphilosophie*, in which industrial modernity is a world that has been disenchanted of its metaphysical horizon. In secular modernity, only remnants of the original sense of a calling remain in the fervent attitude towards work. By treating work in industrial modernity as a moral imperative, rather than

---

11   Max Weber, *Gesamtausgabe I/18*, ed. Ursula Bube and Wolfgang Schluchter (Tübingen: Mohr Siebeck, 2016), 209 ff.
12   Weber, *Gesamtausgabe I/18*, 245.
13   Weeks, *The Problem with Work*, 39.

as a means to a concrete end, the capitalist work ethic is ideal for "an economic system predicated on labor abstracted from the specificity of the working person and the particular task."[14] Labor is performed under the guise of a calling, but no longer with a sense of intention or continuity that existed in a world where one's work was a direct link to God.

DB contains scenes of religious reflection in which Dagny attempts to retrieve this direct link to God. After arriving in Cologne, Dagny seeks out the cathedral, where she kneels to pray. Her desperate plea, which is repeated throughout the book, is, "It's not a matter of happiness this time, dear God" (DB, 13). She has abandoned her hope of happiness; all she needs is a means of survival. But God remains silent, and gives no sign of help to the desperate woman. Dagny laments, "I am unfamiliar with prayer, but everything inside me was written within me. Did he perhaps never learn to read? I must not have been clear enough" (DB, 15). Like the diary, Dagny is a text that can be read; perhaps a text that evades clear reading, jumping from one moment to the next, but nonetheless contains information. Yet God is absent, both as a reader and as a speaker. He does not call to her. How will Dagny find a calling under these circumstances? She wonders out loud:

> Outwardly, I am, as you know, a cabaret artist. Somehow, you must accept this calling, otherwise you could easily get rid of it. But your ways are inscrutable ... So much is connected to one's calling, since it is earthly, but you know and respect this with kindheartedness. You see, I can't give grounds for my calling, but I know you can call on me. Let it be as you wish.

> [Meines äußeren Zeichens bin ich, wie du weißt, Kabarettistin. Du wirst auch mit diesem Beruf einverstanden sein, irgendwie, denn sonst könntest du ihn ja leicht abschaffen. Aber unerforschlich sind deine Wege ... Mit dem Beruf ist ja so vieles verbunden, weil der Beruf irdisch ist, aber das weißt du auch, und du bist gütig und nimmst Rücksicht. Sieh, ich kann meinen Beruf gar nicht begründen, aber ich weiß, daß du mich berufen kannst. Es sei, wie du es willst.]

> (DB, 189)

Dagny cannot substantiate herself and give grounds for her choices (Begründung): only God can do this by calling her (Berufung) to the task she must take on. In subjecting herself to a higher, divine power, the narrator invokes a world order in which work is not simply labor,

---

14 Weeks, *The Problem with Work*, 45.

but represents an existential endeavor. She describes her own choice to be a cabaret artist as a mere "outward" manifestation rather than an active decision—necessary only for earthly survival. Dagny exists in a state of anticipation, hoping that God will become manifest and reveal her calling to her, filling her earthly life with new, transcendent purpose.

The Impoverishment of Work

While Dagny is poor, the world around her is impoverished too, because it offers her no opportunities to pursue a calling under divine auspices. This insight is at the heart of the novel's first scene of crisis, in which Dagny, fresh off the train, reads the job listings in the papers at a café. She desperately needs employment, but finds it impossible to convince herself that she is suitable for any of the listings—though perhaps it is the reverse, and none of the listings are suitable for her.

> "Seeking intelligent young women with good references." No one has ever been foolish enough to recommend me. "Helper for housewife ..." –: I can't even help myself. "Three trained seamstresses, sound knowledge of dress shirts ..." Oh, I'm neither one nor the other ... I move myself to a cigarette factory, sit down, and begin rolling a brand I've only ever smoked, but I won't do that again either. I'm doing unbelievable damage. I'd rather leave work well alone.

> [»Gut empfohlene, intelligente Mädchen finden Beschäftigung.« So leichtsinnig ist noch niemand gewesen, mich zu empfehlen. »Stütze der Hausfrau ... « –: wo ich mich nicht einmal selbst habe halten können. »Drei gelernte Weißnäherinnen, die firm in Manschetthemden sind ... « Ach, ich bin weder das eine, noch das andere ... Ich versetze mich in eine Zigarettenfabrik und drehe sitzend eine Marke, die ich bisher nur geraucht habe, aber ich werde das auch nie wieder tun. Ich richte ja einen unglaublichen Schaden an. Lieber will ich meine Hände von der Arbeit lassen.]

(*DB*, 18–19)

All of these listings are for "pink collar" work and require traditionally feminine attributes of the applicant. The mental preparation Dagny must do to existentially align herself with these jobs is too much for her. She instead fantasizes about factory work, but in this fantasy, she is an anarchic element in the factory, a wrench in the works doing "unbelievable damage" to the entire process. Her internal monologue suggests that she not only feels practically unqualified, but is actively opposed to these positions. She sees no solution but to opt out of an economy that will force her to abstract from her own existence and sell her labor power to make a living. However, there is a big problem with opting out, as she grimly notes: "You can't make a living doing nothing" (*DB*, 18–19).

Dagny begins to unfold an economic logic in which, since she has nothing else to offer, her life is the only form of possible payment. She orders a meal at the café and contemplates suicide:

> What if I ordered a sandwich? I could eat it slowly and slit my arteries with the knife; after eating, of course ... Once you're dead, there's no more counting to be done. It fades away in the throes. As you die, unpaid bills, which you desperately sought to pay when you were alive, become trifles, and belief [*Glauben*] miraculously transforms into certain knowledge [*Erkenntnis*]: "I wouldn't have been able to pay anyhow – now I definitely won't."
>
> [Wie, wenn ich mir ein illustriertes Brötchen bestellen würde? Das könnte ich langsam essen und mir mit dem Messer die Pulsadern aufschneiden; nachher natürlich, nach dem Essen ... Sowie man tot ist, wird nicht mehr gerechnet. Schon während der Agonie läßt das nach. Sterbend werden unbezahlte Rechnungen, um die man sich im Leben verzweifelt bemüht hat, sie zu zahlen, Bagatellen, und wunderbar vertieft sich der Glaube zur klarsten Erkenntnis: »Ich hätte ohnedies nicht zahlen können – jetzt zahle ich erst recht nicht.«]
>
> (*DB*, 21, 23)

Death becomes not only an escape from this particular situation, but the solution to escaping the yoke of the money economy as a whole. The absurd idea of exchanging a life for a sandwich highlights Dagny's desperation. Notably, this scene foreshadows one of the novel's primary insights: when you do not have labor power to pay for things, all you are left with is your own existence. This kind of life is considered worthless by society at large. Yet, as Dagny asserts repeatedly, it is the only certainty she can count on, and therefore the only reality upon which she can build a calling. Furthermore, this logic breaches the horizon of transcendental precarity: it allows Dagny to transform belief—*Glauben*—into knowledge—*Erkenntnis*.

Surreal Economies

DB subsequently chronicles Dagny's experiments in turning her own person into a calling. While prostitution is ultimately the clearest expression of this ambition (more on this later), Dagny also attempts to sell intangible assets that are not commodities in the normal sense: time, air, and her death to come. These are not use-values created by productive labor but frame the conditions of her own existence. Accordingly, her attempts, or fantasies, of exploiting them for monetary value create a surreal economy that drives capitalist exchange to its utmost limits. As we will see, "belief" becomes a key term to validate these assets, which otherwise have no tangible value.

Time is one of Dagny's only plentiful possessions: "I had time, only time, nothing else" (*DB*, 12). In a dream, Dagny envisions an alternative world in which employment offices are replaced by ministries for time. Rather than measuring one's labor power, these ministries give people receipts for the amount of time they possess:

> In the night, I dreamed that time was weighed in an office every day, and that there were time bills. Everyone deposited their packets of time. Names were written on them and receipts were issued.

> [In der Nacht träumte mir, die Zeit würde jeden Morgen in einem Bureau gewogen, und es gab Zeitscheine. Jeder gab sein Paket Zeit ab. Der Name wurde drauf geschrieben und eine Quittung wurde ausgestellt.]

The dream first imagines time as a solid mass that can be traded, weighed, and cataloged. But it quickly morphs into a viscous, bodily substance that quivers with existential vulnerability:

> Time was brought in the form of extremely sensitive material. It was a gray, rubbery, slime-like lump, which left behind no visible trace or dampness. The gray lump was streaked with red veins of blood, and swollen blue and green veins.

> [Denn die Zeit wurde in Form einer überaus empfindsamen Materie gebracht. Es war eine graue, zähe, schleimartige Masse, die gleichwohl weder feuchte, noch sichtbare Spuren hinterließ. Diese graue Masse war durchzogen von roten Blutfäden, und von blau und grün angeschwollenen Adern.]

(*DB*, 37)

This corporeal mass, full of swollen veins and arteries, represents the felt quality of time, its human value and weight. But although time quivers with the weight of human life, it leaves behind no trace as it slips onto the scales. In this dream, time "grow[s] steadily," flooding Dagny, and yet has no exchange value (*DB*, 37). Though time is money, as Benjamin Franklin said, Dagny becomes no richer through her vast supply of time, but begins to understand that time is only worth something in relation to labor, not in isolation from it.

Dagny then attempts to make use of her plentiful time by selling air—more specifically, air freshener tablets made of naphthalene (the primary ingredient in mothballs). She responds to a job advertisement looking for "[p]ersons with free time and a large number of acquaintances," though she admits to having only one of the two requisites (*DB*, 58). She meets a married couple who want to sell off a stockpile of air freshener tablets. Dagny sets out as a door-to-door saleswoman for these tablets, which are marketed as "Ozone Odor" and perfumed with the scent of the impossible: "Flowering meadows in winter." To heighten their absurdity, they are emblazoned with a decidedly half-hearted sales slogan, "Once you have it, you'll never go without it" (*DB*, 59). Adding insult to injury, the promise of "purity" these "ozone tablets" offer is a mere fiction: naphthalene is in fact a fumigant used for household pest control. She eventually gives up her attempts to sell these tablets out of disgust at the product, and her own recognition of the futility of her task: "I won't become the ozone sales representative for all Westphalia, since you can't represent something you don't believe in" (*DB*, 67). Though this is a dry punchline for a satirical episode in her string of odd jobs, her true objection to the matter pulls it back into a religious framework. Dagny voices the idea that work must be something to believe in, and no mere money-making activity. The imperative to believe, as we will see later, leads her to conclude that prostitution is a more honest profession than acting.

Her one successful attempt at selling time is to sell a by-product of its passing: her own hair. She lauds it as her only true productive creation: "Perhaps it was the only real thing my head ever brought to light. The only power and energy, perhaps." Naturally, this act of honest, and unalienated production falls out of the purview of a traditionally structured economy. "'Letting my hair grow' isn't a job I can declare at a hotel, I think," Dagny wryly comments (*DB*, 44–5).

Once Dagny has exhausted a range of options for making a living, she attempts to sell her body to an anatomy institute—in other words, sell off her corpse in advance. This is another satirical high point of the novel, in which Dagny attempts to convert her existence into a commodity with market value. She has been told by a colleage that she can receive up to 300 marks for this effort, and comments: "To receive three hundred marks for something quite passive—who wouldn't be tempted by that, once in their lives? To make a deal out of death?" (*DB*, 201). However, this idea is not taken up in jest, but again with the idea that Dagny must embody the promise of her own corpse and spark belief in herself. As the confused doorman at the anatomy institute becomes more and more alarmed by

Dagny's rambling attempts to sell her corpse, she finally blurts out: "I forbid the slightest doubts about my sanity. I feel professional as a corpse, and perhaps that's why you find me absurd" (*DB*, 207).

Dagny hopes to appeal with her professionalism—a displaced form of belief, as we have seen with Weber—to prove that she has serious intentions. She begins to price her most precious resource: "I demand three hundred marks, I won't hawk myself off for less. Just so you know. If your institute doesn't want me, fine. I don't mind. I'll find other anatomical institutes that will, so to speak, roll out the welcome mat" (*DB*, 207). Yet Dagny has no real bargaining power. The doorman explains that her body is not rare enough to be worth 300 marks; only if she had some kind of bodily abnormality would she be interesting to science. As it is, she leaves the anatomy institute empty-handed and exhausted.

These three vignettes show Dagny attempting to turn passive features of existence into income, yet none approach her ideal of a calling. In this vision of her work, she must find a pursuit in which, above all, she can offer belief—in her own existence.

Beruf Incarnate

The central problem of *DB* is that Dagny must become her own calling. This can only happen through two major terms: belief and substantiation—that is, existential embodiment. Prostitution is a nexus that connects these two qualities to one another, becoming a form of work that (sometimes) mirrors the creative act and allows Dagny to become God-like, capable of extending salvation to the world that has sent her to her ruin.[15] Yet Dagny's work as a prostitute is also characterized by profound trauma, an abject pain and loss of sense of self: "Something inside me is full of cracks and bloody threads. I don't know what. It hurts and is sore. I don't know why" (*DB*, 232). Powerful imagery of wounds circumscribes her pain. The sex acts she undertakes are only mentioned as things which cannot be mentioned or shared: "there are things on earth that are unspeakable" (*DB*, 150). The reader is cast adrift amid these very different characterizations of prostitution. Prostitution is part of a shifting, indeterminate field that allows the narrator to explore the relationship between calling, belief, and embodiment from the position of withdrawal she otherwise occupies.

---

15 Behrmann emphatically argues that Dagny is not a martyr in the text: see Behrmann, *Geburt der Avantgarde*, 155. I would add, however, that there is a difference in presenting oneself as a martyr and as God-like, and that in *Das Brandmal*, the narrator does the latter.

Dagny's first foray into prostitution occurs after she rejects wage labor and experiences an initial sexual violation. After a near meltdown in the café, Dagny is saved by her acquaintance, the actor Titus Matschke, who pays for dinner but then demands sexual favors in return.[16] Titus himself takes part in a similar exchange as a companion to a (presumably wealthier) woman. He scorns ordinary work and suggests that Dagny do the same: "What a strange sermon he held! Work destroys the human spirit, and it is impossible to iron shirts in an intellectual fashion." While Titus is presented to us as a bohemian, with far more self-assurance and none of the structural disadvantages of our narrator, his critique of work still resonates with Dagny. As she imagines praying once again to God for an answer, Titus's voice intrudes "like a dream in reality," and offers the answer that God withholds from her: she must sell herself. Yet Titus does not advise her to sell sex outright, but rather to master the art of desire; "I should set the senses of others asway." He advises, "You must wield your personality as skillfully as the violin virtuoso plays his instrument" (*DB*, 27). The art of selling sex involves stimulating the customer's senses and fantasies through one's person. While Titus means his advice to be straightforward, Dagny transforms it through her own religious ideas into something less mundane: the production of belief itself.

Throughout the novel, the narrator claims repeatedly that though she is a prostitute, she does not sell sex so much as belief to her clients. This belief is once again coupled to the possibility of a fulfilled calling:

> I am within grasp, made of flesh and blood ... I can make only myself into a calling. I believe deeply in myself, my own existence, and hope others will believe in it too. Can those who embrace me not believe in that moment that I am reality? That I am nature? I am matter.

> [Das Greifbare bin ich selbst, von Fleisch und Blut ... Ich kann nur mich selbst zum Berufe machen. Am tiefsten glaube ich noch an mich selbst, an mein Dasein, und ersehne, daß auch die andern daran glauben möchten. Wer mich umarmt, glaubt er im Augenblicke nicht, daß ich die Realität bin? Bin ich dann nicht die Natur? Ich bin die Materie.][17]

(*DB*, 68–9)

16 This argument is made by Christiane Schönfeld, who thinks that Titus rapes or demands sex from Dagny by the Rhine. I have found this interpretation increasingly convincing over several re-readings. See Schönfeld, *Dialektik und Utopie*.

17 This may also be an ironic rebuke to a typical Expressionist division between man, the thinker, and woman, the feeling animal. See Marion Adams, "Der Expressionismus und die Krise der deutschen Frauenbewegung," in *Expressionismus und Kulturkrise*, ed. Bernd Hüppauf (Heidelberg: Verlag Carl Winter, 1983), 105–30.

By turning herself into her calling, Dagny makes belief into the basis of her work. In certain ways, this stands the Weberian idea of work on its head: if work in capitalism is traditionally undertaken because of an inherited form of belief that has cast labor into a moral mold, her work instead offers up belief (the moral mold itself) as a good. In Dagny's own language, she imparts belief in fixity for a moment. Countering Benjamin's vision of the prostitute as human become pure commodity,[18] in *DB* the prostitute is someone—or something, i.e., matter—"to believe in."[19] She becomes a God-like figure that can cleanse the world of sin through belief: "I must cleanse the whole city; this is my heavy task. Wade through all the swamps. Then, when I will have sunk to my lowest—taken willingly—I will say in perfect surrender, 'Do you believe in me?'"[20] (*DB*, 95).

However, the coupling of belief and matter must be read in a different sense too: as the artist's longing to become one with her creation. As Dagny reflects upon her previous acting jobs, she notices that they always involve a displacement of self, though her "material," so to speak, is her own self. The perfect artistic fantasy, by contrast, is to join with the material and incarnate it:

If I were a fulfilled calling, I would be like God.

Now I am playing my own role. But can I truly arrive in it? Love allowed God to become human, and this was a calling: the creator became his creation. But what artist can turn himself into his own statue, his own work? It's all too unreal, like a fairy tale.

[Wäre ich erfüllter Beruf, wäre ich gottähnlich.

So aber spiele ich mich hinein. Komme ich denn aber wirklich hinein? Die Liebe ließ Gott Mensch werden, und das war Beruf,

---

18   See Schönfeld, *Dialektik und Utopie*, 88, and her commentary on the relevant passage in Benjamin. Walter Benjamin, "Paris, Capital of the Nineteenth Century," in *The Arcades Project*, trans. Howard Eiland and Kevin McLaughlin (Cambridge, MA: Harvard University Press, 1999), 14–26.

19   Dagny tries to remove herself from the money economy by claiming that she performs her role out of a feeling of "Hingabe" (sacrifice/surrender), which, with its root word "Gabe" (gift), already points to an economy of the freely given. For more on *Gabe* and its Christian connotations in *DB*, see Behrmann, *Geburt der Avantgarde*, 323–7.

20   This overwrought passage is ironized by the preceding paragraphs, which describe a painful childhood memory: a man in Dagny's village tries to force himself upon her but fails, and she continues to greet him against her will, describing this as a form of sacrifice.

daß Schöpfer zum Geschöpf wurde. Welcher Künstler aber verwandelt sich in seine eigene Statue, in sein eigen Werk? Alles ist zu unwirklich, märchenhaft.]

(*DB*, 68–9)

An actor can never truly become her character, and is thus distanced from what she produces. Instead, Dagny longs to participate in an act of complete incarnation: not just to have a fulfilled calling but *become* it. In fact, this is how she defines the calling anew. The creator must become his or her own creation. By becoming her calling, she will become like God, incarnating her purpose just as God became human to save humankind.

Hennings' writings from the period in which she wrote *DB* further develop ideas of incarnation and embodiment. In a letter to Hugo Ball in 1915/16, she voices a deep, urgent desire to become one with the act of creation:

> When we left Berlin, you said we are wanderers in the night, tightrope walkers in the dark. And that we could remain so, forever ... I love great adventure and the conquest of adventure. Yes, I'll admit I want to become an adventure myself, one that can never be forgotten.

> [Als wir von Berlin fortfuhren, sagtest Du, wir sind wie Nachtwandler, Seiltänzer noch im Dunkeln. Daß wir es bleiben dürften, immer ... Ich liebe das große Abenteuer und die Überwindung des Abenteuers. Ja, ich gestehe, ich selbst möchte ein Abenteuer werden und sein, daß man nie vergißt.][21]

Walking a tightrope and embarking upon an adventure, the great unknown of artistic production, is invoked by Hennings not as something that she wants to do, but something she wants to become. Incarnation and embodiment are key to her idea of artistic creation. Only by incarnating the work itself can she become a fulfilled calling, disappearing into it completely and defining herself only through it. This ambition is once again connected to an act of withdrawal, as Hennings imagines disappearing into the slipstream of an event. Behrmann characterizes Hennings' cabaret performances in similar fashion: "Her performances must have been so disturbing because she no longer appeared as female allegory with a referent, but instead staged the event itself, behind

---

21 Hennings, *Hugo Ball. Sein Leben in Briefen und Gedichten* (Berlin: S. Fischer, 1930), 104.

which she, as its author, disappeared completely."[22] The complete collapse of author into an event, into her material, marks the true power of Hennings' work. Through this disappearance, the author (or, in this case, the narrator) becomes but a shadow figure suggested through her own absence—she is at one with her text.

Yet this language, which suggests a messianic role for the prostitute/artist, is offset by Dagny's repeated laments that she is irrevocably damaged and powerless. She is fundamentally unable to communicate about her life and to express the pain she has suffered:

> I will keep and hold everything inside me, because it is my fate to keep. Everything is written inside me. And inside me, everything is new, as if the past were happening again and again. The living image repeats itself inside me, becoming even more alive. If only it didn't hurt so much! Those are the reflex pains: when you can't see anything, but it's all there ... But I can't speak.

> [So will ich denn alles in mir behalten und bewahren, denn es ist meine Bestimmung, zu behalten. Alles steht in mir. Und in mir ist alles neu, als geschähe die Vergangenheit immer wieder. So wiederholt sich das lebendige Bild in mir und wird immer lebendiger. Wenn es nur nicht so schmerzte! Das sind die Reflexschmerzen: wenn man nichts mehr sieht, und doch alles da ist ... Ich aber kann gar nicht sprechen.]

(DB, 149)

In this passage, Dagny describes herself as a "living image" (reminiscent of her prayer to God, in which she is a "living text") behind which her person disappears. Her withdrawal or disappearance has taken place—but it is one in which she is left a mute shell, and the image or text remains invisible, while she suffers from the excess of life that continues to repeat and expand within her. The reflex pains,[23] which are prolonged and severe, are the only haptic sign of her distress. In part, this is because she has not been able to author the text that is contained within her. Instead, it is impressed upon her by the outside world: she describes herself as "a living mirror," behind which only she can see with "the eyes of the mind."[24] (DB, 82)

---

22 Behrmann, *Geburt der Avantgarde*, 234.
23 Reflex pains are a form of prolonged pain in which the body continues to produce a pain response long after the triggering event.
24 For more on Dagny as medium/text, see Behrmann, *Geburt der Avantgarde*, 155; 233–4; Berg, "Writing the Inner Strife."

The process of writing is cast as a negative one, in which her own withdrawal into the text impressed upon her makes communication impossible. Instead, words loose themselves from her of their own accord:

> I write here, alone. How weak everything is. The words written here came from the heart, but the letters are black. And a living person wrote them, a person who has never been able to turn to someone else with these words, since there are some things on earth that are unspeakable. Words escape me when someone touches the stigma. When someones bumps against me, all I can do is flinch away and cry. That's my only answer.

> [Ich schreibe hier nieder und allein. Wie schwach ist alles. Hier steht nun, was aus dem Herzen kam, aber die Buchstaben sind schwarz. Und ein lebendiger Mensch hat sie geschrieben, der mit dem Wort sich noch nie hat an einen anderen Menschen wenden können, denn es gibt Dinge auf Erden, die unaussprechlich sind. Die Worte entfallen mir, wenn jemand das Brandmal berührt. Wenn jemand an mich anstößt, werde ich nur zusammenzucken und weinen. Das ist meine einzige Antwort.]

(*DB*, 149–50)

The act of writing is solitary and intended to compensate for a speaking that is impossible. But this writing is, in a sense, merely a private compensation (in the form of a diary) for her fundamental inability to communicate. "Words escape me" can be read in two ways: words mentally escape her in the moment of attempted communication; or words "fall out" of her grasp, into the world and away from the living text of her body. Only the loosening of language itself, its falling-away from the narrator, can enable this text to speak of the unspeakable. In a sense, Dagny has become her material; but rather than being able to present it to others as a whole, she can only incarnate the material through a process of gradual dissolution. This is how *DB* portrays ultimate impoverishment.

As the novel comes to its conclusion, Dagny is rescued from her acting job (which she describes as just another form of prostitution) by a bad fever, in which her consciousness fractures into dreams, prayers, and visions, and her body "dissolves into diamond dust." Matter, the body that others could believe in, has now dissolved into white, crystalline powder that can blow away in the gust of a breeze. Nothing but a trace is left behind. This fever is not a fitting punishment for the protagonist's immoral life, but is instead a natural conclusion to a work that explores the dissolution of self into language, which begins to run riot, floating away and playing at rhymes: "My name dances around in waves of sound. My name, like my self, can't be realized. But people don't believe me, and try to grab my thighs"[25] (DB, 232). Dagny's name and self cannot be grasped; they dissolve into waves, withdraw—yet even this act of withdrawal remains fundamentally unrecognized by those who try to catch a handful of flesh. Dagny's ultimate impoverishment is being denied the ability to withdraw completely, while she is inwardly already elsewhere. She fails once again—a failure that marks her gender and lack of power.

Coda

In this chapter, I have argued that DB is a novel about the failure to turn work into a calling, an activity that goes beyond labor in industrial capitalism by looking towards a metaphysical horizon. Yet this metaphysical horizon is at best self-posited and does not carry an active promise of redemption. When Dagny talks to God, she receives no answer. Indeed, her doubts become part of her practice of prayer: "Oh, Christ Kyrie, let me go over the waves. Can you accept my doubts as prayers? Because my doubts concern you too" (DB, 242). The novel does not offer a fulfilled metaphysical alternative to labor, but peters out quietly in Dagny's thoughts. The critique of modernity the novel attempts to offer is complicated by narrative failure on multiple fronts, which the narrator blames on her feminity, her poverty, and her prostitution. From the very beginning, she is condemned to muteness. The critique of wage labor is therefore embedded within an aesthetics of failure that proffers acts of withdrawal as the only possible way to exemplify systematic powerlessness, since it cannot be escaped from. No single factor—gender, sex, capitalism, religion, or work—can explain or resolve the conflicts at the heart of Das Brandmal. Instead, the novel gives its readers a sense of interpretive precarity: they must constantly move between standpoints to understand the fragile web that holds Dagny's universe together.

---

25 "Mein Name macht die Runde und ist eine Schallwelle. Mein Name läßt sich, wie mein Ich, nicht begreifen. Aber das glauben die Leute nicht, und sie wollen mich immer um die Hüften greifen."

Works Cited

Adams, Marion. "Der Expressionismus und die Krise der deutschen Frauenbewegung." In *Expressionismus und Kulturkrise*, edited by Bernd Hüppauf, 105–30. Heidelberg: Carl Winter, 1983.

Behrmann, Nicola. *Geburt der Avantgarde – Emmy Hennings*. Göttingen: Wallstein Verlag, 2018.

Benjamin, Walter. "Paris, Capital of the Nineteenth Century." In *The Arcades Project*, translated by Howard Eiland and Kevin McLaughlin, 14–26. Cambridge, MA: Harvard University Press, 1999.

Berg, Mirjam. "Writing the Inner Strife: Emmy Hennings's *Das Brandmal. Ein Tagebuch* (1920)." In *Women in German Expressionism: Gender, Sexuality, Activism*, edited by Anke Finger and Julie Schoults. Ann Arbor, MI: University of Michigan Press, forthcoming.

Bersani, Leo and Ulysse Dutoit. *Arts of Impoverishment: Beckett, Rothko, Resnais*. Cambridge, MA: Harvard University Press, 1993.

Greaney, Patrick. *Untimely Beggar: Poverty and Power from Baudelaire to Benjamin*. Minneapolis, MN: University of Minnesota Press, 2008.

Hemus, Ruth. *Dada's Women*. New Haven, CT: Yale University Press, 2009.

Hennings, Emmy. *The Branding: A Diary*. Edited, translated, and with an introduction by Katharina Rout. Peterborough, ON: Broadview Press, 2022.

Hennings, Emmy. *Das Brandmal, Das Ewige Lied*. Göttingen: Wallstein Verlag, 2017.

Hennings, Emmy. *Hugo Ball. Sein Leben in Briefen und Gedichten*. Berlin: S. Fischer, 1930.

Nebrig, Alexander. "Expressionismus, Neue Sachlichkeit." In *Handbuch Literatur und Religion*, edited by Daniel Weidner, 181–5. Stuttgart: J.B. Metzler, 2016.

Schönfeld, Christiane. *Dialektik und Utopie: Die Prostituierte im deutschen Expressionismus*. Würzburg: Königshausen und Neumann, 1996.

Weber, Max. *Gesamtausgabe I/18*, edited by Ursula Bube and Wolfgang Schluchter. Tübingen: Mohr Siebeck, 2016.

Weeks, Kathi. *The Problem with Work: Feminism, Marxism, Antiwork Politics, and Postwork Imaginaries*. Durham, NC and London: Duke University Press, 2011.

Eight   Typists as "billige Ware": White-Collar Women's Work in Weimar Literature

Mary Hennessy

Richard Oswald's romantic comedy film *Arm wie eine Kirchenmaus* (*Poor as a Church Mouse*, 1931) opens with bank director and baron Thomas von Ullrich (Anton Edthofer) returning home from a business trip to the United States. Impressed by the speed and efficiency with which American business is conducted, von Ullrich is determined to introduce principles of rationalization—of "Tempo! Tempo! Tempo!"—to his own sleepy Viennese bank. After firing his glamorous secretary—during the Great Depression—for being too friendly and too feminine, von Ullrich secures the secretarial services of Susi Sachs (Grete Mosheim), the film's titular "church mouse."

Sachs is an ideal candidate; in addition to being modestly dressed, she speaks English and French, and is well versed in both typing and stenography. In a trial dictation, Sachs appears beatific, smiling and encouraging von Ulrich to speak faster and faster, appearing to anticipate his words before he speaks. "Use my labor power!" she tells him. "Faster!" Her hands, framed in a quick close-up, fly over the typewriter keys at almost superhuman speed. Impressed, von Ullrich hires Sachs on the spot, later telling a male colleague that his new employee is not a young woman but "part of the typewriter." Sachs's alignment with the machine and her focus on work is so complete that she can forgo such human frailties as eating or taking breaks. Despite (or more accurately because of) her machine-like performance at work, von Ullrich and Sachs fall in love. The film ends with a marriage proposal made by dictation, and with it, the transformation of Sachs from worker to wife.[1]

The cheerful onscreen representation of typists in late Weimar cinema is at odds with the reality of most female typists at the time, who were overworked, underpaid, and often subject to harassment and exploitation by male superiors. This was reflected both in the social reality and language of the time: as Friedrich Kittler argues, "typewriter" came to refer to both machine and female typists beginning in the nineteenth century, as women entered the white-collar workforce in staggering numbers.[2] Even as the typewriter expanded the opportunities for female authors to publish and find audiences, it did so in accordance with gendered logics of production, reproduction, and control that cast women as receivers and consumers rather than producers of texts. These gendered logics have proven durable, marking subsequent media theories that grapple with the collapse or confusion of woman and typewriter in many Weimar-era sources. Kittler, for instance, describes Weimar-era novels written by women as a series of "endless feedback loops making secretaries into writers."[3] Yet, as Katherine Biers notes, Kittler's account ignores "women's own interpretations of the dramatic new place they came to occupy within the late nineteenth-century discourse network."[4]

In this chapter, I consider Siegfried Kracauer's "Das Schreibmaschinchen" (*DS*; "The Little Typewriter"), a short prose text from 1927 that tells the story of a male author's infatuation with his (female) typewriter. I contrast Kracauer's piece with a popular, but critically forgotten novel of the Weimar Republic, Christa Anita Brück's *Schicksale hinter Schreibmaschinen* (*SHS*; *Destinies Behind Typewriters*; 1930), which offers a first-person account of the relentless commodification of women typists.[5] Kracauer and Brück's texts present mirror images of the typist,

---

1 For an excellent article on *Arm wie eine Kirchenmaus* and Wilhelm Thiele's 1931 film *Die Privatsekretärin* (The Private Secretary), see Angelika Führich, "Woman and Typewriter: Gender, Technology, and Work in Late Weimar Entertainment Film," *Women in German Yearbook* 151 (2016): 151–66.

2 See Friedrich Kittler, *Discourse Networks 1800/1900*, trans. Michael Metteer and Chris Cullens (Stanford, CA: Stanford University Press, 1990) and *Gramophone, Film, Typewriter*, trans. Geoffrey Winthrop-Young and Michael Wutz (Stanford, CA: Stanford University Press, 1999).

3 Kittler, *Gramophone, Film, Typewriter*, 221.

4 Katherine Biers, "The Typewriter's Truth," in *Kittler Now: Current Perspectives in Kittler Studies*, ed. Stephen Sale and Laura Salisbury (Cambridge: Polity Press, 2015), 136.

5 Scholarly attention to Brück has been slim. Exceptions include Sara Kristina Farner Budarz, "Inside the City: Gender and the Production of Interior Space in Weimar Republic German Literature, 1929–1933," PhD diss., University of North Carolina at Chapel Hill, 2014; Christiane Nowak,

who is tasked with producing and reproducing words for others, but never for herself. In both texts, we see a juxtaposition of meaning and non-meaning: Kracauer's infatuation with his machine is expressed in the feverish production of nonsense words, while Brück portrays the act of typing as a foreclosure of sense or meaning-making, whereby words, consciousness, and thought are crushed, or "zermalmt," by the typewriter, abusive male bosses, and financial and social precarity. If writing in the age of the typewriter became a form of word processing, as Kittler argues, women themselves became word processors—at great personal cost.[6]

Kracauer, who writes his text from the perspective of the male objectifying subject, describes the relationship between the author and the typewriter as one between a male lover and his female love object. Brück, on the other hand, reveals how the all-pervasive structural challenges in a typist's life gradually strip her of all vitality and make her into an object. By readings these two texts together, I argue that typists in the Weimar Republic were not only subject to a process of capitalist *Verdinglichung*, in which human life and social relationships are reduced to things, but also that this process viciously targeted female white-collar workers, despite their best efforts to resist it.[7] Both texts further reveal the human cost of bureaucratic communication, particularly for women. Far from offering emancipation, the role in which female typists were cast—as reproducers, mediators, transcribers, processors, and networkers—further reduced women to objects, either as objects of male sexual desire or as mechanical objects whose work served the interests of the (male) business world. In Brück's novel, the female typist is denied both mind and body; by serving as a channel or medium for others, she loses her ability to think or create meaning, while the repetitive, strenuous nature of the work saps her of her vitality. The

---

"'Durchschnittsware': Individualisierungskonzepte in den Angestelltenromanen *Schicksale hinter Schreibmaschinen* (Christa Anita Brück) und *Das Mädchen an der Orga Privat* (Rudolf Braune)," *JUNI. Magazin für Literatur und Politik* 47/48 (2013): 103–18; and Liane Schüller, *Vom Ernst der Zerstreuung: Schreibende Frauen am Ende der Weimarer Republik: Marieluise Fleißer, Irmgard Keun und Gabriele Tergit* (Bielefeld: Aisthesis Verlag, 2005).

6   On word processing as gendered labor, see the chapter "Unseen Hands" in Matthew Kirschenbaum's *Track Changes: A Literary History of Word Processing* (Cambridge, MA: Harvard University Press, 2016).

7   *Verdinglichung*, usually translated as reification or objectification, is a concept associated primarily with Georg Lukács's 1923 book *History and Class Consciousness*, which examines, among other topics, rationalization and its effects on workers. See Georg Lukács, *History and Class Consciousness*, trans. Rodney Livingstone (Cambridge, MA: MIT Press, 1972).

hieroglyphic nonsense texts produced by Brück's protagonist, in the last of the five positions she holds in the novel, are reconfigured from a form of inner resistance to one of deep suffering, produced by a subject who has been denied subjectivity.

Mädchen und Maschinchen: Kracauer's "Das Schreibmaschinchen"

In "Das Schreibmaschinchen," a male narrator describes his recently-purchased typewriter as an object of romantic and sexual affection.[8] He assigns to the "little machine" (*Maschinchen*) distinctly feminine characteristics: "From the first moment I loved the machine for its perfection. It is gracefully built, light as a feather and flashes in the dark. The frame that supports the keys has the slenderness of flamingo legs" (*DS*, 589). So entranced is he with his typewriter that at first he is afraid to use it: "At the beginning of our relationship, I only sheepishly caressed her cool parts" (*DS*, 586). The language Kracauer employs to describe the typewriter is drawn from contemporary typewriter advertisements, which deployed words like *leicht* (light), *schön* (beautiful), and *vollkommen* (perfect/complete), to entice consumers. Many typewriter models even bore women's names (Erika, Monika, Diana, and Gabriele). The typewriter in Kracauer's piece is coded female not only by anthropomorphic description and the consonance of *Mädchen* und *Maschinchen* but also in terms of the narrator's "relationship" with "her." When he finally works up the courage to type, the act is framed as a passionate, semi-sexual union: "We spent blissful hours together in twilight, when I could not quite see the keys … Often the keys moved by themselves, so connected was the little machine with me" (*DS*, 586).

The narrator's relationship to the typewriter begins as one of possession: "Recently, I have come to call a typewriter my own" (*DS*, 586). After a time, however, his attachment to the machine grows so intense that he begins to forgo human contact in favor of the typewriter: "It soon mattered more to me than a woman or my friends. We sped forward from the left edge of the sheet into the unknown and back again; every spot of the paper was covered with ciphers. Weeks passed us by

---

8   Siegfried Kracauer, "Das Schreibmaschinchen," in Kracauer, *Werke* 5.2: *Essays, Feuilletons, Rezensionen, 1924–1927*, eds. Inka Mülder-Bach and Ingrid Belke (Frankfurt: Suhrkamp, 2004): 585–9. Hereafter referred to as *DS*. Johannes von Moltke has translated "Das Schreibmaschinchen" into English. His translation appears in Siegfried Kracauer, *The Little Typewriter*, ed. Meghan Forbes and Hannah McMurray (Austin, TX: Harlequin Creature, 2017). The translations in this chapter are mine.

like this" (DS, 586). The narrator no longer uses a strictly first-person point of view, but speaks and writes *with* the typewriter: "I" becomes "we." Whether we understand the typewriter in Kracauer's piece as woman, machine, or feminized machine, the effect "she" has on the narrator is undeniable. The narrator gives himself over to a frenzied, passionate encounter in which he produces "Schriftfiguren" (writing or font figures) that signify nothing. The text he produces is stripped of its referentiality, its meaning, and any discernible commodity or use value. Their union is one of *jouissance*, a utopian flight into the unknown.

The romance between narrator and typewriter is over as quickly as it begins, however, when the key for the cedilla gives out, a seemingly minor glitch that the narrator cannot abide: "The little machine became sick" (DS, 586). When a repairman arrives to fix the machine, he disassembles it, exposing its mechanical insides for the first time: "Now a marvel spread out before me, all spirals and screws, the world in a drop of water. I was moved and unashamed" (DS, 588). The narrator's wonder at seeing inside the typewriter soon gives way to disgust, however, after the typewriter has "submitted" to the repairman's attentions. The narrator finds particularly unbearable the insertion of the repairman's "terrible instruments" into the machine's "entrails" (*Eingeweiden*, S, 588). The "little machine" (*Maschinchen*) is demoted to "machine" in the span of one sentence: "The little machine was in order; the machine was repaired" (DS, 589). The narrator's tone changes suddenly from tender and euphoric to cold and distant: "A strange man came at her brutally, and she was immediately at his behest. The fact that I had cared for her with all my might meant nothing to her. My love for the typewriter disappeared" (DS, 589). The beloved typewriter is now an impersonal, mass-produced object, easily replaceable: "It was just one of many, all of which were artificially made and could be mended as needed. When one was finished, another could be bought. Pursuing it was not worthwhile. There are factories and stores, domestic and foreign brands from which to choose" (DS, 589).

The narrator's disdain for his former love object reflects perhaps the impossible position women occupied in workplaces that viewed them as disposable objects—as worker-machines *and/or* potential sexual partners. In this way, we might read Kracauer's piece as a critique of male sexual hypocrisy and the widespread cultural trope of the boss/secretary romance, a trope that reinforced troubling connections between female sexuality and passivity, in which the typewriter—whether *Mädchen* (girl) or *Maschine* (machine)—was at men's disposal. In a 1932 article called "Working Women," Kracauer describes onscreen representation of female employees in which "cheerful young private secretaries or typists … take dictation for the fun of it and do a little typing" and then marry the boss as "not only the dream of many girls but also a tested means of transforming them into compliant instruments."[9] Read in context of "Working Women" and his ethnography of white-collar employees from 1930, *The Salaried Masses: Duty and Distraction in Weimar Germany* [*Die Angestellten: Aus dem neusten Deutschland*], "Das Schreibmaschinchen" might be understood not only as a misogynist literary experiment but also as a critique of the instrumental treatment of female typists by their male bosses as typewriters and objects, never fully human.[10]

Georg Lukács argues in *History and Class Consciousness* that the distinguishing feature of modern capitalism is its transformation of goods, labor, and people into things. Building on Marx's notion of commodity fetishism, Lukács argues that a person's individual qualities, faculties, and abilities become abstracted into "things which he can 'own' or 'dispose of' like the various objects of the external world."[11] What is striking about Kracauer's modernist engagement with reification is that, for him, women bear the brunt of objectification and of commodity fetishism. The male narrator's treatment of an object as a woman suggests that women are already—and always—objects and *remain* so in their roles as typists or lovers. Kracauer's narrator may suffer disillusionment and fragmentation because of his encounter with the typewriter, but he retains some semblance of self, unlike the lover/typewriter, who is treated as a thing and then discarded. The typewriter in Kracauer's story—whether machine, woman, or both— is an object of male desire or a mere thought experiment, but never a subject in her own right.

Kracauer's narrator emerges from his union with the typewriter disillusioned and disappointed, but otherwise no worse for wear. Proper subjectivity has been restored:

> I go among people again and seek modest pleasures in intercourse with women. I use the machine like a thing. The writing consists of correspondences, bills and reflections of a pleasing nature. My friends are happy with me because they understand the writing and the room is always tidy.

---

9 Siegfried Kracauer, "Working Women," in *The Weimar Republic Sourcebook*, ed. Anton Kaes, Martin Jay, and Edward Dimendberg (Berkeley, CA: University of California Press, 1994), 216.

10 Siegfried Kracauer, *The Salaried Masses: Duty and Distraction in Weimar Germany*, trans. Quintin Hoare (London: Verso, 1998), 28. On Kracauer's usefulness for feminist critique, see Summer Renault-Steele, "Unrepressing Philosophy: Interdisciplinarity as Feminist Critique in the Work of Siegfried Kracauer," *philoSOPHIA* 7, no. 1 (2017): 58.

11 Lukács, *History and Class Consciousness*, 100.

[Ich gehe wieder unter Menschen und suche bescheidene Freuden im Verkehr mit den Frauen. Die Maschine gebrauche ich wie ein Ding. Das Geschriebene besteht aus Korrespondenzen, Rechnungen und Betrachtungen gefälliger Art. Meine Freunde sind zufrieden mit mir, weil sie die Schriftstücke verstehen und das Zimmer stets aufgekehrt ist.]

(*DS*, 589)

If in "Das Schreibmaschinchen," Kracauer's narrator briefly experiences what it feels like to be an object through his communion with a feminized, fetishized machine, by the end of the text, order is reestablished—to the narrator's subjectivity, his room, his relationships with women, and his writing. His writing practice turns from one of joyful non-meaning to "correspondences, bills, and reflections of a pleasing nature" (*DS*, 589). As Heiko Reisch puts it, Kracauer's narrator's almost hallucinatory experience with the typewriter's "magical-erotic" qualities is superseded by the typewriter's status as a "Gebrauchsgegenstand," or object of utility.[12]

Destinies of Women

Ultimately, Kracauer portrays women's objectification and dehumanization as a pleasurable experiment with reification, using a feminized object to reflect on his own compromised subjectivity and sexual-authorial inadequacy in the age of the typewriter. As a contrast, consider Christa Anita Brück's narrator's description of her typewriter as a "living being" in *SHS*: "A typewriter has never been a dead object to me; it has always been, from the very beginning, an unspeakably living entity—it has been my enemy from the first moment I excitedly fumbled around on its keys, gloating maliciously, full of deceit and guile, an antediluvian system."[13] Here Brück's narrator grants subjectivity and even agency to the typewriter, not as a "dead object" or as a feminized object of male desire, but as an enemy and foe. As we will see, in Brück's novel, the seemingly posthumanist strategy of comparing humans to machines emerges as a deeply humanist plea for women to be treated as *more* than objects. As Fräulein Brückner, the novel's protagonist, says to a male colleague who advises her not to fret about her job prospects because she'll soon get married: "Yes, you dismiss us with this, our struggle for a

---

12   Heiko Reisch, *Das Archiv und die Erfahrung: Walter Benjamins Essays im medientheoretischen Kontext* (Würzburg: Königshausen & Neumann, 1992), 52.

13   Christa Anita Brück, *Schicksale hinter Schreibmaschinen* (Berlin: Sieben-Stäbe-Verlag, 1930), 228. Hereafter referred to as *SHS*.

meager living, ten times harder than yours, our struggle for recognition, our desperate resistance against our degradation to a dead machine" (*SHS*, 36). In this passage, the characterization of the typewriter as a "dead machine" likewise serves to highlight Brückner's humanity.

Brückner can be seen as a thinly veiled stand-in for Brück herself, who trained as a stenotypist and worked in Berlin as a typist before writing her novel. The similarity between Brück's last name and the name of the protagonist (Brückner) strengthens the novel's proximity to autobiography. Throughout the novel, Brückner is defined primarily as an employee. She has no social life to speak of, her parents are dead, and she is single with no plans to marry. While the novel includes a handful of scenes that take place in an apartment or on the street, most occur in offices. The protagonist often refers to her coworkers by their first names, but she herself is never addressed by hers. At 362 pages, the novel gives readers a strong sense of Brückner's isolation and the endless, day-to-day grind of an office employee.[14] In contrast to novelist Irmgard Keun's savvy typist-protagonists, who attempt to use modernity's new regimes of labor and looser sexual mores to their advantage, the earnest Brückner is depicted as a victim of labor exploitation and abusive male bosses. The novel's reception was mixed; while Kracauer described it as "an excellent contribution to the inventory of the white-collar world," Kurt Tucholsky dismissed it as "rubbish."[15]

Brückner is twenty-two years old at the beginning of the novel and has already been working for several years. She earns 110 marks per month in Königsberg (now Kaliningrad) as a stenotypist for a nondescript company called Dudenmeyer.[16] The novel begins as Brückner's older colleague, Urschl, returns from a stay at a sanatorium for work-related health problems. The forty-two-year-old Urschl now pretends

---

14   The novel raises many of the same issues circulating in such publications as *Die Rundschau der Frau*, a women's newsletter published by the Zentralverband der Angestellten (ZdA) between 1930 and 1933. *Die weiblichen Angestellten*, also published by the ZdA, was a book-length summary of the results of a questionnaire completed by 5,741 female employees in 300 different German cities. Suhr's study, like *Die Rundschau der Frau*, discussed problems specific to women workers and contributed to a growing understanding of white-collar labor as working-class labor, especially amidst rationalization and economic crisis. See *Die weiblichen Angestellten: Arbeits- und Lebensverhältnisse*, ed. Susanne Suhr (Berlin: Zentralverband der Angestellten, 1930).

15   Siegfried Kracauer, "Ein Angestelltenroman," *Frankfurter Zeitung Literaturblatt*, July 6, 1930. For Tucholsky's review, see Peter Panter, "Christa Anita Brück: 'Schicksale hinter Schreibmaschinen,'" *Die Weltbühne*, December 23, 1930, 940.

16   Salaries for white-collar female employees in Germany in 1930 ranged from 70 marks per month on the low end to 300 marks per month on the high end. *Die weiblichen Angestellten*, 37.

to be well, but secretly relies on coffee and painkillers to maintain some semblance of her former productivity. She fools no one, least of all her sexist, ageist male boss: "Doesn't seem like you've gotten better. If you ask me, women over forty no longer belong in the office" (*SHS*, 10). When Urschl sits down to take dictation from said boss, her pen ominously breaks.

Urschl is soon home sick again, and the precarity of her situation is again apparent. Despite her generally collegial relationship with Brückner, Urschl worries that her coworker, who checks in on her, will report to the boss how ill she is. She eventually admits to Brückner that, although her health improved during her stay at the sanatorium, she returned to work against her doctor's advice out of fear she would be replaced. It is "no wonder" she is ill, she explains, given "twenty-seven years of office work, twenty-seven years of hunching, stuffy air, countless overtime, twenty-seven years of irregular meals, and always rushing, hurrying, under tremendous pressure" (*SHS*, 18–19). In her nearly three decades as a typist, Urschl continues, she has held almost forty different positions, each with its own "variant of torture"[17] (*SHS*, 19). Urschl's complaints reflect contemporary accounts by white-collar women, who reported suffering from nervous ailments, headaches, eye pain, even gynecological problems. Typists in particular complained of hearing problems, swelling in their hands, and nerve pain due to the "rushed and strained work pace" of the modern office.[18]

Chronically ill, Urschl faces an impossible choice. Only forty-two, she cannot receive her pension until she is sixty-five.[19] Yet if she continues to work, it is unlikely she will live that long.[20] In one of the novel's most memorable passages, Urschl levels a scathing and pointed critique at male bosses' treatment of their female employees:

> They're nicer to their dog than their typist. Or it's the other way around, and they permit themselves every indecency. After all, we depend on them. You see, Fräulein Brückner, a typewriter, when it's ruined, costs money. But an employee is fired when she's in need of repair, and replaced with a new, fresh one.

---

17 Torture or "Qual" is a word Brück returns to repeatedly in the novel to describe Brückner's experiences of work.

18 *Die weiblichen Angestellten*, 23.

19 According to Suhr's 1930 study, only 5 percent of women employees in Germany were over age 40. *Die weiblichen Angestellten*, 8.

20 In comparison to most typists, Urschl has managed to keep working as a typist for a remarkably long time; most typists were able to sustain their work for only ten years. *Die weiblichen Angestellten*, 23.

A typist is cheap goods. You rate her by the number of syllables she can shoot off in a minute and that's it.

[Zu ihrem Hund sind die freundlicher als zu ihrer Stenotypistin. Oder es ist umgekehrt und sie erlauben sich jede Ungehörigkeit. Man hängt ja von ihnen ab. Sehen Sie, Fräulein Brückner, so eine Schreibmaschine, wenn sie ruiniert wird, kostet Geld. Aber eine Angestellte setzt man an die Luft, wenn sie reparaturbedürftig ist und holt sich eine unverbrauchte neue. Ein Tippmädel ist billige Ware. Man bewertet sie nach Silbenzahl, die sie in der Minute herunterklappert und damit fertig.]

(*SHS*, 19–20)

Urschl's trenchant observation that a female typist is "cheap goods," more disposable than a typewriter, treated with less respect than a dog, and only valued for the number of words she can produce per minute, will come to reflect Brückner's own experiences as typist. Lying in her sick bed, Urschl urges Brückner to marry so that she might avoid such a fate: "Marry, Fräulein Brückner, marry, marry! ... Think of me, marry at any price!" (*SHS*, 22). Although Urschl's warning is clear—marry or suffer my fate—Brückner believes that she can find satisfaction in her work and refuses to see typing as a temporary stop on the way to marriage. She describes her encounter with Urschl as "waking" her up about her own future: "I gather together everything this night opens up in me, my painful hunger for life, my melancholy at having no home, the furious wish that, one day, my life too may be granted a dreaming garden once again" (*SHS*, 24).

In her work on the novel of the New Woman, Kerstin Barndt has shown how New Objectivity ought not be seen as either a purely aesthetic category or as a reaction to political crisis, but as a realist sensibility with distinctly gendered modes of address and reception.[21] Barndt's argument for the coexistence of sentiment and sobriety is on full display in Brück's novel. Brückner's melodramatic longing—her melancholy (*Wehmut*), lack of home (*Heimatlosigkeit*) and hunger for life (*Lebenshunger*)—infuse the harsh reality of her matter-of-fact description of her everyday life. Her encounter with Urschl at the beginning of the novel sets off a chain of events that give the rest of the novel its structure and communicates that women's suffering is simultaneously individual and communal, personal and structural.

---

21 Kerstin Barndt, *Sentiment und Sachlichkeit: Der Roman der Neuen Frau in der Weimarer Republik* (Cologne: Böhlau Verlag, 2003).

Brückner's encounter with Urschl at the beginning of the novel is crucial for establishing the rest of the novel's structure and form, as Brückner moves from job to job in search of respect and responsibility while finding neither. Each change in position exists as a narrative segment of the novel, each following the same pattern. It becomes clear to the reader, early on—as Brückner oscillates between hope and despair, new beginnings and failures—that she is trapped in a cycle. Like Urschl, Brückner becomes ill, and after her recovery, discovers that she has been replaced and is once again out of work. This depiction of "destiny" suggests the bleak, deterministic view of the world in late nineteenth-century literary naturalism. While her fate may not be determined by the cosmic indifference of the universe, it is nevertheless sealed, from page one, by forces outside of herself: socioeconomic conditions, the typewriter, and her gender.

Typists as Cheap Goods

Brückner has resolved not only to avoid Urschl's fate but also to find meaning and even happiness in her work. While she does not hope for love or marriage, she does plan to rise above the "misery of her fellow employees" through hard work, but this goal proves ever more elusive (*SHS*, 24–5). For example, when Brückner asks for a promotion at Dudenmeyer, she is met with disdain from her boss: "'What nonsense are you talking?' he rumbles. 'You want to be a correspondent in my auto department. You? A girl?'" (*SHS*, 30). When he offers her the position of private secretary, she turns him down, saying she has "higher goals" (*SHS*, 33). Brückner discusses her predicament with a male colleague who addresses her using the diminutive form of her last name, "Brücknerchen," or "Miss Don't-touch-me"—a nickname that suggests he has already sexually harassed her (*SHS*, 33). Like Urschl, he urges Brückner to marry, characterizing marriage as her "only salvation" (*SHS*, 37).

Brückner's male coworker blatantly sexualizes and objectifies her, advising her not to waste her "beautiful, God-given body" behind files and typewriters (*SHS*, 37). When she learns that a less qualified male employee is being considered for the job she wanted, she quits. Brückner's failure to obtain a promotion is unsurprising: most female employees during this time experienced no advancement in position over their entire work lives.[22] As Brückner searches for a new job, she sees an advertisement for a typist that states "Only first-rate workers

---

22 *Die weiblichen Angestellten*, 19–20.

should apply. Average goods are not considered here" (*SHS*, 48). The language here explicitly signals female workers' status as objects (*Ware*), is reminiscent of Urschl's warning to Brückner that a typist is "cheap goods" and foreshadows the difficulty Brückner will encounter finding work as she grows older. In coming years, she sees other advertisements that restrict applicants to women under 20, 24, or 25 (*SHS*, 253).

Brückner's first position after Dudenmeyer is as managing clerk (*Disponentin*) at a fledgling film distribution company. In contrast to later jobs, in which Brückner's mental state begins to deteriorate, Brückner initially suffers under the physical toll of white-collar work. Her boss, "Herr Lichte," at first promises her a contract, a fair wage, and responsibilities, but soon reneges on all three. The rapid pace of work is strenuous:

> Each of us works under extreme exertion. I can't stay at a task for five minutes, can't finish writing a letter without being called away several times. Lichte loves to rush us around when there are customers. It increases the impression of bustle. Always hustle, always bustle, bustle.

> [Jeder von uns arbeitet unter äußerster Anstrengung. Ich kann nicht fünf Minuten bei einer Arbeit verweilen, nicht einen Briefbogen zu Ende schreiben, ohne mehrere Male abgerufen zu werden. Lichte liebt es, uns durcheinander zu hetzen, wenn Kundschaft da ist. Das erhöht den Eindruck der Betriebsamkeit. Immer Tumult, immer Tempo, Tempo.]

> (*SHS*, 73)

Lichte sends his employees on wild goose chases, asking them to look for films or posters he knows are not available, seemingly for his own amusement or to impress customers. Working conditions are both unsafe and uncomfortable: the boss and the customers smoke cigarettes in the office, despite the lack of ventilation and the presence of highly flammable celluloid.

Brückner describes her four years in this position as deleterious to her health, her nerves, and her will: "They have ruined me. My nerves sometimes no longer obey. The constant mental pressure has led to all kinds of disturbances" (*SHS*, 134). Once again, she experiences a kind of awakening, this time as she "sleepwalks" through the busy street "mechanically" when a glimpse of a raised river bridge reminds her of the natural world—framed as the happy alternative to her own life of office work and urban drudgery—and awakens in her a desire for "the space and freedom of the ocean, a journey into endless blue" (*SHS*, 137).

Soon after this moment of renewed hope, she secures, against all odds, a similar position at another film distribution company with a higher salary and more responsibility. She is hopeful, "almost happy," noting that the films offered at her new company are nearly all "films of good reputation" (*SHS*, 141).

But the protagonist's happiness is short-lived as Brück relentlessly unfolds her fatalist narrative. Brückner learns more about her new boss, "Herr Murawski," when she is trained by the *Disponentin* she is replacing and notes the woman's "deep sorrowful shadows under the eyes" (*SHS*, 150). When Brückner asks why the woman is leaving after only one year on the job, the *Disponentin* tells her she is "broken." Since both humans and things can be "broken," we can read in this answer another subtle acknowledgment of female employees' status as objects or *Ware*. Murawski, Brückner soon learns, abuses his employees, threatening to fire or withhold employee salaries to maintain control. The office runs on a system of sexual coercion, and Brückner grows increasingly desperate in her attempts to resist Murawski's advances. Murawski forces his employees to stay in the office for up to sixteen hours a day.[23] He claims that he keeps them so late to prevent them from pursuing relationships with men: "Because if you're free, other guys will have you" (*SHS*, 174).

Still intent on improving her lot, Brückner uses her first paycheck to advertise her skills in the *Film-Kurier* but receives no offers. The employment office warns Brückner not to resign, because there are "perfect typists" who "offer themselves" (*sich bieten*) for 70 marks per month, barely a living wage (*SHS*, 186). This language recalls Urschl's warning to Brückner that typists are cheap goods ("billige Ware"). She therefore acts to protect herself and others as best she can. When another female employee is home with a fever, and Murawski orders Brückner to write a letter of dismissal, she refuses to do so. She also manages to avoid his sexual advances, refusing to accompany him on a business trip because she knows that the trip is merely a ruse. After only two months of employment, in which she narrowly escapes Murawski's assault, she is pushed to her breaking point and flees to Berlin to look for a new job.

The job search in Berlin proves fruitless, and Brückner is forced to return to Königsberg and assume a position at a bread factory, which is free of overt sexual harassment but grinds her down through the sheer monotony of the work. Brückner describes the experience of

---

23 Unpaid overtime was an especially salient issue for women employees, because they had the added responsibilities of housework and caring for aging parents or sick relatives. Including their commute, most women's work days exceeded ten hours, not counting their unpaid domestic labor. *Die weiblichen Angestellten*, 24.

taking dictation as a form of increased dissociation, until she becomes a typing automaton: "I have no idea what I'm writing. My hand does it all by itself. Somewhere in my head, an independent machine crushes the meaning of what the hand, antenna-like, catches"[24] (*SHS*, 255). For Brückner, to be automated is to lose consciousness; it is danger and death. In contrast to her previous role as *Disponentin*, a position that included various tasks, she now does nothing but type letters, upwards of 150 per day (*SHS*, 234). In this part of the novel, Brück uses repetition to capture the endlessness of these letters, these "waybills, waybills, waybills" (*SHS*, 238). As Brückner sees it:

> After only three days it was mechanical work, a shadowy interaction between eyes and fingers, in which consciousness played no part. Every seventeen-year-old girl who has attended advanced training school does it just as well as I do, perhaps even better, because a certain resistance rising from within, the rebellion against the spiritual withering, quarrels and admonitions of burdened conscience, they all hinder the speed. And speed alone is important in my work.

> [Schon nach drei Tagen war es nur mehr mechanische Arbeit, eine schattenhafte Wechselwirkung zwischen Augen und Fingern, an der das Bewußtsein keinen Anteil hat. Jedes siebzehnjährige Mädchen, das die Fortbildungsschule besucht hat, macht das genau so gut wie ich, vielleicht sogar besser, denn ein gewisser aus dem Innern heraufsteigender Widerstand, die Auflehnung gegen die geistige Verdorrung, Streit und Mahnung des belasteten Gewissens, sie alle behindern das Tempo. Und auf das Tempo allein kommt es bei meiner Arbeit ein.]

> (*SHS*, 238)

In this passage, Brück contrasts consciousness and spirit with the (mechanical) body—eyes and fingers. She also gestures to a certain amount of self-will and *Eigensinn* (obstinacy) in her protagonist, a "resistance rising from within," to the role in which she has been cast. Brückner must also contend with residual trauma from her previous positions. She experiences moments of malfunction (perhaps another form of inner resistance), similar to what we now call PTSD, wherein she is suddenly with her former bosses, freezes, cannot speak or take dictation, and writes down undecipherable "hieroglyphics" instead

---

24 Kittler, too, describes typewriting hands as "antenna-like" in his discussion of automatic writing. Kittler, *Gramophone, Film, Typewriter*, 222.

of shorthand (*SHS*, 235). And while Brückner's latest boss treats her decently, his uncle, who is involved in the business, touches her constantly.

While in previous jobs Brückner's body has borne the brunt of the destructive effects of her work, this position targets her last remaining refuge: her mind. Monotony is not simply boring, but actively destroys what little subjectivity she has left: "It would be a relief if I could take shorthand from time to time, file mail, or fill in the card index. But I am hopelessly caught up in the machinery of crushing monotony" (*SHS*, 251). The verb "zermalmen"—to crush or to grind—seems to represent exactly what these jobs do to Brückner's sense of self, as she continues to deteriorate both mentally and physically: "Physical exhaustion keeps apace with the mental kind. Perhaps one is conditioned by the other" (*SHS*, 251). Here, Brück emphasizes a view of the human subject that encompasses body and mind, corporeality and consciousness. To be objectified as a white-collar worker is not only to experience one's body as an object or thing but also one's mind. That capitalism reifies workers' bodies and minds is one of Lukács's arguments in *History and Class Consciousness*. To Lukács's point we might add that reification also acts as a tool of gendered social control; despite its emancipatory promise, the white-collar workforce wore women down by wresting from them their time, energy, body, and minds.

Brückner frames the consequences of rationalized work environments in terms no less than life and death. Her work is so monotonous that days, weeks, and seasons pass in such a way that she questions whether she is still alive: "Am I sure that I'm alive? Didn't I die seven years ago?" (*SHS*, 256). In contrast to her description of the typewriter as a "living entity" earlier in the novel, the typewriter has now become a death-dealing machine[25] (*SHS*, 228). To be alive for Brückner is to have consciousness and spirit; a physical body is not enough. As both an extension and victim of her typewriter, Brückner is drained of her life force. Though in a very different sense, she, like the typewriter in Kracauer's "Das Schreibmaschinchen," has been transformed from "living entity" into lifeless object.

Brück's protagonist, who remains hopeful that a good job is just around the corner, is trapped in a cycle of "cruel optimism," Lauren Berlant's term for the constant adjustment to, management of, and negotiation with perpetual crisis that characterizes life under global neoliberalism. Brück's book captures this sense of ongoing

---

25 For a recent book on the relationship between mortality and labor, death and capitalism, see James Tyner, *Dead Labor: Toward a Political Economy of Premature Death* (Minneapolis, MN: University of Minnesota Press), 2019.

crisis—many decades earlier—through immediate, present tense narration and through the depiction of the protagonist's oscillation between hope (as she searches for and finds a new job) and despair (as she begins and leaves a job). For Berlant, optimism is a form of attachment that becomes cruel when the object of one's desire "actively impedes the aim that brought you to it initially."[26] Brückner's attachment to the idea that work can offer her fulfillment has become "cruel."

This "cruel optimism" plays out once again in the novel, this time when Brückner sees an ad for a student organization and thinks, yet again, that this might finally be what she has been looking for. After all, it is not a company or a factory but a non-profit organization that helps young people study abroad. Unsurprisingly to the reader, this position is as dysfunctional as all her previous ones; her colleagues and boss blatantly undermine her success. She continues to deteriorate as she carries out her day-to-day tasks: "Without inner involvement, I scribble all over the pages of my shorthand pad. After my lunch break, I begin with the transcription. Since one can very well forget oneself in this work, I cannot decide to stop after closing time" (*SHS*, 320). Brückner "loses herself" in the act of transcribing shorthand (which she's written in her stenography pad) to long form (which she types). Succumbing, finally, to the self-effacing logic of textual reproduction demanded by secretarial work, Brückner has become little more than a dissociated wanderer in a world of hieroglyphics; any vestige of inner resistance, the last stronghold of her subjectivity, has vanished. She realizes it is futile, "laughable" even, to expect any kind of "mental work" (*Denkarbeit*) (*SHS*, 324). *Denkarbeit*, Brück seems to suggest, was never a real possibility for Brückner, given the curious role of the typist—to serve as a channel or interface for the words and thoughts *of others*.

Finally, Brückner becomes ill and must stay home. But, as Brückner's colleague, Urschl, had done at the beginning of the novel, Brückner returns to work before she is well. She is barely able to hold her pen, cannot take dictation, and falls asleep on her typewriter. She is so desperate to keep her job that she accepts without argument news from her boss that her salary will be reduced. When she is home sick again, her boss replaces her without warning. Brückner returns to work and learns that what Urschl predicted has come to pass: no longer useful or productive, she has been discarded like an old or malfunctioning typewriter. In one final moment of self-reflection, she lays out her suffering in a speech to the boss: "I no longer have parents and have no friends, I have no job and no way to make money, I no longer have confidence and my ability to work is broken. A few years ago I was a

---

26   Lauren Berlant, *Cruel Optimism* (Durham, NC: Duke University Press, 2011), 2.

brave, confident, trusting person" (*SHS*, 352). Here, Brückner charges work with destroying her relationships, her sense of self, and, indeed, her very ability to work. Her "labor power" (*Arbeitskraft*) is broken, just as Kracauer's "little machine" is broken.

Despite realizing that work has destroyed her and that her optimism has been utterly cruel, Brückner once again feels renewed hope after spending six weeks in the provinces recovering amidst "sky, water, silence and good brown farmland" (*SHS*, 354). At the end of the novel Brückner resolves to go back to Königsberg and seek out a new position. This ending, it warrants emphasizing, is far from happy. The reader is left with no reason to imagine that things will be any better than they were before. Given the five jobs Brückner has already been through and the fact that her happiness is clearly tied to nature and to her *Heimat* (a fact that gestures to the rather conservative view of the city as the desert of modernity),[27] the reader is left to assume Brückner's future will be more of the same.

Conclusion

The literary texts I have examined in this chapter offer remarkable perspectives on both the typewriter and the *Verdinglichung* of female typists in Weimar Germany. Both Kracauer and Brück suggest—from very different, gendered perspectives—that technology under capitalism has reified humans, human-object relations, and relations among humans, making them into things. What for Kracauer is a feminized, sexualized object is for Brückner an instrument of (male) oppression. When compared to Kittler's account of the typewriter and to Kracauer's "Schreibmaschinchen," however, Brück's novel suggests that there are no better experts on women's lives than women themselves. Looking to women's own accounts of their experiences allows us to see women typists not only *as* the typewriters at which they worked but also as workers and subjects who were not satisfied with the roles afforded them by the typewriter (nor their alignment with it) and who questioned unfair structures of power as much as they accommodated them. The very existence of Brück's novel suggests a kind of performative contradiction between her insistence on the impossibility of writing, of meaning-making, and of subjectivity in the age of the typewriter, on the one hand, and the reality of the novel—written by a former typist—sitting before us, on the other.

---

27   Brück's novel is full of contradictory discourses, some quite conservative. Even as Brückner seeks success through work and expresses no desire to marry or have children, she reflects at one point on women's natural roles as mothers.

In Brück's case, writing about her experiences at work becomes a means of describing the transformation of women workers into commodities and the toll of this transformation on women's minds, bodies, lives, and relationships. While capitalism transforms all workers into commodities, what is especially disturbing about white-collar work is not only its false promise of emancipation but also the highly gendered social control it exercised over female subjects. In *The Problem with Work*, Kathi Weeks notes that "we tend to focus more on the problems with this or that job, or on their absence, than on work as a requirement, work as a system, work as a way of life."[28] Through dramatic irony and repetition, Brück's novel does both; it critiques "the problems with this or that boss" and "the system that grants them such power."[29] Brück suggests that any optimism under capitalism and patriarchy is cruel, and that the typewriter has only intensified that which was, for women, always already cruel.

Works Cited

Barndt, Kerstin. *Sentiment und Sachlichkeit: Der Roman der Neuen Frau in der Weimarer Republik*. Cologne: Böhlau Verlag, 2003.

Berlant, Lauren. *Cruel Optimism*. Durham, NC: Duke University Press, 2011.

Biers, Katherine. "The Typewriter's Truth." In *Kittler Now: Current Perspectives in Kittler Studies*, edited by Stephen Sale and Laura Salisbury, 132–53. Cambridge: Polity Press, 2015.

Brück, Christa Anita. *Schicksale hinter Schreibmaschinen*. Berlin: Sieben-Stäbe-Verlag, 1930.

Farner Budarz, Sara Kristina. "Inside the City: Gender and the Production of Interior Space in Weimar Republic German Literature, 1929–1933." PhD diss., University of North Carolina at Chapel Hill, 2014.

Führich, Angelika. "Woman and Typewriter: Gender, Technology, and Work in Late Weimar Entertainment Film." *Women in German Yearbook* 151 (2016): 151–66.

Kirschenbaum, Matthew G. *Track Changes: A Literary History of Word Processing*. Cambridge, MA: Harvard University Press, 2016.

Kittler, Friedrich. *Discourse Networks 1800/1900*. Translated by Michael Metteer and Chris Cullens. Stanford, CA: Stanford University Press, 1990.

Kittler, Friedrich. *Gramophone, Film, Typewriter*. Translated by Geoffrey Winthrop-Young and Michael Wutz. Stanford, CA: Stanford University Press, 1999.

Kracauer, Siegfried. *Die Angestellten: Aus dem neuesten Deutschland*. Frankfurt: Suhrkamp, [1930] 1971.

Kracauer, Siegfried. "Das Schreibmaschinchen" (1927). In *Werke*, vol. 5.2: *Essays, Feuilletons, Rezensionen, 1924–1927*, edited by Inka Mülder-Bach and Ingrid Belke, 585–89. Frankfurt: Suhrkamp, 2004.

---

28 Kathi Weeks, *The Problem with Work: Feminism, Marxism, Antiwork Politics, and Postwork Imaginaries* (Durham, NC: Duke University Press, 2011), 3.

29 Weeks, *The Problem with Work*, 3.

Kracauer, Siegfried. "Ein Angestelltenroman." *Frankfurter Zeitung Literaturblatt,* July 6, 1930.

Kracauer, Siegfried. *The Little Typewriter.* Translated by Johannes von Moltke and edited by Meghan Forbes and Hannah McMurray. Austin, TX: Harlequin Creature, 2017.

Kracauer, Siegfried. *The Salaried Masses: Duty and Distraction in Weimar Germany.* Translated by Quintin Hoare. London: Verso, 1998

Kracauer, Siegfried. "Working Women" (1932). In *The Weimar Republic Sourcebook,* edited by Anton Kaes, Martin Jay, and Edward Dimendberg, 216–18. Berkeley, CA: University of California Press, 1994.

Lukács, Georg. *History and Class Consciousness.* Translated by Rodney Livingstone. Cambridge, MA: MIT Press, 1972.

Nowak, Christiane. "'Durchschnittsware.' Individualisierungskonzepte in den Angestelltenromanen *Schicksale hinter Schreibmaschinen* (Christa Anita Brück) und *Das Mädchen an der Orga Privat* (Rudolf Braune)." *"Erzählte Wirtschaftssachen: Ökonomie und Ökonomisierung in der Literatur und im Film der Weimarer Republik."* JUNI. *Magazin für Literatur und Politik* 47/48 (2013): 103–18.

Oswald, Richard, dir. *Arm wie eine Kirchenmaus.* 1931.

Panter, Peter [Kurt Tucholsky]. "Christa Anita Brück: 'Schicksale hinter Schreibmaschinen.'" *Die Weltbühne,* December 23, 1930.

Reisch, Heiko. *Das Archiv und die Erfahrung: Walter Benjamins Essays im medientheoretischen Kontext.* Würzburg: Königshausen & Neumann, 1992.

Renault-Steele, Summer. "Unrepressing Philosophy: Interdisciplinarity as Feminist Critique in the Work of Siegfried Kracauer." *philoSOPHIA* 7, no. 1 (2017): 45–62.

Schüller, Liane. *Vom Ernst der Zerstreuung: Schreibende Frauen am Ende der Weimarer Republik: Marieluise Fleißer, Irmgard Keun und Gabriele Tergit.* Bielefeld: Aisthesis Verlag, 2005.

Suhr, Susanne, ed. *Die weiblichen Angestellten: Arbeits- und Lebensverhältnisse: Eine Umfrage des Zentralverbandes der Angestellten.* Berlin: Zentralverband der Angestellten, 1930.

Tyner, James. *Dead Labor: Toward a Political Economy of Premature Death.* Minneapolis, MN: University of Minnesota Press, 2019.

Weeks, Kathi. *The Problem with Work: Feminism, Marxism, Antiwork Politics, and Postwork Imaginaries.* Durham, NC: Duke University Press, 2011.

Nine   Unemployment, Organization, and Reproductive Self-Determination in *Kuhle Wampe*

Ulrich Plass

Poverty, unemployment, eviction, suicide: among the filmic and photographic records of the final years of the Weimar Republic, starting with the Wall Street crash of 1929 and culminating in the National Socialists's seizure of power in 1933, the film *Kuhle Wampe* (*KW*), released in 1932, stands out for its sober acknowledgment of the miseries of the Great Depression, counterbalanced by its aesthetically complex endorsement of grassroots political organizing. *KW* portrays bodies taking control of themselves: both collectively, in athletic contests, and individually, as a woman struggles for her sexual and reproductive freedom. Responding to state censorship demands, the film's aesthetics emerge from a tension between what can be seen on the surface and what is only implied. *KW*'s rhetoric of constructivist montage requires that the viewer read the film's images not in isolation or in a linear progression, but rather in dialectical conversation with one another. This entails the reading of what is no longer visible: the censored and lost scenes that can be reconstructed only based on the extensive censorship records. In this chapter, I argue that is it precisely in the negative space of its most elusive and even illegible passages that we can detect the feminist, revolutionary core of *KW*.

Collaboratively made by a team of communist avant-gardists (director Slatan Dudow, composer Hanns Eisler, and writers Ernst Ottwalt and Bertolt Brecht), *KW* breaks with the aesthetics of left-wing issue films such as *Mutter Krausens Fahrt ins Glück* (*Mother Kraus' Journey to Happiness*; 1929) or *Cyankali* (*Cyanide*; 1930), which depict the increasingly desperate social and economic circumstances of the German working class through conventional naturalism. Instead, drawing on the techniques of Brecht's epic theater and citing a variety of cinematic predecessors,[1] *KW* combines visual documentation of mass unemployment with a politics of mutual aid, autonomous mass organizing, and class and gender solidarity. In stark contrast to a film such as *Cyankali,* which centers on the drama of an unsuccessful illegal abortion, *KW*'s Anni is not punished with *theatrical* suffering and death for seeking an abortion but rewarded with *discreet* emancipation from the bourgeois family. It is "discreet" because political pressures forced the creators of *KW* to tell this feminist story by means of metaphorical condensations and metonymic slippages, displacements, and substitutions.

Post-1933 reception of the film has tended to read *KW*'s visual and musical aesthetics as an indication that, in the final years of the republic, Brechtian modernism had arrived at an artistic and political impasse.[2] According to such skeptical verdicts, the film's contrasting depictions of mass unemployment and mass organizing remain stuck in a dualism of bad and good collectivity that is "resolved" negatively and retroactively, in the aesthetics of fascism.[3] Thus the sequence depicting a large sports festival was in retrospect seen as "unwittingly anticipating Nazi parades,"[4] with its "young revolutionaries resembl[ing] those youthful rebels who in numerous German films of the opposite camp are finally ready to submit or to enforce submission."[5] Similar readings filter everything through the dark lens of the caesura of 1933; they project onto the politics of *KW* a bad teleology that treats the defeat of the organized working class as predestined and so diminishes the complexities of proletarian politics to either "procommunist"

1   Because it uses such disparate modes of cinematic representation, Stefanie Diekmann describes *KW* as a "patchwork" and an "anthology" of styles. See "Ein Kino, das zum Anthologischen neigt," in *Brecht und das Fragment,* ed. Astrid Oesmann and Matthias Rothe (Berlin: Verbrecher, 2020), 47–58.

2   In contrast, the first reports about and reviews of *KW*, as it was still in production and immediately after its release, were mostly enthusiastic. See Wolfgang Gersch and Werner Hecht, *Kuhle Wampe oder Wem gehört die Welt: Filmprotokoll und Materialien* (Leipzig: Reclam, 1971), 151–96. Abbreviated as KWPM.

3   As Marc Silberman argues, the film's political aesthetics depended on the existence of a "class-conscious spectator" and the historical conditions for *KW*'s aesthetics simply disappeared with the "total elimination of the left-wing public sphere" in 1933. See Marc Silberman, "Whose Revolution? The Subject of *Kuhle Wampe,*" in *Weimar Cinema: An Essential Guide to Classic Films of the Era,* ed. Noah Isenberg (New York: Columbia University Press, 2009), 326.

4   Lotte Eisner, *The Haunted Screen: Expressionism in the German Cinema and the Influence of Max Reinhardt,* trans. Roger Greaves (London: Thames & Hudson, [1952] 1969), 335.

5   Siegfried Kracauer, *From Caligari to Hitler: A Psychological History of the German Film* (Princeton, NJ: Princeton University Press, [1947] 2004), 247.

or "protofascist" positioning.[6] Such one-dimensional understandings of late Weimar politics encourage a hollowly formalist reading of the film that easily obscures its self-reflexive and essayistic nature[7] as an inquiry into self-determination and dispossession under the conditions of the increasingly anti-democratic German welfare state.[8] To correct such one-sided readings of *KW*, this chapter proposes that the film can be read dialectically: beneath its visible documentation of real misery, the film subtly probes a politics of solidarity and liberation that lies concealed within the catastrophe of the global economic crisis.

A close reading of the film's visual rhetoric needs to account for the fact that the social precarity it depicts also dictated its conditions of production. *KW*'s completion was delayed not only by the bankruptcy of its first production company, Prometheus Film, but also by numerous cuts demanded by the state censor's office, the Berlin *Film Examination Board* [*Filmprüfstelle*], which warned that screening *KW* would endanger "public order and security." The office demanded that all references to the state's responsibility for the suicide in part 1 of the film be removed, as well as the abortion subplot. No footage of the censored scenes has survived, and the detailed notes kept by the *Filmprüfstelle* constitute their only historical record. In my reading, the nearly-erased abortion subplot is pivotal, because it articulates *KW*'s most sophisticated political and economic argument: revolutionary change requires not only organized mass action but also the process of learning to embrace the absence of work and production – including the intentional termination of unborn labor power.

KW has a tripartite structure; the three parts are joined by two non-verbal intermezzi that, just like the prologue, set music and image against one another to create a shock effect of recognition.[9] Wolfgang

---

6   For a recent example of this, cf. Bastian Heinsohn, "Film as Pedagogy in Late Weimar and Early Nazi Cinema: The Role of the Street in Mobilizing the Spectator," in *Continuity and Crisis in German Cinema, 1928–1936*, edited by Barbara Hales, Mihaela Petrescu, and Valerie Weinstein (Rochester: Camden House, 2016), 51–69.

7   For a reading of *KW* as an essay film, see Nora Alter, *The Essay Film after Fact and Fiction* (New York: Columbia University Press, 2018), 62–75.

8   This was a state that granted the modest achievements of the German worker's movement, such as unemployment insurance benefits, only at the high cost of punitive control of the unemployed, a repressive police force, an authoritarian judiciary, and the growing influence over politics by wealthy industrialists (who would eventually do away with the republic altogether). A canonical account of Weimar's terminal crisis can be found in Detlev Peukert, *The Weimar Republic*, trans. Richard Deveson (New York: Hill and Wang, 1992), 247–72.

9   See Theodor Adorno and Hanns Eisler, *Composing for the Films* (London: Continuum, 2007), 17.

Gersch and Werner Hecht's "scene segmentation," to which I will refer in this chapter, further divides the film into eight "acts."[10] The plot, to give the briefest summary, is structured episodically: The first act, titled "Ein Arbeitsloser weniger" ["One unemployed worker less"] shows workers on bicycles looking for jobs. In the second act, we meet the Bönike family. Both father and son are unemployed; they haven't paid their rent in six months. After the son is reproached by his parents for not trying hard enough to find a job, he jumps to his death out of the window of their modest tenement apartment. The movie's second part is titled "Das schönste Leben eines jungen Menschen" ["The best years of youth"]. It begins with the Bönike daughter Anni's futile attempt to prevent her family from being evicted. When she fails, Anni's boyfriend Fritz offers them temporary housing in the suburban tent colony Kuhle Wampe (act 3).[11] After Anni, during the fourth act, finds out that she is pregnant, Fritz urges her to have an abortion. Unable to afford a safe procedure, Fritz reluctantly agrees to an engagement. The subsequent celebration (act 5) ends with Anni leaving Fritz and moving in with her coworker Gerda. In the third part (and opening sixth act), Anni helps to organize a proletarian sports festival. It is implied that Anni has been able to secure an abortion. Fritz, who has in the meantime lost his job as a cab driver, attempts to win Anni back by attending the sports meet with her. The film moves away from Anni and Fritz after they have presumably reconciled, and focuses almost fully on the athletic contests, the socializing afterwards (act 7), and the train ride back to the city, during which the young workers argue with other passengers on the train about the need for global revolutionary change (act 8).

The plot, however, is only the narrative vehicle for the concatenation of episodes that document a progression from misery and despair to self-help and hope. The agents of optimism are young proletarians whose activism clashes with the lethargy and escapism of an older generation of workers, drawing a contrast, as Siegfried Kracauer pointed out,[12] between

---

10 As far as I am aware, this is the terminology used by the *Filmprüfstelle*, which was subsequently adopted by scholars of the film.

11 "Kuhle Wampe" was the name of a tent colony at Berlin's Müggelsee, founded in 1913. Because the lake's most desirable shore locations were already occupied by private estates, the proletarians seeking to escape the unhealthy dampness and darkness of their tenement apartments had to make do with the lake's coldest cove—hence the name "Kuhle Wampe." The film was first conceived as a celebration of the weekend as a chronotope of proletarian freedom from the toils of the workweek, the factory, and the slums. Brecht's draft screenplay bears the title *Weekend – Kuhle Wampe* and the solidarity song's draft titles were "Sonntagslied der freien Jugend" [Sunday Song of the Free Youth] and "Das Lied vom roten Weekend" [Song of the Red Weekend].

12 Siegfried Kracauer, "Kuhle Wampe verboten!," *Frankfurter Zeitung* April 5, 1932.

politicized communist workers and depoliticized non-communist (presumably social-democratic) workers. Yet the contrast is not only between communist and social-democratic, or young and old, but also between petty-bourgeois institutions (the neighborhood pub frequented by the Bönike father, but also Anni and Fritz's engagement party as a ritual of mindless, alcohol-fueled bonhomie) and proletarian organizing as exemplified by the young athletes, who were played mostly by members of Berlin's "Fichte-Wandersparte" [*Fichte Hikers*], a large youth organization engaged in leisure and sports activities. However, *KW* does not, *contra* Kracauer, glorify youth. Rather, the film presents collective organizing as a way out of the atomized powerlessness that drives Anni's brother to suicide.

Debates in and about *Kuhle Wampe*

KW's essayistic approach to cinematic storytelling is indicated in its subtitle: *Wem gehört die Welt?* [Who Owns the World?], and in the final two lines of the film's musical leitmotif, the "Solidarity Song": "Wessen Straße ist die Straße/Wessen Welt ist die Welt?" ["Whose street is the street?/Whose world is the world?"] The song is used both extra- and inner-diegetically.[13] It functions as a soundtrack during the sports scenes and in the film's final scene, and it is sung by the athletes on their way to the festival and at its conclusion. Both the song's collective subject – the singing masses—and the universal claims of "street" and "world" articulate a decidedly non-bourgeois notion of ownership. Indeed, *KW* suggests that, if left in the hands of the bourgeoisie, the economic violence that had become shockingly manifest during the Great Depression would only continue.

This lesson is articulated in the film's final act, when the protagonists, Kurt, Gerda, Anni, and Fritz are riding home in a train car jam-packed with other young workers and a cross-section of Berliners. One passenger, reading a newspaper, comes across a news item that he shares loudly with the other passengers: "In Brazil they burned 24 million pounds of coffee."[14] After eliciting skeptical and stunned responses from some of the other passengers, he continues, now agitated: "We have expensive

---

13 For an informative discussion of sound in *KW*, see Nora Alter, "The Politics and Sounds of Everyday Life in *Kuhle Wampe*," *Sound Matters: Essays on the Acoustics of Modern German Culture*, ed. Nora Alter and Lutz Koepnick (New York: Berghahn Books, 2004), 79–90.

14 Bertolt Brecht, *On Film and Radio*, ed. and trans. Marc Silberman (London: Methuen, 200), 247. Abbreviated as BFR.

wheat and unemployed industrial workers while Argentina has expensive industrial goods and unemployed farmers. And it is all called the world market and is a crying shame" (BFR 248). The ensuing debate pitches a nationalist "man with starched collar" (the original screenplay refers to him as a "right-wing politician"[15]) against Kurt, who speaks for the workers. The former argues that "if we had colonies, then we'd have coffee too" (BFR 251), and Germans would at last benefit from the simultaneous existence of excess commodities and mass misery. If able to exploit intentional scarcity to drive up commodity prices, Germany would find itself on the winning side of global economics: "then ... we'll cut the deal" (BFR 251). In contrast to this personification of smug chauvinism, the character of Kurt (the film's foremost representative of the worker-athletes, whom the filmmakers placed on the train to be the spokesperson for practical materialist reason) inquires: "I keep hearing 'we.' Who is this: we?" After gesturing at several other people on the train, he states: "So, 'we' cut a deal? Come on, man, you don't really believe that" (BFR 251). The lesson here is clear: those who profit from driving up the prices by reducing the supply of commodities do not spend their Sunday afternoons riding on a packed S-Bahn car.

After Kurt appears to have won the argument that a shift in the balance of imperialist powers will not change the unjust structure of the world economy, and after some additional back and forth on the train, one passenger notes apathetically to another: "Yeah, the two of us, we're not going to change the world either," to which Kurt replies emphatically, "Right!" (BFR 255). He then points at other passengers, each time remarking that they won't change the world, either. Finally, he turns to the right-wing politician and states: "This man here will not change it either. After all, he likes it the way it is now." Framed in an extreme close-up at a slightly low angle, the right-wing politician retorts sharply, addressing both Kurt and the audience: "And who will change it?" The next and final shot on the train shows Kurt's girlfriend Gerda. We see her at a less claustrophobic close-up than the previous shot, at a slightly elevated angle. Looking directly into the camera, she proclaims slowly and clearly: "Those who do not like it" (BFR 257) ["Die, denen sie nicht gefällt." (KWPM 82)].[16]

---

15   Bertolt Brecht, *Werke: Große kommentierte Berliner und Frankfurter Ausgabe*, ed. Werner Hecht, Jan Knopf, Werner Mittenzwei, and Klaus-Detlef Müller (Berlin, Weimar and Frankfurt: Aufbau/Suhrkamp, 1988–1998), vol. 19, 553. Abbreviated as *GBA*.

16   All DVD captures are from the 2020 Atlas Film edition, which reproduces the "restored" *Deutsche Kinemathek* version. © Prometheus-Film AG, 1932. All rights reserved.

Figure 9.1 *KW* 1:10:43: Kurt.
Figure 9.2 *KW* 1:10:53 "Right-Wing Politician."
Figure 9.3 *KW* 1:10:56: Gerda.

In their article on *KW* for the *Brecht Handbuch*, Burkhardt Lindner and Raimund Gerz lament the claustrophobic feel of the train scene and note that the discussion "about a peripheral subject matter" appears to be a substitute for a real political debate—the kind of debate direly needed "in face of the fatal crisis of the Weimar Republic"[17] but rendered impossible due to heightened censorship rules presumably designed to protect "vital state interests" against "political violence."[18] Moreover, Lindner and Gerz claim that the young agitators violate a fundamental rule of political organizing: rather than establishing common cause with the older passengers on the train over the high cost of coffee, they rhetorically reinforce the split between old and young. Lindner and Gerz echo the criticism of Kracauer, who argued, "The gravest blunder committed in *Kuhle Wampe* is its gross attack against the petty-bourgeois mentality of the old workers—an attack obviously designed to stigmatize social democratic behavior."[19]

Kracauer, Lindner, and Gerz all associate the film's politics with those of the Communist Party, which during The Depression became "the party of the unemployed par excellence,"[20] and whose fight against the "social fascism" of the SPD and the unions purportedly weakened the left and facilitated National-Socialist gains among workers. *KW*'s state censor arrived at a similar conclusion when he

17 Raimund Gerz and Burkhardt Lindner, "Kuhle Wampe," in *Brecht Handbuch* vol. 3, ed. Jan Knopf (Stuttgart: Metzler, 2002), 432–57, 454.
18 *Dritte Verordnung des Reichspräsidenten zur Sicherung von Wirtschaft und Finanzen und zur Bekämpfung politischer Ausschreitungen. Vom 6. Oktober 1931* http://www.documentarchiv.de/wr/1931/wirtschaft-finanzen-ausschreitungen_reichspraesident-vo03.html#t7
19 Kracauer, *From Caligari to Hitler*, 246.
20 Richard Evans, *The Coming of the Third Reich* (New York: Penguin, 2004), 237.

declared in March 1932: "This motion picture contains a sharp attack on the Social Democratic party and its politics" (KWPM 125; my translation). Since the Social Democratic Party (SPD) had committed itself to the "democratic republic" as the "form of state necessary for the liberation struggle"[21] of the working class, the censorship office correctly understood that overthrowing the state meant jettisoning social democracy, and vice versa. Even though *KW* does not mention any political party, the film censor, Kracauer, and subsequent viewers have identified the petty-bourgeois milieu of the Bönike parents and their neighbors with the SPD's quietism, which is contrasted with the young people, who stand in for the politics of the Communist Party, and who "want to change the given conditions not through toleration but through violence," as the censor put it (KWPM 125). As futile as the KPD's piecemeal attempts at revolutionary action remained throughout the Weimar years, "change through the toleration of conditions" reads like a self-parody of the "conformism which has marked the Social Democrats from the beginning," to borrow Walter Benjamin's acerbic assessment from 1939.[22] In *KW*, the conformism preached by the Bönike parents is depicted as a dead end, which their son's suicide literalizes. They abstain from politics and try to blame others for their misery, including reproaching their son for not having greeted their landlord—to whom they owe six months of rent, as their daughter reminds them. It is Anni who sums up the bleak reality evoked in the montage sequences at the film's beginning: "There are no jobs" (BFR 217).

Kracauer concluded his review by claiming, "The film invalidates its cause by expressing differences of attitude through differences between generations."[23] Yet the film's central question of "who owns the world" does not merely hint at generational conflict, it also speaks directly to the unemployed masses. If, according to the political rhetoric of the Social Democrats, individuals were meant to acquire their share of the world through a more equitable distribution of productive labor, the Great Depression destroyed the party's stated goal of abolishing class rule.[24]

21 SPD, *Heidelberger Programm* (1925) https://www.marxists.org/deutsch/geschichte/deutsch/spd/1925/heidelberg.htm

22 Walter Benjamin, *Selected Writings*, 4 vols., trans. Edmund Jephcott and others, ed. Howard Eiland and Michael Jennings (Cambridge, MA: Harvard University Press, 1996–2003), vol. 4, 393.

23 Kracauer, *From Caligari to Hitler*, 247.

24 See *Heidelberger Programm*.

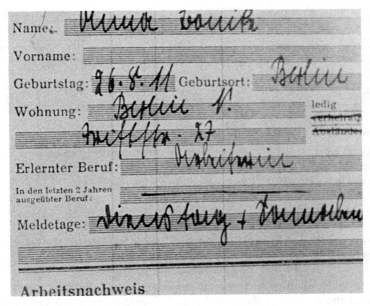

Figure 9.4 *KW* 0:35:14: Anni's employment ID card.

Significantly, the crisis of mass unemployment affected most severely those born in the years immediately preceding the First World War—like Anni, whose "Arbeitsnachweis" [employment identity card] shows that she was born in 1911. The unemployed in *KW* all belong to Weimar's "lost generation," which Detlev Peukert has described as a "distinct generation" arising from the "absolute and relative increase in the numbers of young people" due to an especially high birthrate between 1910 and 1913.[25] *KW* did not have to demonstratively link together youth, unemployment, and communism because this association was obvious in the proletarian neighborhoods of Germany's industrial cities. With more than half of *KW* shot on site in working-class areas of Berlin, the movie's fictional dimension was transparently embedded within a documentary representation of proletarian life.[26]

---

25 Detlev Peukert, "The Lost Generation: Youth Unemployment at the End of the Weimar Republic," in *The German Unemployed: Experiences and Consequences of Mass Unemployment from the Weimar Republic to the Third Reich*, ed. Richard Evans and Dick Geary (New York: St. Martin's, 1986), 190, 173.

26 Dudow's 1930 documentary short *Wie der Berliner Arbeiter wohnt*, his only feature prior to his directing *KW*, provides a close look at overcrowding and domestic work largely absent in the latter.

Figure 9.5 *KW* 0:3:38: "Four million!"

Figure 9.6 *KW* 0:3:47: "More than 5 million unemployed and furloughed."

Figure 9.7 *KW* 0:3:49: "Unemployment keeps rising."

Representing Unemployment: *Kuhle Wampe*'s Proletarian Aesthetic

KW depicts unemployment as a personal, potentially fatal hardship within the context of the global crisis of capitalism. The acceleration of the crisis is indicated through a montage of newspaper headlines that note ever-rising unemployment numbers over the course of the year 1931. Snippets of other economic and political news items are also visible, for instance, the news about the destruction of "985,105 bags of coffee" that inspires the film's concluding debate about belonging and revolution. The draft screenplay even juxtaposed German unemployment numbers with news from Japan and England to show that the crisis explained not only "the conditions in Germany, but in all capitalist states in the world."[27] Although the film, unlike the draft screenplay, includes only a few references to the global dimension of the Great Depression, *KW* nonetheless addressed a question with which Brecht had begun to wrestle in the 1920s: how can hidden connections between seemingly isolated economic facts and events be represented in non-reified form?[28] Brecht summed up this challenge in a frequently-cited passage from his *Threepenny Lawsuit*, written immediately before *KW*: "The situation has become so complicated because the simple 'reproduction of reality' says less than ever about that reality. A photograph of the Krupp works or the AEG reveals almost nothing

---

27 Brecht, *Werke* 19, 442.

28 Brecht's increasing interest in economic processes and their concrete manifestations was reflected in a tendency towards "de-narrativizing" in his dramatic works; see Matthias Rothe, "Die Temporalität der Kritik: Bertolt Brechts Fragment *Jae Fleischhacker in Chikago* (1924–1929)," in *Brecht Yearbook* 40 (2016): 28–50.

about these institutions. Reality as such has slipped into the domain of the functional. The reification of human relations, the factory, for example, no longer discloses those relations" (BFR 164–5). One may gloss this observation by noting that the destruction of coffee in Brazil says more about the causes for mass unemployment than the labor inside a factory, for it illuminates the contradiction between productive forces and the relations of production at the heart of the crisis (that is, according to the Marxist crisis theory that was authoritative for Brecht and his fellow filmmakers[29]). This contradiction, as Friedrich Pollock wrote in 1933, "expresses itself in the contradiction between the unlimited economic-technological possibilities and the limited goal of capital valorization, which has a tendency to become ever more difficult to realize."[30]

In Pollock's interpretation of the crisis, capitalism failed to employ the productive forces it had developed to fulfill the needs of all members of society. But instead of seeking to balance productive potentiality with actual insufficient distribution and consumption, capital decided to fight the crisis by destroying raw materials and idling human labor power. Unemployment, Pollock stated, was a much more comprehensive "destruction of productive forces than the idling of factories or the trashing of machines."[31] Readers of daily newspapers, he noted, were not confronted with the full scope of capital's destructive measures; as one notable exception to this rule, he cited newspaper reports about the destruction of coffee in Brazil. Similar to the workers' own analysis in *KW*, Pollock saw such forms of destruction culminating in "measures directed against the unfolding of the 'greatest productive force,' the working class."[32]

For Pollock, all attempts to resolve the economic crisis without changing the relations of production amounted to undermining the "growing ability of the working class to organize itself."[33] Economic

---

29 There is, of course, not one unified Marxist crisis theory, but regardless of whether Marxists theoretically emphasize falling rates of profit or the "underconsumptionist" realization of capital crisis, *KW*'s political-economic argument relies on the insight of Marx's "law of capitalist accumulation" that the generation of surplus value leads to the periodic proliferation of unemployed surplus populations. In this vein, Fredric Jameson has provocatively argued that Volume 1 of Marx's *Capital* is not primarily a book about politics or value but unemployment. Fredric Jameson, *Representing Capital: A Commentary on Volume One* (London and New York: Verso, 2011).

30 Friedrich Pollock, "Bemerkungen zur Wirtschaftskrise," in *Zeitschrift für Sozialforschung* 2, no. 3 (1933): 321–54, 321 (my translation).

31 Pollock, "Wirtschaftskrise," 341.

32 Pollock, "Wirtschaftskrise," 342.

33 Pollock, "Wirtschaftskrise," 343.

measures seemingly designed to address the crisis would also politically undercut the very working-class power that Pollock considered the "precondition for a new organization of society."[34] Pollock's
Depression-era theoretical reflections resonate with *KW*'s pictorial
argument. The athletic competitions are a means of maintaining the
"organizability" of the proletariat during a time of mass unemployment, while the debate over the destruction of goods such as coffee,
wheat, or cotton (all mentioned by the workers on the train) at the conclusion of the film is not, *pace* Lindner and Gerz, an episodic aberration,
but rather a staging of *KW*'s core theoretical argument. The phenomenon of mass unemployment is not an "exogenic" disaster that can be
remedied with frugality, self-sufficiency, protectionism, or new wars.[35]
Because it is endemic to capitalism, its solution can only be a revolutionary change of the relations of production on a global scale.

   Truthfully documenting the plight of Weimar Germany's "lost generation," young Bönike's matter-of-fact suicide is a fulfillment of his
assigned role in the economic order: he participates in the necessary
destruction of productive forces. In the spirit of Brecht's suggestion in the
Threepenny Lawsuit that social realism is constituted by functions rather
than things, the suicide plot not only draws on filmic precedents, such
as *Mutter Krausens Fahrt ins Glück*, but also on the fact that many unemployed proletarians were driven to the same conclusion.[36] In his "Short
Contribution to the Theme of Realism," written in the spring of 1932 after
the filmmakers' meeting with the Film Inspection Board, where they
received a "short course on realism. From the perspective of the police"
(BFR 209), Brecht has the censor cry out: "Your film proposes that suicide
is typical, that it is not simply the act of this or that (pathologically dis-
posed) individual but rather the fate of an entire social class!" (BFR 208).
Brecht records the censor's reaction to the "explicitly demonstrative"
and "mechanical" gesture of the son taking off his wristwatch before he
jumps: "Good God, the actor does it as if he were showing how to peel
cucumbers!" (BFR 208–9). Brecht makes the censor sound like a parody
of Georg Lukács in his more dogmatic moments,[37] as when Brecht ven-
triloquizes the censor reproaching the film's depiction of suicide "for
not being sufficiently *human*" (BFR 208). The reproach implies that the

---

34 Pollock, "Wirtschaftskrise," 343.
35 Pollock noted that every crisis renews the "praise of poverty" (342) and wars are
    continuations of crises by other means (344).
36 See Moritz Föllmer, "Suicide and Crisis in Weimar Berlin," in *Central European
    History* 42 (2009): 195–221.
37 For Brecht's rejoinder to Lukács's declinist critique of modernist technique, see
    Adorno, Benjamin, Bloch, Brecht, Lukács, *Aesthetics and Politics* (London: Verso,
    1980), 68–9.

actor failed to create a persuasive illusion of a "flesh-and-blood person ... with his particular worries, particular joys and finally his particular fate" (BFR 208). According to Brecht's rendition of their exchange, the censor portrays his criticism as an "*artistic* reproach" (BFR 208); of course, the censor's overlapping use of *artistic* and *human* is one of the core tenets of the bourgeois aesthetic Brecht and his collaborators sought to overcome.

The involvement of proletarian cultural organizations in the production process was crucial for the creation of a proletarian aesthetic. Just as Brecht and Eisler's *Die Maßnahme* in 1930 (directed by Dudow) featured workers' choirs, and their 1932 production of *Die Mutter* agit-prop performers, three different proletarian organizations were credited for participation in *KW*. The participation of non-professional actors contributed to the film's aesthetic effects of documentary accuracy and unsentimental matter-of-factness. At the same time, *KW*'s use of location shooting and amateur actors differs crucially from the use of these techniques in other contemporaneous films, such as *Menschen am Sonntag* [*People on Sunday*; 1930], which pursues an apolitical aesthetics of authenticity.[38] The differences between *Menschen am Sonntag*'s author-director team, Edgar Ulmer, Robert Siodmak, and Billy Wilder, and *KW*'s collective makers have been well-expressed by Sergei Tretiakov's notion of "operativity."[39] In Benjamin's succinct definition, the "operative writer's" "[m]ission is not to report but to struggle; not to play the spectator but to intervene actively."[40] Leftist bourgeois art, Benjamin asserted in 1934, puts the writer-as-producer outside the dominant apparatus of production, and, by extension, sets the intellectual apart from organized proletarian struggle. For the makers of *KW*, however, "operativity" meant not only including unemployed workers in the production but also redefining the artist's relationship to the work of art.

Concretely, "operativity" meant "organization." As Brecht stated in his notes on making *KW*, "the organization of the work caused us a lot more trouble than the (artistic) work itself, that is, we gradually came to see the organization as an essential part of the artistic work" (BFR 204). Brecht was alluding to the difficult and drawn-out process

---

38   Cf. Lutz Koepnick,"The Bearable Lightness of Being: *People on Sunday*," in *Weimar Cinema: An Essential Guide to Classic Films of the Era*, ed. Noah Isenberg (New York: Columbia University Press, 2009), 237–53. For a critique of this and similar nostalgic readings, see Carrie Collenberg-Gonzalez, "Rape Culture and Dialectical Montage: A Radical Reframing of *Menschen am Sonntag*," in *Feminist German Studies* 35 (2019): 85–109.

39   On *KW* and operativity, see Sabine Hake, *The Proletarian Dream: Socialism, Culture, and Emotion in Germany, 1863-1933* (Berlin and Boston: De Gruyter, 2017), 319–33.

40   Benjamin, *Selected Writings*, vol. 2, 770.

of preparing the film's production. "Fresh from our experiences of the *Threepenny* lawsuit" (BFR 204), which had taught Brecht that the contractually guaranteed right of free artistic expression was in practice subordinated to the production company's profit-making imperative, he oserved that the conditions of film production resembled the conditions of capitalist production in general, since the workers, manual and intellectual alike, were deprived of control over the means of production. In his *Threepenny Lawsuit*, he noted:

> The migration of the means of production away from the producers signals the proletarianization of the producers. Like the manual labourer, the intellectual worker has only his naked labour power to offer, yet he is his labour power and nothing more than that. And, just like the manual labourer, he needs these means of production more and more to exploit his labour power (because production is becoming ever more 'technical'): the horrible vicious circle of exploitation has begun here too!
>
> (BFR 162)

KW attempted to reverse this process in the interest of the "socialization of the [cinematic] means of production." The "technical apparatuses" were to "supersede the traditionally untechnical, anti-technical, 'transcendent' 'art' associated with religion" (BFR 162)—that is, the type of art that dominates mass culture as much as it dominates the old bourgeois artistic forms of the novel and the drama. In artistic production, too, the contradiction between forces of production and relations of production prevailed. In the case of *KW*, the forces of artistic production were inhibited not only by funding difficulties after *Prometheus*'s insolvency but also by the politics and aesthetics of the censorship office, which twice prohibited the film's release. *KW*'s short theatrical release came only after a concerted protest campaign in the left-wing press. In 1933, the new Nazi regime banned all further screenings.

As Brecht noted, working with Münzenberg's *Prometheus* had enabled him and his collaborators to obtain a contract "that made us, the film makers, the holders of the copyright in a legal sense. This cost us our right to the usual remuneration, but we gained for our work otherwise unobtainable liberties" (BFR 204). The "great financial pressure" under which the shooting took place required quick work; "a quarter of the entire film [was shot] in two days." The disadvantages of a precariously low budget and small production team were ameliorated by working with proletarian organizations on and off the set. Off the set, "communist armed squats" protected the crew from attacks by "Nazi storm troopers."[41] For the music and sporting sequences, the film benefited from the collaboration between Eisler, Robert Scharfenberg (the set designer), and the worker-athletes; all rehearsals took place after regular work hours. Looking back at the production process, co-producer George Hoellering noted: "In fact, it was the smoothest and simplest production I've seen. I've worked in the commercial cinema and things did not go as smoothly as they did on *Kuhle Wampe*."[42]

Hoellering also recalled that Prometheus had wanted to produce a low-cost movie on the youth movement that "would glorify sport for the workers."[43] Although the film's seventh act still reflects some of that original intent, the placement of the sports scenes in a film about unemployment changes their meaning from "a 'positive' film"[44] to something that is better described as critical utopianism. From the beginning, the movie visually suggests that the athletic competitions are more than glorifications of youth: the first images of the film depict young men looking for work, riding their bicycles from one employer to the next in vain. They behave as a group, acting almost in unison and out of routine, rather than as individual competitors trying to outrace one another. What we see is, in Brecht's words, "the search for work as work" (BFR 205). The work-like nature of the group's bicycling is underscored by medium shots that make the spinning feet and wheels seem like machine parts of a larger, invisible whole—a metonymic reference to the effects of "rationalization," the replacement of workers (variable capital) by automated production processes and machinery (constant capital).

The collective character of the futile search for employment combined with Alfred Schäfer's eerily mechanical performance of young Bönike's fate as an interchangeable specimen of the "lost generation" establish a mimetic relationship between the film's first and seventh acts. Mere futility in the first act—as the camera follows the wheels spinning on the street and ends with the son's bike, hanging motionless from the ceiling of the small apartment—reappears in the seventh act as the instantiation of a learning process that mimetically repeats the lessons of defeat in preparation of eventual victory.

KW does not articulate what it means to "learn to win" politically (a utopian projection), but it is evident that the rhythmic patterns of the young worker-athletes' physical exercises function dialectically

---

41 "Making *Kuhle Wampe*: An Interview with George Hoellering," *Screen* 15, no. 4 (winter 1974): 71–8, 76.

42 "Making *Kuhle Wampe*," 76.

43 "Making *Kuhle Wampe*," 71.

44 "Making *Kuhle Wampe*," 71

Figure 9.8 *KW* 0:6:35: Searching for work as work.
Figure 9.9 *KW* 0:46:31: Automated work.
Figure 9.10 *KW* 0:52:41: All play, no work.

(this is underscored by Eisler's repetitive yet developing music). Corporeally, the athletes reenact the submissiveness of the workers inside and outside the factory to economic forces beyond their control. At the same time, this reenactment makes visible the workers' unrealized collective power: their organized cooperation, their solidarity. Their ability to organize is grounded in the exhortation to remember one thing: "Vorwärts! und nicht vergessen/Die Solidarität!" ["Forward and no forgetting/Our solidarity!"]. Amid mass unemployment, "forward" does not mean a return to full employment, but rather a replacement of labor through automation and play. The intermezzo between the second and third parts shows industrial production occurring without any visible expenditure of human labor power; likewise, the motorcycle race during the sports meet is presented as a joyful liberation from the toil of bicycling at the beginning of the movie.[45]

The Solidarity Song's rhythm dominates the film's third part. But before the audience hears the words sung by a group of young workers marching through the streets of Berlin-Wedding on their way to the sports festival, we hear the theme in an orchestrated arrangement in Eisler's *Suite 3*, accompanied by a montage of images of industrial production, featuring moving cranes and dollies, but no humans. This "musical intermezzo" reminds the audience that industrial production requires ever fewer workers. At first glance, we see a representation of production without employment. This representation does not disclose, to use Brecht's phrase from the *Threepenny Lawsuit*, the agential "human relations" that make up what our reified vision one-sidedly apperceives

---

45   See also Christoph Schaub's analysis of *KW*'s "politics of form" as practiced in the film's cycling and athletic sequences: "Labor-Movement Modernism: Proletarian Collectives between *Kuhle Wampe* and Working-Class Performance Culture," *Modernism/Modernity* 25, no. 2 (2018): 327–48, especially 333–7.

as "factory" or "industrial production." Yet the relationship between Eisler's stirring music and the images of production suggests that a crisis in one social order can be liberation in another. In capitalism, losing a job has catastrophic consequences for the worker. In communism, on the other hand, work could become automated for the benefit of the workers: a reduction of necessary labor-time would not mean immiseration but rather liberation from drudgery and the possibility of exercising one's corporeal powers for purposes other than the production of surplus value.

Rehearsing Solidarity: "Learning to Win"

Coupled with "emergency degrees" that cut welfare benefits, the labor crisis translated into a housing emergency. Young Bönike's suicide shows the domestic sphere to be the setting in which the crisis viscerally takes shape, first in the destruction of human life, then in the family's eviction from their apartment. After the eviction notification, Anni attempts to secure a postponement, illustrated in a quick montage of shots showing her being rejected by various authorities. Her efforts are futile, just like her brother's search for work. But just as the futile search for work has its dialectical antithesis in the playful motorcycling in the film's third part, the family's eviction finds its dialectical antithesis in a performance by the agitprop troupe "Das rote Sprachrohr" ["Red Megaphone"] during the sports festival.

Agitprop groups mushroomed during the last years of the republic as unemployed young workers turned to artistic organizing in their neighborhoods to translate "found materials" into public performances that would illustrate and lend support to everyday struggles against representatives of the ruling class, such as police and landlords: "It was theater that staged pieces of reality through the lens of its working-class performers."[46] Agitprop gestures, stances, motion, and speech were intentionally terse and nondramatic.[47] "Aesthetic values" were replaced with "combat values."[48] Perhaps the most well-known agitprop group, "Red Megaphone" insisted on the radically collective character of its work. Its founder, Maxim Vallentin, argued in *Die Linkskurve* that the specialized "bourgeois" division of labor typical for the

---

46 Jessi Piggott, "Acts of Commitment: Prefigurative Politics on the Agitprop Stage" (PhD diss., Stanford University, August 2019), 60.

47 Hake, *Proletarian Dream*, 251–53.

48 Maxim Vallentin, "Agitpropspiel und Kampfwert," in *Die Linkskurve* 2, no. 4 (1930): 15–16.

theater no longer applied. Although the *Linkskurve* editors dismissed Vallentin's praise of non-specialized collective work as a "retrograde utopia,"[49] Red Megaphone's performance at the sports meet is a successful, almost spontaneous reenactment of an omnipresent fear haunting proletarian families: eviction.

The reenactment is cast in almost classical form: accompanied by drums and banjos, "the scene of eviction is both spoken in solo voice and sung in solo and chorus using large, clear gestures" (BFR 244), thus imbuing the banal degradation of eviction with the dignity of a tragic *sujet*. However, the lesson of the performance is not that eviction is an inevitable tragedy, but that it can be averted if the neighbors gather to oppose it: "The neighbours, proles, are building a circle. The furniture mover asks, he discusses, until even … the last one understands" (BFR 245). The neighbors' spontaneous act of solidarity forces the landlord to yield. This was articulated unequivocally in the rest of the scene, which was cut to placate the censor: "The neighbours are standing like one man, that's why the masters are yelling … no one gets in. The landlord, the bailiff, the police, under pressure they'll release the apartment" (BFR 257).

In his warning about the scene (see KWPM 123), the censor correctly understood Red Megaphone's performance of spontaneous solidarity to be an appeal to resistance. The eviction experienced by the Bönike family in the second act was different, however. They only received help from Fritz, who drove them and their belongings to Kuhle Wampe. Red Megaphone's performance is thus a critical reenactment of what could have happened to the Bönikes had the neighbors acted in their common shared interest. Similar to a theatrical performance, the performance of the eviction skit ends with the audience applauding. This almost perfunctory round of applause is followed by the collective singing of the Solidarity Song,[50] which concludes the skit's lesson: spontaneous solidarity does not emerge out of thin air, but requires the existence of an organizable collective, and the primary purpose of the sports festival is the rehearsal of organized collectivity. As Brecht noted, the athletic competitions in part three "are brilliantly organized" and thus have a "political character." The exercises in which the worker-athletes engage have "the mark of militancy" (BFM 205).

Nonetheless, no work of art is immune to the risk of aestheticizing and depoliticizing its subject, and some of the participating *Fichte*

---

49 *Linkskurve* 2.4 (1930): 17.
50 Stefanie Diekmann reads the audience's participatory reaction as a "counter-image" to the aestheticized fascist stagings of masses in films such as Riefenstahl's "Triumph of the Will" and "Olympia." See Diekmann, "Ein Kino, das zum Anthologischen neigt," 51.

athletes complained that *KW* lacked revolutionary radicalism. They felt that the "beautiful transition" of the film's plot from the "most dire need of the unemployed" to the semi-idyllic Kuhle Wampe had betrayed their struggle: "As class-conscious workers, we reject this film decisively, because it gives a totally screwed-up [*völlig versaut*] rendition of our athletic activity and our view of life" (GBA 19, 727; my translation). *Ex negativo*, the participants' perception of the film's failure to provide a naturalistic representation of their lives touches on the dialectical technique with which the camera registers cityscape and landscape. Rather than documenting the immediate appearance of social misery, the camera shows suburban outdoor spaces and city streets *as if* they belonged to the workers. The camera sees both what is and what *could* be.

The only departure from the dialectical sequence that chronicles unemployment and self-organization are the opening sequence shots of dark and rundown tenement buildings. However, the film then goes on to link these iconic images of proletarian housing to economic factors and, in the third act, to the state's role in evicting tenants. In a scene faulted by the censor for "evoking the impression that the state does not protect the families of the unemployed," we see a judge reading the eviction verdict, to quote again from the censor's report, in "an indifferent, mechanical manner" (KWPM 122).

According to the judge's verdict, the eviction is valid because the Bönikes' "current difficulties must be seen as their own fault [*selbstverschuldet*]" (BFR 21). The film highlights these kinds of state and class domination with artful brevity: the 18-shot montage sequence showing Anni's futile attempts to avert her family's eviction is less than two minutes long. Yet there is one form of domination that is shortchanged by the movie's economy of expression: in the final, censored version of *KW*, Anni's resistance to the social and legal domination of her gender

Figure 9.11 *KW* 0:3:12: Berlin-Wedding, where the unemployed dwell.
Figure 9.12 *KW* 0:19:24: Evicted, "in the name of the people."
Figure 9.13 *KW* 0:56:42: Red Megaphone averts the eviction, retrospectively.

and sexuality is barely legible, due in large part (though not entirely) to the censor's fears about the film's "incitement to abortion" and "morally corrosive effect" (KWPM 134 and 135).

"My body belongs to me": Lessons in Self-Liberation

The politics of abortion have played a mostly marginal role in *KW*'s lively scholarly reception.[51] For the censorship office, however, the lesson that "solidarity extends even to getting over an abortion" (KWPM 123), clearly demonstrated that the movie's politics of class and gender-based "anti-statist" politics of self-help had gone too far. The censors correctly understood that the film's rhetorical argument elevated collective solidarity above state-sanctioned networks of kinship support. The idea of a female protagonist leaving her fiancé to engage in collective organizing was intolerable, especially in light of Anni and Fritz's eventual reconciliation, which came about only after Fritz accepted Anni's choice of the collective over the family.

In a conventionally plot-driven film, Anni and Fritz's relationship would have been a central narrative device, especially since Ernst Busch (Fritz) and Hertha Thiele (Anni) were by far the two most well-known actors participating in *KW*. In the movie's third part, however, their story is entirely relegated to the sidelines. Agitprop performances strictly excluded professional actors, and during Red Megaphone's performance, we can first spot Anni right next to the stage. However, the next audience shots show Anni farther back, now standing next to Fritz, but not paying attention to him. Anni's doubled presence at the performance, both as one spectator amongst many and as Fritz's companion, creates a slight but noticeable distancing of Thiele and Busch among the mass of unknown proletarians and between the characters of Anni and Fritz—their story is over, but the film and the fight go on.

The two protagonists, then, appear as strangers in their own film,[52] an impression underscored by the increased focus on Adolf Fischer's Kurt and Martha Wolter's Gerda in *KW*'s final part. While Fischer had

---

51 Notable exceptions are Ursula von Keitz's perceptive close reading of the theme in *Im Schatten des Gesetzes: Schwangerschaftskonflikt und Reproduktion im deutschsprachigen Film 1918 bis 1933* (Marburg: Schüren, 2005), 350–74 and Robert Heynen's treatment of the theme in the context of his monographic interpretation of Weimar politics of the body in *Degeneration and Revolution: Radical Cultural Politics and the Body in Weimar Germany* (Chicago, IL: Haymarket, 2016), 572–5.

52 See Patrick Primavesi, "Wie im (falschen) Film: Brecht und die Arbeit mit nicht/ professionellen Akteuren," in *Brecht Yearbook* 45 (2020): 86.

Figure 9.14 *KW* 0:55:12: Anni by herself, upper center.
Figure 9.15 *KW* 0:56:34: Anni with Fritz, watching Red Megaphone perform.
Figure 9.16 *KW* 0:57:21: Busch and Thiele, strangers in their own film.

played a bit part in Pabst's *Kameradschaft* (in which Busch had starred as well), Wolter, a seamstress, had been "discovered" by Dudow, who instructed her to do nothing but "play herself."[53] The proletarian lay actors were tasked with playing themselves, whereas Thiele and Busch, whose unmistakable identity as professional actors was inseparable from the roles they performed, were tasked with not stealing the limelight from the lay actors.

Busch was Germany's most famous communist actor and singer and had also performed in the first staging of Brecht and Eisler's *Die Maßnahme* in 1930. Thiele was hired for *KW* just before she became a star for playing the lead role in Leontine Sagan's *Mädchen in Uniform* [*Girls in Uniform*], released in 1931. Her character in that film, Manuela, "embodies youth in its utter vulnerability," as Kracauer noted.[54] Only the spontaneous solidarity of the other girls at her oppressive Prussian boarding school prevents Manuela from throwing herself to her death at the end of the film. Thiele's Manuela comes from an aristocratic family; she suffers theatrically. In *KW*, by comparison, Thiele's Anni is unflappable even in the wake of her brother's suicide and her family's eviction. She embodies the "New Woman" not only in her appearance, but in the role she plays in her family and her relationship, and in her self-contained *gestus*, her trademark soldier-like walk which we witness in act 3, as she walks alone from one office to the next seeking to obtain an extension on the family's eviction, and, in act 6, as she marches with a group of worker-athletes to the sports festival singing the solidarity song.

---

53 *Film-Kurier*, March 9, 1932, cited in Primavesi, 90.
54 Kracauer, *From Caligari to Hitler*, 227.

Figure 9.17 *KW* 0:20:33: Anni seeking to postpone the eviction.
Figure 9.18 *KW* 0:52:07: Anni with the *Fichte* athletes.

While Anni's mother runs the household and her unemployed father doesn't do much at all, she works in the device testing section of what appears to be AEG's plant for electronic devices in Berlin-Treptow.[55] Most importantly, however, "Anni precedes Fritz in liberating herself."[56] For Anni, self-liberation means claiming control of her reproductive labor power. The film contrasts her taking control of her body to the "measureless" and "unceasing" fertility of nature depicted first in the musical interlude between the first and second act and during the "sex scene" at the end of act 3, where the camera shows nothing but meadows and trees moving in the wind, with a voice-over by Helene Weigel performing Brecht's poem "Der Frühling" [Spring], which ends with the line "Und es gebiert die Erde das Neue/Ohne Vorsicht" (KWMP 35). ["And the Earth gives birth to the new/Without heed."][57] *KW* strikingly contrasts aestheticized sexual pleasure and natural fertility with Anni's actual pregnancy, and this contrast between ideological image and disenchanted reality leads to an immediate rupture between the lovers. When we next see Anni and Fritz, their distant body language reflects their words: he inquires whether she has investigated her abortion options. Anni replies, "It's too dirty there. I am not going to ruin my life" (BFR 229). Between Fritz's question and

---

55 As Peukert notes, "cheap female labour was better placed in the crisis than was male labour." ("The Lost Generation," 78)
56 Kracauer, *From Caligari to Hitler*, 246.
57 Brecht, *Collected Poems*, trans. David Constantine and Tom Kuhn (London and New York: Livermore, 2018), 410.

Anni's response there is a gap noticeable only because of a slight jump cut.[58] In a scene cut at the censor's behest, Anni tells Fritz that the abortion will cost more than she can afford, 90 marks. In another cut scene, we learn that after Anni and Fritz's falling out, Gerda and the *Fichte* comrades lent Anni the money needed "and now everything is okay" (BFR 257).

In the approved version of *KW*, the audience is given just enough information to intuit that since Fritz is unwilling to support the pregnant Anni, her rejoining the *Fichte* collective is crucial for the process of "self-liberation." We learn in passing that Anni had previously left the sports organization because Fritz thought that Anni "didn't have the stuff for your athletics" (BFR 241). The plot thus suggests a condensed dialectical *Bildungsroman*, leading from the initial collective (Anni's *Fichte* membership) to a bourgeois relationship (the antithesis of the former) and then into a reconciliation between the two. Such a synthesis, however, becomes possible only on two narrative conditions: Fritz must relinquish his egotistic "freedom"[59] for Anni's needs, and both must accept their demotion from protagonists to supporting cast. Consequently, during the third act of the film (*KW*'s dialectical synthesis, as it were), the workers Kurt and Gerda emerge as the leading couple, without, however, any hints of romantic infatuation. Their two qualifications for becoming the leading couple are their selfless commitment to the *Fichte* collective and their deliberate use of reproductive autonomy: as the sports meet is winding down, Kurt and Gerda are shown with a man selling brochures. Kurt notes that he already has a copy of *Birth Control*[60] and instead purchases a copy of *Factory and Union* (BFR 245).

Abortion in Weimar Germany was illegal, as the film originally reminded its viewers in a spoken title cut to appease the censor: "Criminal Code §218, Sec. I. Off-voice: A woman who kills her foetus in the womb or who permits the killing by someone else will be punished with imprisonment." (BFR 257) In a comment from 1930, Brecht anticipated *KW*'s interpretation of the law's political function: it was designed to extend the state's monopoly on violence to all spheres of human existence. The state, Brecht noted, "prohibits us from preventing our offspring from life [*unsere Nachkommen am Leben zu verhindern*]; the state wants to do this itself. The state reserves for itself the right to

---

58 Earlier copies of the film contain a noticeable "cracking sound" where the cut was made; see von Keitz, *Im Schatten des Gesetzes*, 356.

59 Advised to marry Anni, he responds: "Nonsense. I want my freedom" (BFR 230).

60 Earlier in the film, an image showing an advertising for *Fromms* condoms was censored.

abort adult humans capable of doing work [*arbeitsfähig*]."[61] Brecht not only had a general political but also a personal stake in the matter of abortion rights: his collaborator and lover Margarete Steffin, a member of the *Fichte* organization and participant in *KW*, had an abortion in 1932, about which she noted: "Wer keine Stellung hat muß sorgen/Daß er keine Kinder hat" ("He who is unemployed must ensure/that he has no children").[62] Then as now, punishment for abortion was meted out unequally: it disproportionately affected proletarian women. As Atina Grossmann has shown, the politics of abortion came to a head as unemployment rose. For proletarian women, an additional child could spell the difference between poverty and destitution. Massive protests for the abolition of Paragraph 218, in which the communists played a major role, doubtlessly influenced *KW*'s choice to represent the search for work and the search for an abortion "as dual emblems of capitalist crisis."[63]

But *KW* also introduces a third "emblem of capitalist crisis": the calamities of homelessness and food insecurity, aggravated by the Brüning government's emergency decrees gutting unemployment benefits (which are mentioned in a censored reference in the second act), are comically mirrored by the excess consumption on display at Anni and Fritz's engagement party.[64] The guests devour the free food and drinks as if it were their last meal. The engagement scene which concludes the film's second part ends with an intoxicated guest named "Uncle Otto" attempting to go for a swim in the lake. He fends off his wife, who is trying to pull him back inside the tent, by exclaiming, "My body belongs to me" (BFR 238). This sentence, of course, would have come out of Anni's mouth had it not been for the tactical need to outsmart the censors. Instead, Uncle Otto's slogan is linked to Anni's reclamation of her autonomy only contiguously (metonymically): as the party unravels, Anni decides to leave Fritz and move in with her friend Gerda. In the act's final shot, we see Gerda and Anni about to enter Gerda's apartment. Gerda instructs Anni: "So, now you are going to live with me, next Sunday you'll come with me to the athletic games and you can forget Fritz" (BFR 239).

Gerda has anticipated this turn of events. In an earlier scene, Gerda and Anni are shown at work, testing electronic devices in a booth

---

61 GBA 21: 373. I thank Matthias Rothe for alerting me to this statement.

62 Cited in Werner Hecht, *Brecht Chronik* (Frankfurt: Suhrkamp, 1997), 336.

63 Atina Grossmann, *Reforming Sex: The German Movement for Birth Control and Abortion Reform, 1920–1950* (New York: Oxford University Press, 1997), 86.

64 One of *KW*'s conceptual origins was Brecht's comedic one-act play *Die Kleinbürgerhochzeit* (1919), on which Dudow in 1930 based a draft for a film script bearing the same title (GBA 19: 718).

marked with the sign "Danger! Life threatening," and Anni confides: "I can't stand it anymore. If it goes on, I'm moving away from there" (BFR 230). The setting of this scene, however, communicates more than the solidarity Gerda will offer to her troubled coworker. The charging and discharging of electrical power the two women are performing indicates a twofold shift of authority: a shift from the earlier scenes of natural fertility to the productivity of rationalized Taylorist industrial labor. The lack of work, perhaps even lack as such,[65] is associated first with Anni's father and brother, and later with Fritz after he loses his job as a cab driver. Indicated here is a shift not only in the gender of workers but also the workers's relationship to their work: the passivity stereotypically associated with women doing assembly work here extends to the male workers. Young Bönike's relationship to work is exemplified in his suspended bicycle, which metaphorically anticipates his imminent suicide; Fritz's is expressed in the phallic yet subordinate gesture of washing the underbody of his cab; Anni and Gerda's coworkers are portrayed as if their hands are detached from their bodies as they assemble electronic devices along a conveyor belt. In each of these cases, the workers are passive towards or detached from their work.

Set against these images of passivity, Anni and Gerda embody the risk of getting too close to the invisible energy for which they are testing. Their work is no longer productive in the narrow sense but is closer to the testing and supervising associated with managerial work. Viewed as an ensemble, these scenes depicting relations between workers and their work thus underscore the growing divergence between skilled and unskilled labor that was beginning to divide the working

Figure 9.19 *KW* 0:10:09: The son's bicycle, suspended.
Figure 9.20 *KW* 0:33:12: Fritz washing a car.
Figure 9.21 *KW* 0:31:35: No idle hands on the assembly line.

---

65 See von Keitz, *Im Schatten des Gesetzes*, 364.

class. The inherent dangers of this historical and technological process are inscribed in the scene's composition: sitting back-to-back, fenced in like "dangerous animals,"[66] each holding a pair of pistol-like testing devices, Gerda and Anni resemble a caged two-headed centaur—an allegory of capitalist history birthing monsters, but also an allegory of the desire to escape, together.

However, this visual diagnosis of the divide in capitalist labor and its gendered underpinnings is not *KW*'s final articulation of how the abstract and global totality of the Great Depression affects the concrete lives of Berlin workers in the early 1930s. Instead, *KW* visually proposes a utopian reading of mass unemployment through visual montage. The film's third part, "Wem gehört die Welt?" ["Who Owns the World?"],[67] quickly transitions from the intermezzo of scenes of industrial production to a group of worker-athletes engaged in the unpaid work of organizing Berlin's proletarian neighborhoods to attend and participate in the athletic festival.

Figure 9.22 *KW* 0:32:32: Anni and Gerda at work, discussing Anni's escape.

---

66 Von Keitz, *Im Schatten des Gesetzes*, 364.
67 This intertitle is noted in the censor's records but is missing from *KW*'s DEFA Film Library and Deutsche Kinemathek restored versions.

In contrast to Gerda and Anni's repetitive, monotonous, and dangerous work at the factory, they print flyers and paint banners for the festival in an atmosphere of joyful anticipation. Here, tools and machines serve a fully decommodified, collective purpose. The subsequent images of the proletarian athletes, which show them liberated from both the drudgery of wage labor and the listlessness of unemployment, convey the cathartic power of the competitions: we see Kurt on a motorcycle and Gerda in a row-boat, alongside dozens of other worker-athletes. The film suspends its plot, just as it shows the temporary suspension of everyday life in favor of more meaningful activity. These scenes are superfluous to the extent that they do not advance the story, yet this is precisely what makes them essential. Their political meaning is highlighted by the lyrics of Brecht's "Von den Hinterhäusern kommend" [Coming from the crowded tenements], sung by Ernst Busch, who temporarily steps out of the role of Fritz and instead assumes his default role as a performer of working-class battle songs.

The combination of image and sound emphasizes the contrast between the liberating athletic activity—itself a fusion of work and play, individual and collective effort—and the everyday living conditions of the Berlin proletariat. As the viewers see a fast-moving montage of swimmers, rowers, and motorcyclists racing towards the finish line, they hear Busch's unmistakable tenor intone, "Kommend

Figure 9.23 *KW* 0:48:29: *Fichte* worker-athletes: decommodified work.

von den vollen Hinterhäusern/Finstern Straßen der umkämpften Städte .... // Aus den zermürbenden Kämpfen um das Notwendigste/ Für wenige Stunden/Findet ihr euch wieder zusammen/Um gemein-sam zu kämpfen./Und lernt zu siegen!" (*KW* 63–4) ["Coming from the crowded tenements/From the dark streets of the embattled cities .... // Out of the crushing struggle/For the bare necessities/For a few hours/ Once more you gather to fight the common fight/And learn to win!"][68] The crucial qualifier in this battle song is "for a few hours"—it under-scores the extraordinary character of the athletic festival.

In the film's total seventy minutes, this scene takes up less than ten minutes, and only a little over two minutes show the actual competi-tions. According to the original draft screenplay, the sporting events had been initially envisioned in a more critical context, followed by a satirical scene about a traffic jam and an "intermezzo" showing scenes of mass tourism. Crucially, these scenes were intended to have an orchestral accompaniment in the "rhythm of machines," while the *Sportlied* sung by Ernst Busch was to accompany groups of athletes marching to the meet. The lyrics were also different, culminating in an almost eschato-logical acclamation of collective action as judgment by battle: "Uns treibt nicht der Ruhm/der erste zu sein/Im Kampf ist der einzelne nichts/ Wir halten zusammen, wir/stehn nicht allein/Am Tage des Kampfger-ichts." ["We are not driven by the glory/to be the first,/The individual is nothing in our fight./We stand together, we/do not stand alone/on the day of judgment by combat."] The athletic contests, Brecht's orig-inal lyrics tell the viewers, are metaphors for the "great game" of the world revolution: "Wagt mit uns das große Spiel/Denn es stehen die Millionen/Aller Länder, aller Zonen/Im Endkampf ums Ziel" (GBA 19: 522) ["Venture with us the great game/for the millions/from all countries and spheres/stand in the final battle to win" (my translation)].

The draft screenplay emphasized the internationalism of revolu-tionary struggle, and the hunt for labor was to be shown in a montage sequence featuring unemployed workers from America, Italy, and China, all cycling to find work. In the finished film, the international dimension of the struggle remains invisible, and the sports meet seems politically and spatially isolated: it is the precarious utopia of a safe space, but it is bereft of a visual aesthetics that can translate the metaphor of sports into the arena of political struggle.[69] Instead, the mediation between sports as a playful "learning exercise" and the practice of politics is left to the

---

68   Brecht, *Collected Poems*, 410-1.
69   For a critique of Brecht's (futile) attempts to harness the metaphor of sports for left-wing politics, see Kai Marcel Sicks, "Sollen Dichter boxen? Brechts Ästhe-tik und der Sport," in *Hofmannsthal Jahrbuch zur europäischen Moderne* 12 (2004): 365–404.

film's soundtrack. Both the solidarity song and the final debate about global political economy use verbalization to deliver lessons to the audience. At the very end of the film, we once again hear Busch's famous voice singing the solidarity song, ending with the lines, "Denn wir wissen, das ist nur ein/Tropfen auf den heißen Stein./Aber damit kann die Sache/Nicht für uns bereinigt sein." (KWPM 83) ["For we know that these are only/Drops in the ocean of our need/We are angry, we are hungry/On such crumbs of comfort we'll not feed."[70]] The proverbial "Tropfen auf den heißen Stein" is a remnant of the eponymous poem Brecht had intended to be the film's signature song. Thanks to Dudow's insistence on using a more "concise" and "mobilizing" song, Brecht and Eisler quickly came up with the solidarity song (see KWPM 111). Dudow's anecdote illustrates *KW*'s commitment to a "rationalized" economy of representation that asks the viewers to draw conclusions at which the film's visual rhetoric merely hints. Partially as a result of pressure from the censors, the narrative of Anni's emancipation, which places the feminist politics of reproductive control at the center of proletarian liberation, remains hidden beneath the visible surface of the collective corporeal empowerment portrayed in the sports festival.[71]

Before *KW* arrives at its finale, it has instructed its viewers to see the bodies of the athletes not as atomized bodies but as interconnected forces of political struggle. In the fourth act, a stream of images pass through Anni's mind in quick succession as she and Fritz walk past a group of young children, and form the anticipatory counterpoint to *KW*'s celebration of collective organizing in the sixth and seventh acts. The images include children's faces, baby products and toys, a display of coffins in a store window, and business signs for a gynecologist's practice, a pregnancy counseling service, and a funeral institute. However, the montage associates death not with Anni's abortion but rather with her brother's suicide and the theme of unemployment: not only do we see the courtyard where he killed himself, his dead body under a sheet, and a police ambulance, but also two pieces of paperwork related to Anni's potential future employment situation, her employment ID card and a notification of employment termination due to "lack of work" [*Arbeitsmangel*]. As the image of the "pink slip" fades, the faces of the group of children walking past Anni and Fritz appear to her as a prefiguration of a future reserve army of the unemployed.

---

70 Brecht, *Collected* Poems, 407.
71 I disagree with Rippey, who reads *KW* as rescuing the body from ideological appropriation and for aesthetic experience. To claim, as Rippey does, "corporeality's resistance to becoming coextensive with politics," presupposes a nonpolitical "outside" of pure art and play, which runs the risk of reinscribing a strict nature/culture divide. See Theodore F. Rippey, "*Kuhle Wampe* and the Problem of Corporal Culture," in *Cinema Journal* 47.1 (2007): 21.

Figure 9.24 *KW* 0:34:46: Anni's vision of unemployment …
Figure 9.25 *KW* 0:34:48: … due to "lack of work."
Figure 9.26 *KW* 0:34:46: Future reserve army of the unemployed.

Figure 9.27 *KW* 0:30:57: Anni: "I don't want to ruin my life."
Figure 9.28 *KW* 0:35:44: Fashion anticipates the transition to comradeship.
Figure 9.29 *KW* 0:35:56: The soon-to-be-unemployed Fritz departs for work.

Anni's *gestus* throughout tells the viewer that she rejects a future in which her commitment to family and children would deprive her of political agency. Instead of relating to Fritz as the father of her future child, she visually closes the gendered hierarchy between them: while the plot only chronicles their relationship crisis, Anni's androgynous appearance signals a claim to sexual equality, which is gesturally sealed by their parting handshake. Their similar appearance not only indicates an ambition for equal partnership; shirt and tie also suggest a generic work uniform. If read prefiguratively, this *gestus* communicates a utopia in which the strict separation between labor and leisure has disappeared, and with it also the power of the social institutions that rule over it: employment (waged labor) and the family (unwaged labor).

The dialectical reading of *KW* proposed in this chapter dissolves the dualistic categories (such as, art/propaganda, modernism/realism, politics/sports, mass/individual, success/failure) that have shaped most readings of the film. Instead, I have sought to underscore the potential for liberation that lies within the crisis of capitalism—a potential that the film's visual rhetoric encodes in phenomena of social violence (immiseration, unemployment, homelessness, poverty). While a teleological reading of history would read these only as portents of doom, dialectical readings decipher the possibilities of change arising from autonomous organized efforts to overcome the present misery in playful, anticipatory enactment of what could be. The censorship-induced near-erasure of Anni's abortion as a practice of self-liberation has surely contributed to critical readings which argue that the final two acts do not live up to the film's revolutionary ambition. Less melancholy readings, however, will see in the film's visual depiction of unemployment, idleness, sports, and taking control of one's own body the possibility of a society in which the destruction of productive forces is not destined to lead to catastrophe.[72]

Works Cited

Adorno, Theodor and Hanns Eisler. *Composing for the Films*. London: Continuum, [1944] 2007.

Adorno, Theodor, Walter Benjamin, Ernst Bloch, Bertolt Brecht, and Georg Lukács. *Aesthetics and Politics*. London: Verso, 1980.

Alter, Nora. "The Politics and Sounds of Everyday Life in *Kuhle Wampe*." In *Sound Matters: Essays on the Acoustics of Modern German Culture*, edited by Nora Alter and Lutz Koepnick. 79–90. New York: Berghahn Books, 2004.

Alter, Nora. *The Essay Film after Fact and Fiction*. New York: Columbia University Press, 2018.

Benjamin, Walter. *Selected Writings*, 4 vols. Translated by Edmund Jephcott and others. Edited by Howard Eiland and Michael Jennings. Cambridge, MA: Harvard University Press, 1996–2003.

Brecht, Bertolt. *Werke: Große kommentierte Berliner und Frankfurter Ausgabe*, 30 vols. Edited by Werner Hecht, Jan Knopf, Werner Mittenzwei, and Klaus-Detlef Müller. Berlin, Weimar and Frankfurt: Aufbau/Suhrkamp, 1988–98.

Brecht, Bertolt. *On Film and Radio*. Edited and translated by Marc Silberman. London: Methuen, 2010.

Brecht, Bertolt. *Collected Poems*. Translated by David Constantine and Tom Kuhn. London and New York: Livermore, 2018.

Brewster, Ben and Colin MacCabe. "Making *Kuhle Wampe*: An Interview with George Hoellering." *Screen* 15, no. 4 (winter 1974): 71–8.

Collenberg-Gonzalez, Carrie. "Rape Culture and Dialectical Montage: A Radical Reframing of *Menschen am Sonntag*." *Feminist German Studies* 35 (2019): 85–109.

---

72 I thank Cecilia Sebastian for her corrections and suggestions, and I thank Matthew Garrett for his generous bounty of comments and ideas (many more than I could include here).

Diekmann, Stefanie. "Ein Kino, das zum Anthologischen neigt." In *Brecht und das Fragment*, edited by Astrid Oesmann and Matthias Rothe, 47–58. Berlin: Verbrecher, 2020.

Eisner, Lotte. *The Haunted Screen: Expressionism in the German Cinema and the Influence of Max Reinhardt.* Translated by Roger Greaves. London: Thames & Hudson, [1952] 1969.

Evans, Richard. *The Coming of the Third Reich.* New York: Penguin, 2004.

Föllmer, Moritz. "Suicide and Crisis in Weimar Berlin." *Central European History* 42 (2009): 195–221.

Gersch, Wolfgang, and Werner Hecht. *Kuhle Wampe oder Wem gehört die Welt: Filmprotokoll und Materialien.* Leipzig: Reclam, 1971.

Gerz, Raimund and Burkhardt Lindner. "Kuhle Wampe." *Brecht Handbuch*, vol. 3, edited by Jan Knopf, 432–57. Stuttgart, Metzler, 2002.

Grossmann, Atina. *Reforming Sex: The German Movement for Birth Control and Abortion Reform, 1920–1950.* New York: Oxford University Press, 1997.

Hake, Sabine. *The Proletarian Dream: Socialism, Culture, and Emotion in Germany, 1863–1933.* Berlin and Boston: De Gruyter, 2017.

Hecht, Werner. *Brecht Chronik.* Frankfurt: Suhrkamp, 1997.

Heinsohn, Bastian. "Film as Pedagogy in Late Weimar and Early Nazi Cinema: The Role of the Street in Mobilizing the Spectator." In *Continuity and Crisis in German Cinema, 1928–1936*, edited by Barbara Hales, Mihaela Petrescu, and Valerie Weinstein, 51–69. Rochester, NY: Camden House, 2016.

Heynen, Robert. *Degeneration and Revolution: Radical Cultural Politics and the Body in Weimar Germany.* Chicago, IL: Haymarket, 2016.

Jameson, Fredric. *Representing Capital: A Commentary on Volume One.* London and New York: Verso, 2011.

Von Keitz, Ursula. *Im Schatten des Gesetzes: Schwangerschaftskonflikt und Reproduktion im deutschsprachigen Film 1918 bis 1933.* Marburg: Schüren, 2005.

Koepnick, Lutz. "The Bearable Lightness of Being: *People on Sunday.*" In *Weimar Cinema: An Essential Guide to Classic Films of the Era*, edited by Noah Isenberg, 237–53. New York: Columbia University Press, 2009.

Kracauer, Siegfried. "Kuhle Wampe verboten!" *Frankfurter Zeitung*, April 5, 1932.

Kracauer, Siegfried. *From Caligari to Hitler: A Psychological History of the German Film.* Princeton, NJ: Princeton University Press, [1947] 2004.

Primavesi, Patrick. "Wie im (falschen) Film: Brecht und die Arbeit mit nicht/professionellen Akteuren." *Brecht Yearbook* 45 (2020): 81–114.

Peukert, Detlev. "The Lost Generation: Youth Unemployment at the End of the Weimar Republic." In *The German Unemployed: Experiences and Consequences of Mass Unemployment from the Weimar Republic to the Third Reich*, edited by Richard Evans and Dick Geary, 172–93. New York: St. Martin's, 1986.

Peukert, Detlev. *The Weimar Republic.* Translated by Richard Deveson. New York: Hill and Wang, 1992.

Piggott, Jessi. "Acts of Commitment: Prefigurative Politics on the Agitprop Stage." PhD diss., Stanford University, Stanford, CA, August 2019.

Pollock, Friedrich. "Bemerkungen zur Wirtschaftskrise." *Zeitschrift für Sozialforschung* 2, no. 3 (1933): 321–54.

Rippey, Theodore F. "*Kuhle Wampe* and the Problem of Corporal Culture." *Cinema Journal* 47, no. 1 (2007): 3–25.

Rothe, Matthias. "Die Temporalität der Kritik: Bertolt Brechts Fragment *Jae Fleischhacker in Chikago* (1924–1929)." *Brecht Yearbook* 40 (2016): 28–50.

Schaub, Christoph. "Labor-Movement Modernism: Proletarian Collectives between *Kuhle Wampe* and Working-Class Performance Culture." *Modernism/Modernity* 25, no. 2 (2018): 327–48.

Sicks, Kai Marcel. "Sollen Dichter boxen? Brechts Ästhetik und der Sport." *Hofmannsthal Jahrbuch zur europäischen Moderne* 12 (2004): 365–404.

Silberman, Marc. "Whose Revolution? The Subject of *Kuhle Wampe*." *Weimar Cinema: An Essential Guide to Classic Films of the Era*, edited by Noah Isenberg, 311–30. New York: Columbia University Press, 2009.

Vallentin, Maxim. "Agitpropspiel und Kampfwert." *Die Linkskurve* 2, no. 4 (1930): 15–16.

Ten "Hidden Stockpiles of Words and Images": An Interview with Thomas Heise

Matthias Rothe

I interviewed filmmaker Thomas Heise via Zoom on November 30, 2021. His films—*The House 1984* [*Das Haus 1984*], *The People's Police 1985* [*Volkspolizei 1985*], and *Why a Film about These People?* [*Wozu denn über diese Leute einen Film,* 1980]—are particularly suited for reflecting on the specific kinds of precarity present in East Germany. How did instability and vulnerability manifest themselves in the GDR, and, if they are understood as products of social circumstances, which circumstances brought them about?

Precarity in the GDR—and I write from the position of someone born there—seems to me largely due to the omnipresence of a paternalistic state which claimed it was infallible. The state felt responsible for the well-being of its subjects from birth to death, and historically legitimated this responsibility through antifascism for which "successful lives" in turn had to serve as evidence. Under these circumstances, the refusal to adapt or follow a predetermined course became not only an individual failure (an odd confluence with neoliberal ideology) but was also—perhaps first and foremost—political failure. Hence precarity in the GDR did not predominantly manifest as economic insecurity (this could have been a consequence) but delegitimized citizens' existences and limited their chances to participate in society. Precarity was legislated, i.e., produced through § 249, the so-called "antisocial paragraph" of the criminal code. Hence, it could be a crime to not have steady employment or engage in various forms of social activism or alternative ways of life (being a punk, for example). According to *Mitteldeutscher Rundfunk* (*MDR*), in 1989 circa one-quarter of all prisoners behind bars had landed there because of this paragraph. This data challenges the deep-seated belief that the East German state held back in the 1980s or lost interest in the lives of its citizens. Perhaps the connections to antifascism had weakened, but bureaucracy continued to spin its wheels regardless. This is made clear in Heise's radio feature, *First Name: Jonas* [*Vorname Jonas*, 1983], which was banned in the GDR. After all, Heise himself was subject to considerable political and economic precarity when he was thrown out of film school in the 1980s.

In general, Heise's films—and not only those about the GDR—focus intensely on bureaucracy and the encounter between human beings and the state, and the ways in which this encounter can bring about precarity (though this would not be Heise's preferred term). His films depict ritualized forms of this encounter (*The House 1984*) as well as moments in which it seems as though the state's functions, abstract and violent, might be taken into possession by the people (*Material*, 2009), just as Marx described the uprising of the Paris commune. Heise's most recent film, *Heimat is a Space in Time* [*Heimat ist ein Raum aus Zeit*, 2019], portrays this encounter, the 'administration of life," as a meeting of micro- and macro-history in a longue durée.

The work that Heise made in the GDR, though it could not be shown there, is unique for yet another reason. Literature and film from the 1950s and early 1960s imagined precarious lives as belonging to people who had not yet come around to East German socialism, who were mired in skepticism, or lost within another time altogether. They had to prove their worth by integrating into the collective. But the tide turned in the 1960s, and now the maladjusted protagonist became a singular "genius hero" who challenged the socialist collective to rethink its customs and labor norms, and recognize its own corrosions (from *Traces of Stones* to *The Quest for Christa T.*, to *The New Sorrows of Young W.* to *Kippenberg*, etc.). These challenges lapsed, in the 1980s, into defiant claims that GDR socialism could never be reformed (in Volker Braun and Wolfgang Hilbig, for example). But despite—or even because—of this pathos of radical denial or refusal, these works still remained wedded to the East German project, imagining a different future for it or lamenting its failure.

By contrast, Heise was not committed to the East German project, neither through praise nor radical critique. And yet he did not leave the country; instead, he "detached from within," images and words were "'put into storage' for the future." The future became simply "a time after." Those who watch his films must become archeologists. One could argue that this perspective is typical for the documentary films of the 1980s. As Claus Löser has noted, documentary films then were subject to greater freedom (they were not centrally monitored, and since they did not have large audiences, the state was not very interested in them). It became possible to make films such as Helke Misselwitz's *After Winter Comes Spring* [*Winter Adé*, 1988] or Dieter Schumann's *whisper & SHOUT* [*flüstern & SCHREIEN*, 1988]. All these films come with an un-ideological, sober view of "social reality" in East Germany. But no one brings his subject so close to his audience as Heise does, only to distance it again radically. He is the documentarian of a future already past, a (past) "reality of the possible." This is not a convention of the genre. The images and words that beset us always seem to come from elsewhere (indeed, they have often been repurposed, turned into material anew), and precisely because of this, they live on in a highly concrete timelessness.

*

M: I'm very happy to meet you. I rewatched a lot of your films in advance of our conversation, and I think that the topic of precarity, which this book focuses on, is quite fitting.

T: I really can't speak to that. It's not my topic, and I really don't care through which lens one views my films. It's an academic approach, which is quite different from an artistic one. I'm always suspicious when artists begin to analyze their work. It's a sign that something is wrong. When you make a film, you try to pin something down conceptually, express a concept and the film then stands for it, but it's not about the message or the audience. I don't believe in that—it's completely irrelevant. Of course, that's my own issue, and I know where it comes from.

M: Then I'll try to ask more specific questions and would like to begin with *The House* and *The People's Police*, your films from the 1980s. They depict everyday scenes in East German administration as state functionaries and citizens interact at the Berolina House on Alexanderplatz. This is the department for social services, and we meet a pensioner whose pension isn't sufficient, a single mother who can't get by with her money, and a woman whose housing and work situations are highly unstable. How did you come to this theme and this place?

T: It's very simple. In the same year, that is to say, in 1984, I was working on *Silent Village* [*Schweigendes Dorf*]. It's a story in which the narration and mediation are more important than the actual events. It's about a train full of concentration camp inmates from the Neuengamme A3 subcamp. The train traveled from a region around Morsleben, near Magdeburg, from the south to the north, up to the coast. This narrow strait was a remnant of the German Empire, surrounded by the Russians to the east and the Americans, English, and French to the west. The freight train was carrying six thousand women. They had been working in underground tunnels in Morsleben for the weapons industry. Forced labor. They were evacuated when the front moved in, and they were supposed to be brought to ships and then shipped away. And the story goes that the train stopped in a village called Sülstorf, ten kilometers outside Schwerin, and couldn't keep going because the signal was red. This happened because the station workers one village further knew what the train was carrying and didn't want anything to do with it, so they turned the signal to red. The train came to a stop, remained there for three days, and then continued. It arrived in Hamburg just as the British army marched into the city. Two years later, a mass grave was discovered in Sülstorf, with fifty-three dead. Right by the train station. Back then, in 1947, the media reported on this. The new authorities ordered the dead to be reburied and for a cenotaph to be set up. Willy Bredel wrote a story about it. There are several versions of that story, but he never managed to write down what actually happened, and the story that was finally published is very strange. There's an architecture student who has a girlfriend who lives in the village, and the student tells his professor this story, which he didn't experience personally but only heard about. And the story ends happily. Then, based on this story, there was an opera called *Silent Village* [*Schweigendes Dorf*], and as it turns out, Anna Seghers also wrote about it. She decided to set it as a fairy tale, because she thought it couldn't be reported on realistically but needed a new form, something very simple.

I felt *Silent Village* should become a documentary, but that wasn't possible. This wasn't the way in which the Nazi era was supposed to be remembered in the GDR. Also, subcamp A3 was used by the GDR as a depository for nuclear waste. I couldn't do it, and so I wrote it down, and made a documentary film in writing. Then Henschel, which is really a theater publisher, said to me, you know what, we'll call it a play and give it to the theater in Potsdam. Then actors put on something that was really meant to be a documentary film, and this was in 1984. And in that context, I realized that relatively few authentic administrative records from the Nazi era have been preserved. There are transcripts of interrogations, but they never include the situation; it's about the information but the situation disappears, and really you need both. Then you'd understand how it worked. That's why *The House* is effective: because you can see how the administration works. That's why the film is timeless.

M: You once said that you wanted to "make hidden stockpiles of words and images" …

T: Exactly. But you have to hide them well; they can't come to light. If you use iconic images, they will become mute, because their meaning changes.

M: Does making "hidden stockpiles" mean you are doing this for future generations, or for another time altogether?

T: Yes, exactly. At least, not for our time. It would make me happy if you went into the woods and found not only mushrooms but a box, and there was something exciting in that box. I leave behind boxes.

M: In the case of *The House*, was it filmed with the idea that all of this— East Germany, socialism—would be over one day?

T: What does "being over" mean? Either socialism would change, or it would cease to exist, but when, where, and how wasn't clear. It could have kept going for another hundred hears. *The House* and *Volkspolizei* are two films which had a constrained concept, a frame in which we had to move. That means we had to deposit material, practice a kind of preventative archeology. We left behind artifacts. That's why the year is part of the title: *The House 1984* and *The People's Police 1985*. The titles are two short messages. *The House* and *1984* will bring up something for everyone who flips through index cards looking for "administration," and then you watch it. You can't *not* think of Orwell. It's the same thing for *The People's Police* and *1985*. Police, a clear time frame. That was the transition to Gorbachev. *The House* practically begins with a surveillance camera. It was a scandal back then, the surveillance cameras on Alexanderplatz.

M: The protagonists of the film, those who visit the department of social services, don't seem to acknowledge the filmmakers' presence at all. How did you manage that?

T: There was no managing anything. It's quite funny. There was always a feeling of solidarity between the people in front of and behind the camera in the GDR—at least in documentary film. We trusted each other. We trusted TV less. That was something different. Of course, I had no idea what was going on. I decided that on Monday, we'd go to that office, on Tuesday to the next, and so on. We did this from eight in the morning until whenever. Then we had a sampling without searching for protagonists or cases. The wedding, for instance, was the first wedding on September 1, 1984, at the city hall in Berlin-Mitte. Of course, we got lucky, because everything was so sparse and rigid, but precisely because of it, the images became charged with meaning and we can interpret them.

M: There are some very clear interventions on your part, such as the intertitles.

T: Yes, I had a thing for intertitles back then. I wanted to do critical things with them, like [Alexander] Kluge. Sometimes it worked, and it was fun. It was a challenge to summarize an entire scene in a sentence. Sometimes three sentences summarize three hours of conversation, and that's what's left.

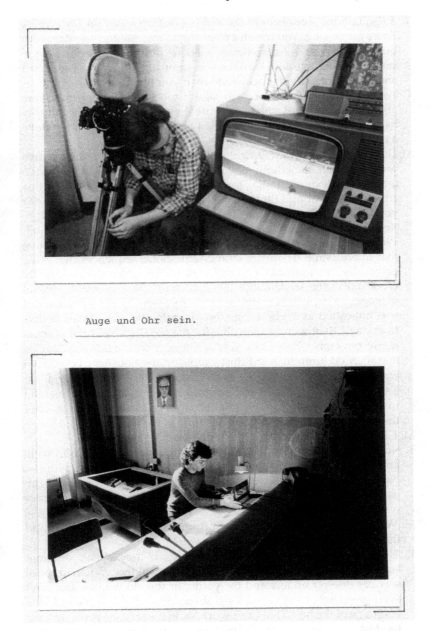

Auge und Ohr sein.

Figure 10.1 Peter Badel and Thomas Heise on the set of *Volkspolizei 1985 (People's Police 1985)*. © Thomas Heise. All rights reserved.

M: I also find the story behind the making of *The House* and *The People's Police* interesting. You weren't planning to make a documentary film but instead you were commissioned to produce material for the state's film archive, and then the film came together in the process of shooting, indirectly or backhandedly if you like.

T: Yes. I had to be careful not to take it too far. The intertitles were already too much, of course, because they are commentaries, simply because they repeat what has already been said. But we didn't have a concept for the film.

M: But you did have what I might call a "double purpose." The pictures were made for something they weren't used for—instead you made a film. That's quite similar to *Material*, and I wonder whether this situation of creating a film "on the sly" produced an aesthetic imprint you later consciously pursued?

T: Not necessarily. I only ever do what is possible in a given moment. When I can make something like *The House*, I find a perspective that interests me. There are strange situations, sequences that often end badly. For example, you feel very happy when things actually work out in the scene about the aquarium: the responsible official manages to explain something to the mother. On the other hand, I was interested in the housing administration because it was Berlin-Mitte, and they were responsible for me too. I thought the woman might remember me—"Oh, you're the man who made the film"—and then I'd jump forward thirty spots on the housing queue. That was what I really wanted. It was the same for *The People's Police*. I had a score to settle with them. Then I told myself that if we were going to do something like this, we might as well go straight to the office of the guy I had unfinished business with.

M: Did the people at the station end up watching the film?

T: No, I only showed it to the captain. I had gotten to know him well, and liked him as a person. He only ever told stories about failures. Nothing worked out. For example, the one with the copper: the guy escaped to the west, and then he was gone. Before 1961, the border was just a line on Brunnenstrasse.

M: What do these situations, these encounters between the people and the state or administration reveal to you?

T: How they relate to each other. After all, they speak different languages. In *The House*, you can clearly see that the woman in social services doesn't understand the young or the old woman and can't even grasp what they're talking about. She only understands the language of the law. That can't work, even if everyone is trying their hardest. You can see that. It's the same situation in the department of interior affairs: the young woman wants to prove to the clerk that she has a job. She pretends as though she does, but the clerk isn't even interested—all she wants to do is check a box: "antisocial." You can see that. And you can see the same behavior in the young woman as she attempts to behave appropriately in the interview.

M: There's a moment in which the "antisocial" woman mentions that she wants to go live in the west. That seems like a thorny issue—how did you feel about it?

T: Yes, it was odd.

M: And the clerk ignores it. She only comments on her drinking.

T: Yes, that's right. But what could she have done? She had to let her go.

M: Can we talk about your 1980 film, *Why a Film about These People (Wozu denn über diese Leute einen Film)*? How did you find your protagonists, and why were they willing to participate in the project?

T: I was looking into a different matter in Prenzlauer Berg and was by the water tower, where a friend lived. I went to visit him. He told me that his motorcycle had been stolen, and that he knew who had done it. We went there, faster than the police. We got there and the mother was all worked up because she knew what had happened. Something was always up when someone showed up, and the boys were just sitting there, watching cartoons. They seemed very relaxed. I said immediately, let's follow this story. We'll make something of it.

M: It's remarkable how naturally they talk about themselves.

T: Yes, it was another time. They had no prejudices against the camera, no problems with having their picture taken. Or being taped on a tape recorder.

Figure 10.2 Norbert and Bernd Weber, from: *Wozu denn über diese Leute einen Film? [Why a Film about These People?*, 1980]. © Thomas Heise. All rights reserved.

M: How did the situation evolve, how did you come to make a film?

T: I simply asked them if they'd work with me on the day we met each other, and they said, "Yeah, sure." They were open about it. I found it interesting that committing delinquencies in their spare time came so naturally to them—it went without saying that I wouldn't have considered it natural, and that was an important experience for me, to accept it and say, that's just the way it is. I have to respect that. And that's the story the film tells, because it takes them seriously without moralizing. And then the film introduces the victim, the person whose property has been stolen, who says that he comes from similar social circumstances. He knows what those circumstances mean.

One scene I shot came about by chance, but I didn't include it in the film. One of the boys was sitting at a bar, drinking, and then the guy whose motorcycle he stole comes in with his helmet. Then they sit together and have a beer. I turned the camera off, because I thought, no one will believe it and they'll think I staged it.

M: Just like *First Name: Jonas*, your radio feature, this film was never shown. It must have been quite provocative to show that a so-called antisocial life was something natural, a possible way of life. After all, wasn't that rather unusual in East German art?

T: I didn't see it in the context of art, the topic simply interested me.

M: Why were *First Name: Jonas* and *Why a Film about These People?* rejected?

T: It was very odd. With the film, it happened in several steps. First, it was discussed in a pre-screening, and I was critiqued for my "cold eye." And then they said that the story was politically all wrong, and soon afterwards, it was censored. Better yet—it wasn't officially censored, but simply not released for rental. Nothing was censored. My film was still shown at the student film festival, but the screening broke off after barely ten minutes, and then the curtain was suddenly lowered. I went into the screening room, and they told me that something had broken. You get used to it. But it changes the way you think. Something similar happened with *First Name: Jonas*, and the works that followed. So that led to a film like *The House 1984*. When something like that has happened to you five times in a row, when you've been put through the mill with that nonsense, you do things differently.

I made a feature called *Resistance and Conformity – Strategies for Survival* [*Widerstand und Anpassung – Überlebensstrategien*] about the actor Erwin Geschonneck. It came about like this: Geschonneck was in the hospital, and I was out of work. I went to see him and saw that he was all alone. And so we came up with the idea of doing something on the theater in the Dachau concentration camp, where he had been kept prisoner from 1938–45. He was the oldest prisoner in his block. It was about the relationship between resistance and conformity. Nothing heroic about it. The result went all the way up to the central committee of the communist party, and they censored it flat out. Then it was published in the literary journal *Sinn und Form*, and then they wanted to get rid of *Sinn und Form*.

M: Why did they react like this?

T: Because among other things, the feature discussed the Soviet Union, the non-aggression pact, and the purges. Those were all part of his story. Geschonneck emigrated right at the beginning of the Nazi era, was in Czechoslovakia and then went to the USSR, where he worked in various itinerant theater troupes. They were all sent away, expelled from the USSR, in 1937/38 as part of the purges. And then, in Communist Czechoslovakia, he practically collided with the invading German Wehrmacht, and they packed him off to Dachau. In 1939, he learned about the non-aggression pact between Stalin and Hitler. The end. And he put on theater in the Dachau concentration camp, the knight play, "The Night of Blood on the Rock of Horrors" ["Die Blutnacht auf dem Schreckenstein"], for the prisoners and the SS, in front of the disinfection station. In 1945, he was taken on a prisoner convoy to Hamburg and put on the "Kap Arkona," which was bombed by the British in the harbor and sank. Most prisoners drowned. He was one of few prisoners to survive the bombing and the shipwreck, because he somehow managed to swim back to land.

He felt that some things should be said openly. The head of the radio drama department then ruled out "any further work" with me. I had to find new work.

M: Can we discuss *Material*? The aesthetic premise of *Material* is that the shots in the film have been taken out of completely different contexts and reused: they were either left over from other projects or made for a completely different purpose. What's the advantage of using ready-made images?

T: I've always done that. After all, in doing that, you represent an idea, and the image of that idea becomes the film. For me, that's an appropriate narrative form.

M: Another important aspect of *Material*, which becomes a theme, is the relationship to theater: the Fritz Marquardt staging of *Germania, Death in Berlin* [*Germania. Tod in Berlin*]. The topic of the play by Heiner Müller, as well as Müller's methods, are quite similar to your film. It's about large historical arcs, but history is portrayed as accumulation. Did Müller's play inspire the structure of your film?

T: Yes, of course. That's certainly the case, and that's where I learned this technique. For example, I recorded a curious conversation between Wolfgang Heise and Heiner Müller as part of *Heimat is a Space in*

Time and because I transcribed it, I knew it almost by heart and had it in my head. It was on my mind for a long time, and I ended up using it in my work. The question of whether it is still possible to just go ahead and tell stories, or just show things firsthand, is also at the heart of that conversation. *Material* then moves from the general to the individual. *Heimat* does too. And that's because you must talk about yourself to get people to listen.

M: *Material* contains so many surprising and disturbing shots, such as the prison scenes. Were they intended for another project as well?

T: During that time, I simply shot things, and I was on the street after November 4, 1989. A colleague of mine wanted to shoot a film on prisoners, and the head of the prison called him up and asked him if he could help. The prisoners were revolting and asking for someone from TV to come and speak to them. My colleague called me up and asked me, "Will you come?" I said, "Of course." I didn't know what I would do. Then I realized I could just set up a camera, and everyone could say, quite democratically, what they had to say. That was it. Everyone thought we were from "Public TV." It was a VHS camera, and that calmed down the situation and made them talk.

The prisoners also issued a declaration, and I made sure that it was broadcast on the radio.

The scenes in the prison are like *The House*. It's stunning what comes out of it, and the material improves with time: ten, twenty years, or even longer. The fact that the prisoners and the guards are talking about improvements to the penal system shows how much potential there was at the time. The reality of the possible. One can see it. It has nothing to do with what we now call "stories of the *Wende*." Those are only about the Wall, only about escape. The only thing you could do with your life, supposedly, was to escape. That's what's left of the GDR, and it's unbelievable how quickly that idea spread. That's where *Material* intervenes with its own reality.

M: That's what's so fantastic about this film, that it can produce this sense of possibility, for example in the party discussions about involvement with the secret police, or in the renters' meeting. The film manages to make visible a potential that completely disappeared in the years following the fall of the Wall. How did you put the film together? After all, the shots aren't just thrown together, otherwise they wouldn't achieve that effect.

T: It was clear that it had to start with the play [Fritz Marquardt's staging of *Germania, Death in Berlin*]. But I wanted to precede it with Peter [Badel]'s images of the evacuation of Mainzer Strasse. It was important to have a contrast to the calm and focus of Fritz and the play, the stage and the audience, above and below. It all happened at the same time. And the battle at the beginning is a street fight, a war between people on the roof and the national police, who are below. And it's about how they talk to each other. Citizens and the state. It's the same question as with *The House*. The whole film might just be about the fact that sometimes, something shifts, something is created, and people do something like communicate with one another before lapsing back into silence. The music is by Charles Ives, and it describes a shipwreck, and the reactions of the people watching the ship sink. Montage is fun, after all, and in principle *Material* is a score ...

M: Yes, it has very musical qualities.

T: Or perhaps it's closer to Hesse's *Glass Bead Game*. It's tempting just to play, because you can discover so many things through play. There's no plan that tells you to do this or that.

M: My experience as a viewer, with *Material*, as well as with *The House* and *The People's Police*, was that I was at the mercy of the images or the events that the images relate. There's little context and the camera is slow. I don't know what exactly is happening and what exactly I'm seeing and I'm forced to create meaning, and empathetic or identificatory strategies don't work. The images challenge me to develop an almost ethnographic gaze.

T: This is anthropological research. It's the archeology of real life, and you need a cold gaze to do this. The more distance I have, the more clearly I can see.

Figure 10.3 "Gestern lernte ich Pjotr Velargowitsch kennen" [Yesterday, I met Pjotr Velargowitsch], from *Heimat ist ein Raum aus Zeit* [*Home is a Space in Time*, 2019]. © Thomas Heise. All rights reserved.

M: I was born in the GDR in 1966, and for me, these shots bring up many memories. How does an audience react when it can't make these associations? Are you afraid of losing that point of contact?

T: No. *The House* was just screened in Japan. There must be something that's working, you can't control that.

M: In contrast to *Material*, when I saw your wonderful film, *Heimat is a Space in Time*, I had the feeling that where *Material* really tries to open up history, history has already become inaccessible in *Heimat*. There's a melancholy to *Heimat*, which might have to do with the fact that it tells the story of generational change and aging. The film has a heaviness to it, and its approach to history seems quite different.

T: Yes, it's different, but that has to do with the material too. You have all these boxes with family things in front of you—and I had no idea. But there are lots of points at which the family story becomes very general.

M: The story spans one hundred years …

T: I could have kept going with my mother's story, but that would have required a different form of storytelling, and it always depends on the material I'm working with.

M: Yes, by treating it as material you already depersonalize it …

Figure 10.4 "… froh, dass die unheilvolle Stille vorbei ist" [… glad that the ominous silence is over], from *Heimat ist ein Raum aus Zeit* (*Home is a Space in Time*; 2019). © Thomas Heise. All rights reserved.

T: Yes, and I didn't make a single change. Nothing was written just for the film. Nothing was changed—I kept it as it was, even though that means some things remain unclear.

M: Does it change something when the material comes from your own family?

T: No, and I always wonder why it's talked about as my "own" family. Really, it's enough to say family, but the "own" is always there.

M: Did your relationship to the GDR change through your work on films such as *Material* or *Heimat*?

T: No, I don't think so. It was always an estranged relationship. At one point, I tried to escape to the west, but that didn't work out. And then I decided that I would turn the GDR into my research project. This became clear in my work, and even became a point of critique: I was criticized for being too descriptive. That leads to something like *The People's Police*. You stand there without any preconceived ideas and observe what they're doing.

M: This curious attitude, which turns the subject at hand into a foreign object, makes me think of a poem by Bertolt Brecht about the drama fragment *Jae Fleischhacker*. And I know that you staged this fragment at the Berliner Ensemble. In the poem, the speaker wants to tell a story about financial speculations in wheat, but then realizes that those who aren't born yet and will live in a liberated society will not be able to understand the poem, so the speaker then tries to tell this story for the not-yet born. The typical style of narration, which depends on tension and anticipation, breaks down and the object becomes foreign as it is described for a foreign perspective. It creates a mound of material, words and images that are in need of new meaning. I have the impression that many of your films, such as *The House*, are addressed to those who are not yet born, and that the story is told from the perspective of posterity.

T: But that doesn't have anything to do with the GDR as such. Yes, with *The House*, for example, it was conceived so it could be told to the two following generations. My career was at a standstill, I'd just been thrown out of film school and managed to get a job in film documentation because they worked with freelancers and you didn't have to show your diploma. Peter [Badel] passed the job on to me. Then I suggested that we should do something on "administration" after I learned what film documentation was actually for. We had to collect material that might be used in the future to make documentaries. So that was the situation, and the rest was simply a matter of organization, setting times, and showing up. And then we had the material.

M: This attitude or gesture of looking at things as if they've already happened …

T: Yes, it's odd, so I'd best not think about it.

M: ... it's present in many of your films, and *Jammed – Let's Get Moving* (*Stau. Jetzt geht's los*) has a similar attitude, doesn't it? It also has this ethnographic gaze.

T: I wanted to get to know the Nazis, learn about what kind of people they were. That gave me a reason to make it. I had to make money, and I was interested in the topic. The funding was good and I got to do research for three months. That's not possible anymore.

M: And there are shots from the premiere of this film, *Jammed*, which appear in *Material*?

T: It's not the premiere, but an avant-premiere that I held in Halle, in 1992 on the day of German Unification.

M: Those shots are unbelievable. The "well-behaved" audience, glass of wine in hand, retreats as the movie theater is attacked, and watches from their corner while the film continues to play. I thought I had misunderstood or missed something ...

T: The attack ended just as the film reached the closing titles. It was an attack orchestrated by a group of leftists who had thought the event was fascist and had come to the movies too late.

  Material then draws a link back to the beginning, to the street fight that continues to be waged in houses, in movie theaters.

M: I've read interviews with you and know many of your films, and my impression was that it's always, one way or another, about using the distanced gaze to redeem something: a particular kind of experience, a way of being in a world that is in danger of being lost—in other words, to do justice to something fragile and precarious.

T: I suppose so. There's something to that. One critic wrote a review titled, "When in doubt, protect the weak." That means roughly the same thing. It's not about saving something, but about taking seriously what usually isn't.

  In other words, let's see what Nazis are actually like. I know they're shit; I don't need to hear that again. That's not necessarily political.

M: But isn't it like that with *Material* too? You give voice to or redeem the fragile sense of possibility that we all had in 1989?

T: And it shows that people had clearly repressed something. It became evident at the Berlinale. But the film didn't have a lasting effect, and they're still selling those postcards where everyone is standing on the Wall, looking towards west Berlin. Not a single person is looking towards the east, though they climbed up from the west, since the east of the Brandenburg Gate was still off limits. No one could climb up from there. So it doesn't add up. But there's nothing we can do, that's the way it will stay. These fairy tales. That's also why I didn't shoot during the fall of the Wall, because it made no sense. What business did I have there?

M: Like *Jammed*, you were interested in what did not fit into sanctioned narratives.

T: Yes, that's right. And the reason I wanted to get to know the Nazis in the first place were the reports on the Nazi riots and attacks on refugee homes in Hoyerswerda. I thought, *we have to do something that takes these people seriously.* I didn't necessarily want to do it myself, but I was asked by a producer. They still had some subsidies for the former east left over, and someone from the ministry of labor wanted a film. So we had funding. The money had to be spent quickly so they could get new funding for the coming year. I had to make a decision, otherwise I probably wouldn't have done it.

I can tell you the story of how I met these people.

M: Yes please!

T: I'd gotten the address of a meeting-spot from the youth welfare office. I only wanted the meeting-spot, nothing else. I went there and parked my car a bit further away, it was around Christmastime and snowing, there was slush everywhere, and I walked to the "Roxy." The street by the apartment buildings was rather dark, and I walked past a woman. Then the woman called out to me, and asked me whether I was going to the "Roxy" too. I stopped, and said yes. She said, "My son's in there, and I don't dare go in. I need to talk to him."—"Sure, what's his name?" And then I had a good reason to go in. Burn your bridges so you can't go back, only forward. I had to go in. I wanted to learn something, and I could only do that if I went in, you can't just choose.

M: It seems to me that *Jammed* attempts to give an overarching explanation. The images at the beginning, the camera panning over the new apartment blocks, the monotonous routines, the probing look at everyday life—it suggests to me that it's about the lack of possibilities, the impossibility of imagining a different situation for oneself, which, after all, is caused by political and economic circumstances, and which hardens these lives ... Is my impression wrong, or does this film have a stronger leading narrative than the other films?

T: There's a sequel, the *Newtown* (*Neustadt*) film, in which that aspect is even more pronounced. Everyone is exhausted. It's a film about exhausted people. In the first film, they still had a bit of energy. You couldn't organize them through the NPD [National Democratic Party], or something like that. They did their own thing. That was one way in which the east differed from the west. And Konrad, the skinhead, who's sitting on the Kyffhäuser mountain with his girlfriend—who by the way is now the leader of the Volkssolidarität in Halle—that Konrad, in the sequel, has become the regional chairman of a right splinter party called "Volks-Block."

M: Would it be incorrect to say that your films are very concerned with this sense of possibility, or what happens to people when they lose their sense of possibility? In *Material*, you open it up; in *Jammed*, you show the consequences of people lacking such a sense; *Heimat* is about the disappearance of possibilities within the historical process; in *The House* and *The People's Police*, in this timeless, ritualized encounter between citizen and state, this sense cannot even develop.

T: I didn't try to put it together like that; I've never thought about it. I can't think about it like that, I can't see it from the outside. It's what happens in the conversation between Müller and Heise—they talk past each other, but there are still brief moments of contact, maybe one and a half words, and then it's over again, and yet something still happens.

M: A sort of spontaneous montage. You have different elements or levels that come together, and then something new is created.

T: Yes—it's very strange.

M: Thank you very much for the conversation.

Trans. Sophie Duvernoy

Works Cited

Works by Thomas Heise:

Wozu denn über diese Leute einen Film, 1980; *Vorname Jonas*, 1983 (Radio Feature); *Das Haus 1984*, 1984; *Volkspolizei 1985*, 1985; *Schweigendes Dorf*, 1985; *Widerstand und Anpassung – Überlebensstrategie*, 1989 (Radio Feature); *Stau, Jetzt geht's los*, 1992; *Jae Fleischhacker* (Brecht fragment), first performance at Berliner Ensemble, text version and direction, 1998; *Neustadt (Stau – Der Stand der Dinge)*, 2000; *Kinder wie die Zeit vergeht*, 2007; *Vaterland*, 2002; *Material*, 2009; "Archäologie hat mit Graben zu tun," *Thomas Heise Material*, Berlin: Edition filmmuseum 56, 2011. *Heimat ist ein Raum aus Zeit*, 2019.

Other Works

Beyer, Frank, dir. *Die Spur der Steine*. DEFA, 1966.
Brecht, Bertolt. "Diese babylonische Verwirrung der Sprache" (1927). In *Werke: Große kommentierte Berliner und Frankfurter Ausgabe*, 30 volumes. Edited by Werner Hecht, Jan Knopf, Werner Mittenzwei, Klaus-Detlef Müller. Berlin, Weimar and Frankfurt: Aufbau/Suhrkamp, 1988–98, vol. 13.3, 256–8.
Bredel, Willi. *Das schweigende Dorf*. Rostock: Hinstorff, 1948.
Hesse, Hermann. *Das Glasperlenspiel*. Zurich: Fretz & Wasmuth, 1943.
Ives, Charles. *Orchestral Set No. 2 III. From Hanover Square North, at the End of a Tragic Day, the Voice of the People again Arose* (composed between 1915 and 1919).

Löser, Claus, "DEFA Dokumentarfilme zur Wende," in *Bundeszentrale für politische Bildung*, 2019. https://www.bpb.de/gesellschaft/bildung/filmbildung/299301/defa-dokumentarfilme-zur-wende.

Marquardt, Fritz. Production of Heiner Müller, *Germania, Tod in Berlin*. Berliner Ensemble, 1989.

Marx, Karl. "Der Bürgerkrieg in Frankreich" (1871). *In Marx-Engels-Werke*, 44 volumes. Berlin: Dietz, 1956–2018, vol. 17, 313–365.

Misselwitz, Helke. *Winter Adé*. DEFA, 1988.

Müller, Heiner. *Germania, Tod in Berlin*. Berlin: Rotbuch, 1977.

Noll, Dieter. *Kippenberg*. Berlin: Rotbuch, 1979.

Plenzdorf, Ulrich. *Die neuen Leiden des jungen W.* Berlin: Sinn und Form, 1972.

Schumann, Dieter, dir. *flüstern & SCHREIEN*. DEFA, 1988.

Stedler, Wiebke. "Asozialen-paragraph in der DDR, ein Stigma mit Folgen." *MDR Geschichte*, 2021. https://www.mdr.de/geschichte/ddr/politik-gesellschaft/asozialenparagraph-arbeitslos-opposition-arbeitslager-zwangsadoption-100.html.

Sinn und Form, journal for literature and culture, founded in 1949.

Wolf, Christa. *Nachdenken über Christa T.* Halle (Saale): Mitteldeutscher Verlag, 1968.

Eleven   Biopolitics and Superstition
in Barbara Albert's
Böse Zellen

Lena Trüper

Lying in the bed of an Austrian hospital after a medical examination, a little girl named Yvonne asks her aunt Gerlinde: "What are they testing me for all the time? It hurts so much." Covered by the white sterile sheets of the hospital bed, two latex-gloved hands grasp her head from behind. A mouth plug turns her mouth into an infinite dark hole, leaving Yvonne helplessly exposed to the doctors' probing. The sounds of her choking and swallowing are accompanied by the monotonous rattles and wheezes of a medical instrument. A large tube is pushed down her pharynx. "They're just checking for evil cells inside you," her aunt explains to her. "They did the same thing for me. They're doing it to everyone. But we don't have any, they just wish we did."[1]

Yvonne's medical examination in Barbara Albert's *Böse Zellen* (2003) leaves us feeling uneasy; not only have we witnessed the invasive examination of a child, but we, too, are not told what Yvonne is being tested for [Figure 11.1]. Like Gerlinde, we are unable to answer Yvonne's question. The medical staff stays out of the picture and the camera frames them so that their faces remain hidden; we can only see their hands using medical equipment.[2] *They* do not give explanations.

---

1   In the German original (with the local Austrian dialect), these lines read as follows: Yvonne: "Was untersuchen die die ganze Zeit in mir, das tut so weh." Gerlinde: "Nur ob du nicht vielleicht böse Zellen in dir hast. Des ham's bei mir a gmacht. Des machen's mit jedem. Aber wir ham keine, auch wenn se's noch so gern hätt'n."
2   Critics have noted that observation and surveillance are key themes in the film; see for example Imke Meyer, "Metonymic Visions: Globalization, Consumer Culture, and Mediated Affect in Barbara Albert's *Böse Zellen*," in *New Austrian Film*, ed. Robert von Dassanowsky and Oliver C. Speck (New York and Oxford: Berghahn Books, 2011), 96. The camera often shows people from a rear view and framing sometimes hides people who are talking off screen. This becomes especially apparent in scenes of hospitalizations. While the medical staff processes the treatment, they are shown from behind with their heads cut off by the picture frame.

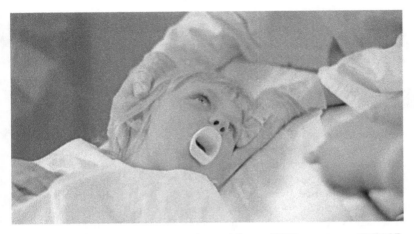

Figure 11.1 *Böse Zellen,* dir. Barbara Albert. DVD capture, 00:36:25. © Coop99, 2003. All rights reserved.

But who are *they*, exactly? Are they physicians? And what are they searching for? Gerlinde's intimations make us skeptical. She lacks the reassuring authority typical of adults that will soothe the little girl. Instead, her voice sounds weak, almost broken. Gesturing at wishes and "evil" things, she seems frightened. Why, indeed, do the medical staff remain nameless and faceless? And why would any medical professional "wish" to find "evil cells"? Talking about wishes sounds more like something a child would say. Scientists are expected to hypothesize, determine, and provide explanations. Wishes and evil belong to fantasies, dreams, and myths, not to science.

The characters in *Böse Zellen* accept their passive lives and helplessness before anonymous, unintelligible higher forces as normal. The film is composed of several plots: the first begins with Yvonne's mother, Manu, who survives an airplane crash but dies shortly thereafter in a late-night car accident involving a group of teenagers. Her death leaves the story without a protagonist and a gap in the lives of those who were close to her.[3] In a collage of storylines, the film portrays the emotional

---

3   The lingering pain caused by her death affect Andreas, her widower, and her best friend, Andrea; both quickly find themselves in an unhappy relationship. Her brother Lukas, a high school teacher, also remains hurt and flees into a parallel world of mathematical fractals to find a sense of universal order. Manu's sister Gerlinde, who choses Yvonne as her ally, grows desperate over the world's mendacity. The teenage driver of the car, Kai, carries the unbearable guilt of having killed Manu, while his girlfriend is left paralyzed in a hospital. Similarly

development of different characters affected by the accident. Their pain, however, is not shared: they rarely show compassion for one another. Instead, the characters are focused on pursuing their careers and personal success—a daunting task in the neoliberal labor market. As service workers in childcare, cashiers in grocery stores, and vacuum cleaner salesmen, their occupations are easily replaceable. Economic success is a matter of luck rather than the reward for hard work. The character's lives are defined by social alienation, while the city's shopping mall becomes the key location for social integration, mediated by wage labor and consumption. To make sense of social alienation, the characters engage with different epistemic systems, such as Protestantism, spiritualism, psychology, and popular science, none of which provides the guidance and security they seek. Instead, the characters are forced to cope with persistent insecurity, because they inhabit a state in which systems outside of their control prompt them to repeatedly search for new explanations for their world.

Böse Zellen's episodic narrative technique further destabilizes viewers by confronting them with heterogeneous montages showing images of Christian revelation, natural catastrophes, commercials, TV shows, fractals, and Easter bunnies. The film's montage technique creates the paranoid impression that these disparate phenomena fit together compellingly and fatefully; at the same time, causal links remain inexplicable. For example, when a butterfly flaps its wings, a metonymic montage suggests that it has caused the thunderstorm in which Manu's plane crashes. As the plane takes off, the gray sky fades to the white curtain of the church in Manu's hometown, then pans towards a choir singing Martin Luther's Christmas choral "From Heaven above to Earth I Come."[4]

Due to the central role of the shopping mall as a space of social encounter, *Böse Zellen* has often been described as a critique of commercialism and social alienation, and the nationalist undercurrents of these

---

desperate remains Belinda, a middle-aged woman who tries to commit suicide after an aborted love affair and loses a leg, while her Afro-Austrian daughter Sandra tries to disarm Lukas's racial bias by wanting to fall in love with him.

4   Martin Luther, "Vom Himmel hoch da komm ich her." In this choir scene, some of the future protagonists are introduced: the middle-aged mother Belinda, who desperately falls in love with the policeman Karl, as well as the choir leader becoming friends with Belinda. The Protestant chorale signals their status as a marginalized group, since Protestants are a minority in majority-Catholic Austria.

phenomena.[5] The film thematizes surveillance and observation, as the camera is often situated above or behind the characters, thus enhancing feelings of an elusive, omnipresent threat.[6] Furthermore, the film makes recurrent references to chaos theory, in particular through two popular references: fractals and the "butterfly effect."[7] Scholars have often interpreted these popular scientific references as merely decorative components, "mysteries," or part of a "quicksilver aesthetic" that highlights the complexity of postmodern societies or the general unpredictability

---

5   *Böse Zellen* is set in a superficial and faceless environment of commercial spaces and suburban housing which avoids specific references to Austria; this makes the story transferrable to other countries. According to Robert von Dassanowsky and Oliver Speck, this omission of national specificities or *Heimat* are characteristic for Austrian New Wave Cinema. See Robert von Dassanowsky and Oliver C. Speck (eds.), "Introduction," *New Austrian Film* (New York and Oxford: Berghahn Books, 2011), 3. On consumerism, see Meyer, "Metonymic Visions," 102; Mary Wauchope, "Place and Space of Contemporary Austria in Barbara Albert's Feature Films," *New Austrian Film*, ed. Robert von Dassanowsky and Oliver C. Speck (New York and Oxford: Berghahn Books, 2011), 114; Beret Norman, "Carousel of Consumerism: Austrian Filmmaker Barbara Albert's Critique of Contemporary Society in *Böse Zellen*," *Glossen* 32, no. 2 (2011); Elly Derek, "Free Radicals," *Film Reviews Locarno* (Performing Arts Periodicals Database, 2003), 24; J. Hoberman compares the feeling of loss, loneliness, and isolation to the films of Ingmar Bergman, see Hoberman "Voice Choices: Butterfly Affects Suicide Attempt, Bad Sex, Mall Construction," *The Village Voice* 49, no. 29 (2004): 54.

6   Meyer, "Metonymic Visions," 102. Claudia Lenssen mentions Albert's fascination with the "uncanny, the haunted, the beyond." See Claudia Lenssen, "Raffiniert collagierte Parallelgeschichten, Barbara Albert und ihre Filme," *Eine Eigene Geschichte: Frauen Film Österreich seit 1999*, ed. Isabella Reicher (Vienna: Sonderzahl, 2020), 34.

7   Questioning the possibility of precise measurement, linear narratives, and predictable futures, chaos theory became one of postmodernism's favorite ideas. On chaos theory and postmodernism, see Warren Smith and Matthew Higgins, "Postmodernism and Popularisation: The Cultural Life of Chaos Theory," *Culture and Organization* 9, no. 2 (2003): 93–104. The "butterfly effect" is a basic part of chaos theory describing that a small change in initial conditions of a phenomenon can cause an enormous change on the large scale of seemingly unrelated phenomena, like a butterfly flapping its wings causing a thunderstorm. It is referenced in *Böse Zellen* when Manu's plane crash is apparently caused by a butterfly in the Brazilian rainforest. On the butterfly effect see Peter Dizikes, "When the Butterfly Effect Took Flight," *MIT Technology Review*, February 22, 2011. Other popular representations of chaos theory are images of mathematical fractals. In *Böse Zellen* they connect associations of organic growth with economic and urban development. On chaos theory and urban development, see P.A. Longle and M. Batty, "The fractal simulation of urban structure," *Environment and Planning* 18 (1986): 1143–79, and R.D. Smith, "Social Structures and Chaos Theory," *Sociological Research Online* 3, no. 1 (1998), 82–102.

of life.[8] Overall, *Böse Zellen* has frequently been criticized for being overladen with details, not providing "conclusive answers," or even for being conceptually unsatisfying.[9]

However, it is precisely the film's visual juxtaposition of scientific, spiritual, and commercial images that constitutes its epistemic project. It thereby exceeds an open, fragmented narrative, and delivers a critique that interrogates the authority of accepted knowledge systems.[10] Reminiscent of paranoid, conspiratorial meaning-making, the imagery of *Böse Zellen* creates metaphoric connections that trip up those who attempt to rationally explain the events.[11] By inserting visual metaphors of science into a story about neoliberal working conditions, the film proposes that precarity is not defined solely by economic factors. Rather than focusing on economic inequality, the film emphasizes the characters' adherence to immaterial systems of knowledge production. At the same time, powerful social institutions, such as the medical apparatus, the nation state, or the economic order resemble invisible and unintelligible spiritual forces. Precarity is thus portrayed as a state of diffuse consciousness, in which personal knowledge becomes unreliable and insignificant compared to the omnipresent pull of overpowering

---

8   Sylviane Gold, "All the Lonely People," *New York Times*, July 18, 2004; Jeff T. Dick, "Free Radicals," *Library Journal* 130, no. 7 (2005): 133. Some critics have understood chaos theory as reflecting the "multilayered reality" of the film, but have not gone into further detail. See Wauchope, "Place and Space," 115. Others have noted a correlation between chaos theory and the fractured narrative reminiscent of "essential interconnectedness." Wendy Everett, "Fractal Films and the Architecture of Complexity," *Studies in European Cinema* 2, no. 3 (2005): 165; see also Kristin Jones, "FREE RADICALS," *Film Comment*, no. 4 (2004): 74.

9   Wauchope, "Place and Space," 116. See, for example, Elly Derek's review: "though fiercely intelligent, [*Böse Zellen*] is a movie in which a Big Picture doesn't satisfyingly emerge from the mass of minute details. There is also an underlying feeling that Albert herself has taken on too ambitious a theme at this early stage in her feature career." Elly Derek, "Free Radicals," 24.

10 In his book *The Third Lens: Metaphor and the Creation of Modern Biology*, Andrew Reynolds states that "cell theory provides both a powerful reductionist perspective and a unifying generalization about life and all its diverse forms" (Andrew S. Reynolds, *The Third Lens: Metaphor and the Creation of Modern Cell Biology* [Chicago, IL: University of Chicago Press, 2018], 2).

11 Reynolds describes metaphors as epistemic tools which "allow us to get a grasp or handle on some aspect of the world so that we can dissect it, identify the parts, put them back together, and in some cases redesign them so as to better suit our own specific ends," see Reynolds, *The Third Lens*, 7. Similarly, Donna Haraway has argued that metaphors are essential for testing the boundaries of accepted knowledge systems. See Donna Haraway, *Crystals, Fabrics, and Fields: Metaphors that Shape Embryos* (Berkeley, CA: North Atlantic Books, 1976), 2. In a similar way, the metaphor of "evil cells" in *Böse Zellen* can be understood as testing objective systems of knowledge production and circulation.

systems. By being subject to this insecurity, characters are constantly searching for explanations to regain control. *Böse Zellen* proposes that this mode of superstition, highlighted by the filmic montage, is inherent to systems of scientific knowledge production, which supports the very mechanisms of exploitation and exclusion at the core of capitalist societies.

Precarious Epistemologies and Superstitious Beliefs

The metaphor of the "evil cell" is a paradigmatic example for invisible power structures and superstitions that develop out of neoliberal social precarity. Because the film's titular "evil cells" are only mentioned once, in the hospital scene I touched upon at the beginning of this chapter, critics have barely commented on them.[12] However, it is safe to assume that they play a larger role in the film, given their importance for the title. On an individual level, the "evil cells" might reflect Yvonne's inner psychic deprivation in the wake of losing her mother.[13] Instead of working through Yvonne's psychic wounds, her father Andreas subjects her to physical medical testing to detect the "evil cells" that sicken her. However, interpreting "evil cells" as an expression of individual grief risks shortchanging a broader conceptual reading. It has been argued that "evil cells" represent a general "fear of foreignness," both on an individual and on a societal level.[14] A closer look at the role of illness and hospitalization in the film reveals, however, that this "general foreignness" is decisively racialized and gendered. Yvonne is not the only character in the film who receives medical treatment: throughout the film, *all* female characters suffer either physical or mental afflictions, while male characters enjoy physical integrity.

---

12 The English title does not reference them at all, but instead mentions "free radicals" and moves the meaning further away from the organism. In biology, free radicals are understood as unstable atoms with a dual function, which can damage cells causing illness and processes of aging but can also be helpful to the body when produced by the normal life functions of cells. See Pham Huy, Lien Ai, Hua He, and Chuong Pham-Huy, "Free Radicals, Antioxidants in Disease and Health," *International Journal of Biomedical Science* 4, no. 2 (2008): 89–96.

13 See Meyer, "Metonymic Visions," 103.

14 See Meyer, "Metonymic Visions," 102: "The film repeatedly examines a fear of foreignness – both figuratively via the suspected 'evil cells' in the human body, and literally via the presence of 'others' in a formerly homogenous society." On National Socialism in Austrian cultural memory, see Jaqueline Vansant, "Challenging Austria's Victim Status: National Socialism and Austrian Personal Narratives," *The German Quarterly* 67, no. 1 (1994): 38–57.

Furthermore, the types of illnesses the female characters suffer are contingent on their apparent national affiliation: white women identified as Austrian lose physical integrity, while women marked as "other" struggle with mental health issues. Thus, illnesses are a central topic of *Böse Zellen*, and crystallize in the metaphor of "evil cells." This metaphor draws connections between bodily affliction, national affiliation, and so-called racial properties.[15] Such unmediated connections suggest that the health of each individual directly translates into the health of society or the state, that national affiliation is hereditary, and that non-white racial characteristics, as well as diseases, can be considered "biological errors."

If these ideological assumptions expressed in the film's metaphor of the "evil cell" are left unexplained, they might be accepted as *literal* or naturally given.[16] It is thus worth highlighting how these assumptions date back to hygienic paradigms developed within bacteriology in nineteenth-century European science. At the time, Western European public health systems started a "war" against germs by identifying certain groups of people as the "infectious other" that should be suppressed and excluded to secure national unity and colonial possessions. A biopolitical reading of *Böse Zellen* allows us to draw historical and functional links between the hygienic dispositive of the nineteenth century and the neoliberal economic systems of the twenty-first century.[17] It suggests that the discursive logic of nineteenth-century nationalism, partially constituted by identifying the "infectious other" or "evil cell" as a danger to the national community, has reemerged in neoliberal societies. In the contemporary world, the entire scientific and political apparatus has been recast as an invisible "poison" infecting the body of the people—for example, in the form of a vaccine. Given contemporary anti-vaccination movements across the US and Europe, it is imperative to better understand these metaphoric slippages within discourses on "national health" that relate medical treatment and economic precarity.

---

15 "Evil cells" thus might "literally" mark the "presence of 'others' in a formerly homogenous society," as Meyer has argued in "Metonymic Visions," 102.

16 Reynolds and Haraway have described metaphor as community based. In such a community, the knowledge gained by the connections that metaphors draw might be accepted as "literal" fact. See Reynolds, *The Third Lens*, 178. By installing "evil cells" as metaphor in the film, *Böse Zellen* presupposes and at the same time questions its ideological implications as a "community possession" of the audience. On metaphor as community possession see Haraway, *Crystals, Fabrics, Fields*, 3.

17 On the hygienic dispositive, see Sarah Jansen, *Schädlinge: Geschichte eines wissenschaftlichen Konstrukts 1840–1920* (Frankfurt: Campus Verlag, 2003), 13.

"Evil Cells" in Nineteenth-Century Science

While analogies between body and state can be traced back to antiquity, questions about the division of singular entities and their collaboration in larger corporations were revived when cells and their membranes appeared under the microscopes of European scientists in the mid-nineteenth century. "The history of the concept of the cell is inseparable from the history of the individual," the French philosopher Georges Canguilhem wrote in his 1965 book *Knowledge of Life*.[18] This is especially true for European countries, in which industrialization accompanied by the formation of nation-states and individual citizenship came about at the same time as scientific cell theories. Cells became a metaphor for healthy and productive workers who contributed to the wealth of the nation as a larger whole by taking their place within the social division of labor.[19]

One of the first scientists to draw connections between multicellular organisms and the German nation state was the liberal microbiologist Rudolf Virchow. While conducting research on cellular pathology, Virchow imagined a liberal "cell state," in which individuals—like cells in a multicellular organism—divided labor and were endowed with individual rights to act responsibly in order to contribute to the health and wealth of the community.[20] However, as a social reformer of the *Deutsche Fortschrittspartei* (German Progress Party), he did not attribute the cause of diseases to specific cells like bacteria—a view which his colleague, the microbiologist Robert Koch, supported by the end of the nineteenth century. Instead, Virchow argued that hunger crises and poor living conditions of proletarians were causing the spread of diseases like typhus.[21] Such socialist attitudes were unpopular with the new conservative government of the German Empire that rose to power after the Franco-Prussian War in 1871.

---

18 Georges Canguilhem, *The Knowledge of Life*, ed. Paola Marrati and Todd Meyers, trans. Stefanos Geroulanos and Daniela Ginsburg (New York: Fordham University Press 2008), 42.
19 Andrew Reynolds has argued that the metaphor "cells are (social) organisms" is still one of the most common in modern biology, see Reynolds, *The Third Lens*, 4.
20 Laura Otis, *Metaphors of Invasion in Nineteenth-Century Literature, Science and Politics* (Baltimore, MD and London: The Johns Hopkins University Press, 1999): 18, and Reynolds, *The Third Lens*, 124; Paul Weinding, *Health, Race and German Politics Between National Unification and Nazism, 1870–1945* (Cambridge: Cambridge University Press, 1989), 38.
21 Rudolf Virchow, *Über den Hungertyphus und einige verwandte Krankheitsformen: Vortrag gehalten am 9. Februar 1868, zum Besten der Typhuskranken in Ostpreussen* (Berlin: Verlag von August Hirschwald, 1968): 23–4.

To counter socialist claims that diseases were caused by social miseries and poor working conditions, the conservatives funded microbiological research to show that diseases were caused by bacteria and could be transferred from one person to another. This scientific hypothesis delivered simple explanations for social miseries which could be communicated publicly and addressed by hygienic measures instead of social reform.[22] By supporting microbiology and introducing a sophisticated public health system, the German Empire thus aimed to reduce social tensions and further national unity. This led to a professionalization of medicine under governmental supervision. On an institutional level, new hospitals and health care facilities were built to secure public health. In the private realm, new hygiene measures began to define everyday life. State-driven programs for public education on health and hygiene were introduced to reduce the spread of diseases. Furthermore, the press frequently circulated news about the latest medical discoveries and shaped popular knowledge about biology. By bringing medical care under state control, the German Empire also pushed back against alternative healing methods like hydrotherapy and so-called quackery [Kurpfuscherei], which provoked resistance especially in highly industrialized Saxony and the small towns of Württemberg, where these methods had a long tradition (and which today are epicenters of anti-vaccination resentment and activism).[23] While the working class profited from new possibilities of medical care, the increasing number of hospitals and state-funded research facilities and universities provided new opportunities for work and upward mobility for the middle class to meet the growing need for well-trained medical professionals.[24]

But new hygiene measures were not only meant to support inner political peace. They also became central strategies of occupation in the late colonial expansion of the German Empire towards territories in East, South, and West Africa (now Cameroon, Togo, Namibia, and Tanzania), Brazil, New Guinea, and China, beginning in 1884.[25] In this context, bacteriology took on an increasingly militaristic vocabulary. Robert Koch, for example, who became the leading bacteriologist in the

---

22 Weinding, *Health, Race, and German Politics*, 4.
23 Weinding, *Health, Race, and German Politics*, 21. On governmental bans of lay therapists and anti-vaccination protests around 1900 in Stuttgart, Karlsruhe, Munich, Dresden, and Berlin see Weinding, 24.
24 Weinding, *Health, Race, and German Politics*, 31.
25 Jansen, *Schädlinge*, 275.

colonial expansion of the German Empire, referred to his research on germs as a *Vernichtungskrieg* (war of extermination).[26] Colonial bacteriology, or so-called *Tropenmedizin*, had two goals: the elimination of diseases in the belief that it would make the colonies easier on the colonizer's bodies, while simultaneously immunizing or curing the bodies of native workers in order to make them exploitable for colonialism.[27] Although European colonizers were the ones who carried germs back and forth between countries, in the imperialist mindset it was the colonized people who were identified as "germs" themselves, intruding on the body of the homeland. In a preposterous inversion, the invaded were turned into the invaders.[28]

In this nationalist framework, cells were imagined as metaphors for healthy productive workers who would support the likewise "healthy" nation state. However, this metaphorization also enabled the denigration of individuals as unproductive "others" endangering the nation state and its productivity. Marked as "germs" or "evil cells," individuals became subject to exclusion or—as later in National Socialism—extermination. By the end of the nineteenth century, the hygienic methodology employed in the colonies was expanded to include Eastern European populations. Jewish people migrating from Russia and passing through the German Empire between 1880 and 1914 were accused of transmitting cholera and similar illnesses. Furthermore, during the invasion of German soldiers in Poland during the First World War, the invaders' mission to "clean the East" was described as a "giant laboratory of delousing."[29] The metaphorical meanings of "germs"

---

26 Robert Koch, "Ergebnisse der vom Deutschen Reich gesandten Malariaexpedition," *Verhandlungen der Deutschen Kolonialgesellschaft*, Division Berlin-Charlottenburg (Berlin: Reimer, 1902), 442. As Laura Otis has shown, in his experiments in *Stephansort* in New Guinea involving native people, Robert Koch developed a system of centralized disease control to eradicate germs following the principles of *Identifikation, Ausrottung, Vernichtung* (identification, elimination, extermination). See Otis, *Metaphors of Invasion*, 34–5. On the use of similar vocabulary in newspaper articles from Dar es Salaam, Tanzania, see also Sílvio Marcus Correa de Asouza, "'Combating' Tropical Diseases in the German Colonial Press," *História, Ciencias Saude Manguinhos* 20, no. 1 (2013): 77.

27 Correa de Asouza, "Combating Tropical Diseases," 91.

28 Otis, *Metaphors of Invasion*, 5. On healthcare systems as authoritarian tools of control in colonialism see also Frantz Fanon, "Medicine and Colonialism," *A Dying Colonialism* (New York: Grove Press, 1965): 125–6. See also Jansen, *Schädlinge*, 257.

29 Monika Urban, *Von Ratten, Schmeißfliegen und Heuschrecken: Judenfeindliche Tiersymbolisierungen und die postfaschistischen Grenzen des Sagbaren* (Konstanz and Munich: UVK Verlagsgesellschaft, 2014), 114.

and "vermin" were thereby cross pollinated. Both derived their metaphorical potential as "lower" animals by living *under* the earth or *under* the human skin and therefore presenting an invisible threat.[30]

(In)visibilities of Medical Power in *Böse Zellen*

Böse Zellen revives the nineteenth-century notion of the invisible "evil cell" imagined as a social menace. Rather than dealing with infectious germs endangering the vision of a healthy nation state, the film transfers the metaphor into a general reflection on how different bodily conditions play out in a neoliberal society of service workers, in which the division between "productive" and "unproductive" labor has become blurred. The ubiquitous and unquestionable biopolitical power structures are represented as off-screen medical authorities in *Böse Zellen* who refuse to give explanations, while racialized and female-gendered bodies are excluded from the economic realm.

In several scenes in *Böse Zellen*, white female characters are hospitalized. Their paralyzed bodies are hooked up to life-sustaining machines. Medical authorities remain noticeably absent: their bodies and faces are awkwardly cut off in the frame, while only hands operating medical instruments remain fully visible. For example, when Gabi is left paralyzed after the car crash that killed Manu, her full body is seen connected to medical instruments, while only the hands of medical staff appear in the picture, and commands are given from off screen [Figure 11.2]. Similarly, during Yvonne's testing, only hands operating the medical machines are shown [Figure 11.3]. The same goes for Belinda after her botched suicide attempt. Positioned in a row with other injured bodies, Belinda is connected to life-sustaining machines, while her daughter Sandra sits at her bed. The nurses, however, stay in the background. None of them interact with Sandra or give explanations [Figure 11.4].

---

30   Urban, *Von Ratten, Schmeißfliegen und Heuschrecken*, 69. As Monika Urban mentions, the metaphorical adaptation of "germs" and "vermin" for marginalized groups was facilitated by the increasing acceptance of Darwinism throughout the nineteenth century, which broke with the essential split between humans and animals established by the Enlightenment and suggested a spectrum of human races in which some could be visualized as "closer" to the animal than others, or even excluded as "non-humans." Tiago Saraiva has extended this processual view of fascism, reading it as a modernism forming alongside the development of biopolitical breeding structures of plants and animals, see Tiago Saraiva, *Fascist Pigs: Technoscientific Organisms and the History of Fascism* (Cambridge, MA: MIT Press, 2018), 5.

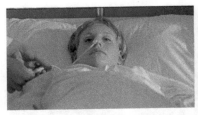

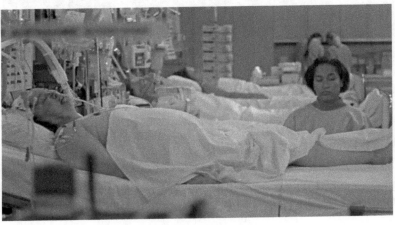

Figure 11.2 *Böse Zellen,* DVD capture, 00:52:13. © Coop99, 2003. All rights reserved.

Figure 11.3 *Böse Zellen,* DVD capture, 00:36:22. © Coop99, 2003. All rights reserved.

Figure 11.4 *Böse Zellen,* DVD capture 00:52:13. © Coop99, 2003. All rights reserved.

It is not unusual in the filmic medium to express both deindividualization and hidden lust or crime through hands that appear detached from the rest of the body.[31] *Böse Zellen* further highlights this de-personalized vision by supplementing the examining hands with tubes and wires connected to the female body. The medical apparatus performs a double function, sustaining life but rendering it dependent

---

31 As the filmmaker Harun Farocki once stated: "The hand that commits a crime seems to engender desire" [Figure 11.5]. On Farocki's film *Ausdruck der Hände,* see also Volker Pantenburg, "Aus Händen lesen," *KulturPoetik* 3, no. 1 (2003), 56. Regarding *Böse Zellen,* one could also discuss the role of legs, as two characters are depicted as one-legged. Compared to the depersonalizing, yet active operationality of hands, the loss of legs could be interpreted as a loss of individuality or personal standpoint.

The hand that commits a crime seems to engender desire.

Figure 11.5 *Ausdruck der Hände*, dir. Harun Farocki, DVD capture, 00:03:37. © Harun Farocki GbR, 1997. All rights reserved.

on medical technology and labor. The invisibility of the medical staff suggests a parallel between this medical complex and the equally invisible economic forces. Together, they determine people's lives, forming an indeterminate, powerful, almost spiritual sphere which creates dependency while remaining cognitively inaccessible. When Gerlinde states that "they" will test everyone for "evil cells," she alludes to vague and intermingling technological, economic, and spiritual forces that can neither be controlled nor understood. Female bodies thus present the material surface on which invisible biopolitical power structures become apparent. As female characters are the primary agents driving the film's narration, their vulnerability can be interpreted as a filmic strategy to destabilize the naturalization of biopolitical power structures to which they are subjected.

Hospitalizations, Spiritualism, and Mass Media

By hiding the medical personnel, the film emphasizes that medical professionalization and social alienation have produced a power vacuum which enhances the characters' helplessness and dependence. In *Böse Zellen*, this vacuum is filled by the TV show *Verzeih mir* (*Forgive Me*), in which a moderator mimics the role of medical professionals. In this show, Gabi's boyfriend Kai, who lives in constant guilt for having caused the car accident that has left her paralyzed, asks her publicly for forgiveness. Formerly concealed by the walls of the hospital, Gabi experiences a medial resurrection when she is invited to the show. While the film never shows a physician examining her condition during her stay in the hospital, the TV moderator, dressed in a white coat, enacts this role in *Verzeih mir*, asking her a series of questions: [Figure 11.6, 11.7 and 11.8] Apparently, Gabi has been left in the dark about her medical condition. Television, by contrast, seems to offer an alternative path to self-knowledge through enactment and visualization.

Similar to television, occult powers make a visual "appearance" in the spiritualistic séances in which the highschooler Patrizia and her classmates conjure the spirits of the past [Figure 11.9]. The affinities between medicine, mass media and spiritual "mediums" are neither unusual nor coincidental. They rely on popular fads and practices that emerged in the eighteenth and nineteenth centuries, a period during which the healing powers of human spiritualistic trance mediums became filtered through modern conceptualizations of mass media.[32] In substituting for absent medical authorities, the TV moderator in *Böse*

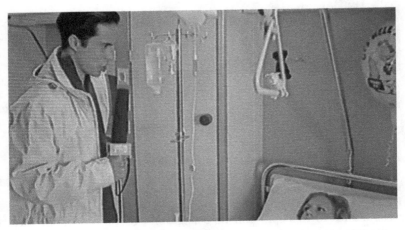

Figure 11.6 *Böse Zellen*, DVD capture 1:33:17. © Coop99, 2003. All rights reserved.

---

32 See Erhard Schüttpelz, "Trance Mediums and New Media: The Heritage of a European Term," *Trance Mediums and New Media: Spirit Possession in the Age of Technical Reproduction*, ed. Anja Dreschke and Martin Zillinger (New York: Fordham University Press, 2014), 62.

Figures 11.7 and 11.8 *Böse Zellen,* DVD capture, 1:32:57. © Coop99, 2003. All rights reserved.

Figure 11.9 *Böse Zellen,* DVD capture, 1:13:58. © Coop99, 2003. All rights reserved.

Zellen mimics the social and spiritual role of human "mediums" who were considered responsible for psychological healing before the institutionalization of medicine took hold in the late nineteenth century.[33] By fusing science, spiritualism, and media technologies, *Böse Zellen* thus alludes to this spiritualistic background of Western modernity, while at the same time questioning its own filmic qualities as a medium of knowledge production.

---

33 See Erhard Schüttpelz, "Trance Mediums and New Media," 74. Schüttpelz claims that mass media carry the same duality of passivity and activity of spiritualist mediums when understood both as passive mass-medial "hypnotization" and active empowering forces manipulating the masses.

Wage Labor as a "Cure" for Social Disobedience

With the metaphor of "evil cells," the film not only transposes a notion of social exclusion from the nineteenth to the twenty-first century, combining skepticism towards established scientific knowledge with the effect of economic precarity; it also implies that the hospitalization of its female characters is the price to be paid for momentary pleasure (going on vacation, spending a night dancing and drinking, or having a sexual affair) experienced outside of the compulsory economic cycle of exploitation. As punishment for social disobedience, "evil cells" or female disease in *Böse Zellen* resemble what Susan Sontag has identified as the moral condemnation of the patient in achievement-oriented societies.[34] Wage labor, by contrast, appears as a form of social integration. This becomes apparent in the representation of Manu's initial plane crash. While the film omits showing her hospitalization and convalescence, her filmic resurrection occurs in a supermarket as she stacks beverage containers and monotonously scans goods at the cash register [Figure 11.10]. With her green and yellow apron, she visually blends into her commodity environment.

Figure 11.10 *Böse Zellen*, DVD capture, 00:08:08. © Coop99, 2003. All rights reserved.

---

34 In *Illness as Metaphor*, Susan Sontag argues that moralistic evaluations of diseases changed from an initial Christian perception of illness as punishment to the definition of disease as a "weakness of will" during the Enlightenment and, by the middle of the twentieth century, coupled illness to specific characters, such as the manic depressive "cancer personality." See Susan Sontag, *Illness as Metaphor* (New York: Farrar, Straus and Giroux, 1978), 53.

Manu's visual assimilation into her workplace resembles her husband Andreas' workplace mimicry. Andreas's oversized blue jacket matches the color scheme of the self-serve vending area at the local cinema *Lollywood Selbstbedienung* (Lollywood Self-Service) where he works as an usher [Figure 11.11]. His blue jacket also blends in with the barrier tape directing foot traffic. As a good Austrian service worker, Andreas ensures proper social segregation.

Fateful illnesses affect the (white) female characters of *Böse Zellen* as punishment for their desire to escape the monotonous rhythms of wage labor. Similarly fateful, male characters' economic success is more a matter of chance than a consequence of hard work. In his daily ritual, Andreas neurotically scratches away at numbers hidden behind each of thirty-eight "cells" in a labyrinth on the glossy pages of the Shopping World advertising brochure, symbolizing the paths of fate [Figure 11.12]; after completing this weekly raffle "challenge," he wins a newly built single-family house in a fenced-in subdivision.

Manu's brother Lukas experiences success in a similar fashion. Employed as a mathematics high school teacher, he finally succeeds in representing seemingly "natural" and uncontrolled growth of fractals on his private computer screen. For him, these patterns visualize the ultimate mathematical rule by which the chaos of the universe can be ordered. When he explains the structures to his students, he is almost

Figure 11.11 *Böse Zellen*, DVD capture, 09:33. © Coop99, 2003. All rights reserved.

Figure 11.12 *Böse Zellen*, DVD capture, 00:10:06. © Coop99, 2003. All rights reserved.

consumed by his ideas [Figure 11.13].[35] As uncontrollably growing structures that infinitely expand their inner borders, the fractals resemble Andreas' "cells" in his weekly raffle card labyrinth.

While Andreas represents the obedient employee, Lukas embodies the bourgeois dream of becoming a scientist. Unlike Andreas, the precarious worker who believes in scratch-off lotteries to make his life meaningful, the middle-class intellectual Lukas engages in DIY science. However, through visual similarities *Böse Zellen* suggests that these knowledge systems are two sides of the same coin—they are just different ways of coping with precarity and biopolitical control under neoliberal working conditions, in which the absence of cognitively graspable power structures fosters people's mystic self-guidance. Blossoming in the hands of the white male DIY scientist, the fractals can also be read as a fantasy of infinite economic growth. In this, they resemble the maze-like pattern of the new subdivision of single-family houses adjacent to the shopping mall, the only site of material production seen in the film.

---

35 As Mary Ann Doane has argued, "The concepts of absorption and inhabitation, the fascination of being incorporated or enveloped by an image, are symptoms of an uncertainty and anxiety about the individual's relation to an increasingly incomprehensible social network [...]." Mary Ann Doane, "The Location of the Image: Cinematic Projection and Scale in Modernity," *The Art of Projection*, ed. Stan Douglas and Christopher Eamo (Stuttgart: Hatje Cantz, 2009), 164.

Figure 11.13 Böse Zellen, DVD capture, 00:14:59. © Coop99, 2003. All rights reserved.

Visual Othering and Mental Illness

Andreas' and Lukas' respective economic success illustrate that the nineteenth-century work ethic has been decoupled from nationalist ideals and dissolved into a fateful system of chance and superstitious beliefs. Oddly enough, however, fate seems to take national affiliation, racial properties, and gender into account. The reproductive bodies of white women who can be identified as Austrian are endangered by physical illnesses. In comparison, women marked as "other" due to their visual appearance suffer from mental health issues and are often depicted as excluded from the socially integrative compulsion of waged labor. The Afro-Austrian woman Sandra, for example, is depicted as a good worker who regularly visits a psychological self-help group. Unlike Gabi, who is excluded from the labor market due to the "higher power" of the car accident, Sandra loses her job in a drug-store when her dark skin color is rendered visible by an industrially standardized tone of make-up she is presenting to a white customer [Figures 11.14 and 11.15].

Like in the hospitalization scenes, Sandra's hand is detached from her body. It serves as an instrument or screen that renders the implicit racism of industrial color standards visible. While during the nineteenth century governmental institutions and popular beliefs conceptualized "evil cells" as reasons for exclusion from the nation state, Sandra's example shows that in neoliberal capitalism these structures are transferred to standardized medical-scientific power structures which are organized according to visibilities and invisibilities. Industrial standards

Figures 11.14 and 11.15 *Böse Zellen*, DVD capture, 00:27:23 and 00:27:46. © Coop99, 2003. All rights reserved.

converging with nationalist convictions categorize Sandra's cells as "evil" and mark her as subject to exclusion from the labor market.

A similar function of visual othering plays out in the character of Gerlinde, who is marked as a "strange Eastern species" by dressing up in a wide fur coat that looks odd against the glossy surface of the Austrian shopping mall [Figure 11.16].[36]

Like Sandra, she does not suffer physical affliction but is depicted as mentally unstable. As such, she is excluded from the official labor market and makes a living as a sex worker satisfying a one-legged man who provides her with a place to stay.[37] Gerlinde's deviant behavior is especially connected to hygiene. On the one hand, during a verbal tantrum in the shopping mall, Gerlinde herself makes use of hygienic vocabulary by insulting the other customers in the mall as "fat smelly humans" who don't care that other people die and are tortured while they are shopping. On the other hand, she is herself punished by her pimp after a one-night stand with womanizer Reni, after which her pimp commands her to wash off her sin and "take a bath." When she rises from the bathtub representing something in between baptismal font and a liquid grave, she exclaims: "Ich lebe noch!" [I am still alive]. Despite biopolitical control mechanisms and sexual violence, her body seems to resist. Together with Yvonne, she engages in a liberating dance between the puddles of an undeveloped lot on the outskirts of the city. While Gerlinde engages in a wild dance, Yvonne observes the fractal-like structures of a shimmering film of oil in a puddle—a looking glass into a future yet to come.

---

36 In reference to the eastward expansion of the EU in 2004, her "Eastern-ness" is even more highlighted when she is shown peacefully collecting flowers on a traffic island next to a huge Euro sign, surrounded by the rushing of cars.

37 According to Beret Norman "Albert provides a glimpse of hope for change through the unlikely figure of the homeless and unemployed Gerlinde and her distinctly anti-consumerist role in the film" (Beret Norman, "Carousel of Consumerism").

Figure 11.16 *Böse Zellen*, DVD capture, 00:59:06. © Coop99, 2003. All rights reserved.

Conclusion

Böse Zellen develops a critical vision of a globalized capitalist society and argues for the many ways in which superstitious beliefs and alternative knowledge systems conjoin with the forces of the market economy to replace the control mechanisms of state power. Productive wage labor is transformed into seemingly futile service work and is therefore uncoupled from the ideal of material productivity, while institutional guidance and scientific authority are mostly absent. The characters are unable to understand the power structures they are subjected to and lapse into superstitious ritual practices. However, as Yvonne's dubious medical testing illustrates, the ideological power of a nationalistic hygienic dispositive still lingers in the background. The hygienic ideal of the healthy, white, male, working-class hero persists and leads to social exclusion.

Transferring the nineteenth-century metaphor of the "evil cell" into a neoliberal society, the film presents a specifically gendered version of bodily affliction that is closely tied to the economic exploitability of the body, national affiliation, and racialized properties. The bodily vulnerability of female characters destabilizes the naturalization of invisible biopolitical power structures. *Böse Zellen* thus highlights that mistrust of established scientific authority is closely linked to economically-conditioned feelings of powerlessness. However, Albert's film also highlights that the bourgeois dream of being a scientist can lead to even more speculations. While in the nineteenth century, cells served as metaphorical structures defining national, exclusionary identities, these structures seem to vanish in the twenty-first century. The film might therefore give a clue to the recent radicalizations of contemporary anti-vaccine movements. In the imagination of these movements, it appears plausible to accuse the entire governmental health system of introducing "evil" in the guise of a vaccine into the healthy national body.

Works Cited

Canguilhem, Georges. *The Knowledge of Life*, edited by Paola Marrati and Todd Meyers and translated by Stefanos Geroulanos and Daniela Ginsburg. New York: Fordham University Press, [1965] 2008.

Correa, Sílvio Marcus de Asouza. "'Combating' Tropical Diseases in the German Colonial Press." "O 'combate' às doenças tropicais na imprensa colonial alemã." *História, Ciencias Saude Manguinhos* 20, no. 1 (2013): 69–91. https://doi.org/10.1590/s0104-59702013005000003.

Dassanowsky, Robert von, and Oliver C. Speck, eds. "Introduction." In *New Austrian Film*, 1–21. New York and Oxford: Berghahn Books, 2011.

Derek, Elly. "Free Radicals." *Film Reviews Locarno*, Performing Arts Periodicals Database 391, no. 1 (2003): 24.

Dick, Jeff T. "Free Radicals." *Library Journal* 130, no. 7 (2005): 133.

Dizikes, Peter. "When the Butterfly Effect Took Flight." *MIT Technology Review* (February 2011). https://www.technologyreview.com/2011/02/22/196987/when-the-butterfly-effect-took-flight/.

Doane, Mary Ann. "The Location of the Image: Cinematic Projection and Scale in Modernity." In *The Art of Projection*, edited by Stan Douglas and Christopher Eamo, 151–65. Stuttgart: Hatje Cantz, 2009.

Everett, Wendy. "Fractal Films and the Architecture of Complexity." *Studies in European Cinema* 2, no. 3 (2005): 159–71. https://doi.org/10.1386/seci.2.3.159/1.

Fanon, Frantz. "Medicine and Colonialism." In *A Dying Colonialism*, edited by Adolfo Gilly and translated by Haakon Chevalier, 121–46. New York: Grove Press, 1965.

Haraway, Donna. *Crystals, Fabrics, and Fields: Metaphors that Shape Embryos.* Berkeley, CA: North Atlantic Books, 1976.

Hoberman, J. "Voice Choices: Butterfly Affects Suicide Attempt, Bad Sex, Mall Construction." *The Village Voice* 49, no. 29 (2004): 54.

Jansen, Sarah. *Schädlinge. Geschichte eines wissenschaftlichen Konstrukts 1840–1920.* Frankfurt: Campus Verlag, 2003.

Jones, Kristin M. "FREE RADICALS." *Film Comment* 40, no. 3 (2004): 73–4.

Koch, Robert. "Ergebnisse der vom Deutschen Reich gesandten Malariaexpedition." *Verhandlungen der Deutschen Kolonialgesellschaft*. Division Berlin-Charlottenburg, 422. Berlin: Reimer, 1902. https://edoc.rki.de/bitstream/handle/176904/5207/435-447.pdf?sequence=1&isAllowed=y.

Lenssen, Claudia. "Raffiniert collagierte Parallelgeschichten, Barbara Albert und Ihre Filme." In *Eine Eigene Geschichte: Frauen Film Österreich seit 1999*, edited by Isabella Reicher, 27–39. Vienna: Sonderzahl, 2020.

Longle, P.A. and Batty, M. "The Fractal Simulation of Urban Structure." *Environment and Planning* 18 (1986): 1143–79. https://journals.sagepub.com/doi/pdf/10.1068/a181143.

Meyer, Imke. "Metonymic Visions: Globalization, Consumer Culture, and Mediated Affect in Barbara Albert's *Böse Zellen.*" In *New Austrian Film*, edited by Robert von Dassanowsky and Oliver C. Speck, 94–107. New York and Oxford: Berghahn Books, 2011.

Norman, Beret. "Carousel of Consumerism: Austrian Filmmaker Barbara Albert's Critique of Contemporary Society in *Böse Zellen.*" *Glossen* 32, no. 2 (2011). https://blogs.dickinson.edu/glossen/archive/most-recent-issue-322011/beret-norman-glossen32/.

Otis, Laura. *Metaphors of Invasion in Nineteenth-Century Literature, Science and Politics.* Baltimore, MD and London: The Johns Hopkins University Press, 1999.

Pantenburg, Volker. "Aus Händen lesen." *KulturPoetik* 3, no. 1 (2003): 42–58. https://www.jstor.org/stable/40621658.

Pham Huy, Lien Ai, Hua He, and Chuong Pham-Huy. "Free Radicals, Antioxidants in Disease and Health." *International Journal of Biomedical Science* 4, no. 2 (2008): 89–96.

Reynolds, Andrew S. *The Third Lens: Metaphor and the Creation of Modern Cell Biology.* Chicago, IL: University of Chicago P, 2018.

Saraiva, Tiago. *Fascist Pigs: Technoscientific Organisms and the History of Fascism.* Cambridge, MA: MIT Press, 2018.

Schüttpelz, Erhard. "Trance Mediums and New Media: The Heritage of a European Term." In *Trance Mediums and New Media: Spirit Possession in the Age of Technical Reproduction*, edited by Anja Dreschke and Martin Zillinger, 56–76. New York: Fordham University Press, 2014.

Smith, R.D. "Social Structures and Chaos Theory." *Sociological Research Online* 3, no. 1 (1998): 82–102. https://journals.sagepub.com/doi/pdf/10.5153/sro.113.

Smith, Warren and Matthew Higgins. "Postmodernism and Popularization: The Cultural Life of Chaos Theory." *Culture and Organization* 9, no. 2 (2003): 93–104. https://doi.org/10.1080/14759550302803.

Sontag, Susan. *Illness as Metaphor.* New York: Farrar, Straus and Giroux, 1978.

Urban, Monika. *Von Ratten, Schmeißfliegen und Heuschrecken: Judenfeindliche Tiersymbolisierungen und die postfaschistischen Grenzen des Sagbaren.* Konstanz und Munich: UVK Verlagsgesellschaft, 2014.

Vansant, Jaqueline. "Challenging Austria's Victim Status: National Socialism and Austrian Personal Narratives." *The German Quarterly* 67, no. 1 (1994): 38–57. https://www.jstor.org/stable/408117.

Virchow, Rudolf. *Über den Hungertyphus und einige verwandte Krankheitsformen: Vortrag gehalten am 9. Februar 1868, zum Besten der Typhuskranken in Ostpreussen.* Berlin: Verlag von August Hirschwald, 1968. https://archive.org/details/b21990979/mode/2up.

Wauchope, Mary. "Place and Space of Contemporary Austria in Barbara Albert's Feature Films." In *New Austrian Film*, edited by Robert von Dassanowsky and Oliver C. Speck, 108–21. New York and Oxford: Berghahn Books, 2011.

Weinding, Paul. *Health, Race and German Politics between National Unification and Nazism, 1870–1945.* New York: Cambridge University Press, 1989.

Twelve   Precarious Lives and
Social Decline in Marlene
Streeruwitz's *Jessica, 30.*
and Kristine Bilkau's
Die Glücklichen

Lisa Wille

In the post-war Germany of the 1950s and 1960s, the proletariat and
social issues of poverty appeared to have been rendered obsolete by
the "economic miracle" set in motion by the Marshall Plan and the
"Rhenish" model of a regulated, socially fair and democratic capitalism
(*soziale Marktwirtschaft*). Poverty and destitution were now considered
things of the past. However, the deregulation of the labor market following the 1993 recession and the consequences of a performance-ori-
ented social order created a social landscape that was rife with precarity,
despite the expectations held in the decades following the Second
World War. A social contract that had guaranteed a stable, middle-class
life and the possibility of advancement through education was now
eroded. Since the 2000s, the term "precariat" has been used repeatedly
to describe not only fundamental changes in the labor market but also
in the social fabric of society.[1] "Precariat," a neologism coined from precarity and proletariat, was first introduced in Italian ("precarito"), then
French, and then made its way into German and English. It has since
been taken up by the media and in everyday language, as shown by
its 2009 inclusion in the *Duden* and 2018 inclusion in the *Oxford English
Dictionary*. The term refers to a "part of the population, which, particularly because of chronic unemployment and a lack of a social safety net,

---

1   See Klaus Kraemer, "Ist Prekarität überall?," in *Von "Neuer Unterschicht" und
Prekariat. Gesellschaftliche Verhältnisse und Kategorien im Umbruch: Kritische Perspektiven auf aktuelle Debatten*, ed. Claudio Altenhain, Anja Danilina, Erik Hildebrandt et al. (Bielefeld: Transcript 2008), 139.

lives in poverty or is threatened by poverty, and has few opportunities for upward social mobility."[2] The *Duden* also describes precarity as the "entirety of labor conditions without welfare" as well as a "difficult state; [a] problematic social situation."[3] The former definition was only recently added as a semantic expansion of the term.

The precariat is often discussed as a new, exploited class. However, the term "class" implies a form of unity and collective amalgamation that is not applicable to the precariat. Instead, the precariat is a fractured set of sub-groups. There are clear differences between unemployed young people with academic degrees, delivery men without higher education, and foreign contract workers. The precariat is often discussed as a neoliberal phenomenon, constituted primarily through competition between individual job-seekers. Its neoliberal cast becomes particularly visible when precarity is apprehended within society as an individual experience and blamed on a person's own insufficiencies, in the sense of "life is what you make it."

A significant section of the contemporary precariat is comprised of overqualified degree-holders, who have often allowed themselves to be exploited for the sake of self-fulfillment, and struggle to achieve a minimum of stability and security. This is particularly the case for the urban middle class, which is increasingly afflicted by the fear of downward mobility and precarious life conditions. In *The End of Illusions*,[4] sociologist Andreas Reckwitz sees within contemporary western society a late-modern culture of the subject, which has developed since the 1970s and 1980s in contrast to the industrial culture of the subject of the 1950s and 1960s,[5] and propagates maxims of self-fulfillment that have been taken up by the urban middle class in the twenty-first century. According to Reckwitz, the subject culture of late modernity has "brought forth intractable paradoxes through consumer capitalism, the demands of the post-industrial working world, and the structures of our digital culture of attention," which promise absolute subjective fulfillment to the individual and moreover suggest that individuals "have a right to realize this goal."[6] This "promise" has, in reality, turned out to be no more than a "phantasm"[7]—as the

---

2   "Prekariat," *Duden online.* https://www.duden.de/rechtschreibung/Prekariat.
3   "Prekarität," *Duden online.* https://www.duden.de/rechtschreibung/Prekaritaet.
4   Andreas Reckwitz, *The End of Illusions: Politics, Economy, and Culture in Late Modernity*, trans. Valentine A. Pakis (Cambridge: Polity, 2021).
5   See Reckwitz, *The End of Illusions*, 115.
6   Reckwitz, *The End of Illusions*, 111–12 (translation modified).
7   Reckwitz, *The End of Illusions*, 112.

danger of precarization despite education and *the late-modern individual's weariness of self-actualization* reveal.[8]

In *Germany's Hidden Crisis: Social Decline in the Heart of Europe*, sociologist Oliver Nachtwey describes contemporary Germany as "society in which collective fear of downward mobility seems to be universal,"[9] and diagnoses that "societies of ascent and social integration … have become societies of downward mobility, precariousness and polarization,"[10] thus reconstituting class stratifications once thought to have been overcome. In particular, he describes literature as a "sensitive seismograph for this transformation."[11] When "literature [turns toward] the present, it tells stories of failure, uncertainty, decline, and downfall."[12] Consequently, literature can reveal, describe, and make tangible the consequences of social precarity as experienced by the urban middle class. Contemporary novels such as Marlene Streeruwitz's *Jessica, 30.* (2004) and Kristine Bilkaus's *Die Glücklichen* (*The Fortunate*; 2015) can contribute to the debate about a "new social question" and the dangers of precarity through their narratives, which chronicle social exclusion and the fear of economic and social decline. Both novels feature protagonists who live under precarious circumstances. *Jessica, 30.* focuses on a single woman who has obtained a PhD, but lives in financial precarity and works as an intern, and is continually struggling within a competitive framework. *Die Glücklichen* tells the story of Isabell and Georg, a couple who live in a large German city and consider themselves "fortunate," since they have achieved the dream of self-actualization (with dream jobs and a life as a bourgeois small family in a trendy neighborhood). However, once they both lose their jobs, they progressively lose the possibility of an economically secure future.

Through an analysis of *Jessica, 30.*[13] and *Die Glücklichen*,[14] this chapter will seek to establish how precarious living and labor conditions among the urban middle class are represented in contemporary German literature. Though a number of literary works—particularly since

---

8   See Reckwitz, *The End of Illusions*, 111–30.

9   Oliver Nachtwey, *Germany's Hidden Crisis: Social Decline in the Heart of Europe*, trans. by David Fernbach and Loren Balhorn (London and New York: Verso, 2018), 1.

10   Nachtwey, *Germany's Hidden Crisis*, 8.

11   Nachtwey, *Germany's Hidden Crisis*, 2.

12   Nachtwey, *Germany's Hidden Crisis*, 9.

13   Marlene Streeruwitz: *Jessica, 30.* (Frankfurt: Fischer 2004). Hereafter abbreviated as *J*.

14   Kristine Bilkau: *Die Glücklichen* (Munich: Random House 2017). Hereafter abbreviated as *G*.

2010—examine precarity in late-modern society,[15] I have chosen to investigate two texts that treat similar themes (existential uncertainty, neoliberal competitive paradigms), but were published about one decade apart (2004 and 2015), and I will focus on how the topics have developed and transformed with time. The analysis centers on the following questions: what range of precarious experiences do these novels chronicle? To what extent are they described as forms of uncertainty or destabilization? How is social precarity experienced by the figures? And how do the novels relate to social and economic situations in contemporary Germany and Austria?

Marlene Streeruwitz: *Jessica, 30.*

Jessica's story begins with the words: "... Everything will be all right" [... Alles wird gut] (*J*, 5). But as the novel goes on, it becomes increasingly clear that for Jessica, nothing is going right. The novel is divided into three stream-of-consciousness chapters, breathless and unpunctuated except for many commas, which present Jessica's thoughts. Jessica Somner, who has just finished a PhD in Cultural Studies (*Kulturwissenschaft*) goes by "Issi," is thirty years old, intelligent, and good-looking. She has neoliberal virtues: she is flexible, mobile, and highly motivated and ambitious. She has lived in New York and Berlin, and now resides in Vienna. She embodies the ideal neoliberal, metropolitan citizen, and yet lives in poverty, since "there's no money there either" [es ist ja auch kein Geld da] (*J*, 100–1). She tells herself to stop thinking "about all that money crap" [an diesen Geldscheiß] all the time (*J*, 19). Though Jessica's stomach may not fall prey to hunger, Ina Hartwig writes that "Jessica still feels hungry. Hungry in her soul. Hungry for a future. Hungry for security."[16]

Jessica works in media and writes as a freelance journalist for a lifestyle magazine whose "ideal reader [is] 30, attractive, independent, and financially successful" [die ideale Leserin ... 30, attraktiv, unabhängig und gut verdienend]. Claudia, her editorial director, wishes that Jessica and her colleagues would be so too, "but then she would have to pay them something" [aber dann müsste sie auch etwas zahlen]. But

---

15   Till Mischko's dissertation examines precarity in contemporary literature. See: Mischko, *Prekarität in deutschsprachigen Romanen der Gegenwart* (Frankfurt: Peter Lang, 2022).

16   Ina Hartwig, "Jessicas Lauf gegen die Weiblichkeit," in *"Aber die Erinnerung davon:" Materialien zum Werk von Marlene Streeruwitz*, ed. by Jörg Bong, Roland Spahr, and Oliver Vogel (Frankfurt: Fischer, 2007), 137.

this isn't necessary, since magazines like Claudia's "can always find enough girls who are happy just to take part" [finde(n) ja immer genug Mäuschen, die schon vom Mitmachen zufrieden sind], so that Jessica is forced to ask herself, "does Daddy still help them with their rent" [zahlt denen auch allen der Papa noch etwas zur Miete]?, since even "the ones with contracts don't make that much" [die Fixen ... auch nicht so viel bekommen] (J, 14). Observations of this kind clearly describe the life conditions of the (primarily female) "internship generation." They are "girls," women who are not taken seriously and instead exploited for cheap labor. The fact that many are happy "simply to participate" points to a lack of transparency in accessing the media and culture world for "people like me, who are fully educated" [Leute wie mich mit einer vollgültigen Ausbildung] (J, 165). Despite her best efforts, Jessica has not managed to get a real job anywhere. She concludes, "I might as well have dropped the PhD, it's worth nothing anyways" [das Doktorat hätte ich auch sein lassen können, das ist sowieso nirgends etwas wert], betraying her feelings of worthlessness (J, 71). The erstwhile promise of advancement through education ("Aufstieg durch Bildung") has become obsolete and irrelevant in Jessica's world.

Marta Wimmert, in reference to Britta Claus,[17] notes that novels about single women, like *Jessica, 30.*, typically revolve around women in the media business. However, Streeruwitz's novel reveals "significant breaks with the character portrait typical of the genre; instead, it strongly thematizes the issues of living costs and career."[18] Jessica's workplace holds a double function in this context: while, on the one hand, it promises the possibility of financial security and independence, the workplace also becomes a "place of coercion and conformity ... that prevents the protagonist from self-actualization."[19] Jessica's reflections about her friend and colleague Tanja reveal the extent to which those in her environment are affected by precarity as well:

> Tanja is smart, she's the smartest one of us by far, and I don't judge her because she works for a tabloid, it's a shame about her studies, of course, but maybe she's projecting that on me, on us, we were ambitious, more ambitious than most, and since she's a psychologist, she thinks she's gone down a step, become a

---

17 See Britta Claus, *Kein Leben zu zweit: Darstellungen des weiblichen Singledaseins in deutschsprachigen Romanen der Jahrtausendwende (1996–2006)* (Würzburg: Ergon, 2012), 143.

18 Marta Wimmer, "Von brüchigen Familien und unglücklichen Singles – zu einem aktuellen Thema deutschsprachiger Gegenwartsromane," in *Convivium: Germanistisches Jahrbuch Polen* (2015): 254.

19 Wimmer, "Von brüchigen Familien," 254.

traitor, because she wanted to be a therapist and help others and wouldn't have made any money for a long time, I get it, I get that you might want a decent life, we have a right to a nice life after all, and then you have to do things like this, I wouldn't have imagined that one day I'd be writing a sex column and Foucault wouldn't matter anymore.

[Die Tanja ist intelligent, sie ist die Intelligenteste da, überhaupt, und ich verachte sie doch nicht, weil sie für so ein Massenblatt arbeitet, es ist natürlich schade um ihre Ausbildung, aber vielleicht projiziert sie das auf mich, auf uns, wir waren da ehrgeizig, ehrgeiziger, und dass sie als Psychologin da, findet sie das einen Abstieg, findet sie das einen Verrat, weil sie ja eigentlich etwas Therapeutisches machen wollte und da noch lange kein Geld verdient hätte, ich verstehe das doch, ich verstehe doch, dass man es jetzt ordentlich haben will, wir haben auch ein Recht auf einen Lebensstil, und dann muss man halt solche Sachen machen, ich hätte ja auch nicht gedacht, dass ich einmal Sexratgeber schreiben werde und Foucault auch keine Rolle mehr spielt.]

(J, 84)

Similar to Jessica, who is condemned to precarity despite her doctoral degree, Tanja is forced despite her degree in psychology to work for this "tabloid," betray her ideals, and conform to the system, since her own chosen profession has no possibilities for "breadwinning." Jessica and Tanja are typical for a generation that has failed to achieve stable work conditions despite their motivation, ambition, and flexibility. Yet they believe that because they have invested in their educations and received high qualifications, they should have a right to a carefree life.

The protagonist in Streeruwitz' novel exemplifies one member of the academic precariat in a neoliberal, post-industrial working world that has replaced solidarity with competition. Jessica notices that her friends, who work at the same magazine and live under similarly precarious circumstances, have begun conspiring against her. Ever since Jessica has moved out of their shared apartment, they "put down my projects in editorial meetings" [in den Redaktionskonferenzen gegen meine Projekte], or snap up each other's assignments, so that one "should really only walk around with a pitch that's been notarized" [eigentlich ... nur noch mit notariell beglaubigten Vorschlägen da überall hingehen] (J, 15). Jessica, 30. does not only portray a competitive atmosphere that friendships can no longer withstand, but also the Darwinist motto, "Survival of the fittest." Jessica's fear when she goes running, that "I'm the slowest jogger ... everyone runs past me" [ich bin die langsamste Läuferin ... alle ziehen an mir vorbei] (J, 18) is symbolic and reappears with Georg in Die Glücklichen. The title already suggests that Jessica is not unique, but stands for an entire generation: her age, 30, points to "a feeling specific to a group, and thus is both a marker of individual and broader generational identity."[20]

Existential fear rears its head once Jessica realizes that she may no longer receive any assignments from the magazine. She tells herself, "it's going to get really tight, my dear, you're not the only freelancer buzzing around, and the others do everything they're told" [wird es wirklich eng, meine Liebe, du bist nicht die Einzige, die da als freie Mitarbeiterin herumschwirren will, und die anderen, die machen alles, was von ihnen verlangt wird] (J, 64). And "if I don't watch out, being a waitress won't do, my dear, there are plenty of girls more eager than you, they can do a much better job, and you don't look young enough anymore for those jobs, you won't even get one." [wenn ich nicht aufpasse, kellnern geht nicht mehr, meine Liebe, da gibt es viel Eifrigere als dich, die das viel besser können, und du schaust nicht mehr jung genug aus, für solche Jobs, die kriegst du gar nicht mehr] (J, 79). She fails to negotiate her contract with Claudia: "once again, [we didn't] talk about money" [über Geld (ist) wieder nicht gesprochen worden] (J, 101). At the very end, Jessica will no longer work for Claudia, and finding another steady position seems like an impossible goal. Jessica expresses her experiences in the post-industrial working world in her monologues, which are increasingly stripped bare of illusions. When literary texts, as Felix Maschewski and Nina Peter have written, focus on the post-industrial working world, they often describe jobs that involve technology and which are shaped by "flexible, rapid forms of communication as well as figurations of absolute entrepreneurship, which results in some degree of 'creative destruction' under the dictates of efficiency and productivity."[21] This flexible, rapid communication is not only present in Jessica's work life, but in her stream of consciousness, which attests to the internalization of post-industrial labor structures in her own thoughts and communications. The narrative style of *Jessica, 30.* markedly portrays how existential uncertainty inflects the thoughts of the protagonist. Jessica's thoughts, and thus her narration, rush breathlessly through her head, lose themselves in new trains of thought, which often break off and begin anew. Jessica's thoughts do not contain a single period, which symbolically implies that Jessica herself cannot come to a stop, since she is driven along by her environment.

---

20 Claus, *Kein Leben zu zweit*, 133. Cit. in Wimmer, "Von brüchigen Familien," 253–4.
21 Felix Maschewski and Nina Peter, "Finanz- und postindustrielle Arbeitswelt in der Gegenwartsliteratur," in *Handbuch Literatur und Ökonomie*, ed. Joseph Vogl and Burkhardt Wolf with Alexander Mionskowski (Berlin: De Gruyter, 2019), 643.

The novel also reflects upon the difference between generations, such as when Jessica realizes that her mother's life unfolded in a much more straightforward and stable fashion:

Mom's still got the things she had when she was thirty: the job and the kid, only the man changed, and I don't have a job, a kid, and men come and go, no one's really come along since Alfred and all the troubles of a relationship and no hope of finding something that will last.

[Die Mama hat heute nur, was sie schon mit 30 gehabt hat, den Job, das Kind, nur der Mann hat gewechselt, und ich habe keinen Job, kein Kind und die Männer sind Wechselbälger, seit dem Alfred nur noch irgendwelche und die Beziehungsproblematik und keine Aussicht auf eine Festigkeit.]

(J, 48)

The lack of stability that Jessica bemoans in her work and personal life she attributes "much less to social developments that are beyond her reach. Instead, she blames individual choices in life."[22] In addition, these precarious working conditions contribute to the fact that potential family planning is pushed aside, since "no one can afford to feed a family" [niemand eine Familie ernähren könnte] (J, 53); in addition, Jessica thinks that she "could never put a child through this, this insecurity, plus it might have to live with its grandparents" [(könnte) das keinem Kind antun, diese Unsicherheit und dass es dann ja doch vielleicht bei den Großeltern leben muss] (J, 53–4). The worst-case scenario that Jessica imagines—being unable to provide her own child with adequate care—becomes a concrete reality and obstacle for Georg and Isabell in *Die Glücklichen*.

The intractability of her existential situation leads Jessica to indulge in escapist moments of nostalgia, in which she reminisces about her childhood in the countryside. Thus, the novel thematizes her extended family in Hartberg, upper Austria, in contrast to her current situation in Vienna. There, conditions were clear and stable, since everyone "had exactly one role to play" [ganz genau eine Stelle einnehmen (musste)] (J, 201). Isolde Charim notes that "for Jessica, Hartberg comes to symbolize true freedom, and especially the true happiness of 'belonging.'"[23]

---

22   Wimmer, "Von brüchigen Familien," 254.
23   Isolde Charim, "Nichts als Einsatz: Neoliberalismus im Werk von Marlene Streeruwitz," in *"Aber die Erinnerung davon:" Materialien zum Werk von Marlene Streeruwitz*, ed. Jörg Bong, Roland Spahr and Oliver Vogel (Frankfurt: Fischer, 2007), 37.

Jessica stages a protest at the end of the novel by escaping from the clutches of the lifestyle magazine and breaking off contact with Claudia. Jessica now attempts to chart out her own path. At the very end, she is off to Hamburg to present an investigative story on a prostitution scandal among politicians to a *Stern* reporter. The novel does not tell readers whether she succeeds in escaping precarity once and for all.

Kristine Bilkau: *Die Glücklichen*

While competitive pressure and individual struggle are leitmotifs from the very beginning in *Jessica, 30.*, the lives of the protagonists in Kristine Bilkaus *Die Glücklichen* at first seem untroubled. The novel tells the story of Georg and Isabell, a city-dwelling, middle-class couple in their late thirties and early forties, who have recently become parents, achieved their dream jobs, live in a sprawling prewar apartment with French doors, and consider themselves fortunate—until both lose their jobs in rapid succession and are threatened by downward mobility. The novel uses a multi-perspectival narrative to tell the story, switching off between Georg and Isabell's perspectives between and within chapters. This narrative form enables the novel not only to lay bare the thoughts of both figures but also to chart the minute nuances of their developing fears of social decline. The text is divided into two: *Part 1 (Winter Will Come Soon)* encompasses chapters 1 to 19, while *Part 2 (Spring is Here)* covers chapters 20 to 41. While part 1 narrativizes their uncertain work situations and the potential threat of social decline, the second part tells the story of the couple's unemployment and their gradual downward mobility.

The pair live in the trendy neighborhood of a large city, such as Berlin or Hamburg, close to a yoga studio, a gourmet food shop and bistro, and an overpriced concept store ("rose soap from Portugal, alpaca wool blankets from Norway, knitted sweaters made by a southern French manufacturer" [Rosenseife aus Portugal, Alpaka-Decken aus Norwegen, Strickpullis einer südfranzösischen Manufaktur])—all "of this was home" [alles (ist) ihr Zuhause] (*G*, 10). Georg and Isabell live a cozy, privileged, and unworried life. This well-situated, bourgeois life, which they can observe in the prewar apartments and houses in their neighborhood on evening walks (full bookshelves, stylish ceiling lamps, and bright curtains in childrens' rooms) is evidence of a "good life" and their middle-class social status. Consumption is not the only factor to play an important role—the sense of keeping up with others becomes clear and inescapable as they lose their jobs and enter precarity. Suddenly, they have to give up their distinctive consumption and leisure patterns, such as going to the movies or restaurants, using delivery services, or buying organic food (see *G*, 199).

Isabell is a cellist and works in a musical orchestra. This may not correspond to her ideal situation (such as a record deal, or playing in a renowned quartet), but Isabell is satisfied, since her job is compatible with motherhood—during her nightly concerts, Georg takes care of their son Matti, who is roughly one year old. When Isabell resumes her position after one year of maternity leave, she feels estranged from the orchestra, though she tells herself, "there's no reason to be afraid, she's here, her third evening after a long break, she's here, it's as if she'd never been away" [es gibt keinen Grund sich zu fürchten, sie ist hier, den dritten Abend nach einer langen Pause, sie ist hier, als wäre sie nie weg gewesen] (G, 15). Everything is familiar, and yet she fails to successfully reintegrate into her job: the pressure and tension get to her, and so her hands begin to tremble when she plays her solo. "Everyone could see it: she had lost her sound and her ease" [jeder konnte ihr dabei zusehen: Sie hatte den Klang verloren, und die Leichtigkeit] (G, 18). From then on, the trembling comes back at inopportune moments, and Isabell quickly realizes that she will lose her job if she cannot control her "deficit" (see G, 25). Isabell's self-doubts and sense of her own inadequacy grow dramatically over the course of the novel, such as when Isabell listens to a piece by Pablo Casal, "who suffered from stage fright his entire life, but it didn't do him any harm, fright can't touch a genius" [der lebenslang unter Auftrittsangst litt, aber geschadet hat es ihm nicht, einem Genie kann die Angst nichts anhaben] (G, 81). The neoliberal implications of this interpretation become clear as Isabell blames her failures on personal weakness. Just as Jessica Somner blames herself rather than society, the same goes for Isabell: "The trembling is *her* weakness, *her* fault" [Das Zittern ist *ihre* Schwäche, *ihre* Schuld] (G, 211).

Merciless competition reigns in the orchestra, not only concerning musical talent, but the musicians' contracts. The concertmaster, Alexander, asks the second chair violin, Sebastian, whether his contract has been extended: "Once you've cleared *that* up, you'll be less frustrated. You're all so tense!" [Mach *das* mal klar, dann bist du weniger frustriert. Ihr seid ja alle so verspannt!] (G, 101). This leads Isabell to uneasily speculate, "Alexander's contract was renewed, but why now? And why only his?" [Alexanders Vertrag wurde verlängert, wieso eigentlich jetzt schon? Wieso nur seiner?] (G, 103). In addition, Isabell's fixed-term contract is threatened by digitalization—the contracts of the string players of the (shrinking) orchestra are not renewed, since their voices can easily be digitally reproduced (see G, 223). Isabell's contract is not renewed after she takes a sick leave only shortly after returning from maternity leave to escape the psychic pressure of the job ("she is unbearably tired" [sie ist unsagbar müde] (G, 108). Her problem isn't an "uncontrollable trembling" [unkontrolliertes Zittern], quite the contrary: "it appears, quite precisely, when she is vulnerable" [es kommt auf den Punkt genau, wenn sie verwundbar ist] (*G*, 79). The trembling is highly metaphorical in the text, since it does not just exist in Isabell's hands, but is symptomatic of her existential fear for the future. The trembling affects Georg, too: online, he reads rumors that the daily newspaper where he works is on the brink of bankruptcy. "The end is near. Trembling in crisis. About to fold. Will it sell on the brink?" [Das Ende droht. Zittern in der Krise. Kurz vor dem Aus. Verkauf auf der Kippe] (*G*, 113). These rumors make him nervous, and he feels "an oppressive pain in his neck" [Anspannung im Nacken, die ihn niederdrückt] (*G*, 113). As a newspaper reporter, Georg has also succeeded in getting his dream job and is happy with this, although he did not manage to become a foreign correspondent. Georg's profession has also been restructured by various crises: he barely has time to do reporting any more, since "there's no time for being on the road" [für das Unterwegssein bleibt immer weniger Zeit] (*G*, 69). Instead, he organizes and edits pieces by others and has to "manage spreadsheets with news topics" [Tabellen mit Themenplänen pflegen] (*G*, 69); he sits "at his desk and in meetings every day" [jeden Tag am Schreibtisch und in Konferenzen], since "the scant staff must be present" [die knappe Belegschaft muss anwesend sein] (*G*, 69). Georg only seldom has the time to drive out and do research—in the novel, he interviews a couple who has dropped out of society and lives on an old farmstead. Georg's.

> work is shaped by the word *deficit,* the product is *deficient,* someone from management explains that to them at least twice a year, and it always sounds as if they were a group of children who should be thankful that someone was still bothering to feed them.
>
> [Arbeit ist geprägt worden von dem Wort *Defizit,* das Produkt sei *defizitär,* mindestens zweimal im Jahr erklärt ihnen das jemand aus dem Management, und es klingt dann, als wären sie eine Horde Kinder, die dankbar sein sollte, dass sie noch jemand mit Müh und Not durchfüttert]
>
> (*G*, 69)

This passage references the newspaper crisis that has affected Georg's line of work and is thematized in other texts of the same period, such as the novel *Möbelhaus* (*Furniture Store;* 2015), written by a former journalist under the pseudonym Robert Kisch, which tells the story of his "own decline from talented writer to furniture salesman."[24] In exemplary fashion, these texts describe the "transformation of a whole branch of

---

24 Nachtwey, *Germany's Hidden Decline,* 3.

employment that only a few years ago promised professional prestige, autonomous activity and a good income. This world of journalism no longer exists—or only for a few, if at all."[25] Even though Georg has a permanent position (unlike Jessica, who also works in the media industry), this does not help him in the long run. After the company is sold and the editorial staff are informed of the new situation, the consultant tells the editors in chief that he has made all possible calculations, but layoffs are unavoidable. He casually lets slip a remark, "That must have been clear to you." [Das muss Ihnen auch klar gewesen sein] (*G*, 127). For Georg, this remark betrays "a lack of mercy that is supposed to be considered normal. As if the fact that they were working here, hoping that they had a future with the company, and were now mired in uncertainty, was nothing more than their own stupid mistake" [eine Gnadenlosigkeit, die als selbstverständlich gelten soll. Als wäre die Tatsache, dass sie hier arbeiten, dass sie auf eine Perspektive hoffen und nun im Ungewissen hier sitzen, nichts als ihr eigener dummer Fehler] (*G*,127). When Georg finally loses his job, it becomes clear to him and Isabell that "things are really going downhill" [Es geht wirklich abwärts] (*G*, 221–2).

Reckwitz notes that late-modern subjects, such as Isabell and Georg, not only wish to achieve self-actualization (a romantic ideal developed around 1800) but also feel entitled to a high social status, due to their achievements and investments (as shaped by the "bourgeois" ideal). For Reckwitz, these aspects of late-modern subjectivity are epitomized by the "new, well-educated middle class in Western metropolitan regions."[26] Georg is a child of this generation; he comes from a modest background and is the only one in his family to have an advanced degree. In contrast, the "uneducated reverence" [bildungsferne Ehrfurcht (*G*, 45).] of his father, who manages an electronics store, *Radio and Television,* stands for the bygone era of industrial modernity. Georg embodies the paradigm of social advancement through higher education, but the novel unmasks this paradigm as hollow and mendacious. While Georg has assumed that his educational and professional accomplishments will be awarded with economic security, he finds himself professionally and economically stagnant and disillusioned at the age of forty-two. He considers himself a "failure" [Versager] (*G*, 238) and "can't figure out how he will make a living in the future" [keine Antwort darauf, womit er in Zukunft sein Geld verdienen soll] (*G*, 199). Unlike his former colleagues,

25   Nachtwey, *Germany's Hidden Decline*, 3.
26   Reckwitz, *The End of Illusions*, 115.

who "seem to succeed so easily, carry on, start fresh, the next job is always the best" [alles so mühelos zu gelingen (scheint), weitermachen, neu anfangen, der nächste Job ist immer der beste] (*G*, 199), Georg feels "sick, damaged, unqualified," when he thinks of them, "and it's my own fault" [kränklich, beschädigt, disqualifiziert, und das selbst verschuldet] (*G*, 199). He is overqualified for the jobs he is offered. He interviews for a position as a "local reporter—without a permanent position at first, but with prospects for more" [Lokalreporter – vorerst ohne Festanstellung, aber mit Aussichten auf mehr] (*G*, 177), in a small town seventy kilometers away. When Georg is told his potential salary, he forces:

> ... a sporting smile. To be honest, he should have laughed, as if it were a bad, no, a good joke—he was too qualified and too old to agree to the offer. But what was the use? For five months, he had tried not to undersell himself, with the result that he had not sold himself at all.
>
> [ein sportliches Lächeln ab. Eigentlich hätte er lachen müssen, wie über einen schlechten, nein, einen gelungenen Scherz, er war zu qualifiziert und auch zu alt, um mit dem Angebot einverstanden zu sein zu dürfen. Aber was half es, fünf Monate lang hatte er versucht, sich nicht unter Wert zu verkaufen, mit dem Ergebnis, dass er sich gar nicht verkauft hatte.]
>
> (*G*, 178)

Since the salary won't cover the costs of commuting, only one option remains: "They would have to move" [Sie müssten dort leben]. The idea of living "in some small town, in a small house, that would presumably have a ridiculously low rent" [in einer beliebigen Kleinstadt, in einem kleinen Haus zu wohnen, das höchstwahrscheinlich einen Spottpreis an Miete kosten würde], entices Georg to start imagining a new life and coming up with exit strategies for his family. "The possibility fascinates him" [Die Möglichkeit fasziniert ihn]; he imagines life as a small family in a small town, where it seems as though nothing "would change the situation soon" [an dem Zustand bald etwas ändern]. The price is to give up "everything they are used to" [auf alles, was sie gewohnt sind], but they would receive "peace of mind, security, freedom" [Sorglosigkeit. Sicherheit. Freiheit], "a freedom that only he would understand. The freedom to live a petty-bourgeois, straightforward life. Yes, straightforward! In circumstances that wouldn't overwhelm him" [eine Freiheit, die nur er verstehen würde. Die Freiheit, ein kleinbürgerliches, überschaubares Leben zu führen. Ja, überschaubar! In einem Rahmen, der ihn nicht überforderte] (*G*, 179). Exhaustion and overwhelmedness are traits of the late-modern subject,[27] and are exemplified in the text by Isabell's inability to work. Yet Georg experiences it too as he:

> ... lies awake at night, turning over the same questions in his mind again and again. How long could they go on like this? What would they do when it wasn't possible any more? Where would they live? Who would even take them? Two unemployed people. All he wanted was ... to live a straightforward life.
>
> [nachts wach zu liegen und sich um die immer selben Fragen zu drehen. Wie lange würden sie so durchhalten? Was würden sie machen, wenn es nicht mehr ging? Wo würden sie eine Wohnung finden? Wer würde sie überhaupt nehmen? Zwei Arbeitslose. Alles, was er wollte, war ... ein überschaubares Leben (zu) führen.]

(G, 179–80

The exhaustion of the situation, the threat of entering the precariat, and creeping fears of social decline gradually alienate Isabell and Georg from each other, leading to a serious crisis in their relationship. Both are incapable of discussing their emotions and fears. Instead, they blame each other for their terrible situation and sink into escapist fantasies: while Georg spends his time on real estate websites and looks for picturesque, remote houses in Italy (the "German" place of longing in the 1950s and 1960s) or scours the countryside, Isabell scrolls through social media and becomes fascinated by the posts of a family she does not know who regularly share pictures of their happy, carefree life. Tellingly, their relationship improves only once Georg receives a tentative offer, and they go celebrate the occasion with lunch in a fancy restaurant. "Georg wants to eat a steak that has been aged for at least six weeks, and she will drink red wine" [Georg will ein mindestens sechs Wochen gereiftes Steak essen, sie wird Rotwein trinken] and "spend the day living a pleasant lie, she will allow herself the soft, warm feeling of safety for the day" [den Tag mit einem angenehmen Schwindel verbringen, ein weiches, warmes Gefühl der Sicherheit wird sie sich heute genehmigen] (G, 164). They are finally amid "their kind," again, with "people in suits, or looking deliberately casual in sweaters, jeans, and expensive sneakers" [Anzugträger oder betont Lässige mit Pulli, Jeans und teuren Turnschuhen] (G, 164), who can afford to eat lunch at this restaurant without a second thought. Notably, it is only when the two can sit in this restaurant without worries that Isabell thinks that those around her "really don't matter, those who are doing well, who belong

---

27   See Reckwitz, *The End of Illusions*.

here" [endlich wieder wunderbar egal (sind), die anderen, denen es gut
geht, die hierher gehören] (*G*, 165). The importance of economic success
and social status for their relationship is also revealed in Isabell's reaction to Georg's news:

> The salary is good, more than good, he says, and nods. She sees
> that he is happy, and she cups his face in her hands, because she
> is moved that he is trying to keep his excitement down but can't
> manage.
> [Die Bezahlung sei gut, mehr als gut, sagt er und nickt dabei.
> Sie sieht, dass er sich freut, und sie muss gleich die Hände um sein
> Gesicht schließen, weil es sie rührt, dass er seine Freude versucht
> im Zaum zu halten, aber nicht dagegen ankommt.]
>
> (*G*, 165)

Isabell touches Georg only now, whereas before, when they had no
options and "the chasm between them seemed unbridgeable" [die Kluft
zwischen ihnen unüberwindbar schien] (*G*, 164), there was no space
for intimacy or connection in their relationship. A short while later,
Georg's offer is revoked; "a phone call made them explode with disappointment, fear, and anger" [ein Anruf ließ sie in Enttäuschung, Wut
und Angst zerspringen] (*G*, 165). Yet not only Isabell and Georg fail to
communicate about their worries, fears, and emotions; their social environment is also devoid of emotional support. Isabell meets up with her
longtime friend and former roommate, Miriam, who now lives in London and is in town with her agent to meet a record company (Miriam is
also a musician). After exchanging a few superficial pleasantries, Isabell
suddenly tells her about her performance anxiety, her trembling hands,
and her unemployment. But Miriam is unable to respond adequately
to her friend's problems: "'I know some people to whom that's happened. Who knows, maybe they all take betablockers. Did you know
that betablockers can make your hair fall out?' she jokes, and Isabell
regrets ever having brought it up" ["Ich kenne Leute, denen das passi-
ert ist. Wer weiß, wie viele von denen Betablocker schlucken, Wusstest
du, dass Betablocker Haarausfall verursachen?," sie lacht und Isabell
bereut, mit dem Thema angefangen zu haben] (*G*, 234). When Miriam
tries to minimize the problem ("You just have to find someone good.
You can work on performance anxiety" [Man muss nur wissen, zu wem
man geht. Auftrittsangst, daran kann man arbeiten] (*G*, 234–5) and Isabell resignedly tells her that neither she nor Georg can currently afford
therapy, Miriam "suddenly seems distracted, fiddles with the strap of
her sandal, and doesn't answer" [auf einmal abgelenkt, sie nestelt an
dem Riemchen ihrer Sandale und antwortet nicht], upon which Isabell
is overtaken by "a tremendous feeling of exhaustion, as if all the energy

had drained out of her" [ein Anfall von Müdigkeit, es ist, als wäre alle Energie aus ihr herausgeflossen] (*G*, 235). The resignation Isabell feels also comes up for Georg. When the announcement is made that Georg's publisher is in financial difficulties and there will be a round of layoffs, Georg thinks, bleakly:

He's jealous of everyone who will soon have their career paths behind them. A career path, running down a path laid out for him, sprinting, no, he's running a marathon and he can't catch his breath anymore. His life is a series of steps that always seem to involve being too late. He was born too late to experience digitalization and those fragile capital markets as exotic, far-away lands, which didn't affect his own life, his own personal existence in his own four walls. Too late to trust in his job without the fear of numbers and restructuring. The old colleagues had it good. They radiated with the certainty of having chosen the right job. They went to their own country houses each summer, to Provence or Tuscany, and they had a comfortable pension. Each day, he felt smaller. It was too late to be the father of a family who would build something permanent or buy a house. Living, renting, buying— he felt like a loser when it came to the subject. Reasonable prices were a thing of the past, and they wouldn't be back.

[Er beneidet jeden, der seine Laufbahn bald hinter sich hat. Laufbahn, Laufen, auf der für ihn bestimmten Bahn, ein Sprint, nein, ein Langstreckenlauf, bei dem ihm jetzt schon die Luft aufgeht. Sein Leben besteht aus Etappen, die vor allem davon geprägt sind: ständig zu spät zu kommen. Zu spät geboren zu sein, um den digitalen Wandel und die fragilen Kapitalmärkte als exotische Kosmen, irgendwo, weit weg, zwar wahrnehmen zu dürfen, aber sie nicht sofort aufs eigene Leben, auf die höchstpersönliche Existenz in den eigenen vier Wänden beziehen zu müssen. Zu spät, um an seinen Beruf glauben zu dürfen, ohne Angst vor Zahlen und Umstrukturierungen. Wie gut hatten die alten Kollegen es noch. Sie strahlten diese Sicherheit aus, den richtigen Job gewählt zu haben. Im Sommer ging's ins eigene Landhaus, Provence oder Toskana, und die Rente war auch komfortabel. Er fühlt sich jeden Tag ein wenig kleiner. Zu spät, um ein Familienvater zu sein, der etwas Bleibendes aufbaut. Eine Immobilie anschafft. Wohnen, Mieten, Kaufen, das Thema macht ihn zum Verlierer. Die Zeiten der vernünftigen Preise sind vorbei und werden nicht wiederkommen.]

(*G*, 123)

This passage summarizes the central realization of the novel: the life which the parents of the urban educated middle class enjoyed is no longer possible. Here, Georg reflects upon himself and the "fate" of his generation. The blatant difference between industrial and late-modern or post-industrial society reveals that it is no longer a matter of course to have a steady job or even accumulate wealth. Nachtwey also emphasizes, "Under the surface of a seemingly stable society, the pillars of social integration have long eroded, and declines and collapses have increased."[28] The generation of late modernity is confronted with a world of uncertainty. Investment in education did not allow Georg and Isabell to establish a comfortable, secure life. Though they have, for much of their lives, "assumed they were entitled to security" [sich den Anspruch auf Sicherheit verdient zu haben], they now realize, "there is no guarantee of security" [doch es gibt keinen Anspruch auf Sicherheit] (G, 292). By the end of the novel, neither have found a new job.

Conclusion

Comparing the novels *Jessica, 30.* and *Die Glücklichen* along with their characters reveals important parallels. The protagonists Jessica, Isabell, and Georg, as members of the urban middle class, have assumed that they are entitled to a high social status and financial security, but find themselves in economic stagnation despite their education and qualifications. Their identities are inflected by neoliberal virtues: to advance in their careers and achieve self-fulfillment, they accept poor work conditions and blame their lack of success on personal weaknesses. The modern, post-industrial world demands workers who are efficient, engaged, flexible, creative, and educated, but without providing any guarantee of financial security. While *Jessica, 30.*, which appeared in 2004, primarily focuses on Jessica's current situation and her unpromising prospects for the future, *Die Glücklichen*, which was written eleven years later, focuses on the real danger of social decline. Comparing the two novels reveals that precarity has not only shifted from targeting young, single people to the family, expanding the field of those affected, but that in 2015, the protagonists of Bilkau's novel are not alone in fearing social decline. The texts attest to a normalization of precarity and to the central position of the precariat within society. One look at the usage frequence of "Prekariat" in the Digitales Wörterbuch der deutschen Sprache confirms this: usage of "precariat" peaks in 2009, and then flattens out, suggesting a

---

28 Nachtwey, *Germany's Hidden Decline*, 8.

normalization.[29] It seems as though the precariat has become the norm rather than the exception. A large section of the urban middle class has been greatly affected by this fear, as sociologist Heinz Bude affirms in *Die Gesellschaft der Angst* (*The Society of Fear*). Bude describes the young generation's fear of failure and downward mobility—of leaving the middle class. "Those who have something to lose, who sense what can happen if you make the wrong choice" are afraid, and "feel uncertain of their position on the social ladder."[30] Bude's "society of fear" is mirrored in the fates of Jessica, Isabell, and Georg:

> Even a medical degree or the once-respected Dr. phil. cannot protect anyone from desperate circumstances, or from being pushed out of their universe of values, which has been defined by education, salary, and profession. There are increasing numbers of people who, despite being from highly educated backgrounds, 'lose out' in education, and increasing numbers of people from upwardly mobile families who fail to establish careers.
>
> [Heute schützt einen selbst ein medizinisches Staatsexamen oder der einstmals so honorige Dr. phil. nicht davor, in eine bedrängte Lage zu geraten und in seiner durch Bildung, Einkommen und Beruf definierten Welt der Wertschätzung den Anschluss zu verlieren. Es gibt vermehrt Bildungsverlierer aus bildungsreichen Milieus und Berufsversager aus Aufsteigerfamilien.][31]

The precarious lives of the urban middle class are clearly reflected in contemporary literature. Both novels open up perspectives on characters who live under precarious circumstances. Relating the novels to one another reveals different aspects of social precarity as well as shared features, such as the general uncertainty the protagonists are subject to. The diffusion of the precariat will continue to expand in the future. Literature now seeks to thematize social problems such as precarious living circumstances, social mechanisms of exclusion, and economic hopelessness to formulate a "new social question," which we must apprehend and take seriously. As always, literature remains an important instrument for diagnosing the ills of the present.

Trans. Sophie Duvernoy

---

29 Usage frequency for "Prekariat," *Digitales Wörterbuch der deutschen Sprache*: https://www.dwds.de/r/plot/?view=1&corpus=zeitungenxl&norm=date %2Bclass&smooth=spline&genres=0&grand=1&slice=1&prune=0&window= 3&wbase=0&logavg=0&logscale=0&xrange=1946%3A2021&q1=Prekariat.
30 Heinz Bude, *Die Gesellschaft der Angst* (Hamburg: Hamburger Edition HIS, 2014), 60.
31 Bude, *Die Gesellschaft der Angst*, 72.

Works Cited

Bilkau, Kristine. *Die Glücklichen*. Munich: Random House, 2017.

Bude, Heinz. *Die Gesellschaft der Angst*. Hamburg: Hamburger Edition, HIS 2014.

Charim, Isolde. "Nichts als Einsatz: Neoliberalismus im Werk von Marlene Streeruwitz." *"Aber die Erinnerung davon": Materialien zum Werk von Marlene Streeruwitz*, edited by Jörg Bong, Roland Spahr, and Oliver Vogel, 24–37. Frankfurt: Fischer, 2007.

Claus, Britta. *Kein Leben zu zweit: Darstellungen des weiblichen Singledaseins in deutschsprachigen Romanen der Jahrtausendwende (1996–2006)*. Würzburg: Ergon, 2012.

Hartwig, Ina. "Jessicas Lauf gegen die Weiblichkeit." In *"Aber die Erinnerung davon": Materialien zum Werk von Marlene Streeruwitz*, edited by Jörg Bong, Roland Spahr, and Oliver Vogel, 136–48. Frankfurt: Fischer, 2007.

Kraemer, Klaus. "Ist Prekarität überall?" In *Von "Neuer Unterschicht" und Prekariat. Gesellschaftliche Verhältnisse und Kategorien im Umbruch: Kritische Perspektiven auf aktuelle Debatten*, edited by Claudio Altenhain, Anja Danilina, Erik Hildebrandt, et al., 139–50. Bielefeld: Transcript, 2008.

Maschewski, Felix and Nina Peter. "Finanz- und postindustrielle Arbeitswelt in der Gegenwartsliteratur." In *Handbuch Literatur und Ökonomie*, edited by Joseph Vogl and Burkhardt Wolf under collaboration with Alexander Mionskowski, 642–52. Berlin: De Gruyter, 2019.

Mischko, Till. *Prekarität in deutschsprachigen Romanen der Gegenwart*. Frankfurt: Peter Lang, 2022.

Nachtwey, Oliver. *Germany's Hidden Crisis: Social Decline in the Heart of Europe*. Translated by David Fernbach and Loren Balhorn. London and New York: Verso, 2018.

Reckwitz, Andreas. *The End of Illusions: Politics, Economy, and Culture in Late Modernity*. Translated by Valentine A. Pakis. Cambridge: Polity, 2021.

Streeruwitz, Marlene. *Jessica, 30*. Frankfurt: Fischer, 2004.

Wimmer, Marta. "Von brüchigen Familien und unglücklichen Singles – zu einem aktuellen Thema deutschsprachiger Gegenwartsromane." *Convivium: Germanistisches Jahrbuch Polen* (2015), 245–64.

| Thirteen | Linguistic Precarity in German Film: Discourses of Appropriateness in *German Class* and *Welcome to Germany* |

Lindsay Preseau

Introduction

Language teaching in the United States and Europe increasingly relies on gig economies, outsourcing, and the engagement of semi- and non-professionals.[1] As pandemic-era teaching has necessitated simple solutions to complex problems in online education, even "prestigious" institutions of higher education in the US have turned to companies such as TalkAbroad and Linguameeting, which charge students as little as $10 per 30 minute session for 1-on-1 access to native speaker "partners" or "coaches," most often Spanish-speaking and located in countries in the Global South. Their labor conditions are, of course, not elaborated on in promotional materials, nor in the proliferation of reviews and case studies of the platforms published in fields such as Second Language Acquisition and Computer Assisted Language Learning. Some companies do employ coaches based in the US, where they are also arguably providing unique employment opportunities to workers for whom lack of proficiency in English is a barrier to other types of employment. However, the precarity of such workers remains evident in the fact that this linguistic "deficit" affects their ability to navigate workers' benefits and protections such as workers' compensation.[2]

---

1 Yuliya Komska et al., "Who Pays for Cheap Language Instruction?", *Boston Review*, July 13, 2020.
2 Shannon Gleeson, "Navigating Occupational Health Rights: The Function of Illegality, Language, and Class Inequality in Workers' Compensation." https://digitalcommons.ilr.cornell.edu/articles/1237.

While language and linguistic ability indisputably play a critical role in economic precarity, the definition of a "linguistic precariat" as such has received little attention. Susan Samata, hitherto the only scholar to rigorously define such a category, characterizes the linguistic precariat as "consisting of people whose identity is, or may be, challenged on language/culture affiliation grounds."[3] Samata argues that the linguistic precariat arose as a consequence of serial migration and complex multi-generational resettlement under global capitalism. Samata's precariat includes, for example, persons who have lost or never fully acquired the first languages of their parents and grandparents, persons whose linguistic identities are misidentified on the basis of their ethnic appearance, and persons who translanguage or engage in languaging practices which call into question the idealization of languages as discrete entities linked to singular national and ethnic identities.

This chapter examines how two films frequently used in German-language teaching, *German Class* and *Welcome to Germany*, reify a system in which this linguistic precariat is deficient and disempowered by drawing on "discourses of appropriateness," a concept that Nelson Flores and Jonathan Rosa coin in their argument against so-called "additive" approaches to language education and policy. Additive approaches to language pedagogy seek to validate stigmatized languages and language forms while also acknowledging the importance of teaching standardized, majority languages. For example, the move to teach what was originally termed as "Ebonics," now referred to as Black or African American English (AAE), as a valid, rule-governed language in public schools has long been a matter of public debate in the US. During the early 1990s, linguists praised such approaches as additive, stressing that they encouraged students to take pride in their home language varieties while "adding" standard English to their academic repertoire. Flores and Rosa argue, however, that such seemingly well-intentioned approaches continue to reify monolingual and standardized language ideologies by delimiting what constitutes "appropriate" language in academic contexts in contrast to what language practices which, while allegedly "valid" or "rule-governed," do not have a place in academic contexts.[4]

Additive approaches to language pedagogy stand in opposition to subtractive approaches, whereby speakers are forced to learn

---

3   Susan Samata, "Linguistic Precariat: Judith Butler's 'Rethinking Vulnerability and Resistance' as a Useful Perspective for Applied Linguistics." *Applied Linguistics Review* 10, no. 2 (2019): 163–77, 5.

4   See Nelson Flores and Jonathan Rosa, "Undoing Appropriateness: Raciolinguistic Ideologies and Language Diversity in Education," *Harvard Educational Review* 85, no. 2 (2015): 149–71.

one language at the expense of another. Subtractive approaches are quite transparently a form of linguistic capital dispossession. However, Flores and Rosa's analysis shows that additive approaches likewise create prime conditions for linguistic dispossession. Subtractive approaches to multilingualism result in a near-total and permanent linguistic dispossession which, as Eva Hoffman describes in her memoir, is "a sufficient motive for violence, for it is close to the dispossession of one's self."[5] Linguistic dispossession resulting from additive multilingualism, on the other hand, breeds precisely the linguistic precarity that Samata describes. Linguistic precarity, to be precise, involves a type of linguistic dispossession whereby the precaritized speaker must fight to retain their linguistic self while simultaneously proving the worth of their "added" linguistic repertoire relative to a mythical "appropriate" standard. This is a standard the precaritized speaker will by definition never achieve, as it is defined just as much by linguistic features as by national origin, ethnicity, and other aspects of identity by which languages are ideologically linked to global hierarchies of capital.

Following geographer David Harvey's concept of capital accumulation by dispossession, the dispossession of someone's linguistic capital tends to parallel the geographical logic of the Global North depriving the Global South of wealth and resources. Just as patterns of migration to the Global North reflect heightened economic precarity in the migrants' countries of origin, the linguistic precariat arose as the result of new patterns of linguistic capital dispossession and accumulation. Both *German Class*, a documentary, and *Welcome to Germany*, a comedy, simultaneously reflect and reproduce the accumulation of linguistic capital by monolingual Germans and the dispossession of linguistic capital of migrants in Germany by sanctioning the linguistic precariat as necessary to social progress or "integration." Written art forms allow for disembodied representations of language that distract from the gendered and racialized conditions of linguistic precarity; likewise, the written word can, in its tendency toward a codified standard, obscure the sonic features of linguistic precarity such as "foreign" pronunciations and gendered voices. Filmic representations, on the other hand, not only afford, but moreover demand, sonic and embodied representations of the linguistic precariat. Film is thus uniquely positioned to demonstrate the mechanisms by which linguistic precarity is produced and reproduced. Specifically, these films show that linguistic diversity in the German-speaking world is broadly lauded while simultaneously being relegated to "appropriate" contexts, just as in the

---

5   Eva Hoffman, *Lost in Translation: A Life in a New Language* (New York: E.P. Dutton, 1989), 121.

US. This, in turn, relegates speakers who do not or cannot adapt their language practices to a hegemonic monolingual ideal to precarious conditions. Representations of language in these films reinforce deficit ideologies of multilingualism, condemning their subjects to a linguistic precariat by appealing to neoliberal sensibilities which eschew overt racial, religious, and cultural discrimination. Instead, these deficit ideologies engage in linguicism, or linguistic discrimination, discrimination which, by promoting the acquisition of a mythical and idealized "appropriate" German as a necessary prerequisite to social progress or "integration," nevertheless reinforce the same power discrepancies officially rejected. Sections II and III demonstrate how this is accomplished through image and sound in each film. Section III addresses the widespread use of these films in German-language teaching, illustrating how the pedagogical use of these films reinforces the exploitation of the linguistic precariat for the purposes of language education. Finally, I suggest strategies for teaching these films as German cultural products through a critical lens.

German Class – Every Beginning is Hard ('Klasse Deutsch – Aller Anfang ist Schwer') (Heinzen-Ziob, 2018)

The documentary *German Class* follows teacher Ute Vecchio and her *Vorbereitungsklasse* ("preparatory course") of immigrant youth learning German in preparation to enter the mainstream educational system. Set in Cologne at the Henry-Ford-Realschule, the film is described by its distributor as "a gorgeous black-and-white film about successful integration and a bow to the daily efforts of dedicated educators."[6,7] Director Florian Heinzen-Ziob echoes this sentiment in his director's commentary, explaining that the black-and-white format gives the film a sense of timelessness. His aim is to center the children rather than the political situation of refugees as reflected in the news, underlining that "above all, their teacher, Ute Vecchio, with her mixture of sternness and affection, will remain a role model for them to master the challenges of life."[8] The film is a monument to the reputed role of language teaching in "successful" integration; Frau Vecchio's job is to integrate the students into German society by teaching them not only the German language

---

6 Translations are my own unless otherwise specified.
7 "Ein wunderschöner Schwarz-Weiß-Film über gelingende Integration und eine Verneigung vor der täglichen Leistung engagierter Pädagogen." (Florian Heinzen-Ziob, *Klasse Deutsch – Aller Anfang ist schwer. W-FILM*, 2018).
8 "Vor allem ihre Lehrerin Ute Vecchio wird ihnen mit ihrer Mischung aus Strenge und Zuneigung ein Vorbild bleiben, die Herausforderungen des Lebens zu meistern." (Florian Heinen-Ziob, "Regiekommentar." *Klasse Deutsch - W-Film*).

itself but also the appropriate contexts of language use in German society. The imagined optimal result of students taking on a monolingual habitus, however, can only happen via linguistic dispossession and relegation to a linguistic precariat. While the students' multilingualism is a focal point of the film, validating their human potential and diversity of experiences, it is simultaneously depicted as a hindrance to their ability to achieve what is necessary to acquire linguistic capital—the ability to become linguistically indistinguishable from a monolingual German in the appropriate contexts.

As the film opens, Bach's Goldberg Variations tinkle softly over black-and-white stills of a school building—the schoolyard, gymnasium, cafeteria, and classrooms—culminating with an image of the door to Frau Vecchio's classroom, a place the camera returns throughout the film as students enter and exit. While the stills of the school reveal a barren, unadorned school, the viewer quickly learns to recognize Frau Vecchio's door by the many pieces of paper taped to it, including one displaying a well-known quotation of Ludwig Wittgenstein: "The limits of my language mean the limits of my world."[9] In one of the first scenes inside the classroom, two girls codeswitch between German and Albanian as they puzzle over an exercise in their book. Frau Vecchio is quick to remind them to speak only German. Ironically, she later leans over an English book with one of the same girls, detailing at length in German how to use the glossary. Frau Vecchio's job is to dispossess the girls of their ability to translanguage through discourses of appropriateness. Her message is clear: German is the appropriate matrix language in classroom settings. Other languages, such as English, must exist as discrete and separate entities, only permissible when native speaker in power has established that they are appropriate.

The linguistic dispossession that has taken place for these girls is twofold; first, the girls are dispossessed of Albanian, their mother tongue. While this is no doubt a type of linguistic dispossession, it was not as clear of an example of linguistic *capital* dispossession as the dispossession of their German–English translanguaging. The global and local capital of English is clearly much higher than that of Albanian; the filmmakers themselves enact this by paying someone to subtitle the English in the film, but not Albanian or any other language. And yet, such appropriateness discourses in Germany further dictate the precise conditions under which the value of global English capital increases or decreases. For these girls, English does not have the same capital as it does for a German businessman or the owner of a hip international

---

9   "Die Grenzen meiner Sprache bedeuten die Grenzen meiner Welt."

nightclub in Berlin—as the film reflects and reifies, the capital value of English can only be "cashed in" by speakers who otherwise embody a nonracialized, monolingual German ideal. As Flores and Rosa argue, "nonracialized people are able to deviate from … idealized linguistic practices and enjoy the embrace of mainstream institutions," while "racialized speaking subjects who are constructed as linguistically deviant even when engaging in linguistic practices positioned as normative or innovative when produced by privileged white subjects."[10] In this case, English represents a permissible linguistic deviation—one associated with significant linguistic capital—for nonracialized Germans. For these girls, on the other hand, the use of English correlates with linguistic deviance rather than linguistic capital. Inversely, Frau Vecchio and her approving audience continue to accumulate linguistic capital from English and German–English translanguaging as they dispossess others of the ability to do so.

Ferdi, a fifteen year old from Kosovo, has already learned this lesson. Frau Vecchio is exasperated when, after having been giving many hints, Ferdi asks repeatedly what a word means. She snaps back at him in her Cologne dialect, "that's what I'm asking you, boy!"[11] Ferdi sternly admonishes her, "don't speak Kölsch, Frau Vecchio,"[12] acknowledging a shared understanding that dialect is not appropriate in an academic context. Frau Vecchio retorts in suddenly quite-standard German that the Cologne dialect is not a foreign language, both substantiating Ferdi's criticism but also reinforcing a hierarchy of appropriateness between "foreign" and "non-foreign" linguistic deviation. Frau Vecchio, embodying the idealized monolingual German speaker, is permitted certain deviations from a linguistic standard, particularly a deviation such as the use of regional dialect which simultaneously reinforces her Germanness. As Patrick Stevenson writes, within the German-speaking world, "there is a high level of public awareness of the distinctive characteristics of local and regional speech forms, and in recent years the general resurgence of 'local values' has led to an increase in the prestige, and consequently in the visibility, of these forms in public contexts."[13] Regional dialect, in other words, carries linguistic capital as "non-foreign" linguistic variation in the appropriate contexts.

In addition to translanguaging, two other major features of Samata's linguistic precariat characterize the students in German Class: ethnolinguistic misidentification and alleged failure to acquire a "first"

10   Flores and Rosa, "Undoing Appropriateness," 165; 150.
11   "dat frag ich dich, Jung'!"
12   "Reden Sie nicht Kölsch, Frau Vecchio."
13   Patrick Stevenson The German-Speaking World: A Practical Introduction to Sociolinguistic Issues (New York and London: Routledge, 1997), 63.

language. The former is evident in the storyline of thirteen year old Schach from Kyrgyzstan, who is bullied for his poor German and for being "Chinese." Schach's best friend, Kujtim from Kosovo, is also precaritzed by Frau Vecchio's allegation that he never learned his first language. Kujtim struggles the most of any student in the class; in a final breakthrough scene, Frau Vecchio establishes this as his core problem. As they are working on spelling, Kujtim enumerates his languages: Romani and Albanian (in which he is illiterate) and Italian ("only a bit" after living in Italy for one year). Frustrated, he exclaims, "I'm forgetting my mother tongue,"[14] to which Frau Vecchio replies, "Yes, but you also never learned your mother tongue."[15] Her reply belies a common discourse of appropriateness which claims that adequate language requires literacy. Moreover, however, she underlines the myth of semilingualism (*doppelte Halbsprachigkeit*). Semilingualism, once entertained in mainstream linguistic literature, is the theory that multilingual children often exhibit inadequate, partial competence in both or all of their languages. While the theory was debunked in the 1980s, it continues to circulate unquestioned as a folk belief in media, education, and language policy in Germany.[16] Even if Kujtim is forgetting his Romani, it is improbable if not impossible that he never spoke it fluently. Frau Vecchio therefore echoes a common sentiment when she identifies this alleged deficiency in his first language as the source of all of his academic problems.

The link between these markers of linguistic precarity and the threat of economic precarity is conspicuous. Frau Vecchio encourages Ferdi to stay in school rather than leave to work at a family friend's mechanic shop, but Ferdi explains that he needs work as soon as possible because his father does not have papers. Frau Vecchio is initially concerned, but relieved to hear the work will be an official apprenticeship. He will attend trade school where he will continue to learn German; economic precarity can only be avoided by also averting linguistic precarity. Gymnasium (college-preparatory secondary school) is Frau Vecchio's ideal goal for students, however. "Cool, it's a Gymnasium!,"[17] she exclaims when a student shows her an acceptance letter, sternly reminding Kujtim that if he works hard, he may be accepted to a Gymnasium where Italian is taught. A voice in the background asks,

---

14 "Ich vergesse meine Muttersprache."
15 "Ja, aber du hast auch die Muttersprache nie richtig gelernt."
16 Heike Wiese, "Führt Mehrsprachigkeit zum Sprachverfall? Populäre Mythen vom 'gebrochenen Deutsch' bis zur 'doppelten Halbsprachigkeit' türkischstämmiger Jugendlicher in Deutschland", *Türkisch-Deutscher Kulturkontakt und Kulturtransfer: Kontroversen und Lernprozesse*, ed. Michael Hofmann and Yasemin Dayıoğlu-Yücel (Göttingen: V&R Unipress, 2011), 165.
17 "Cool, das ist ein Gymnasium!"

"What about Arabic?"[18] The question goes unacknowledged, averting the uncomfortable truth that Italian is an academically appropriate language with significant linguistic capital, whereas proficiency in Arabic will only relegate the unseen student to a precarious future.

Welcome to Germany ("Willkommen bei den Hartmanns") (*Verhoeven*)

In stark contrast to the principled idealism and white saviorism of *Klasse Deutsch*, the comedy *Welcome to Germany* is characterized by tongue-in-cheek humor which ridicules the misguided attempts of its white German characters to save and to integrate the Nigerian protagonist, Diallo, into mainstream German society. The film is, at first glance, parodying white savior films like *German Class*. Nonetheless, critics have accused the film of centering its white characters in doing so.[19] Likewise, the film parodies the superficial language-as-integration narrative of *German Class* while simultaneously affirming the same more complex appropriateness discourses which underlie more simplistic understandings of cultural belonging.

Language teaching is central to the film's plot; the matriarch of Diallo's new German family, Angelika Hartmann, is a retired teacher. Angelika attempts to volunteer to teach language at a refugee camp in Munich, but is rebuked by the head of the school. He takes an explicit jab at white saviors like Frau Vecchio, pointing out that there are enough do-gooder language teachers already. Instead, the ever-persistent Angelika decides that her family will take in Diallo, a Nigerian refugee. Angelika teaches Diallo German at home in a montage which parodies the way German is taught and is represented by Frau Vecchio in *German Class*. In a scene reminiscent of one of Frau Vecchio's dictation exercises involving an in-depth narrative about hedgehog gestation, Angelika puts great effort into teaching Diallo words which, while apparently important to her domestic existence as a wealthy retiree, are laughably irrelevant to his daily life – *Eichhörnchen* ("squirrel"), *Buchsbäumchen* ("little boxwood tree"), *Rasenmäher* ("lawn mower"). She exclaims enthusiastically with a twinkle in her eye that "language is the key to integration,"[20] an oft-heard feel-good slogan during the so-called German refugee "crisis."

The audience is intended to laugh at this scene, but only because lawn care vocabulary is clearly not the key to integration, and not

---

18 "Und Arabisch?"
19 Daniel Gross, "The Awkward Attempt to Find Comedy in the Refugee Crisis" *The New Yorker*, Feb 4, 2017.
20 "Sprache ist der Schlüssel zur Integration."

necessarily because the very idea of language being necessary to integration is problematic. In fact, the film validates the "language as integration" sentiment by affirming Diallo's relegation to the linguistic precariat as a successful form of integration. The film ends victoriously with Diallo winning his asylum case after he has first proven his hardship in a heart-wrenching presentation to the class of the youngest Hartmann son, then his moral worth by helping save Angelika's husband from a heart attack. The only sincere doubt expressed after these events before his asylum proceeding is that perhaps his German is not good enough. Though Diallo's German, notably the only language he speaks throughout the course of the film, is obviously communicatively competent, his grammatical errors apparently render his language inappropriate for daily life. Nonetheless, his German is good enough to join the linguistic precariat. Diallo returns to the Hartmanns' garden in the final scene of celebration, supposedly linguistically unprepared for stable employment, but presumably ready to resume the occasional handiwork around the house that he has done throughout the film.

Like the students in *German Class*, Diallo has been relegated to the linguistic precariat for more complex reasons than purportedly not speaking German proficiently. Diallo's ethnolinguistic misidentification is particularly jarring. Eric Kabongo, the actor who portrays Diallo, migrated to Belgium from the current-day Democratic Republic of Congo. He spoke no German at the time of filming, but worked with a coach to read the script as written for him. The script belies no evidence of "Nigerian"-accented German; in a clearly inauthentic and offensive you-Tarzan-me-Jane fashion, Diallo's major linguistic quirk is zero copula in all syntactic contexts, a feature not shared with any major Nigerian language ("Ich $\varnothing$ dankbar"/"Das $\varnothing$ nicht Allah" – "I $\varnothing$ thankful"/"That $\varnothing$ not Allah"). Even in Nigerian English, copula drop is, as in AAE, limited to very specific grammatical contexts involving stative verbs.[21] Diallo's speech thus serves to underline his blackness rather than any ethnic identification with Nigeria, seemingly chosen as a random placeholder for any developing African country.

Likewise, Diallo's apparent semilingualism is implicit in the fact that his first language is never revealed, and he never speaks English, unlike many other characters in the movie such as the successful businessman son. Given that his host family considers his German to be substandard, this grants Diallo no adequate means of communicating in any language. This linguistic deficiency is often implicitly and explicitly linked

---

21   See Ogechi Florence Agbo and Ingo Plag, "The Relationship of Nigerian English and Nigerian Pidgin in Nigeria: Evidence from Copula Constructions in Ice-Nigeria," *Journal of Language Contact* 13, no. 2 (2020): 351–88.

to cognitive and moral deficiency. For example, in a heart-to-heart with host father Richard, Richard explains the linguistic difference between *gehören* ("belong" in the sense of "own") and *gehören zu* ("belong with" in the sense of "have a bond with"). The language lesson takes on a moral tone as Richard explains to Diallo that in Germany, a wife does not belong *to* you, but *with* you. Diallo nods contemplatively.

Towards a Critical Didactization of Linguistic Precarity

The manner in which films such as *German Class* and *Welcome to Germany* sanction the linguistic precariat as necessary to social integration and progress is of particular interest because such films *about* language acquisition are often employed *in service of* language acquisition. Because these films feature characters learning German, they are also understood to be relatable to students of German, and distributors and educators alike capitalize on this opportunity to produce instructional materials to accompany the films in educational settings. Unsurprisingly, these materials often place particular emphasis on the linguistic aspects of the films, both underlining and legitimizing the processes of linguistic accumulation and dispossession in the films and, as I will show, (re-)enacting them in the space of the language classroom itself.

The distributor of *Klasse Deutsch* explicitly recommends their film for educational use in German, German as a Foreign Language, Pedagogy, Psychology, and Ethics courses for students thirteen years and older. They provide a thirty-four page document of pedagogical material to accompany the film which includes—alongside quotations and stills from the film and factual background information about the film, its characters, and the director—review questions for students, suggested activities, links to individual scenes for use in the classroom, and links to literature and other films relevant to the themes of migration and integration.[22]

The affirmation of linguistic hierarchies described in this chapter is, perhaps, inevitable in a documentary without narration. However, the didactic materials make much of the film's implicit messaging explicit. In a scene featuring Schach, the boy from Kyrgyzstan who is misidentified as Chinese, Frau Vecchio seems exasperated that Schach's mother comes to complain about Schach's poor grade in German when she speaks almost no German herself. On the basis of the film alone, one might argue that this scene is not necessarily empathizing with Frau Vecchio's exasperation, but simply showing her naivete, underlining

---

22 Luc-Carolin Ziemann, *Klasse Deutsch: Filmheft mit Materialien für die schulische und außerschulische Bildung*. W-film Distribution.

that she is stretched to her limit and doing the best she can. However, the pedagogical materials make it clear that the production team is in agreement with Frau Vecchio's assessment of the mother. In the summary section of the materials, the author writes:

> The family from Kyrgyzstan places great importance on good grades and, although the mother herself does not yet speak good enough German to speak directly to Frau Vecchio, Schach's 3 in German is clearly not good enough for her. Because Schach is the only one who translates between his parents and the school, he finds himself in a downright absurd situation, because he translates conversations that would have been better off without him [present].[23]

This version of affairs leaves little doubt in the student viewer's mind that both Frau Vecchio and the filmmakers lay blame on the linguistically precarious mother rather than the institutions failing to provide translation services for Schach. The striking phrasing "downright absurd" to describe the fact that Schach translates for his mother belies a clear judgment that the languaging practices of the linguistic precariat are inherently problematic and, while perhaps temporarily necessary, a problem to be fixed. Rather than framing Schach's abilities as a translator as an asset, the filmmakers take a deficit perspective in framing Schach as a victim of his negligent mother, solely on the basis of her linguistic capital. As Elaine Bauer has argued in her work on such "language brokering," whereby children serve as translators for their migrant parents, "although in Western societies interpreting/translating is seen by some as adult work, for many immigrant families, such activities are seen as an essential contribution to their everyday family life and activity."[24] By very explicitly delegitimizing such forms of languaging and language brokering, the didactic materials that accompany the film ensure that students still read scenes involving nuanced language use from a deficit perspective.

---

23 "Die Familie aus Kirgisien legt großen Wert auf gute Noten und, obwohl die Mutter selbst noch nicht gut genug Deutsch spricht, um sich direkt mit Frau Vecchio zu unterhalten, ist ihr Schachs 3 in Deutsch eindeutig nicht gut genug. Da Schach der Einzige ist, der zwischen den Eltern und der Schule dolmetscht, befindet er sich in einer geradezu absurden Situation, weil er Gespräche übersetzt, die eigentlich besser ohne ihn stattgefunden hätten." (Ziemann, *Klasse Deutsch: Filmheft*, 14)

24 Elaine Bauer, "Practising Kinship Care: Children as Language Brokers in Migrant Families," *Childhood* 23, no. 1 (2015), 33.

While the descriptions of the film in the pedagogical materials serve to make the linguistic hierarchies in the film explicit, the suggested class activities serve to (re)-enact the same hierarchies in the classroom. One activity among the pedagogical materials asks students to reflect on how they would feel in Schach's shoes: "consider how you would feel or how you would act if your parents were reliant on your translation in conversation(s) with teachers![25]" Despite the fact that the production company explicitly recommends the film for German as Second Language classes, the subjunctive phrasing of this and other activities assumes that students will not have experienced linguistic precarity, repeatedly encouraging students to imagine they are refugees themselves.

These sort of pedagogical simulations of oppression, long frowned upon in Holocaust education, have proven no more effective in eliciting meaningful empathy for refugees and asylum seekers. As Mark Franke argues, "refugee simulation exercises, fundamentally, are works of performative abstraction. The participants are asked only to conjure and co-author an experience of self, while the refugee is idealized as other-to-self."[26] If such simulations indeed only allow engagement with the self, where the selves are assumed to not to belong to the linguistic precariat, the vague final instructions of the language broker simulation activity are even more troubling: "summarize the outcomes of your small group discussions together with the whole class![27]" In the likely scenario that at least one student can identify with Schach's role as a language broker, the end goal of consolidating individual experience to a "summary" will no doubt decenter any such actual lived experience, given the subjunctive origins of the activity.

The distributors of *Willkommen bei den Hartmanns* offer a similar pedagogical handbook to accompany the film, recommending the film for students ages fourteen and older in subjects such as German, Ethics/ Religion, Social Studies/Politics, and Art. The twenty-seven-page document, like the film, puts the focus on the German hosts rather than the refugees, asking students to consider what critical and supportive statements the film makes about *Willkommenskultur* ("Welcome Culture"). In contrast to the pedagogical materials for *German Class*, the lessons are

---

25 "Überlegt euch, wie ihr euch fühlen würdet, bzw. wie ihr euch verhalten würdet, wenn eure Eltern im Gespräch mit Lehrern auf eure Übersetzung angewiesen wären!" Ziemann, *Klasse Deutsch: Filmheft*, 27.

26 Mark Franke, "Citizens' Auto-Affectation in the Pedagogy of "playing Refugee': Simulating the Experience of Others from Oneself, for Oneself," *Transformations: The Journal of Inclusive Scholarship and Pedagogy* 30, no. 1 (2020), 27.

27 "Fasst die Ergebnisse eurer Kleingruppengespräche im Plenum zusammen!" Ziemann, *Klasse Deutsch: Filmheft*, 27.

entirely de-personalized. Students are asked to analyze the film and its characters, and occasionally events in contemporary German politics, but never their own personal relationships with refugees or personal involvements in *Willkommenskultur*. Franke's critique of refugee simulations points out citizen empathy for refugees needs to start with citizen self-reflection, writing:

> Simulations exercises lose sight of how citizen-participants are already involved in shared experiences of direct relevance to refugees ... Emplaced citizens need only start from where they are ... Citizens can pay attention to the ways in which their own state is involved in political, security, economic, and industrial relations with other states in the world that suppress and discriminate against minority populations and those who face persecution from their own governments. Citizens may confront their own actions and the actions of their compatriots in facilitating the work of their governments in these respects.[28]

By focusing on the film as a self-contained product, the authors miss the opportunity to ask citizen students to, for example, step into the shoes of the Hartmanns in interrogating their own relationships with both refugees and with the state-sanctioned structures such as the (language) education system.

In her critique of intercultural approaches in North American German classrooms, Adrienne Merritt writes of *Welcome to Germany*, "Perhaps the most troubling result of the Hartmann film is its popularity with North American German instructors and professors, particularly those seeking representation of non-white German speakers on film. In my opinion, there exists only one potential framework for Verhoeven's film: critical analysis partnered with historical background about Africans in Germany and critical race theory (whiteness included)."[29] The type of grounded critical analysis that Merritt proposes no doubt might seem a monumental task to instructors and students alike, particularly for those, like myself, without a background in critical film analysis. Starting this thread of inquiry via critical analysis of representations of language, specifically, poses a unique opportunity to lower this affective

---

28 Franke, "Citizens' Auto-Affectation," 30.
29 Adrienne Merritt, "A Question of Inclusion: Intercultural Competence, Systematic Racism, and the North American German Classroom," in *Diversity and Decolonization in German Studies*, ed. Regine Criser and Ervin Malakaj (Cham: Palgrave Macmillan, 2020), 191.

filter by creating a point of entry that every participant in a college language course naturally has some level of personal investment in.

I do not argue that films like *Welcome to Germany* should not be taught. On the contrary, the fact that they generate student and instructor interest due to their language-related subject matter makes them ripe not just for entertainment, but for the kind of *self-reflective* critical analysis that the pedagogical materials for *German Class* try but fail to elicit. Crucial learning objectives for students viewing these films should thus be:

(1) to explain how language functions as a form of capital in the linguistic marketplace
(2) to give historical and contemporary examples of how linguistic capital has been unequally distributed within and outside of the German-speaking world
(3) to identify institutions and processes in the film through which access to linguistic capital is racialized and gendered and reproduces hierarchies of social power
(4) to assess their own roles in the unequal distribution of linguistic capital (without the explicit assumption that all students are complicit benefactors), in particular in their institutional roles as students of German themselves

A "lesson plan" for enacting these objectives is both beyond the scope of this chapter and, moreover, simply impossible to produce in singular due to the wide variances in student language ability, demographics, and other factors which would have to be accounted for in order to effectively guide students to, in Franke's words, "confront their own actions and the actions of their compatriots."[30] Objective (1), which is broad and need not be specific to German, can be accomplished through the plethora of already existing methods for teaching students about cultural capital, in general, many of which feature linguistic capital prominently. Likewise, objective (3) need not require any activity beyond a close reading of the film, scaffolded to student ability. However, heeding Merritt's call to incorporate *historical background* and *critical race theory* into critical analyses, I will make a few suggestions for accomplishing objectives (2) and (4), particularly with North American students in AP and upper and lower-level college courses.

In service of objective (2), students must understand the history of German as a colonial language and the historical accumulation of linguistic capital by speakers of German via the dispossession of linguistic

---

30 Franke, "Citizens' Auto-Affection," 30.

capital of colonized peoples. For advanced students, a paired reading of the chapter "The Negro and Language" from Frantz Fanon's *Black Skin, White Masks* (1952) with introductory literature on the histories of Namdeutsch, Unserdeutsch, Tok Pisin, and/or other languages influenced by colonial German will provide a natural bridge from historical to contemporary discussions of linguistic capital. At lower levels, instructors might consider how the plethora of materials developed for K-16 students to examine language and power through the lens of French creoles might be adapted for German-influenced creoles such as Unserdeutsch (see, for example, Elsa Wiehe's *"Koze!," Kreol, and Colonialism: Language as Archive*).

A major challenge in achieving learning objective (4) for instructors in North America is that students have likely previously experienced any infusion of "culture" into their German instruction as an exercise in understanding the culture of "us" (Americans, prototypically white) vs. "them" (Germans, always white). Instructors will need to do significant work to intervene in these ideologies in order for students to even begin the work of assessing their own roles as learners of German in the linguistic market of the German-speaking world. In other words, this objective comes with a prerequisite learning objective that students must recognize themselves as members of the German speech community.

For advanced college-level courses, a possible point of entry into these discussions might be Baijayanti Roy's Modern India in German Archives (MIDA) piece on the India Institute of the Deutsche Akademie, the predecessor of the Goethe Institute (2021). Most students will be at least passively familiar with the Goethe Institute as a German institution that they themselves have, at minimum, engaged with, and, more likely, explicitly benefited from in the form of study materials, proficiency testing, and funded campus events. Understanding the colonial roots of the organization—in tandem, perhaps, with examples of their contemporary efforts to address the effects of German colonialism, such as were offered in their online magazine, *Latitude*[31]—will help students to understand themselves as part of the linguistic ecosystem of German (post)-colonialism.

For college students at lower levels and, perhaps, students of AP German, a skilled and knowledgeable instructor might, for the same purpose, critically employ the many superficial course materials designed to surprise students with statistics showing how many speakers of

---

31 Subtitled "Rethinking Power Relations – for a decolonised and non-racial world," this publication was available online from 2019 to 2021: https://www.goethe.de/prj/lat/en/index.html.

German: (1) live outside of officially German-speaking countries; and (2) speak German as an additional language. By redirecting the class discussion from who speaks German to the more important question of *why* we are supposed to be surprised that people who are not popularly understood to count as "German" speak German, instructors can guide students to understand themselves as part of the German speech community. Centering the types of problematic materials that students have likely encountered unquestioned in their prior educational histories is necessary if they are to reflect on mechanisms by which speakers of German, themselves included, have accumulated or been dispossessed of linguistic capital.

Conclusion

Both *German Class* and *Welcome to Germany* draw on discourses of linguistic appropriateness to establish their characters as belonging to, or being at risk of joining, the linguistic precariat. As Samata argues, the utility of framing a linguistic precariat as I have in this chapter lies in exposing members' vulnerability and need for protection, thereby providing a ground for resistance against precarious conditions. Neither the students in *German Class* nor Diallo lack valid language, as both films imply. On the contrary, it is the precaritized characters who are multilingual, with dynamic linguistic repertoires and languaging practices, while the characters given linguistic authority are largely implied to be monolingual. The multilingual characters are relegated to the precariat through their portrayal as language learners first and multilinguals second; it is only by acknowledging and exposing such representations that, as Samata argues, we can empower the linguistic precariat to negotiate a more realistic perception of multilingualism and languaging at large.[32]

Particularly because such films are popular in German curricula in K-12 and undergraduate education in the US, it is crucial to investigate the ways in which they reflect monolingual biases and reinforce ideologies of linguistic imperialism and linguicism. Ultimately, these films lend themselves to a more general neoliberal valorization of language acquisition as an instrument of social progress, both promoting monolingual ideologies which ultimately serve to stigmatize normal characteristics of multilingual individuals and communities such as translanguaging, oral multilingualism, and ethnolinguistic self-identification. The problem with using these films pedagogically

---

32 Samata, "Linguistic Precariat," 5.

is not that they are shown at all, but that they are shown in the wrong contexts, often screened "for fun" in the context of extracurricular programming at universities or on days when a non-German-speaking substitute is teaching at a high school. Students who increasingly rely on a precarious digital language learning industry for their own language learning are unlikely to question these representations on their own. However, precisely this fact also means that critical, intentional teaching of these films represents a unique opportunity for students to reflect on their own roles in the linguistic market and, in many cases, their complicity in the processes of linguistic accumulation and dispossession which create the necessary conditions for a linguistic precariat.

Works Cited

Florence Agbo, Ogechi, and Ingo Plag. "The Relationship of Nigerian English and Nigerian Pidgin in Nigeria: Evidence from Copula Constructions in Ice-Nigeria." *Journal of Language Contact* 13, no. 2 (2020): 351–88. https://doi.org/10.1163/19552629-bja10023.

Bauer, Elaine. "Practising Kinship Care: Children as Language Brokers in Migrant Families." *Childhood* 23, no. 1 (2015), 22–36.

Fanon, Frantz. "The Negro and Language." In *Black Skin, White Mask*, 17–140. New York: Grove Press, [1952] 2008.

Flores, Nelson, and Jonathan Rosa. "Undoing Appropriateness: Raciolinguistic Ideologies and Language Diversity in Education." *Harvard Educational Review* 85, no. 2 (2015): 149–71. https://doi.org/10.17763/0017-8055.85.2.149.

Franke, Mark. "Citizens' Auto-Affection in the Pedagogy of 'Playing Refugee': Simulating the Experience of Others from Oneself, for Oneself." *Transformations: The Journal of Inclusive Scholarship and Pedagogy* 30, no. 1 (2020): 16–34.

Gleeson, Shannon. "Navigating Occupational Health Rights: The Function of Illegality, Language, and Class Inequality in Workers' Compensation." *DigitalCollections@ILR*, Jan. 2014. https://digitalcommons.ilr.cornell.edu/articles/1237.

Gross, Daniel A. "The Awkward Attempt to Find Comedy in the Refugee Crisis." *The New Yorker*, Feb 4, 2017. https://www.newyorker.com/culture/culture-desk/the-awkward-attempt-to-find-comedy-in-the-refugee-crisis.

Heinzen-Ziob, Florian. *Klasse Deutsch - Aller Anfang ist schwer*. W-FILM, 2018. https://www.amazon.com/gp/video/detail/B081FKD6PD/ref=atv_dp_share_cu_r.

Heinen-Ziob, Florian. "Regiekommentar." *Klasse Deutsch – Aller Anfang ist schwer*. W-FILM, 2018. https://www.wfilm.de/klasse-deutsch/regiekommentar_469.

Hoffman, Eva. *Lost in Translation: A Life in a New Language*. New York: E.P. Dutton, 1989.

Komska, Yuliya et al. "Who Pays for Cheap Language Instruction?" *Boston Review*, July 13, 2020. http://bostonreview.net/class-inequality/yuliya-komska-alberto-bruzos-moro-roberto-rey-agudo-who-pay-cheap-language-classes.

Merritt, Adrienne. "A Question of Inclusion: Intercultural Competence, Systematic Racism, and the North American German Classroom." *Diversity and Decolonization in German Studies*, edited by Regine Criser and Ervin Malakaj, 177–96. Cham: Palgrave Macmillan, 2020. https://doi.org/10.1007/978-3-030-34342-2.

Roy, Baijayanti. "India Institute of the Deutsche Akademie (1920–45)". In *Das moderne Indien in Deutschen* Archiven *1706–1989 - MIDA Archival Reflexicon*, 2021. https://www.projekt-mida.de/reflexicon/india-institute-of-the-deutsche-akademie-1928-45/.

Samata, Susan. "Linguistic Precariat: Judith Butler's 'Rethinking Vulnerability and Resistance' as a Useful Perspective for Applied Linguistics." *Applied Linguistics Review* 10, no. 2 (2019): 163–77. https://doi.org/10.1515/applirev-2017-0060.

Stevenson, Patrick. *The German-Speaking World: A Practical Introduction to Sociolinguistic Issues*. New York and London: Routledge, 1997.

Index

Please note that page references to Figures will be followed by the letter f

Volumes in the series: